A LITERARY GUIDE TO THE LAKE DISTRICT

Walk and drive to inspiring places
– the famous and the little-known

GREVEL LINDOP

This revised edition published by Sigma Leisure – an imprint of Sigma Press, 5 Alton Road, Wilmslow, Cheshire SK9 5DY, England. (First edition published in 1993 by Chatto & Windus)

British Library Cataloguing in Publication Data
A CIP record for this book is available from the British Library.

ISBN: 1-85058-821-X

Typesetting and Design by: Sigma Press, Wilmslow, Cheshire.

Cover photograph: Grasmere from Loughrigg Terrace *(Graham Beech)*

Printed by: Bell & Bain Ltd, Glasgow

By the same author:

Poetry
Fools' Paradise
Tourists
A Prismatic Toy
Touching the Earth
Selected Poems

Prose
The Opium-Eater: A Life of Thomas De Quincey
The Path and the Palace

Edited
British Poetry Since 1960 *(with Michael Schmidt)*
Thomas Chatterton: Selected Poems
Thomas De Quincey: Confessions and Other Writings
The Works of Thomas De Quincey
Robert Graves: The White Goddess
Graves and the Goddess *(with Ian Firla)*

For
Xanthe, Gerard
and Catrin

What astonishes me more than any thing is the tone, the coloring, the slate, the stone, the moss, the rock-weed, or, if I may so say, the intellect, the countenance of such places. The space, the magnitude of mountains and waterfalls are well imagined before one sees them; but this countenance or intellectual tone must surpass every imagination and defy any remembrance. I shall learn poetry here ...

John Keats to Tom Keats, 1818

Why the Lakes, my misguided friend? You will get wet through, and it is a hell of a way from London.

Arnold Bennett to Hugh Walpole, 1923

HOW TO USE THIS BOOK

The Lake District is as rich in literary associations as in natural beauty. I hope this book will help you to uncover some of this richness, exploring what interests you most.

To find the literary associations of a place, use the Index of Places. For places associated with a particular person, use the Index of People. Each Part of the book traces one main route through the area, with detours as necessary, dealing with places as they appear on that route. The routes could be used for planning tours or excursions; to help with this they are divided into shorter sections by subheadings, but it is not guaranteed that one section can be completed in one day or less.

Read ahead: you may not want to visit every place mentioned. The *Guide* assumes that you have a compass and an Ordnance Survey map with you at all times. It is not a detailed walkers' guide. If you are going on the fells you should also consult Wainwright's *Pictorial Guide to the Lakeland Fells* or a similar work.

Distances are given in miles (m) and yards (yds). Cardinal points of the compass are abbreviated as N, S, E and W, intermediate points as NW (North-West) and so on. Left and Right are L and R. Remember that L and R apply only if you are following the route in the direction given, and that a compass will not give an accurate reading inside a motor vehicle.

Where a building is described as a shop, inn, Youth Hostel etc, it is open to the public *for that purpose only*. For all other buildings which are open to the public at any time, opening times are given immediately following the appearance of the building's name in **bold type**. As these may change from year to year, it is advisable to check with the property concerned, or a Tourist Information Office, before visiting. National Trust properties are indicated by (*NT*).

Where opening times are not given, buildings are **not open**. Please remember that these are people's homes, workplaces or holiday retreats and respect their privacy. For everyone's sake, and even if you are a solitary walker, please keep in mind the implications of John Wilson's comment in *The Recreations of Christopher North* (1842):

> We cannot patronize the practice of walking in large parties of ten or a score, ram-stam and helter-skelter, on to the front-green or gravel-walk of any private nobleman or gentleman's house, to enjoy, from a commanding station, an extensive or picturesque view of the circumjacent country. It is too much in the style of the Free and Easy.

INTRODUCTION

We must blame Mr Gardiner's business for the loss of one of English literature's more promising Lakeland tours. In Chapter 27 of *Pride and Prejudice*, Elizabeth Bennet agrees to join her aunt and uncle on a visit to the
Lakes:

> 'My dear, dear Aunt,' she rapturously cried, 'what delight! what felicity!
> You give me fresh life and vigour. Adieu to disappointment and spleen.
> What are men to rocks and mountains? Oh! what hours of transport we
> shall spend! ...'

Alas, all too soon a letter brings the news that 'Mr Gardiner would be
prevented by business from setting out till a fortnight later'. They are
'obliged to give up the Lakes'.

The suggestion of a Lake District holiday for her heroine is, of course, a
teasing joke on Jane Austen's part. She herself had never been there; and to
exercise Elizabeth's wit on the 'rocks and mountains' would have diverted
her novel into topical satire, for by 1813, when *Pride and Prejudice*
appeared, the tour of the Lakes had been a fashionable commonplace for
nearly twenty years.

Until the mid-eighteenth century the literary history of the area had
been what one would expect of a remote and fairly poor northern agricultural region. In the ninth and tenth centuries, but leaving no written trace,
there must have been an oral treasury of myth, song and folktale enjoyed
by the Norse settlers who carved out small farms from the marsh and forest
of the valleys. Later, from about 1100, there were chronicles and saints'
lives produced in the monasteries, and from the sixteenth century
onwards a scattering of gifted minor poets – Richard Braithwaite of
Burneside, Thomas Hoggart of Troutbeck, Thomas Tickell of Bridekirk,
and all those talented, forgotten individuals who wrote poignant or witty
verses to be carved on gravestones and other things.

The Lake District achieved prominence, and gained an identity, from
the coincidence of several utterly disparate factors. The first was
road-building. After Bonny Prince Charlie's 1745 campaign it was realised
in London that the Union between England and Scotland demanded better
communications. A road-building programme was begun and by 1768 the
main route north through Westmorland and Cumberland, now the A591,
was being levelled and surfaced. Although most roads in the district
remained mere boggy tracks straggling between pothole and boulder, a
central strip from Lancaster to Keswick was now open to private carriages.

At much the same time, educated Englishmen were starting to take an
interest in 'picturesque' landscape. Paintings by, or in the manner of, Poussin, Claude Lorraine and Salvator Rosa were brought back from the Grand
Tour or marketed as engravings, and after 1750 British landscape artists
began to come north to explore Cumbrian landscapes which, with their

lakes, waterfalls and rugged mountain vistas, resembled the work of the French and Italian masters.

The popular idea of the Lake District as a place with an identity of its own, to be explored by touring for the sake of its scenery, was precipitated by the poet Thomas Gray. In October 1769 Gray travelled at leisure between Keswick and Lancaster looking at the scenery. He was equipped with several 'Claude glasses' – small convex pocket-mirrors, plain or tinted, in which a landscape could be viewed (over one's shoulder) and composed into a living picture, supposedly like a composition of Claude Lorraine. The Claude glass had been invented to help painters find subjects, but Gray viewed the landscape itself as a work of art, as 'picturesque', though he does not use the word himself. He described his tour in a series of beautifully-written letters to his friend Thomas Wharton, and after his death the letters (still the best and most delightful account of a Lakeland tour) were published by William Mason in his 1775 *Life of Gray*. They became enormously popular and encouraged literate people to visit the Lakes and seek out the scenes Gray had described.

Publication of Gray's letters was quickly followed by Thomas West's still more popular *Guide to the Lakes: Dedicated to the Lovers of Landscape Studies and to all who have Visited, or Intend to visit the Lakes in Cumberland, Westmorland and Lancashire* (1778). It was the first systematic guide to the area, and it formalised Gray's perceptions by identifying a series of specific 'stations' or standpoints from which the best views might be obtained. Most of these are given in the present book; some are still popular viewpoints. Travelling in the Lakes soon became a popular middle- and upper-class recreation, especially after 1789 when revolution and war made continental travel impossible. *Guides* and *Tours* poured from the press, and have never ceased to do so. The best of them form an important literary *genre*, and I quote from them freely in this book.

As a literary entity the Lake District was already well known when William and Dorothy Wordsworth came to live at Grasmere in 1799. It is, to say the least of it, a curious coincidence that the great poet of nature and human affections should have spent his childhood in a region which was considered the quintessence of grandeur and beauty in English landscape. Born at Cockermouth in 1770 and educated at Hawkshead, Wordsworth had written the early poems of *Lyrical Ballads* mainly in Somerset, but in 1794 he and Dorothy, together for the first time since their troubled childhood, walked from Ambleside to Keswick and resolved to make the district their home. Their arrival at Dove Cottage was followed by a great creative outpouring, including (on William's part) 'Michael', the first drafts of *The Prelude*, 'Resolution and Independence', and much of the 'Immortality' Ode; in fascinating counterpoint to this, Dorothy composed her Journal.

Wordsworth never again lived away from the Lakes, moving merely from Grasmere to Rydal, and his presence attracted others. Coleridge came, then the essayists Thomas De Quincey and John Wilson. Coleridge drew Southey, who stayed long after Coleridge had left again. The notion of a school of 'Lake Poets' arose, a natural journalistic simplification, but (apart from Wordsworth and Coleridge) these writers really had little in common. What they did share, to some extent, was an interest in landscape and an appreciation of the local community, still characterised by the 'Statesmen (or Estatesmen), small farmers who owned their land and were famous for their resilience and independence of outlook.

As Wordsworth's reputation grew in the 1820s and '30s, it added another dimension to the Lake District's literary attractions, and this had important consequences. For the Victorian reader, Wordsworth's poetic authority centred especially upon his long poem *The Excursion* (*The Prelude* did not appear until after his death). A philosophical reflection on man, nature and society, *The Excursion* promoted humane values, including education, social concern and a respect for the relationship between human beings and the rural landscape. Its values had a deep impact upon John Ruskin, who visited the Lakes many times before settling at Brantwood in 1872. Ruskin was what we should now call a passionate conservationist, whose love of the countryside was linked to an interest in manual skills and traditional crafts.

Like Wordsworth, Ruskin attracted friends and disciples to the Lakes, and his influence was extraordinary. One young admirer, H.D. Rawnsley, went on (with Octavia Hill and Sir Robert Hunter) to found the National Trust. Rawnsley's friend Beatrix Potter also became an early supporter, and bequeathed her extensive Lakeland landholdings to the Trust. Ruskin's secretary, W.G. Collingwood, almost single-handedly transformed the historial and archaeological understanding of the Lake District, and for good measure befriended a young journalist called Arthur Ransome. Ransome, imbued with attitudes which are easily traced to Ruskin, invented (with *Swallows and Amazons*, 1930) the modern children's novel, incidentally promoting the idea that children can benefit from outdoor adventure and the acquisition of real skills, from sailing and semaphore to metallurgy and the building of blast-furnaces.

The blast-furnace (it appears in *Pigeon Post*, 1936) deserves its place here, for it would be wrong to think of the Lake District as an agricultural Arcadia untouched by industry. Part of the area's unique flavour comes precisely from the fact that it is a spectacular rural landscape subtly tinged by the marks of industry. Mining, iron-smelting, quarrying and charcoal-burning have gone on here since prehistoric times. In the early industrial revolution Keswick and Caldbeck were mill-towns. Historians have pointed out that a timely accident, in the form of the change from water-power to steam, saved the district from real damage. Had the development of steam-power been slower the availability of abundant heads of water would have outweighed the disadvantages of mountain roads and remoteness from cities, and the Lakes (like the west Pennines) would have been irrevocably industrialised.

Happily, steam came and the demand for coal moved the industries to the Cumberland coast, which is still scarred. Yet in the central Lakes mining went on until recently, and quarrying still does, as the detonations and rumblings to be heard most days in Langdale and Coniston testify. And from most of the higher peaks on a clear day you can see the nuclear installations around Sellafield, now one of the district's chief employers.

Industry, agriculture and, for the past two centuries, tourism have developed a symbiotic relationship in Cumbria: naturally, for all depend on the area's rich and complicated geology. Essentially the district consists of two massive domes of very old and very hard rock, centring on Scafell and Skiddaw, surrounded by belts of red sandstone and white limestone. You will see these in the buildings as you travel. During the ice ages snow from the 'domes' slowly moved downhill, packing into glaciers which scraped out the radiating valleys and left lakes in the deeper hollows when the ice melted. (The lakes themselves are thus quite young geologically – only some twelve thousand years old.) It is with good reason that Lakeland writers have always loved stone, from the Rock of Names carved at Wythburn with Coleridge's penknife to the fragment from Coniston Old Man which Arthur Ransome kept on his desk.

And what of this book? For Wordsworth's Michael, 'the green valleys, and the streams and rocks' were 'like a book' preserving the memory of the work, the triumphs and crises of his life as a hill farmer. Loved landscapes acquire a human meaning, and for centuries the Lake District has fostered not only human life but a harvest of thought and literature whose effect has been felt far beyond this small corner of England. Many writers have lived here; others have come briefly to work or to rest. Some have exploited the place, some have hated it. Some who never came have been inspired by a placename, or the picture on a postcard. To link places with the writing they inspired or allowed, as this book tries to do, is to understand something about how people see and use landscape, and about how places enter people's minds, to change their ways of thinking and feeling.

As for my 'coverage' of literature, I hope I have mentioned all the important matters that a reader might expect to find in a book of this sort, and I have tried to be systematic in dealing with significant minor writers. But the field is endless. Finally, my criteria have been personal and I have included what seemed interesting: scraps of weird information, traces of the quirkiness of human nature, good verse or prose in unlikely places, interesting writing by forgotten authors.

Throughout the task I have been haunted by thoughts of Coleridge, who (having been richly misled by Hutchinson's *History of Cumberland* and other topographical books) stigmatised 'all authors of tours, county histories &c' – a category into which he would certainly have put this book – as 'Damned liars, strong words but true.' Absolute accuracy is not attainable in human enterprises, but I can at any rate claim that this book contains no lies. I have driven every road mentioned here, I have walked every path; I have (almost) climbed every mountain. Except where I indicate otherwise, I have myself seen the things listed. I hope the reader will enjoy these explorations as much as I did, and will take them further.

This revised edition has given me the chance to add a number of new authors, and some old ones I had missed; to update directions and take account of changes in building and landscape; to add the results of recent research on many details; and to correct mistakes, a few of which had become embarrassing. If you have something else to add or correct, please write and tell me.

In the first edition of this book, I thanked a great many people who had helped in its preparation. I remain grateful to all of them, and think especially of those who have since died: George Kirkby (1936-98), finest gardener at Dove Cottage since Dorothy herself; Bill Ruddick (1939-94), friend and colleague; the poet William Scammell (1939-2000), whose characteristically incisive review pointed out things I had missed; and from further back, Pete Laver (1947-83), whose energy and creativity continue to inspire all who knew him. Belatedly, I should also like to thank Hunter Davies and the panel of judges who so encouragingly awarded the first edition of this book Lakeland Book of the Year: The Hunter Davies Prize in 1994. I hope they will find this revised edition a little bit better. (I suppose there's absolutely no chance of another prize?...)

For help with this new edition I am particularly grateful to Brian Wilkinson, who generously gave his time and went to immense lengths to obtain elusive information of many kinds; to Robert Woof, Director of the Wordsworth Trust; and to Jeff Cowton, Curator of the Wordsworth Museum and Library, Dove Cottage, Grasmere. I should also like to thank Michael Baron; Derek Denman; Philippa Harrison and Anthony McConnell; Christine Hughes; William Roberts; Duncan Wu; and the staffs of the British Library, the John Rylands University Library of Manchester, the Portico Library and the Wordsworth Library, Grasmere. I am grateful to Graham Beech at Sigma Press, for seeing that a new edition was needed and helping to make it possible; to Don Williams of Bute Cartographics for his fine work on the maps; and to Jean Stewart, for her care with the manuscript and presentation of the book. Thanks also to my wife Amanda, who as usual heroically kept the household functioning whilst I buried myself in libraries or got lost among the fells.

GREVEL LINDOP

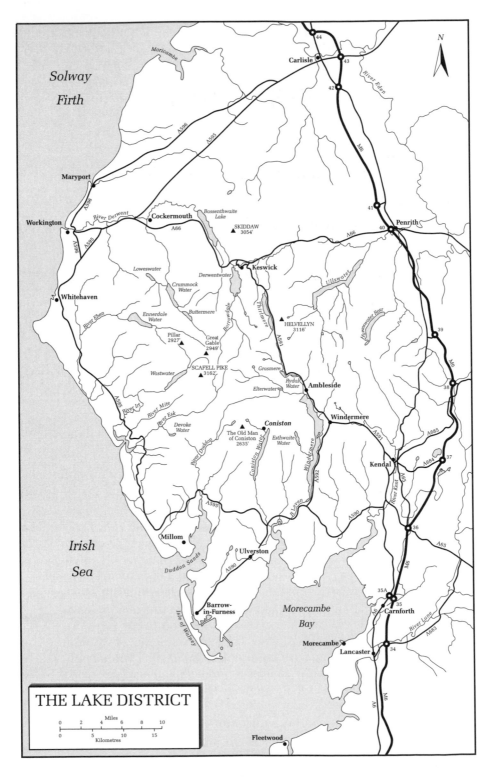

THE LAKE DISTRICT

CONTENTS

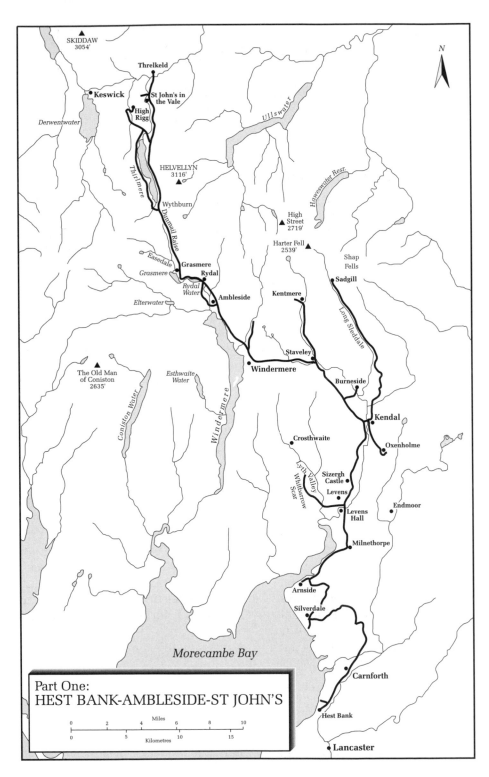

Part One:
HEST BANK-AMBLESIDE-ST JOHN'S

PART ONE

Hest Bank – Ambleside –
St John's in the Vale

Hest Bank and Morecambe Bay

We begin some way outside the Lake District proper, at **Hest Bank**, 6m N of
Lancaster. If you had travelled northward to the Lakes at any time before
1857, this is where your real journey would have started, crossing the
sands of Morecambe Bay at low tide to avoid twenty miles of bad roads and
heavy tolls to Cartmel.

For the point where travellers turned away from land and ventured out
across the Bay, leave the M6 motorway at junction 34, following signs for
Morecambe, then for the Promenade. Go N along the coast road; pass the
Hest Bank level crossing and turn L at sign for Morecambe Lodge and Red
Bank Farm; follow road down to car park. The road continues, unmetalled,
over a belt of pebbles and grass, then disappears into the sand.

The journey across the Bay made a magical beginning to a Lakeland
tour; as Wordsworth put it,

> The Stranger, from the moment he sets his foot on those Sands, seems to
> leave the turmoil and traffic of the world behind him; and, crossing the
> majestic plain whence the sea has retired, he beholds, rising apparently
> from its base, the cluster of mountains among which he is going to wander,
> and towards whose recesses, by the Vale of Coniston, he is gradually and
> peacefully led.

At low tide the sea exposes more than 120 square miles of sand: an extraordinary, shining desert. Crossing it is perilous. There are quicksands, shifting river channels, and an incoming tide which may vary half an hour
either side of the official tables depending on wind direction, and can
arrive as a wall of water six feet high moving faster than a man can run.
Guides have always been essential. In medieval times they were maintained by the monks of Cartmel and Conishead Priories; since the dissolution of the monasteries they have been the responsibility of the Crown.
The Gothic novelist Ann Radcliffe crossed the Leven Sands at the E side of
the Bay on her 1794 tour and tells us that the Guide

> is punctual to the spot as the tides themselves, where he shivers in the
> dark comfortless midnight of winter, and is scorched on the shadeless
> sands, under the noons of summer, for a stipend of ten pounds a year! and
> he said that he had fulfilled the office for thirty years.

The *Lonsdale Magazine* for February 1821 gives a splendid (albeit

CROSSING THE KENT CHANNEL
1882

semifictional) account of the crossing, supposedly written by a cheerful youth on a tour. We begin in the inn at Lancaster:

> I was aroused, by the bustle of preparation, about five o'clock ... I found my father, uncle, and sister already assembled. I was regaling my senses with the fumes of the coffee, when the driver unceremoniously burst into the room: – 'For God's sake,' said he, 'make haste. The tide is down, and we should have been, by this time, at Hest Bank. If you delay, we shall all be drowned.'

They arrive in time, and as they cross the Kent channel,

> A more picturesque, grotesque, *touresque*, or whatever other *esque* scene you may think fit to call it, I think I never saw. There could not be fewer than forty carts, gigs, horses, chaises, etc. with men, women, children, dogs, and I can hardly tell what beside, all in the river at once ... It would have been a fine model ... to draw the Passage of the Red Sea from ... The waves dashing through the wheels – the horses up to the breast in water – the vehicles, some driving one way, some another, in all imaginable confusion – the carriers swearing – the drivers cracking their whips – the women and children screaming – and the apparent impossibility of any of them ever escaping – formed altogether such a *coup d'oeil* as I never had seen nor ever expected to see.

Turner made the crossing on his two Northern tours, and the experience inspired two paintings of 'Lancaster Sands' (1816 and 1825): the first shows the Lancaster coach in heavy rain racing against the incoming tide, the second the arrival of a crowd of travellers at Hest Bank in radiant sunshine.

The perils of the sands feature in Elizabeth Gaskell's short story 'The Sexton's Hero' where a rejected suitor loses his life saving his sweetheart, now another man's wife, from the incoming tide. A good fictional glimpse of the sands and their strange atmosphere is also given in the opening pages of Melvyn Bragg's *The Maid of Buttermere* (1987), where the imposter Hatfield walks out into the solitude of the Bay to practise his new role as The Honourable Alexander Augustus Hope.

In 1857 railway viaducts were built across the estuary, putting an end to most cross-Bay traffic, but the present Queen's Guide to the Sands, Mr Cedric Robinson, still takes parties of walkers across, marking the route in the traditional way with 'brobs', branches of laurel embedded in the sand, which will survive several tides before being dislodged (they can be clearly seen in Turner's paintings). The walks, however, now leave from Arnside, for in 1980 the Kent shifted its bed and the Hest Bank route is now unsafe.

Finally, a footnote from the Lancashire humorist Edwin Waugh, who tells us (in *Over Sands to the Lakes*, 1882) that a gentleman once asked a guide if his colleagues

> were never lost on the sands. 'I never knew any lost,' said the guide; 'there's one or two drowned now and then; but they're generally found somewhere i'th bed when th'tide goes out.'

The very name of **Morecambe Bay** is testimony to the spell cast by books over the landscape hereabouts. Until the eighteenth century the estuary was known simply as 'Kent Sands'. But the Greek geographer Ptolemy, in his *Geographia* (c 150AD), mentions an estuary somewhere in NW Britain called 'Morecambe'. In 1771 Whitaker's *History of Manchester* suggested that Ptolemy's Morecambe might be the Kent Sands. The identification was popularised by Thomas West in his *Antiquities of Furness* (1774), the first guide book to the area; educated tourists began to use it and soon the Bay had a new name. The seaside resort grew later, and now everyone knows Morecambe. (But if you look at a map of the Carlisle area you will see a small estuary just S of the Solway Firth called 'Moricambe'; this is a relic of another, and less popular, attempt at identifying Ptolemy's estuary.)

Silverdale and Arnside

From Hest Bank, take the coast road N, following signs to Carnforth and then Silverdale; if coming directly from the M6, leave at junction 35 and follow signs to **Silverdale**, an attractive coastal village amongst wooded limestone hills. Leave the village going S and after ½m at junction go down small road (signed Jenny Brown's Point). On R you will see **Gibraltar Farm** and **Tower House**, formerly a single property. In the attractive Tower House garden is a square three-storey stone tower. Elizabeth Gaskell often visited the farm, writing in a letter of 1850,

> Silverdale can hardly be called the sea-side, as it is a little dale running down to Morecambe Bay, with grey limestone rocks on all sides, which in the sun or moonlight, glisten like silver. And we are keeping holiday in the most rural farmhouse lodgings, so that our children learn country interests, and ways of living and thinking.

Sometimes the Gaskells rented the Tower as well as rooms in the farm-house. In 1858 Mrs Gaskell reported:

> We live in a queer, pretty crampy house, at the back of a great farm house ... the house is covered with roses, and great white virgin-sceptred lilies, and sweetbriar bushes grow in the small flagged square court ... In the garden, half flower half kitchen is an old Square Tower, or 'Peel' – a remnant of the Border towers.

She was wrong about the tower – it is from the early nineteenth century – but she loved it and found it a good place for work. 'You don't know *how* beautiful Silverdale is,' she told a friend, 'and a tower of our own! think of that!' In 1855 she began her *Life of Charlotte Brontë* here. Large parts of her novels *Ruth* (1853) and *Sylvia's Lovers* (1863) were also written here.

The village of Silverdale provided the model for 'Abermouth' in *Ruth*, whose Chapter 24 portrays

> the black posts, which, rising above the heaving waters, marked where the fishermen's nets were laid ... and grey, silvery rocks, which sloped away into brown moorland, interspersed with a field here and there of golden, waving corn. Behind were purple hills, with sharp clear outlines, touching the sky.

Return to junction and go R (E) up Hollins Lane to rejoin main road; at next junction go L (N). After 100yds private drive on R leads through woods to **The Sheiling**, built by Elizabeth Gaskell's daughters and later the home of the poet and dramatist Gordon Bottomley from March 1914 until his death in 1948. Hard now to believe that this pleasant but rather suburban-looking dwelling, with its red tiles and half-timbering, was once the last word in architectural design and supposed to harmonise perfectly with its rural setting.

The house is described in Edward Thomas's poem 'The Sheiling', written after a visit to Bottomley in November 1916, shortly before Thomas's departure for the Western Front, where he died the following year:

> It stands alone
> Up in a land of stone
> All worn like ancient stairs,
> A land of rocks and trees
> Nourished on wind and stone ...

During the visit Thomas entertained his host with 'a riotous collection of army-songs' and walked in the nearby hills.

The landscape hereabouts has been celebrated in several poems by an almost-forgotten writer of the 1920s, Margot Adamson. 'Easter on Thrang End' surveys the view over farmland and sea from the hills above **Thrang End Farm**, just across the road from The Sheiling – the 'White rocks, green hill grass and wide sky' with the spring sun on brown bracken-stalks and the silver shallows of Morecambe Bay. 'Beyond Slack Head' notes the rich wildlife of this relatively untouched area, where the limestone pavements encourage a plentiful growth of wild flowers.

Continue N following signs (about 4m) to **Arnside**, the quiet and amiable vestige of a minor Victorian seaside resort. This is a pleasant place to potter about; Arthur Ransome enthusiasts will want to follow the promenade W to its end, then take the causeway footpath (signed New Barns Bay) a further 250yds for the shabby sheds of **Crossfield's Boatyard**, where the original dinghy *Swallow*, which was owned by Ransome and helped inspire his *Swallows and Amazons*, was built.

From the promenade also Mr Cedric Robinson's guided walks set out across Morecambe Bay. For details of dates and times, contact the Tourist Information Office at Grange-over-Sands. A walk across the Bay is an exhilarating experience of a strange and beautiful terrain: if you are bound for a walking holiday in the Lakes, why not enter the district in the traditional way, across the sands, and share something of the sublimity tasted by the earliest tourists?

Near the promenade the **Kent Viaduct**, a graceless utilitarian object of squat brick piers and grey metalwork, crosses the estuary. It is the subject of Gordon Bottomley's melancholy poem 'The Viaduct' (1906): the monotonous procession of 'Piled trucks, tarpaulin mounds, and heavy vans' lumbering over the viaduct reminds Bottomley of an Imperial Roman Triumph.

Levens, the Lyth Valley, Crosthwaite and Sizergh

Continue N on B5282 to Milnthorpe, then go L (N) on A6 3m to **Levens Hall** (*open early April to mid-October, Sunday-Thursday, 12-5; closed Friday and Saturday. Car park; admission charge*), a fine country house whose core is a medieval pele tower, around which cluster gabled Tudor wings, some with enormous barrel-like Lakeland chimneys.

Turner sketched the Hall in August 1816, and Edward Lear, landscape painter and nonsense poet, stayed here, sketching the house and gardens, on his Lakeland tour of August-September 1836. From March to June 1897 Mrs Humphry Ward rented the house whilst writing *Helbeck of Bannisdale*, using the Hall as the main model for the novel's 'Bannisdale Hall'. The house delighted her:

> at last we arrived – saw the wonderful grey house rising above the river in the evening light, … & plunged into the hall, the drawingrooms, the dining-room, and all the intricacies of the upper passages & turrets with the delight and the curiosity of a pack of children. Great wood and peat fires were burning everywhere; the magnificent carved chimney pieces in the drawingrooms, the arms of Elizabeth over the hall-fire, the strange stucco birds and beasts running round the hall, shewing dimly in the scanty lamp-light – we shall want about six more lamps – and the beauty of the marvellous old place took us all by storm. Then through endless passages and vast kitchens, bright with long rows of copper pans & moulds we made our way out into the gardens among the yews and cedars, and

LEVENS HALL
Thomas Allom, 1832

had just enough light to see that Levens apparently is like nothing else but
itself, and that there are broad straight gravelled paths among the fantastic
creatures & pyramids & crowns ...

It is hard to stop quoting: one can feel the novelist's imagination taking fire.
The house had everything – even a ghost, the 'Levens Lady', a legend
which figures in the novel.

The dining-room, its walls covered with gilded leather, is clearly
described in the novel: "'It [the leather] is very dim and dingy now,' said
Helbeck, 'but when it was fresh, it was the wonder of the place. The room
got the name of Paradise from it.'" *Helbeck* also describes the grounds,
including the extraordinary topiary-garden. The seventeenth-century
owner was a friend of the diarist John Evelyn, an early enthusiast for land-
scape-gardening, and the garden is the best one of its period still intact.
During Mrs Ward's tenancy several literary visitors came, notably Henry
James, about whose visit (alas) we have no details.

Opposite the Hall gates a walk leads NE alongside the River Kent for 1m.
At the far end, where the A590 now crosses the river, was formerly the 'lit-
tle bridge ... with some steps in the crag leading down to it', where Laura in
Helbeck waits for her secret twilight meeting with Hubert Mason.
Returning across the park she is mistaken for the ghost of 'the Bannisdale
Lady' (modelled, of course, on the Levens Lady).

Immediately N of the bridge by the Hall gates, turn L (W) on A590 for 2m,
then R (N) on to A5074. The road runs up the **Lyth Valley** under the slope of
Whitbarrow Scar, an enormous limestone ridge wooded on its lower
reaches.

The valley is yet another setting for *Helbeck of Bannisdale*, which describes it well in springtime:

> The course of the bright twisting stream was dimmed here and there by mists of fruit blossom. For the damson trees were all out, patterning the valleys; marking the bounds of orchard and field, of stream and road. Each with its larch clump, the grey and white farms lay scattered on the pale green of the pastures; on either side of the valley the limestone pushed upward, through the grassy slopes of the fells, and made long edges and 'scars' against the sky; while down by the river hummed the old mill.

This little-known region is celebrated also in Margot Adamson's poem 'Spring Under Whitbarrow Scar'. Visitors to this 'Wide silent valley/ Beneath whose scree-faced hill the sea birds call' will still see the 'Good, greystone, white-washed farms with northern names' just as she catalogues them in her poem:

> Foulshaw, Rus Mickle, Grassgarth, Flodder Hall,
> Johnscales that's hidden in the shadowing trees,
> High Sampool where the restless lapwings call

– though not quite in that order. To appreciate the area's gentle delights properly, park where you can (not easy) and walk W up the lane that leaves A5074 1m N of the main junction with A590. This tiny road takes you past all the farms mentioned in the poem, and when you reach The Row, a hamlet at the N end of the valley, you can go W past the houses and follow a path up on to the top of the Scar itself – a strange gentle wasteland of grey limestone fragments, remnants of an ancient seabed, with marvellous views.

The naturalist William Pearson gives lively sketches of the area, its wildlife and human goings-on in his *Notes on the Natural History ... of Crosthwaite and Lyth, and the Valley of the Winster* (1839). Few details escaped him, and one is grateful to him for preserving the text of a notice he once found barring the main road up the valley:

> this Rood is stoped
> ites onder Repare
> and is thearfore onpaseable.

1m NW of The Row, follow signs to the tiny village of **Crosthwaite**, home in the eighteenth century of two doggerel rhymesters, John Audland and Jamie Muckelt. Audland, 'once falling foul of some lawyer, Ulverston-way, vented his wrath in these terms':

> God made men, and men made money;
> God made bees, and bees made honey;
> But the Devil himself made lawyers and 'ttorneys,
> And placed them in U'ston and Dalton i Forness.

Continue W through the village to rejoin A5074; after ⅓m round sharp bend to the R, watch for a group of cottages at Low Yews. William Pearson (1780–1856), naturalist, banker and author was born at **The Yews**, a house which formerly stood beside these cottages. The road continues NW to Bowness. We return to the S end of the Lyth Valley and go E on A590 to its junction with A6. Follow signs to **Sizergh Castle** (*NT: open April-October, Sunday-Thursday 1.30-5.30 (gardens 12.30-5.30); closed Friday and Satur-day*). Car park; admission charge.The poet Thomas Gray visited on his Lakeland tour in 1769. He walked in the park, and his account gives a fasci-nating glimpse of the very beginning of the industrial revolution, when its activities were seen as demonic but sublime, like an illustration to *Para-dise Lost*:

> This seat of the Stricklands, an old catholic family, is an ancient hall-house, with a very large tower embattled ... I soon came to the river; it works its way in a narrow and deep rocky channel over hung with trees. The calmness and brightness of the evening, the roar of the waters, and the thumping of huge hammers at an iron-forge not far distant, made it a singular walk: but as to the falls (for there are two) they are not four feet high. I went on, down to the forge, and saw the demons at work by the light of their own fires: the iron is brought in pigs to Milthrop [Milnthorpe] by sea from Scotland, &c. and is here beat into bars and plates.

To reach the walk, take the lane E from the Hall entrance and go under the road. Follow the lane to its end, then turn L (N) until you reach a footbridge. You can follow the river for about 2m. There are no ironworks now, and perhaps Gray means that he went down to Milnthorpe, then a busy little port (the Kent estuary has since silted up).

Kendal

Continue 4m N to **Kendal** (*several well-hidden car parks, and a truly fiend-ish one-way system*), a pleasant town of silver-grey limestone clustered in the Kent valley. Drayton's *Poly-Olbion* (1619) gives us an eloquent intro-duction:

> Where *Can* first creeping forth, her feet hath scarcely found,
> But gives that Dale her name, where Kendal towne doth stand,
> For making of our Cloth scarce match'd in all the land.

'Can', of course, is the River Kent, which flows attractively through the town centre. Kendal was famous as a cloth town from the fourteenth century onwards: hence Falstaff's tall story of the 'three misbegotten knaves in Kendal green' who gave him so much trouble in Shakespeare's *Henry IV* Part One.

Most early visitors mention the cloth industry. Celia Fiennes gives a characteristically breathless sketch in 1698:

> Kendal is a town built all of stone, one very broad streete which is the Market Crosse, its a goode tradeing town mostly famed for the cottons; Kendal Cotton is used for blankets and the Scots use them for their plodds [plaids] and there is much made here and also linsiwoolseys and a great deal of leather tann's here and all sorts of commoditys twice a week is the market furnished with all sorts of things.

KENDAL, FROM THE CASTLE
Thomas Allom, 1832

She visited the King's Arms (now gone), where

> One Mrs Rowlandson she does pott up the charr fish the best of any in the country, I was curious to have some and so bespoke some of her.

The food (including the potted charr) was still good at the King's Arms in 1768 when Arthur Young, busy touring the north of England to report on its economic potential and productivity, recorded:

> A good house, very civil, and remarkably cheap. A brace of woodcocks, veal cutlets, and cheese, 1s. a head, dinner. A boiled fowl and sauce, a roast partridge, potted charr, cold ham, tarts, and three or four sorts of foreign sweetmeats, 8d. a head; three people supped. Another supper; cold ham, tarts, potted charr, anchovies, butter and cheese, 6d. a head. Tea or coffee 6d. a head. Other things proportionably cheap.

Between meals, he found time to glance at Kendal, which he thought

> a well built and well paved town, pleasantly situated ... It is famous for several manufactories; the chief of which is that of Knit stockings, employing near 5000 hands by computation.

Hot on the heels of the economic tourist came the aesthetic one. The poet Thomas Gray visited in October 1769:

> the dusk of evening coming on, I entered Kendal almost in the dark, and could distinguish only a shadow of the castle on a hill, and tenter-grounds spread far and wide round the town, which I mistook for houses. My inn promised sadly, having two wooden galleries, like Scotland, in front of it: it was indeed an old ill-contrived house, but kept by civil and sensible people; so I stayed two nights with them, and fared and slept very comfortably.

(He too was at the inevitable King's Arms.) The 'tenter-grounds' were the many fields around the town where new cloth, dampened during 'milling' to improve its texture, was stretched on frames to dry. The town, which he explored next day, did not appeal to him:

> the town consists chiefly of three nearly parallel streets, almost a mile long; except these, all the other houses seem as if they had been dancing a country-dance, and were out: there they stand back to back, corner to corner, some up hill, some down, without intent or meaning. Along by their side runs a fine brisk stream, over which are three stone bridges; the buildings (a few comfortable houses excepted) are mean, of stone, and covered with a bad rough cast.

In general, the town has appealed most to observers who have taken some pleasure in its industries. Joseph Budworth in 1792 noticed with approval that 'the country people, both men and women, were knitting stockings as they drove their peat-carts into the town', and quite apart from its cloth (today only a memory), Kendal's products have always had their own strongly-marked character. In the early nineteenth century it was known for Kendal Black Drop, a preparation of opium and spices said to have been used by Coleridge; a century later it was noted for Black Kendal Twist, still available from local tobacconists, a pipe tobacco much favoured by Arthur Ransome but described by his friend Edward Thomas as 'strong enough to knock out the unaccustomed southerner like a blow from a battering ram'.

W.H. Auden, in his 1959 prose-poem *Dichtung und Wahrheit*, praises his lover as 'more beautiful than a badger, a sea-horse or a turbine built by Gilkes & Co of Kendal'. Sure enough, you will find **Gilkes's factory** (not open to the public) on the E side of the river, just over the bridge behind the Town Hall, still producing some of the world's best water-turbines.

For a tour of Kendal, the **Town Hall** makes a convenient starting-point. **The Tourist Information Office** was formerly the office where A. Wainwright (1907–91) worked as Borough Treasurer from 1947 to 1967, the period when he was writing and illustrating his incomparable *Pictorial Guide to the Lakeland Fells* (seven volumes, 1955–66).

Turn down Lowther Street (at S side of Town Hall) and at the foot of the street bear L and cross the bridge over the Kent for Gilkes's factory. Walk S along the riverbank. When you come level with a small footbridge over the river turn L (E) into Parr Street which leads to a gate into the Castle grounds. **Kendal Castle** is open at all times because several public footpaths run through the grounds. An impressive ruin (mainly thirteenth-century) with three massive, well-preserved towers, it belonged to the father of Catherine Parr, sixth and last queen of Henry VIII – whence Gordon Bottomley's 1912 poem 'The Pride of Westmoreland' celebrates his marriage to a Kendal girl:

> When I married the pride of Westmoreland
> Youth's wisdom did not floor me,
> I took my pick in Kendal town
> Like Harry the Eighth before me.

Return to the riverbank, continue S to the next bridge, and cross it. Turn L (S); after 200yds, on the W side, you will see the plaque marking the house of the painter George Romney, who in 1802 died here, in his native region, after a successful London career.

Turn back and walk N past the bridge. You will see (on R, between road and river) **Holy Trinity Church**, the beautiful and enormous parish church (said to be the largest in Cumbria). On the wall at the SW corner by the door as you enter is Romney's memorial, a black stone tablet with an urn and the tersely eloquent assertion that 'So long as Genius and Talent shall be revered his Fame will live'. A brass plate on the floor at the E end (under the largest stained glass window) shows a more elaborate eloquence in the verse epitaph composed for himself by Ralph Tyrer, vicar of Kendal (died 1627):

> London bredd me, Westminster fedd me
> Cambridge sped me, my Sister wed me,
> Study taught me, Liuing sought me,
> Learning brought me, Kendal caught me,
> Labour pressed me, sicknes distressed me,
> Death oppressed me, & graue possessed me,
> God first gave me, Christ did saue me
> Earth did craue mee, heauen would haue me.

(Line two presumably refers to a marriage arranged through his sister's influence.)

A less conventional memorial is an old and tarnished helmet hanging high up from a bracket at the E end of the N wall, known as the **Rebel's Cap**. This is said to be a relic of the Civil War, worn by the royalist Robert Phillipson (*alias* Robin the Devil) when he pursued his Parliamentarian enemy Colonel Briggs into the church on a Sunday. Phillipson barely escaped alive from the Puritan congregation and lost his helmet in the melée. Scott used the episode in his poem *Rokeby*: for the full story, see p 243.

An early nineteenth-century Vicar of the church, Matthew Murfitt, is commemorated by Wordsworth in his 1814 sonnet, 'Lines written on a blank leaf in … *The Excursion*'. Murfitt was an early admirer of the poem.

Just N of the church is the **Abbott Hall Museum of Lakeland Life and Industry** (*Open Monday-Saturday (closed Sunday) late January to late December,10.30-5 April-September; 10.30-4 November-March. Car park, admission charge.*) There are displays on local history, industry, agriculture and crafts, as well as a room devoted to the life and work of Arthur Ransome. The Ransome room contains manuscripts, drawings, photographs, letters, and books as well as personal items, including Ransome's desk (with typewriter, lucky holed stone from Coniston Old Man, and a vast array of pipes), his fishing rods, chess set and a Jolly Roger flag. A bookcase displays many of his favourite books, including Homer, *The*

Hobbit, volumes of folktales and Icelandic sagas, and works on natural history.

Behind the Museum is the **Abbott Hall Art Gallery** (*opening times as for the Museum; car park, admission charge*), whose permanent collection includes a range of landscape prints and paintings of the Lake District from the early eighteenth century to the present day. There are also temporary exhibitions as fine as any to be found in the country.

Return to the street (Kirkland) and continue N. Opposite the Town Hall turn L (W) up Allhallows Lane, which becomes Beast Banks. Turn down the narrow lane beside number 27 for **The Obelisk**, commemorating the Glorious Revolution of 1688. It stands on a green hill (Castle Howe) and is a somewhat homely object, built, like most things in Kendal, of slightly rugged limestone. Joseph Budworth in 1792 thought it

> too small ... both for the subject, and the noble rise it stands upon; when we saw it yesterday, it looked like a tall chimney; one could imagine, from its scantiness, there had been a want of money; but, as it was built upon so glorious an occasion, it may rather be attributed to want of taste.

A more political being, the novelist Ann Radcliffe, was here in 1795. Something of a Radical, she was well aware that since the French Revolution any praise of political liberty had become suspect, and her comments are forthright:

> At a time, when the memory of that revolution [of 1688] is reviled, and the praise of liberty itself endeavoured to be suppressed by the artifice of imputing to it the crimes of anarchy, it was impossible to omit any act of veneration to the blessings of this event.

Even to visit the obelisk was, for her, a political act, and she thought the view from the spot 'a scene simple, great and free as the spirit [of liberty] revered amidst it.' The view certainly is a good one – probably the best panorama of Kendal you will find.

Return downhill to the main street (here called Highgate) opposite the Town Hall and continue N. The BeWise clothing store stands on the former site of the **King's Arms**, once Kendal's great coaching inn, of which we have already heard. We may add that Coleridge stayed here in January 1804 on his way from Grasmere to London (he was bound for Malta, where he hoped to lose his opium-addiction); and that in April 1794 William and Dorothy Wordsworth arrived here by coach from Halifax and set out on their three-day walk to Keswick – their first visit to the Lake District together since their family had broken up in 1778. They travelled by Staveley, Ambleside and Grasmere, taking the route of the modern A591 road.

Three doors away are the offices of **The Westmorland Gazette**, the oldest newspaper in Cumbria still publishing. It was edited by Thomas De Quincey in 1818–19 and at that time printed work by Wordsworth, Coleridge and John Wilson as well as the usual news and Tory electioneering. In modern times the *Gazette* has been a notable publisher of books of local interest, including the poems of Margaret Cropper and the original editions of the works of A. Wainwright. Nearly opposite is **Market Place**, birthplace of Isabella Lickbarrow (1784-1847), poet and journalist. A Quaker, she spent much of her life in poverty supporting herself and her sisters by her writing. Her *Poetical Effusions* (1814) and other works show sensitivity to the Lakeland landscape and were admired by Wordsworth.

Continue past the Post Office and turn R (E) into Sandes Avenue, continuing across the bridge. One block ahead on the corner is the **Kendal Museum** (*Open Monday-Saturday 10.30-5; closing 4pm in February, March, November, December; small car park, admission charge*), which besides collections illustrating local natural history and archaeology, has a substantial display relating to Alfred Wainwright (1907–91). Wainwright's manuscript notebooks, annotated maps, sketches and photographs used in preparation of the *Guides* are here; there is also material on his early life, and his work as accountant and Borough Treasurer (including pages of his meticulously neat account-books, with the unmistakable signature appearing here and there).

The Museum also contains a collection relating to John Gough (1757–1825), 'the blind botanist', a citizen of Kendal. Wordsworth knew Gough and mentions him in *The Excursion*, Book VII, claiming that

No floweret blooms
Throughout the lofty range of these rough hills,
Nor in the woods, that could from him conceal
Its birth-place; none whose figure did not live
Upon his touch.

He was uncannily good at identifying plants by touch; when a specimen of moss campion was handed to him in 1817 he is said to have responded 'I have never examined this plant before, but it is *Silene acaulis*' – the correct botanical name. He was also a notable teacher of mathematics: among his pupils at Kendal between 1781 and 1793 was John Dalton, later to become world-famous for his Atomic Theory. The Museum has Gough's barometer, journals and collections of plants.

From the Museum continue SE, then follow sign to Sedbergh into Sedbergh Road. After going under railway bridge, watch for Sedbergh Road unexpectedly branching off to L; follow this branch to 103 Sedbergh Road, otherwise known as **Littleholme**, the house designed by Charles Voysey in 1908 for Arthur W. Simpson (1857–1922), the 'Arts and Crafts' woodcarver and designer. To modern eyes Littleholme is not very remarkable: a small square stone house with front door recessed inside a porch with massive beams and an enormous semicircular arch – but it is the subject of Gordon Bottomley's 1918 poem 'Littleholme', dedicated to Simpson, representing the house as a symbol of Kendal's tradition of craftsmanship, and urging

... the need
For handiwork and happy work and work
To use and ease the mind if such sweet towns
Are to be built again or live again.

Before leaving Kendal, we may note that the town was the home (in the late eighteenth century) of David Patrick, 'known far and wide throughout the North country' as 'the intellectual pedlar'. Wordsworth knew him and used aspects of him for the character of the Wanderer in *The Excursion*. Sara Hutchinson, Wordsworth's sister-in-law and the 'Asra' of Coleridge, spent part of her childhood in his family and claimed that she owed him most of her education.

A final point is a curious tradition, repeated in various forms by most early writers on Kendal. Camden puts it most clearly:

> Lower down in the river Can [Kent] are two falls, down which the water rushes with great noise, one at the little town of Levens, the other more to the south near Betham, which are certain prognosticks of weather to the neighbourhood. For, when the northernmost makes a great noise they expect fair weather, and when the southernmost does the same rain and fogs.

Drayton elaborates this with great Baroque flourishes into a magnificently garbled fantasy:

> Then keeping on her course, though having in her traine,
> But *Sput*, a little Brooke, then *Winster* doth retaine,
> Tow'rds the *Vergivian* Sea, by her two mighty Falls,
> (Which the brave *Roman* tongue, her catadoupae calls)
> This eager River seemes outragiously to rore,
> And counterfetting *Nyle*, to deafe the neighbouring shore,
> To which she by the sound apparently doth show,
> The season foule or faire, as then the wind doth blow:
> For when they to the North, the noyse do easliest heare,
> They constantly affirme the weather will be cleere;
> And when they to the South, againe they boldly say,
> It will be clouds or rain the next approaching day.

Since Levens and Betham are both S of Kendal, their direction differing by only a few points of the compass, and respectively some 5 and 10m away as the crow flies, it is hard to see how any of this can be true. But it provided an oddity of the kind seventeenth-century writers loved.

Oxenholme and Endmoor

Leave Kendal going S on A65, then at signed junction take B6254 for **Oxenholme Railway Station**. If you come to the Lakes by train from the S, the chances are that you will change trains here, as travellers have done for more than a century. Those with time to spare may like to emulate James Murray, the great lexicographer and editor of the *Oxford English Dictionary*. On his way to holiday at Keswick in the 1870s, Murray used to arrive at Oxenholme from London at 3.40am accompanied by his wife, five children and the governess. As the Keswick train did not leave until 7.30 the hyperactive Murray took the children up to the top of 'High Knott' for a dawn view of the mountains. Your only difficulty may be that High Knott cannot now be identified with certainty; a local guess is that it was Benson Knott, 3m N of here, whose summit height is somewhat over 1000ft.

The station features as 'Oxencross' in Eliza Lynn Linton's novel *Lizzie Lorton of Greyrigg* (1866): the heiress heroine Margaret arrives here with her troublesome Aunt Harriet, who thinks the place 'a dreadful hole ... Not a fly to be had – not a cup of tea – and I am sure I cannot understand half the creatures say', whilst Margaret goes happily off to hunt for rare plants.

It also appears as 'Strickland Junction' in Arthur Ransome's *Pigeon Post*, and is clearly shown in the illustration of Roger launching the first pigeon from its basket.

Immediately after the bridge over the railway turn R (SW) for ½m to join A65, then follow it S for 3½m to the tiny village of **Endmoor**. Keats and Charles Brown stayed here (at an inn which cannot now be identified) on their way to the Lakes in June 1818. They were on a walking tour, and according to Brown

> the landlady, eyeing the burthens on our backs, inquired if we provided our own eating; on being answered in the negative, she promised accommodation for the night; though, as she said, she was in a *'squeer, as all her house was whitewashing'*.

Keats tells us that the company included 'an old soldier' who 'had served in America – in the Peninsula – indeed in the Continental war from the time of Sir John Moore to the battle of Waterloo'; and 'an old toper, one Richard Radshaw, drunk as a sponge' who 'Suddenly ... thrust his face forward, made a grasp at my knapsack, and asked if we sold spectacles and razors.' They survived the night and went on to Kendal next day.

Longsleddale

Leave Kendal following signs for Penrith (A6), and after 4m take signed turning L into **Longsleddale**. The beautiful winding road leads along an enchanting narrow valley, little visited, scattered with trees and the occasional small farm. Its literary associations are as diverse as could be imagined: it inspired both the 'Greendale' of John Cunliffe's *Postman Pat* children's books (first written in the 1980s when Cunliffe was a teacher at Castle Park Primary School in Kendal) and the 'Long Whindale' of Mrs Humphry Ward's great Victorian novel *Robert Elsmere* (1888).

The novel compresses the landscape somewhat, shortening the valley to bring its parts within easy walking distance and adding a new church and vicarage; otherwise it gives an accurate picture. The opening pages give a fine description of the valley in spring:

> The narrow road, which was the only link between the farmhouses sheltered by the crags at the head of the valley and [the] far-away regions of town and civilisation ... was lined with masses of the white heckberry or bird-cherry, and ran, an arrowy line of white, through the greenness of the sloping pastures. The sides of some of the little becks running down into the main river and many of the plantations round the farms were gay with

the same tree, so that the farmhouses, gray-roofed and gray-walled, standing in the hollows of the fells, seemed here and there to have been robbed of some of their natural austerity.

Follow the road to its end (about 6m) and you can see a cluster of cottages over a stone bridge across the Sprint. This is **Sadgill**, and features in the novel as 'High Close'.

The old farmhouse at the S end, **Low Sadgill**, is the original of 'Burwood Farm', home of the Leyburns in the novel; you will see the 'long line of grey outhouses' and the group of sycamores, Scotch firs and copper beech as windbreak. It is all as described in the novel except that the new bow-window added by the Leyburns is, happily, a fiction.

Just N of Low Sadgill is **Middle Sadgill**, which seems to be the novel's 'High Ghyll' – a 'gray stone house, backed by the sombre red of a great copper beech, and overhung by crags'. The copper beech is still there. This is the home of Mary Backhouse, who dies after seeing the 'High Fell' ghost. Attending her during her illness brings Robert and Catherine Leyburn together and leads to their marriage. Robert proposes to Catherine in the small wood behind the houses, **Sadgill Wood**.

High Street, Kidsty Pike and Haweswater

This is a fine and fairly strenuous walk. From Sadgill cross the bridge back to the road and continue N on the bridleway. It runs up to Gatescarth Pass. At top of pass near metal gate take footpath W. You are now climbing **Harter Fell** and heading for High Street on a path which figures many times in *Robert Elsmere*, where it is said to be haunted by the ghost of a woman who walks along it at midnight every Midsummer Eve:

> If you see her and she passes you in silence, why you only get a fright for your pains. But if she speaks to you, you die within the year.

Harter Fell itself gives a splendid view of Haweswater. The path continues along the summit ridge and at a large cairn turns E and soon comes over **Small Water**, a little tarn under grey screes. Go down to the tarn if you like. Just below the outlet are the stepping-stones where Robert fatefully takes Catherine's hand as they walk back to Longsleddale from 'Shanmoor' (Kentmere) in Chapter VII.

The main path continues NW on to High Street (if in doubt, use your compass: do not mistake beacon on Thornthwaite Crag, to the W, for trig. point on High Street, NW but not yet visible). As you make your way towards High Street you are walking along the top of Blea Water Crag, above Blea Water, another small tarn ('blea' means blue, and it certainly does look blue in sunshine). Watch your step: Clarke's *Survey* tells us that a man called Dixon fell three hundred feet off the crag while foxhunting in 1763:

> He had no bones broken, but was terribly bruised, and was almost completely scalped, so that now he has no hair upon his head, except a

little above one of his ears. He struck against the rock several times in his fall, but says he was not sensible of it …

As soon as he fell, he instantly raised himself upon his knees, and, in his own dialect, cried out, 'Lads, t'fox is gane out at t'hee end; lig t'dogs on, and I'll come syun;' that is, 'Lads, the fox is gone out at the high end; lay the dogs on, I'll come soon.'

He then fell down 'insensible'. The place was known thereafter as Dixon's Three Jumps.

The path continues to the triangulation pillar on **High Street** (the 'High Fell' of *Robert Elsmere*). It owes its name to the Roman road from Ambleside to Penrith, which runs along its summit ridge. The road, which ran here because the valleys were then full of swamp and forest, is mentioned in an 1826 poem by Wordsworth:

> The massy ways, carried along these heights
> By Roman perseverance, are destroyed
> Or hidden under ground, like sleeping worms

– and certainly the surface of the road is no longer to be found.

The plateau where the triangulation point stands is known as **Race-course Hill**, because until 1830 shepherds from the surrounding valleys met there each July to exchange strayed sheep, hold races and celebrate with 'ale and cakes … supplied from the neighbouring villages.'

Go N along the summit for 1m and then fork R (due E) along another ridge to the top of **Kidsty Pike**, mentioned in Wordsworth's 'The Brothers':

> On that tall pike
> (It is the loneliest place of all these hills)
> There were two springs which bubbled side by side,
> As if they had been made that they might be
> Companions for each other: the huge crag
> Was rent with lightning – one hath disappeared;
> The other, left behind, is flowing still.

The event (which in the poem symbolises the death of one of two brothers) took place, according to Wordsworth, 'some years before 1800'. I have not, however, been able to find any spring here at all. Perhaps it depends on the weather.

Continue E and the path descends to the shore of **Haweswater**, a reservoir formed in the 1930s by damming the Haweswater Beck to expand the former small lake and flood the valley. The village and valley of **Mardale** – by all accounts a particularly attractive valley – exist now only in literature and old photographs. Writing in the 1880s, Mrs Humphry Ward tells us that Mardale (the 'Marrisdale' of *Robert Elsmere*) is 'a long green vale compared to which [Longsleddale] … was the great world itself. Marrisdale had no road and not a single house.' Here the heroine, Catherine Leyburn, comes to reflect on her love for Robert Elsmere.

Eliza Lynn Linton describes Haweswater as it was before damming:

> seen in the calm of evening, with every mountain form repeated with
> tenfold force of line and colour in the black lake, and all these forms so
> grand and severe, it is something well worth travelling far to see.

As for the village,

> in truth, it is all very primitive and rough ... The church is picturesque
> enough, with its gilt weathercock now so seldom seen, but it is by no
> means a rustic cathedral; the royal hotel – and the only one – is a wretched
> wayside public-house, where you can get eggs and bacon and nothing else
> – except the company of a tipsy parson lying in bed with his gin-bottle by
> his side.

Wordsworth tells us that Thomas Holme, the deaf man of whom he
sketches an eloquent biography in Book VII of *The Excursion*, is buried in
Mardale churchyard.

The building of the dam, which flooded the valley to increase Manchester's water supply, and the remote rural community which it destroyed,
are vividly described in Sarah Hall's powerful novel *Haweswater* (2002).
The novel includes an accurate glimpse of the village's brief reappearance
in 1979, when

> a severe drought would take the water levels down further than they had
> been since the flooding, and would turn the lakebed into dry, parched
> skin, [and] the shallow skeleton of the old village would rise again,
> crumbling, out of the desert-looking earth. The bridge in the village would
> be almost perfect,...though the mason's mark on the keystone would be
> eroded almost to nothing.

In the woodland at the N end of Haweswater, just above the road that
runs along the lake's SE shore, is **Wallow Crag**. Coleridge walked here with
Wordsworth in November 1799, and records the local tale that Robert
Lowther, a local landowner and notorious rogue who refused to stay in his
coffin, was banished by a priest to lie under Wallow Crag, the only stone
large enough to keep him down.

Finally, anecdotes of two neighbouring valleys. 5m to the N is
Heltondale. Eliza Lynn Linton describes coming to one of the cottages here
as she and her husband walked towards Haweswater from Pooley Bridge.
They went in 'to ask for bread and milk', and found an idyll of oldfashioned
hospitality:

> The house was a poor-looking, but well-built stone cottage, surrounded by
> a wall that of itself at once inspired the feeling of loneliness ... There was
> no bustle of a farmhouse about; no kine lowing, no horses tramping, ... and
> at first not a human being anywhere; but presently, in a field a little way
> off, we saw a family group haymaking; and when they saw us standing by
> the house-door, they left off work and came to know what we wanted.
> ... They gave us freely of their best; wheaten bread, butter, and a huge
> jug of milk; and the man took down a large cheese from the 'rannel balk'
> (the beam running across the kitchen) piled up with cheeses for their own

MARDALE GREEN
Thomas Allom, 1832

use only, and told us 'to spare nothing, we were kindly welcome.' The place was well furnished in its way – the old settle by the chimney-neuk, the press and clock of black oak, the high-backed chairs, the wealth of 'delf,' giving it a true oldfashioned air and manner of comfort, as understood by these remote farmers. And they were proud of their place, boasting that the Dun Bull (the little inn at Mardale Green) 'hadn't a room the like of theirs, and that they could accommodate more folk than them if they had a mind.'

3m to the SE, and apparently inaccessible by road, is **Swindale**. According to W.G. Collingwood, the church here was remote and neglected, and sometime in the nineteenth century,

> One clergyman, when the parsonage had become too ruinous, lived from house to house, and carried his box of sermons with him. He took one out of the top, when Sunday came, without much picking and choosing, until the old lady with whom he lodged told him to 'stir up that box; they're beginning to come varra thick,' as if they were porridge.

Burneside, Staveley, Kentmere and Ings

From the centre of Kendal keep in the lane for B5284, then (by Methodist Church) take signed turning for **Burneside** (pronounced with three syllables, as if 'Burniside'), a village with a core of attractive old buildings, walled round with dull modern houses and dominated at the centre by James Cropper's paper mill.

The village was the home, for most of her life, of Margaret Cropper (1886–1980), the most underrated Cumbrian poet of the twentieth century. Many of her short poems (published as *Poems* (1914), *The Broken Hearth-Stone* (1927) and *The Springing Well* (1929)) describe local landscape and people; two magnificent longer works, *Little Mary Crosbie* and

The End of the Road, published in the 1930s, give a vivid picture of the life of the Westmorland poor in that period and, though written in standard English, make entirely natural use of local dialect forms and rhythms, something no other poet has achieved. She is currently almost forgotten; not, one hopes, forever.

Taking the turning E (signed Skelsmergh) to **Burneside Hall**, a splendidly dilapidated, fern-and-creeper-grown fortified farmhouse (various later wings added on to a fourteenth-century pele tower; architectural enthusiasts will be further excited to hear that there is a *swept gutter* at the back). It has its own marvellous gatehouse and is embellished with a tiny but pleasant garden complete with Victorian iron railings and gate. It is the essence of the picturesque: one reflects that this is what most rural buildings of similar age must have looked like in the days of Coleridge and Turner (though, more soberly, one wonders if it is not getting a shade *too* dilapidated?).

This was the home of the wit and poet Richard Braithwaite (1588–1673), also known as 'Dapper Dick'. Born here, he studied in London and Cambridge, then returned to Burneside to live as a country gentleman and prolific author of plays, poems and satires. Notable works include his elegy for the wedding party drowned on the Windermere Ferry in 1635 and his doggerel poem *Barnabae Itinerarium, or Drunken Barnaby's Journal* (1638), so popular in the eighteenth century that 'playing Barnaby' became the local expression for getting drunk. The *Journal* tells of Barnaby's wanderings as a horse trader; a short extract gives an idea of its rough-and-ready technique:

> Thence to pearelesse Penrith went I,
> Which of Merchandize hath plenty;
> Thence to Rosley, where our Lot is
> To commerce with people Scottish.
>   By a passage crooktly tending,
> Thence to Ravenglasse I'm bending,
> Thence to Dalton, most delightful;
> Thence to oaten Ouston fruitfull;
> Thence to Hauxides marish pasture;
> Thence to th'seat of old Lancaster ...

Ouston is Ulverston; Hauxide is Hawkshead. Not all Braithwaite's work is so rugged: he can be polished and eloquent.

Return to A591 and continue N. Follow signs to **Staveley**. 'I am always glad to see Staveley;' wrote Dorothy Wordsworth, 'it is a place I dearly love to think of – the first mountain village that I came to with Wm when we first began our pilgrimage together' – that is, their walking holiday in 1794. 'Here we drank a bason of milk at a publick house, and here I washed my feet in the brook, and put on a pair of silk stockings by Wm's advice.'

From the village centre follow the sign (3½m) to the hamlet of **Kentmere** which figures briefly as 'Shanmoor' in *Robert Elsmere*.

KENTMERE HALL
William Green, 1814

Kentmere Tarn was once much larger but it was briskly removed in Victorian times – as explained, in suitably no-nonsense manner, by Harriet Martineau in 1854:

> If familiar with the old description of the district [the traveller] will look for Kentmere Tarn, and wonder to see no trace of it. It is drained away; and fertile fields now occupy the place of the swamp, reeds and shallow water which he might have seen but a few years ago. While this tarn existed, the mills at Kendal were but very irregularly supplied with water. Now, when the streams are collected in a reservoir, which the traveller sees in coming down the pass of Nanbield, and the intercepting tarn is done away with, the flow of water no longer fails.

In fact permanent drainage did not prove possible; if you look S from the church you can still see the tarn, now much slimmed-down and without its reedy shallows.

From the church a bridleway leads ¾m W to **Kentmere Hall**, a well-preserved pele tower with a farmhouse extension and large stone barns, in a beautiful setting in a nook under the fellside. It attracted Turner, who sketched here on August 5 1816 during his northern tour.

The house is said to have been the home of a giant, Hugh Herd, the Cork Lad of Kentmere, son of a nun of Furness cast out into the world at the Dissolution of the Monasteries.

The Cork Lad was a champion wrestler, served King Edward VI of England in his Border battles, amused himself by pulling up trees by the roots, and, single-handed, lifted into place the thirty-foot long chimney-beam whilst the builders were away at dinner. Asked by the King what he liked to eat, he replied, 'Thick porridge, that a mouse might walk on dry-shod, to my breakfast; the sunny side of a wedder [wether] to my dinner when I can get it.' The Cork Lad later lived with his mother at Troutbeck Park.

It was also the home of one Richard Gilpin, said to have killed the last wild boar in England, and the Rev. Bernard Gilpin (1517–83), the 'Apostle of the North', a saintly church reformer who used to travel, preaching and giving alms, in remote parts of Yorkshire and Northumberland where the clergy hardly went.

Return to Staveley and follow signs to A591 (Windermere). After 1m you reach **Ings**. Turn L (S) off main road by petrol station. **St Anne's Church** was rebuilt in 1743 by a local celebrity whose story is told by Wordsworth in 'Michael'. The tablet over the door commemorates 'Mr Robert Bateman, Merchant at Leghorne, Born in this Hamlet'. According to the poem, Bateman, a poor 'parish-boy', set out to seek his fortune in London with a basket of 'pedlar's wares' supplied by kindly neighbours who made a collection in this church. He found work, became a merchant and at length

> grew wondrous rich,
> And left estates and moneys to the poor,
> And at his birth-place built a chapel floored
> With marble, which he sent from foreign lands.

The marble floor is at the E end, and consists of variegated slabs set in a star-and-lozenge pattern like a patchwork quilt. It does not look very exotic, but in eighteenth-century Westmorland it was a wonder: Charles Farish, in *The Minstrels of Winandermere* (1811), tells us that the schoolboys from Hawkshead Grammar School used to come here to see it. When William and Dorothy Wordsworth came here on their walking holiday of 1794,

> The door was open, and we went in. It is a neat little place, with a marble floor and marble communion table, with a painting over it of the last supper, and Moses and Aaron on each side. The woman told us that 'they had painted them as near as they could by the dresses as they are described in the Bible,' and gay enough they are.

Dorothy reported with glee that a local woman told them she had lately met a traveller who claimed to have 'helped to bring [the marble] down the Red Sea, and she had believed him gladly!' The altar painting has gone, but there is elaborately carved wood panelling by Robert Fell, a local craftsman whose carved self-portrait (1910) is on the wall below the pulpit. A brass plate on the N wall of the chancel gives Wordsworth's lines on Bateman, whose portrait is on the same wall.

Windermere and Troutbeck Bridge

Rejoin A591 and continue W. As you approach Windermere watch for Bannerigg Farm on L; just under ½m later, the road goes over the crest of a rise and the lake comes into view. Despite some new building, the traveller can share Wordsworth's pleasure in this view, mentioned in *The Prelude*'s Book IV as he describes his return after a year at Cambridge:

> Bright was the summer's noon when quickening steps
> Followed each other till a dreary moor
> Was crossed, a bare ridge clomb, upon whose top
> Standing alone, as from a rampart's edge,
> I overlooked the bed of Windermere,
> Like a vast river, stretching in the sun.
> With exultation, at my feet I saw
> Lake, islands, promontories, gleaming bays,
> A universe of Nature's fairest forms
> Proudly revealed with instantaneous burst,
> Magnificent, and beautiful, and gay.

Continue into **Windermere** *(some parking near the lakeside; the main car parks are at Bowness, a short walk away).* The town was the creation of the railway, which was built in 1844. Formerly a hamlet called Birthwaite, it was as near the lake as the railway was allowed to come but naturally the company borrowed the lake's name for their station. New building soon swamped the original tiny village.

The abrupt end of the track at **Windermere Railway Station** is testimony to the partial success of local opposition to the railway, led by Wordsworth. Fearing a rash of suburban development, he expressed his fervent views in speeches, letters to the press and even two sonnets. 'Is then no nook of English ground secure/From rash assault?' asks the first, invoking the winds, the rivers and the landscape itself to 'protest against the wrong'; the second addresses the mountains:

> Heard YE that Whistle? As her long-linked Train
> Swept onwards, did the vision cross your view?
> Yes, ye were startled ...

Wordsworth lost the battle to keep trains away from Windermere but happily a plan to carry the line on across the grounds of Rydal Hall, then via Grasmere and a tunnel through Dunmail Raise to Keswick, was dropped.

As a brand-new Victorian village in the Lakes, Windermere aroused much comment. Eliza Lynn Linton gives the flavour of 'the new village of Windermere' in 1864:

> Here everything is modern, wealthy, and well adapted. Natural advantages are made the most of, and natural beauties are respected; becoming sites are chosen for mansions fitted for people of deep purses and liberal education.

On the corner immediately above the station is the drive-entrance to **The Terrace**. In this block of three houses was the home of Arthur Ransome's Great Aunt Susan. Ransome used to escape here whenever he could from his hated prep school nearby. Happily, the aunt was a boisterous old lady, more like the Nancy Blackett of the Ransome novels than

Nancy's own dreadful G.A.; a shareholder in the railway, she liked the noise of the trains on the line below.

Across the roundabout NW from the station is a large sign for the footpath to **Orrest Head**. A winding path leads up ¾m to the summit, which gives a good view of the town, lake and the fells beyond. According to Harriet Martineau, Orrest Head

> was the residence of the noted Josiah Brown, who amused himself, a century ago, with welcoming beggars, whom he supplied with meat and lodging, – sometimes to the number of twenty in a night. He called them his 'jolly companions'; and no doubt he got a world of amusement out of them, in return for his hospitality.

Josiah was also famous for keeping a bull on which he rode about the neighbourhood.

Return almost to the bottom of the path, where a side-path branches off (signed A592, Horse Close Wood). Follow this for ¼m to corner where another path joins it. The long white cottage here (with plaque) is **Christopher North's Cottage**. This was the home from 1807 of John Wilson, *alias* 'Christopher North', editor of *Blackwood's Magazine*, essayist, critic, humorist, sportsman, minor Lake Poet and (extraordinarily) Professor of Moral Philosophy in the University of Edinburgh, a remarkable character. Wilson bought an estate (further down the hill) and settled in the cottage whilst he planned and built (in 1808) the larger house of Elleray. Even after it was built, however, he spent much of his time at the cottage.

Return to the junction by the station and go down the main road W to Phoenix Way. Follow it and turn L alongside playing field, to reach buildings which were formerly **The Old College**, Arthur Ransome's preparatory school from 1893 to 1897. The row of private houses N of playing field were an accommodation block: Ransome slept in 'the dormitory over the gateway in the old square tower that used to rock in high winds.' The tower is the one next to a door marked 'Farr Lawn'.

Return to the main road. 100yds downhill from the sign for the Orrest Head path, opposite the sign for Elleray Road, notice the lodge gates to an unmarked drive. This is **Elleray**, a large Victorian house (now a school) on the site of the original mansion, a rambling one-storey building, built in 1808 by John Wilson ('Christopher North'). During Elleray's construction Wilson had the drawing-room floor covered with turf and held a cock-fight there. It was demolished in the 1860s.

At Elleray he wrote *The Isle of Palms and Other Poems* (1812). He lost his fortune in 1815 and moved to Edinburgh but kept Elleray until 1850, renting it or using it as a holiday home. Walter Scott and J.G. Lockhart (Scott's son-in-law and biographer) stayed here in 1825, when Wilson celebrated Scott's 54th birthday with a regatta on the lake.

Follow the road ⅓m N to a small roundabout. Our route here intersects with that of Part Four: if you are heading for Kirkstone Pass or Bowness, turn to p 249. We continue on A591 to the **Sun Inn**, a favourite with Hartley

Coleridge (1796-1849), poet, alcoholic, and eldest son of the more famous Samuel Taylor Coleridge. It was probably here that he dined with Tennyson and James Spedding in 1835. The meeting was more than successful:

> Coleridge's enthusiasm [we are told] mounted with every gin, until, after the fourth glass, he poured out his thanks to Spedding for introducing them. Then he turned to Tennyson and told him he was far too handsome to be a poet.

He concluded by writing a sonnet, later published as 'To Alfred Tennyson', on the spot.

We are now in the hamlet of **Troutbeck Bridge**: Julius Caesar Ibbetson (1759–1817) lived hereabouts between 1799 and 1802, having fled London to escape his creditors. He was a fine painter of Lakeland landscapes (his last work was a picture of Ambleside market place) and 'As a painter of cattle and pigs,' says the *Dictionary of National Biography* solemnly, 'he has hardly been excelled in England': high praise indeed.

Continue 250yds and take turning signed 'Lakes School'. The road passes the swimming pool and continues W for walkers only to **Calgarth Hall**, a magnificent rambling farmhouse with huge cylindrical chimneys, various wings and extensions acquired over the centuries and a history as robust as its exterior. Clarke in 1789 calls it '*Crow-garth*, alias *Calf-garth*, alias *Cold-garth*, now commonly called *Caw-garth*, be it which it will'. In the seventeenth century it was the home of Robert Philipson, alias 'Robin the Devil', who was besieged on Belle Isle by the Parliamentarians during the Civil War and lost his helmet, as we have seen, in Kendal church. At the Hall until the late eighteenth century were, according to the sceptical Clarke,

> two human skulls, of which many strange stories are told: they were said to belong to persons whom Robin had murdered, and that they could not be removed from the place ... but always returned, even though they had been thrown into the Lake; with many other ridiculous falsehoods of the same stamp: some person, however, has lately carried one of them to London, and as it has not yet found its way back again, I shall say nothing more on so very trivial a subject.

More recent folklore adds that if the skulls were removed from the house, they *screamed*.

Return to A591 and continue N to bridge on corner. Just after the bridge, on L (SW) is the private drive to **Calgarth Park**, a large and rather dull Georgian house, home of the redoubtable Richard Watson, Bishop of Llandaff (1737–1816), who was much too grand to live in the old Hall and built this instead. Watson performed the amazing feat of holding the Oxford chairs of Divinity and Chemistry simultaneously. He knew nothing about chemistry when elected, but worked it up rapidly enough to give effective lectures and make several discoveries, among them (in 1787) an improved method of making gunpowder, using charcoal 'distilled' in iron cylinders. It was a timely invention: two years later the French Revolution began, and in the ensuing wars the good bishop reckoned his 'cylinder powder' had saved the British government at least a hundred thousand pounds a year.

He was a keen and belligerent pamphleteer, and managed to engage a remarkable variety of literary opponents, including Gibbon (with whom he argued over the fifteenth chapter of the *Decline and Fall*); Tom Paine, whose scepticism he attacked in *An Apology for the Bible*; Blake (who wrote furious marginal notes in a copy of the *Apology*, declaring Paine 'a better Christian than the Bishop'); and Wordsworth, who wrote his *Letter to the Bishop of Llandaff* (1793) as an answer to Watson's defence of the French monarchy.

Nonetheless he was a great entertainer and visitors to Calgarth included Coleridge, De Quincey (who wrote an entertaining account of Watson in his *Recollections*), John Wilson, Charles Lloyd and even (in his later years) Wordsworth, whose politics were by then more conservative than the Bishop's.

He was also a keen agriculturist and 'improver' of his extensive estates. Not one to indulge in undue modesty, he viewed his life at Calgarth with unmixed satisfaction:

> I ... laid, in the summer of 1789, the foundation of my house on the banks of Windermere. I have now spent above twenty years in this delightful country; but my time has not been spent in field-diversions, in idle visitings, in county bickerings, in indolence or intemperance: no, it has been spent, partly in supporting the religion and constitution of the country by seasonable publications; and principally in building farm-houses, blasting rocks, enclosing wastes, in making bad land good, in planting larches, and in planting in the hearts of my children principles of piety, of benevolence, and of self-government.

Ellen Weeton even claims (in 1810)

> that to increase his property, he proposed, about twenty years ago, the draining of Windermere, a considerable part belonging to him. He expected to gain some hundred acres by it. It was found to be practicable, as I am informed, but the expense of doing it would have greatly exceeded the advantage, and it was given up.

All this left little time for religion, and he visited his diocese at Llandaff (near Cardiff) only once every three years.

Just N of Calgarth is **Whitecross Bay**. You may like to search at the lakeside here and at Ecclerigg Crag (the promontory at the N side of the bay) for the elaborately-lettered rock inscriptions said to have been cut in the 1830s by John Longmire, an eccentric Ambleside constable. They range from political messages about the Corn Laws and the National Debt, to the names of famous writers and Windermere oarsmen. Some were removed when stone was quarried for Wray Castle but many are said to be still here. I have not investigated them myself.

1½m N of the Calgarth Park drive take road R (signed Troutbeck, Town End) ⅓m to **Briery Close**, a huge complex of buildings expanded from the already large house where Charlotte Brontë stayed in August 1850, seeing the Lake District for the first time as guest of Sir James Kay-Shuttleworth, industrialist and educationalist. She found her host suffocatingly conventional, commenting

> Decidedly I find it does not agree with me to prosecute the search for the picturesque in a carriage ... I longed to slip out unseen, and to run away by myself in amongst the hills and dales.

But she thought the countryside 'exquisitely beautiful, though the weather is cloudy, misty, and stormy; but the sun bursts out occasionally and shows the hills and lake.' She adds 'Mrs Gaskell is coming here this evening.' Elizabeth Gaskell thought Charlotte 'a little lady in a black silk gown, altogether *plain* ... nothing overstrained but everything perfectly simple'. The two novelists at once became firm friends and seven years later Mrs Gaskell wrote the first biography of Charlotte Brontë.

Lowwood and Waterhead

Return to A591 and continue to the **Low Wood Hotel**, built in 1850 to replace an older inn. Somewhere hereabouts, before the shoreline was tidied in Victorian times for picnics and boating, Dorothy Wordsworth saw her brothers William and John off 'at the turning of the Lowwood bay under the trees' on their tour into Yorkshire on May 14 1800. She shed 'a flood of tears', and

> walked as long as I could on the stones of the shore. The wood rich in flowers ... Crowfoot, the grassy-leaved rabbit-toothed white flower, strawberries, geranium, scentless violets, anemones two kinds, orchises, primroses ... Met a blind man, driving a very large beautiful Bull, and a cow – he walked with two sticks.

Thomas West in 1778 mentions that

> No other inn in [this] route has so fine a view of a lake ... A small cannon is kept here to gratify the curious with those remarkable reverberations of sound, which follow the report of a gun &c. in these singular vales.

The Hotel, and the inn it replaced, have entertained a distinguished list of visitors. Wordsworth dined here with Lord and Lady Holland in 1807, and in October 1813 Shelley and Harriet Westbrook stayed briefly on their way to Edinburgh. John Stuart Mill on his 1831 tour of the Lakes 'stopt to dine at Low-wood Inn' and made notes on the colours of the lake ('alternately of a deep lead colour; a beautiful iron-grey; a lightish blue; a glittering white sparkling with the rays of the sun ...') before travelling on to Ambleside and the Salutation for the night. Nathaniel Hawthorne stayed in July 1855 and admired the view across the lake. And in July 1907 E.M. Forster was here: '12/- a day', he told a friend, 'but I must admit they do you prettily there as well as well – no beastliness: I can strongly recommend it though of course only to fools'.

Look N from the lakeside and you will see, half way up the fellside, a gabled house with frilly decorative bargeboards. This is the house traditionally known as **Dove Nest**, now a hotel and renamed The Samling, whose drive slants up from the road on the corner ¼m N of Lowwood. It was built in the late eighteenth century by John Benson (who also owned Dove Cottage) as a simple cottage with 'Gothic' turreted side wings; the present large gabled wings are Victorian.

A lively account of daily life here between 1809 and 1811 is given in the journal of Ellen Weeton, who was governess. Miss Weeton's years here were not easy: her employer, Edward Pedder, was an odious coward, bully and miser; her pupil, Gertrude, accidentally set her apron on fire and burned to death. But Miss Weeton records everything with unperturbed Jane Austenish sharpness, varied with touches of surprisingly Rabelaisian humour. Her record was published as *Miss Weeton: Journal of a Governess* in 1936.

The poet Felicia Hemans (1793–1835) lived here during the summers from 1829 to 1831 and came to know the Wordsworths. She was a considerable literary celebrity, and though Sara Hutchinson thought her affectation 'perfectly unendurable', she earned herself a mention amongst other dead friends in Wordsworth's 'Extempore Effusion on the Death of James Hogg'. Her work clings minimally but tenaciously to public memory by the opening of her poem 'Casabianca' (1829): 'The boy stood on the burning deck/Whence all but he had fled'.

From 1853 Dove Nest was the home of the Rev. Robert Perceval Graves (great uncle of the modern poet Robert Graves), also a friend of Wordsworth's, who wrote a life of the astronomer and mathematician William Rowan Hamilton.

In 1794 William and Dorothy Wordsworth picnicked by (and drank from) the beck that flows down through the wood past the Dove Nest drive, on their walk through the Lakes. Wordsworth celebrated it in a sonnet, 'There is a little unpretending Rill': the beck is 'humbler far than aught/That ever among men or Naiads sought/Notice or name'; for the poet, however, 'The immortal Spirit of one happy day/Lingers beside that Rill, in vision clear.'

Continue N to Waterhead. If you bear L on A5075 (signed Langdale, Coniston) you pass near the head of the lake and **Galava Roman Fort** (*NT*). Camden (1586) tells us that

> At the upper point of Winandermere lies the carcase as it were of an antient city with great ruins of walls, and of buildings without the walls still remaining scattered about ... the British brick, the mortar mixed with fragments of brick, the small urns, glass vessels, Roman coins frequently found ... and the paved roads leading to it plainly bespeak it a Roman work.

The area between the road and the lake is the 'North Pole' of Arthur Ransome's *Winter Holiday*. A summerhouse here (long since demolished) inspired the building to which the children race through the blizzard at the end of the novel.

Ambleside

Continue N to **Ambleside** (*large car park at N end of town; follow signs to Main Car Park*). A small market town, placed where a route from Kirkstone comes down to the head of Windermere, Ambleside was an early centre of tourism. It was well known to the Wordsworths; Dorothy came here almost daily for letters and supplies during their years at Dove Cottage, as her *Journal* records, and in 1810 the family stayed here for six weeks to escape the scarlet fever at Grasmere.

Wordsworth praised the town (and the homely pall of smoke that over-hung it each day from the domestic fires) in one of his last sonnets:

> While beams of orient light shoot wide and high,
> Deep in the vale a little rural Town
> Breathes forth a cloud-like creature of its own
> That mounts not toward the radiant morning sky,
> But, with a less ambitious sympathy,
> Hangs o'er its Parent.

The town's great coaching-inn was the **Salutation**. Despite much enlargement it still has character, and its former identity as a coaching-inn with yard and outbuildings is clearly visible. It was probably here that Gray *nearly* stayed in 1769:

> I now reached Ambleside, eighteen miles from Keswick, meaning to lie there; but on looking into the best bed-chamber, dark and damp as a cellar, grew delicate, gave up Wynander-mere in despair, and resolved I would go on to Kendal directly, fourteen miles further.

Things must have improved, for it quickly became a tourist centre. Keats stayed here in June 1818; Joseph Budworth explored the fells with one Robin Partridge, 'who acts as guide, as boots, postillion and boatman, at the Salutation Inn', portraying him in his *Fortnight's Ramble to the Lakes* (1793) as a comic, sceptical rustic, a sort of Sancho Panza to his own Don Quixote.

Wordsworth, in a draft for his *Guide to the Lakes*, assumes that visitors will start from here and is fairly cynical about how travellers were hustled along:

> From Ambleside to Keswick (explains the bustling leader of a party of Tourists, glancing his eye carelessly on the map in his hand or casting a look towards the clouds for information concerning the state of the weather) is how far? 16 miles. Is there anything worthy of notice on the road? Nothing but what all Travellers see as they pass along – will probably be the answer of mine host of the Salutation if the question be asked at the height of the season & he is anxious to have his horses back again for a fresh job.

John Stuart Mill stayed here in July 1831, as did Tennyson and Edward Fitzgerald in May 1835. Tennyson was working on his 'Morte d'Arthur' and trying to convert Fitzgerald to Wordsworth's poetry.

50yds SW of the Salutation is the **Post Office**, a dull modern building on the site formerly occupied by the house of William Green (1761–1823), Ambleside's best-known landscape artist. Most visitors to the town went to see his studio, and he features extensively in Ellen Weeton's *Journal of a Governess*.

Jessie Harden visited the house on her honeymoon in 1803, and her journal gives the upper-class view – the artist as genteel pauper:

> We have just been viewing some Drawings of the Lakes by Mr Greene who has been here some years and has taken a very great number of accurate views of them. He sells a good many and every visitor gives him a shilling by which means I dare say He picks up a tolerable sum in the course of the season and very deservedly I think.

Her husband, of course, was an *amateur* painter, a very different thing.

Next door (a far older and pleasanter building) at number 5, now Brown's Taxis, was the **Old Post Office**. Here in 1835 Owen Lloyd, curate of Ambleside, minor poet and friend of Wordsworth, wrote the Ambleside Rushbearing Hymn, which explains why the Rushbearing procession which makes its way to the church annually on a Saturday in July always stops outside the building to sing the hymn.

For Ambleside's most surprising cultural association, return uphill towards the Salutation and go behind the Market Hall, then take steep lane curving up R by St Johns Ambulance hall; continue up steps and on to a group of three tall stone terrace houses. The middle one is **2 Gale Crescent**, home from 1945 to 1948 of the German Dadaist poet, sculptor and painter Kurt Schwitters (1887–1948).

Schwitters, one of the great pioneers of collage and abstract painting (best known for his 'Merz' series of constructions using bus-tickets, packaging and other printed matter) was driven from his home in Hanover by the Nazis in 1937 as a 'Degenerate Artist'. He took refuge in Norway and reached Ambleside in 1945 with his English friend and nurse, Edith Thomas. He was seriously ill but continued to work, painting realistic portraits and landscapes, as well as continuing with his abstract works. He and Edith lived at Gale Crescent 'very romantically,' as Schwitters wrote, 'with a splendid view … and share the housekeeping: cooking, cleaning, piano playing, painting.' He used to play chess in the Ambleside cafés with Dr Harry Pierce of Langdale, who gave him the barn where his last major sculptural work was carried out (see p 286). He died of asthma at Kendal in January 1948, and was buried in Ambleside cemetery.

Return to Market Place and head S, then turn R (W) into Church Street. Next to the corner (up steps, with plaque) notice **The Old Stamp House**, Wordsworth's office when he was Distributor of Stamps for Westmorland (collecting a government tax on legal documents) from 1813 to 1843. He kept the stamps and money in his house, and rarely used the office. Continue downhill to the **churchyard**. Kurt Schwitters's grave is at the far side of the church, not easy to find. Look for tall conifer down steep slope at

SW corner of building; the small grey slate headstone is 63yds SW of the tree. Strictly speaking, this is not a grave at all, for Schwitters's body was exhumed in recent times for burial in Germany. The memorial identifies him simply as 'Creator of Merz', a word he invented for his own art by taking the syllable from a torn piece of paper originally reading 'Kommerz' (German for 'business') in one of his own collages.

Return to the main street (Lake Road) and continue S for a small hotel called Lakes Lodge. This was formerly a Victorian house, **Laurel Villa**, where the nineteen-year-old Beatrix Potter stayed with her parents in April 1885. A highlight of the stay was Ginnet's Travelling Circus. 'Very good,' she noted in her journal, 'wonderful performing bull'. She saw the same circus again in August 1895 and noted:

> Mr Ginnet himself hath gone-off in appearance since I last saw him on the same spot ten years since, when he rode a young red-roan bull. He has subsided into a most disastrous long frock-coat and long, tight trousers with about a foot of damp at the bottom of them …
>
> The scornful Madame Ansonia was arrayed in blue and silver, and, alighting from her piebald, put on galoshes publicly in the ring. The fair-haired enchantress did not appear unless indeed she had shrivelled into Madame Fontainebleau, who displayed her remarkable dogs in an anxious cockney accent, and twinkled about in high-heeled French boots and chilly apparel.

These recollections provided inspiration for her circus novel *The Fairy Caravan*.

Finally, the N end of the town. Opposite the main car park is St Martin's College, a large Victorian house with modern extensions. This was formerly **Scale How**, a private house where F.W. Faber worked as tutor from 1840 to 1842.

Faber was well known in his day as a poet and at Scale How wrote *Sir Lancelot* and other now-forgotten poems. The house must also have witnessed some painful heart-searchings: Faber was an Anglican clergyman during his time here, but is remembered today mainly as 'Father Faber', a leading convert to the Catholic church, which he joined in 1845, inspired by the example of Newman.

The poet Fleur Adcock was Writer-in-Residence here in 1977–78 and wrote *Below Loughrigg*, an attractive sequence of poems about the area. Return to the road and go R (NW) along it. After 150yds, between houses called 'Helvellyn' and 'Haven Cottage' a short private drive leads to **The Knoll** (large square stone house on rise). It was built by the journalist and novelist Harriet Martineau in 1846. Wordsworth, with whom she was on cautiously friendly terms, planted two pine trees in the garden and helped choose the inscription for the sundial, 'Come, Light! Visit me!'

Martineau was a highly individual figure, well known locally for her atheism, her interest in hypnotism, her agricultural experiments (she ran a small model dairy farm from The Knoll and wrote a pamphlet on her meth-

THE KNOLL, AMBLESIDE
Harriet Clarke, 1846

ods) and her championing of poachers in *Game Law Tales*. Much of her writing (mainly popularising essays and stories on social and economic themes) was done here; she contributed to Dickens's magazine *Household Words* and published a *Complete Guide to the Lakes* in 1854.

She had innumerable literary visitors. Among them were Charlotte Brontë, who stayed for a week in 1850, met the Arnold family at Loughrigg Holme and, according to Canon Rawnsley, allowed Miss Martineau to hypnotise her; and Emerson, who stayed in 1848.

High Sweden Bridge and Scandale Tarn

Serious walkers tend to neglect Ambleside, but away from the crowded centre there are wonderful walks which have the added interest of being the favourites of Victorian visitors, representing what the Lake District meant to educated tourists in the mid-nineteenth century. As Eliza Lynn Linton wrote in 1864:

> Many and beautiful are the walks about Ambleside: walks within a reasonable distance for any fair pedestrian, and which all but very fine ladies, or very delicate ones, may take without too much fatigue, and without risk or danger if they are moderately careful

– a statement which should not be taken too lightly, as she speaks elsewhere of 'a delicious day's walk of only twenty-six miles in all'.

One such walk – strenuous or reasonable depending on where you turn back – is to Scandale Tarn *via* Sweden Bridge. From the Salutation go 100yds N up North Road for the **Unicorn**, a pleasant inn with many Lake

District memorabilia. Fleur Adcock's poem 'In the Unicorn, Ambleside' (1983) celebrates colourful (and unreliable) Wordsworthian gossip here: 'He drank in every pub from here to Ullswater,/and had half the girls. We all know that …' Continue L up the precipitous Sweden Bridge Lane, then at fork go R (signed Ellerigg Road, Kirkstone); the road continues to the gate of **Eller How**. Anne Clough (1820–92), sister of the poet A.H. Clough, ran a girls' school here. Her pupils included Mary Arnold (later the novelist Mrs Humphry Ward) in 1858–60. An account of the school is given in T.C. Down's 'Schooldays with Miss Clough' (*Cornhill Magazine*, 1920), a delightful essay which deserves to be better known, with its glimpses of Mary Arnold and a school-friend down in the cellar counting the bottles of hated gooseberries 'to see how many more there were for us to eat', practising the piano in a bitterly cold room by candlelight, and (Miss Clough mysteriously summoned to Florence, where her poet-brother was dying) sleeping in her huge, curtained feather-bed and having 'a high old time making tents and playing Red Indians'. Anne Clough was a pioneer of women's education and later became first Principal of Newnham College, Cambridge.

Turn back to the junction and continue N up Sweden Bridge Lane, which soon becomes a stony bridleway running parallel with Scandale Beck. After roughly 1m it emerges from a small wood and reaches **High Sweden Bridge**, a picturesque packhorse bridge. Mrs Humphry Ward recalled how in childhood, as a boarder at Anne Clough's school, she had sometimes been rescued for an afternoon by her father, Thomas Arnold and his friend Arthur Clough. They would walk up the lane to the bridge, while she went 'wandering, and skipping, and dreaming by myself':

> every rock along the mountain lane, every boggy patch, every stretch of silken, flower-sown grass, every bend of the wild stream … were to me the never-ending joys of a 'land of pure delight' … It was a point of honour with me to get to Sweden Bridge … before my companions; and I would sit dangling my feet over the unprotected edge of its grassgrown arch, … queening it there on the weather-worn keystone of the bridge, dissolved in the mere physical joy of each contented sense.

At this point you can honourably turn back. Alternatively, continue N 2m to the top of Scandale Pass (stone wall with stile). Go L along wall after crossing stile; when wall is joined by iron fenceposts, go due W a few yds for **Scandale Tarn**, a tiny funnel-shaped pool which makes a good picnic place.

You may like to hunt for an inscription said to be carved on a boulder overhanging the water at the tarn's N side, reading 'Harry Boyle and Percy Laidlaw stocked this tarn with gudgeon fish on 5th July, 1878'. The inscription is under the overhang, so you have to lie on the rock and look over the edge to see it. I failed to find it, but Boyle's widow says in her life of Boyle (who lived at Eller How and became a prominent diplomat) that it was clearly visible in 1937.

Stockghyll Force and Wansfell

A second Victorian favourite was Wansfell *via* Stockghyll Force. Go round to the back of the Salutation car park and follow the lane uphill alongside the wooded hill. Take the gate into Stockghyll Park and follow the paths up to the waterfall, **Stockghyll Force**. The best of many descriptions is by Keats, who visited in June 1818:

> It is buried in trees, in the bottom of the valley – the stream itself is interesting throughout with 'mazy error over pendant shades.' Milton meant a smooth river – this is buffetting all the way on a rocky bed ever various – but the waterfall itself, which I came suddenly upon, gave me a pleasant twinge. First we stood a little below the head about half way down the first fall, buried deep in trees, and saw it streaming down two more descents to the depth of more than fifty feet – then we went on a jut of rock nearly level with the second fall-head, where the first fall was above us, and the third below our feet still – at the same time we saw that the water was divided by a sort of cataract island on whose other side burst forth a glorious stream – then the thunder and the freshness. At the same time the different falls have different characters; the first darting down the slate-rock like an arrow; the second spreading out like a fan – the third dashed into a mist – and the one on the other side of the rock a sort of mixture of all these.

There is a bridge at the top of the Force, so you can go up one side and down the other. To go further, join the road at the gate by the top of the falls and follow it ½m uphill. Soon after the road turns away from the wood, a signed path leads steeply uphill from a stile to Wansfell. It descends on the far side (as Nanny Lane) into Troutbeck.

Wansfell is addressed in a sonnet, 'Wansfell! this household has a favoured lot…', by Wordsworth, who could see it from Rydal Mount, felt it deserved its niche in English poetry, and gave it one on Christmas Eve 1842.

Under Loughrigg

To reach this delightful nook, which has a rich literary history, leave Ambleside following signs for Coniston and Langdale, then as you cross the bridge over the Rothay look for a small sign, 'Under Loughrigg'. This leads to a narrow and most beautiful road which runs along the riverside under the wooded slopes of Loughrigg Fell to Rydal. If possible walk along it: one of its charms is lack of traffic. The road was a favourite with Dorothy Wordsworth, who often chose this way between Ambleside and Grasmere (she calls it 'Clappersgate' because the road branches off the Coniston route at the edge of Clappersgate). On May 14 1800, she noted

> Came home by Clappersgate. The valley very green; many sweet views up to Rydal head, when I could juggle away the fine houses; but they disturbed me … one beautiful view of the Bridge, without Sir Michael's.

('Sir Michael's' was Rydal Hall – then an obtrusive new house.) It was on

STOCKGHYLL MILL
H. Gastineau, 1832

this walk that she resolved to 'write a journal' – a resolve she kept until 1803.

⅓m along the road, on the W side, is the gate to **Miller Bridge House**. In the early nineteenth century this was the school run by Parson Dawes for the sons of local gentlefolk. Pupils at various times included the future minor poets Owen Lloyd (son of Charles Lloyd) and Aubrey De Vere; Hartley and Derwent Coleridge; and Wordsworth's sons Willie and John.

Another ¾m brings us to **Fox How**, on the N side of the road. This was the holiday home of Dr Thomas Arnold (1795–1842), Headmaster of Rugby School, who bought the land with Wordsworth's encouragement and had the house built in 1833. Wordsworth himself advised on the architecture, insisting on a local vernacular style with unplastered stone walls, cylindrical chimneys and traditional porch.

Dr Arnold loved the house, though always austerly impressing on his children that 'mere mountain and lake hunting' was 'time lost'. The house passed into the hands of the second great Arnold, the poet and critic Matthew, on his father's death. Matthew spent many holidays here and his poem 'The New Sirens' was composed (?1843) 'While walking up and down on a soft gloomy day in the field by the Rotha' below the house. (Or so the standard edition of his poems has it. His biographer tells us that it was 'a soft *bloomy* day': it is characteristic of this area that either could be correct, and equally pleasant.)

Dr Arnold's grandaughter Mary, later Mrs Humphry Ward (1851–1920), spent part of her childhood here and describes it in *A Writer's Recollections*. Separated from her parents (who lived mostly in Ireland) she cannot have been very happy. She lived in the house only for a year (1856–57) before being boarded out (aged seven) at Anne Clough's school in Ambleside, returning to Fox How for the weekends.

She recalled it – with the casual grandeur of the prosperous Edwardian – as

> a modest building, with ten bedrooms and three sitting-rooms. Its windows look straight into the heart of Fairfield, the beautiful semi-circular mountain which rears its hollowed front and buttressing scaur against the north, far above the green floor of the valley.

There was also the garden, with

> its little beck with its mimic bridges, its encircling river, its rocky knolls, its wild strawberries and wild raspberries, its queen of silver-birches rearing a stately head against the distant mountain, its velvet turf, and long silky grass in the parts left wild.

She portrayed the house as 'Ravensnest' in *Milly and Olly or A Holiday Among the Mountains* (1881), a work of great interest (despite its insufferable prose style) as the first children's novel to take a Lake District holiday as its theme.

Continue 250yds to **Fox Ghyll**, home of Thomas De Quincey from 1820 to 1825, the period when he wrote *Confessions of an English Opium-Eater* and established himself as a writer with the *London Magazine*. Most of his writing, however, seems to have been done on trips to London. The De Quinceys were evicted by Dorothy Wordsworth's friend Letitia Luff when she bought the house in 1825. She enlarged it and landscaped its grounds. Her parrot – a 'sportive bird/By social glee inspired' – is described in Wordsworth's 'The Contrast: The Parrot and the Wren', which compares it unfavourably with a wren that haunted the moss-hut at Rydal Mount.

100yds further N is **Loughrigg Holme**, home of Edward Quillinan (poet and Irish half-pay captain), and Dora (Wordsworth's daughter), after their marriage in 1841. Wordsworth had strenuously opposed the match but Quillinan became in time his valued friend and occasional collaborator. Visitors included Harriet Martineau (often), and Charlotte Brontë in 1850, at which time Matthew Arnold met both ladies there. He liked Charlotte Brontë, but noted:

> Talked to Miss Martineau (who blasphemes frightfully) about the prospects of the Church of England, and, wretched man that I am, promised to go and see her cow-keeping miracles ... – I, who hardly know a cow from a sheep.

More decorously, he commemorated the occasion in his poem 'Haworth Churchyard', an elegy for Charlotte Brontë.

In 1861 Henry Alford, Dean of Canterbury and a poet who deserves to be better known, spent the late summer and the wet autumn here with his family, sketching and working on his translation of the *Odyssey*. His account (in 'A Letter to America') gives us a wonderful glimpse of a Victorian family holiday:

> Then our holiday came: in Rydal valley we spent it,
> Snug in our 'own hired house' beneath the elbow of Loughrigg.
> O but to think of the rain that pelted us all that Autumn,
> Flood, and mizzle, and shower, and shower, and flood and mizzle,
> Rothay over his banks, and all the waterfalls roaring,
> I in Macintosh case, and sometimes Alice and Mary,
> Splashing away to the Ambleside Post-office nightly for letters.
> If strong waters are bad for the human constitution,
> Then are all we four done up and ruined for ever.
> Still we drew and walked, and made our hay when the sun shone:
> Or at Fox How sometimes at croquet played with the Arnolds,
> Or in cars to neighbouring lakes attempted excursions.
> So dripped on the weeks: and about the end of October
> Homeward sped we again to all our habits and duties.

A further ¼m brings us to **Stepping Stones** (originally 'Lanty Fleming's Cottage'), home during his first marriage of Edward Quillinan. Later it belonged to Wordsworth's son William, and after that to Gordon, the poet's grandson, who arranged and annotated Wordsworth's voluminous manuscripts there. The house takes its modern name from the picturesque stepping-stones across the Rothay opposite.

The road continues another ½m to join the A591 at Rydal. Both roads run alongside the **River Rothay**. Somewhere near here (on July 19 1855) the American novelist Nathaniel Hawthorne (author of *The Scarlet Letter*) paused during a walk on his tour of the Lakes and reflected

> The Rothay is very swift and turbulent today, and hurries along with foam-flecks on its surface, filling its banks from brim to brim, a stream of perhaps twenty feet across. Perhaps more, for I am willing that the good little river should have all it can fairly claim; it is the Saint Lawrence of several of the English lakes, through which it flows, and carries off their superfluous waters. In its haste, and with its rushing sound, it was pleasant both to see and hear; and it sweeps by one side of the old churchyard where Wordsworth is buried.

Rydal

Rydal is a hamlet of few buildings but great interest. Leave A591 by the side road (signed Rydal Mount): there is a little parking on this road. To the R (E) is **Rydal Hall** (*house not open; gardens open daily; car park for visitors*), now a conference and retreat centre for the Diocese of Carlisle, formerly the family home of the Le Flemings. Sir Daniel Le Fleming, a pioneer of Lake District topography, wrote here a *Description of the County of Westmoreland* (1671), the first history of the county, and a *Survey of Westmoreland and Cumberland in 1671*, one of the earliest topographical descriptions. In 1652 he commissioned paintings of

'Becky and Tiza jumping from one stone to another like little fawns':
ROTHAY STEPPING STONES
Willy Pogany, from Mrs Humphry Ward's *Milly and Olly*, 1907

Rydal Hall and garden (out of ye Round Close), of ye grotto (out of ye Little House) and of ye Vale from Rydal Hall to Windermere-water out of ye best Chamber window

– probably the first ever Lakeland landscape paintings. More of 'ye grotto' later.

The Hall had been newly enlarged and repainted in 1799 when Coleridge and Wordsworth walked through the grounds to visit the Cascades. They were met by a servant who 'came to us ... to reprove us for having passed before the front of the House': a trespass Coleridge thought roughly equal 'with the Trespass on the Eye by his damned White washing!'.

To reach the **Rydal Cascades**, follow the drive below the house and along in front of it to a stone bridge. Close to it are the Lower Falls; higher up you will see the Upper Falls, spanned by a second bridge. Beside the first bridge is a small stone hut, the **Grotto**. This is a 'viewing-house', built in 1669 and probably the oldest in England. Its large rectangular window, facing the Falls, was designed to frame the view. It provides a perfectly-composed living picture and may claim to be the birthplace of the 'picturesque' appreciation of landscape.

The Grotto is now used for prayer and contemplation and is not open (perhaps the present owners might consider a regular hour or day when the Grotto could be open to visitors?).

So much has been written about the Cascades that one could compile a complete history of taste from the descriptions. They first became famous when William Mason (in 1775) lamented Thomas Gray's failure to visit them:

His greatest loss was in not seeing a small waterfall visible through the window of a ruined summer-house in Sir Michael's orchard. Here Nature has performed every thing in little that she usually executes on her largest scale; and, on that account, like the miniature painter, seems to have finished every part of it in a studied manner; not a little fragment of rock thrown into the basin, not a single stem of brushwood that starts from its craggy sides, but has its picturesque meaning; and the little central stream dashing down a cleft of the darkest-coloured stone, produces an effect of light and shadow beautiful beyond description. This little theatrical scene might be painted as large as the original, on a canvas not bigger than those which are usually dropped at the Opera-house.

Joseph Budworth preserves for us with great freshness a momentary glimpse of the living picturesque here in 1792:

At the instant I am writing, a man with his hay-day dress, with a rake and a stone bottle, is passing over the bridge: the back shade makes his frame and dress so distinct I shall never forget the figure. It would have been a happy moment for a painter.

Many painters did indeed visit, and there are notable pictures of the falls by Joseph Farington, Francis Towne, Julius Caesar Ibbetson and Joseph Wright of Derby.

John Stuart Mill was here in July 1831, not expecting much ('a waterfall, in itself gives me little pleasure', he noted dourly), but found it

the finest specimen of its kind which ever I saw. The bed, or trough down which it rushes, seems as if it had been chiselled several feet deep in the living rock: the sides of the ghyll are green, and richly wooded, but over the stream the rock is laid bare, and shews itself in crags above, and slabs and fragments below, superior in wildness to every thing I have seen of this class. The falls are only, in a stream of this character, like the most brilliant passages in a fine piece of music. The stream is all waterfalls.

Eliza Lynn Linton in 1864 uses the same terms as Mason, but now with scathing irony. She thought the falls

so pretty and well-arranged that surely their fittest place is the back scene of some pastoral opera, where the shepherds dress in velvet tights and silk stockings, and the shepherdesses dance in muslin and wreaths of roses! Certainly they are pretty – but they have been so trimmed and cared for – the trees have been so artistically disposed – the vistas so cunningly contrived – the channels have been so scientifically deepened – the resting-basin so tastefully arranged – and the summer-house is such a bit of picturesque trick, that one loses all perception of nature, and cannot but regard those very elegant waterfalls as artificial altogether; to the extent of easily believing in a forcing pump or a steam-engine somewhere out of sight and hearing.

C.L. Dodgson ('Lewis Carroll') and a friend walked here from Ambleside on August 28 1856. Dodgson noted in his diary:

It rained nearly all day, and at last, in despair of better weather, we sallied out in waterproofs to look at Rydal Falls: they are not imposing either in height or breadth; the scenery around is beautiful.

Possibly it was at Rydal that he was inspired to begin his parody of Wordsworth's 'Resolution and Independence', which appeared in *Through the Looking-Glass* as the White Knight's Song, 'A-sitting On a Gate'; at any rate, he noted that he 'finished' it on September 5, eight days later.

Wordsworth describes the lower waterfall in *An Evening Walk*, and it appears again in a late and little-known poem, 'Lyre! though such power do in thy magic live' (1840), whose imagery was 'supplied,' said Wordsworth, 'by frequent, I might say intense, observation of the Rydal torrent'.

The Wordsworths often took guests to see the falls: on December 6 1800, for example, Dorothy notes, 'Sara [Hutchinson] and Wm. walked to the waterfalls at Rydale'.

The parkland which stretches from here almost to Ambleside was also a favourite place for Wordsworth walks. 'To M.H.' ('Our walk was far among the ancient trees'), the first poem Wordsworth completed after moving to Dove Cottage, describes a walk in Rydal Park with Mary Hutchinson, who was to become the poet's wife, along

> A track, that brought us to a slip of lawn,
> And a small bed of water in the woods ...
> The spot was made by nature for herself,
> The travellers know it not, and 'twill remain
> Unknown to them; but it is beautiful; ...
> And therefore, my sweet Mary, this still Nook,
> With all its beeches, we have named from You!

Mary's Nook is still unknown to travellers, for no-one has identified the pool with certainty. Equally elusive is 'The Haunted Tree', a 'time-dismantled Oak' in the Park about which Wordsworth wrote a poem in 1819.

The Park makes a fictional appearance in Marjorie Lloyd's *Fell Farm Campers* (1960), which gives a lively account of the Hound Trails which are still held here.

A little uphill from the Rydal Hall gate is **Rydal Mount** (*open March to October 9.30–5; November to February 10–4 except Tuesdays; admission charge*), home of William Wordsworth

RYDAL MOUNT
John M'Whirter, 1882

and his family from 1813 to 1850. Originally a farmhouse called Keens, it was enlarged in the eighteenth century and renamed in 1803. Wordsworth rented it from Lady Diana Le Fleming of Rydal Hall.

Socially, the house represented a large step up from Dove Cottage, putting the poet on calling terms with the local gentry. Simple pleasures, however, appealed as much as ever; in summer he often spent days gardening or haymaking, and *The River Duddon* describes with gusto the Christmas minstrels' visit to Rydal Mount in 1819.

The house is still lived in but is displayed much as it was in Wordsworth's day, with elegant but comfortable furnishings and fine gardens. The dining room has chair seats embroidered by Mary and Dorothy Wordsworth and Sara Hutchinson; the Drawing Room displays a small statuette of a boy holding a shell to his ear, which suggested a passage in *The Excursion* Book IV:

> I have seen
> A curious child, who dwelt upon a tract
> Of upland ground, applying to his ear
> The convolutions of a smooth-lipped shell ...
> Even such a shell the universe itself
> Is to the ear of faith.

There is a good range of portraits of the poet and his family, including the only known portrait of Dorothy.

Major works written at Rydal Mount (often initially composed whilst walking in the garden) include *The River Duddon, Ecclesiastical Sonnets*, the 1820 *Miscellaneous Poems* and the revision of *The Prelude*, which appeared just after Wordsworth's death in 1850.

Literary visitors have been countless. The Scottish poet James Hogg, 'The Ettrick Shepherd', stayed in 1814 and, after dining with Wordsworth, De Quincey, Charles Lloyd and John Wilson, watched a display of brilliant meteors from the terrace. Hogg ventured the pleasantry that it was 'a triumphal airch *[sic]*, raised in honour of the meeting of the poets', offending Wordsworth, who resented being lumped together with such minor authors. Hogg took his revenge by gently parodying Wordsworth in 'The Flying Tailor' and other pieces.

Keats called on his June 1818 walking tour, but Wordsworth was out convassing for the Lowther (Tory) interest in the approaching election:

> He was not at home [wrote Keats] nor was any member of his family – I was much disappointed. I wrote a note for him and stuck it up over what I knew must be Miss Wordsworth's portrait and set forth again & we visited two Waterfalls in the neighbourhood.

Other visitors included William Wilberforce and his family, who stayed nearby from August to October 1818; Scott and J.G. Lockhart, who came with John Wilson in 1825 and (a less welcome guest) William Godwin, elderly anarchist philosopher, who visited in 1816. In youth, Wordsworth had been greatly impressed by Godwin's plans for an egalitarian society; now, a keen Tory, he lectured Godwin so fiercely that his guest left in a huff. Tennyson and James Spedding came in May 1835. At some time on the same holiday Tennyson climbed Loughrigg Fell opposite and looked across at Rydal Mount. 'Never was a poet more comfortably housed,' he reflected, perhaps with a touch of envy.

In 1849 there was a curious encounter when the twelve-year-old Algernon Charles Swinburne, an elfin figure with a mass of red-gold hair, was brought by his parents to meet the aged Wordsworth, who read him Gray's 'Elegy' – 'a poem which Swinburne ever after thoroughly disliked', according to a biographer. When Wordsworth said goodbye, adding 'I do not think, Algernon, that you will forget me,' the future author of *Poems and Ballads* burst into tears.

In Wordsworth's old age Rydal Mount was a place of pilgrimage for American visitors. Emerson came in August 1833:

> [Wordsworth's] daughters called in their father, a plain looking elderly man in goggles & he sat down & talked with great simplicity ... There may be in America some vulgarity of manners [said the poet] but that's nothing important; it comes out of the pioneer state of things; but ... I fear they are too much given to making of money & secondly to politics.

In 1846 Harriet Martineau brought the American feminist Margaret Fuller. Hawthorne, who waited until 1855, had to be content with a tour of the late poet's garden.

A footnote on Rydal Mount is supplied by Mrs Humphry Ward, who with her daughter rented the house in September 1911. The daughter slept in the 'corner room, over the small sitting-room'; late one night, as she recalled, she suddenly awoke:

> My first impression was of bright moonlight, but then I became strongly conscious of the moonlight striking on something, and I saw perfectly clearly the figure of an old man sitting in the arm-chair by the window. I said to myself – 'That's Wordsworth!' He was sitting with either hand resting on the arm of the chair, leaning back, his head rather bent and he seemed to be looking down, straight in front of him with a rapt expression ... As I looked – I cannot say, when I looked again, for I have no recollection of ceasing to look, or looking away – the figure disappeared, and I became aware of the empty chair. – I lay back again, and thought for a moment in a pleased and contented way – 'That was Wordsworth.' And almost immediately I must have fallen asleep again.

Mrs Ward adds, 'We did not know it till afterwards – that the seer of the vision was sleeping in Dorothy Wordsworth's room', where Wordsworth must often have sat with his sister in her last years of illness.

Wordsworth gave great care to the garden, which is still beautiful. He himself made the terraces which run W from the house, and describes one of them in 'The Massy Ways, carried across these heights' (1826):

> On the mountain's side
> A poet's hand first shaped it; and the steps

Of that same bard – repeated to and fro
At morn, at noon, and under moonlight skies
Through the vicissitudes of many a year –
Forbade the weeds to creep o'er its grey line.

According to Dora Wordsworth, the impulsive Hartley Coleridge used to compose sonnets here, running up and down the terrace whilst thinking. Several poems mention the view from the garden. 'I watch, and long have watched, with calm regret' (1819) describes Wordsworth's feelings on watching a 'slowly-sinking star' vanish behind the 'rocky parapet' of Loughrigg Fell opposite; a sonnet of 1819 addresses 'a projecting point of Loughrigg, nearly in front of Rydal Mount' across the lake:

Aerial Rock – whose solitary brow
From this low threshold daily meets my sight
When I step forth to hail the morning light;
Or quit the stars with a lingering farewell

– and imagines decorating it with an 'imperial Castle' in gratitude for the pleasure it has given.

The lawn – 'the sloping one approaching the kitchen-garden' – is described in a somewhat moralising poem of 1839:

This lawn, a carpet all alive
With shadows flung from leaves – to strive
 In dance, amid a press
Of sunshine, an apt emblem yields
Of worldlings ...

For a pleasant walk to Grasmere (which we shall later deal with from the other end) go uphill from Rydal Mount and take the signed bridleway W along the hillside, or reach it from the gate at the top W corner of the Rydal Mount garden.

We return to the road in front of Rydal Mount and go down to **St Mary's Church**, formerly known as Rydal Chapel, built for the benefit of local people in 1823 by Lady Le Fleming in what had been her orchard. Wordsworth wrote a poem 'To Lady Fleming on ... the Erection of Rydal Chapel' and later became a 'chapel warden' there. The poem praises the chapel 'Lifting her front with modest grace/To make a fair recess more fair' but privately he thought the chapel's design inappropriate and found the interior cramped. It was enlarged in 1884.

The Wordsworth family pew was the front one on the N side; Dr Arnold and his family from Fox How had the front pew on the S side. It must have made a daunting prospect for the preacher (though sometimes Arnold himself preached here). In 1830 the eleven-year-old John Ruskin, on a Lakeland tour with his parents, attended the chapel, and wrote in his diary:

We were lucky in procuring a seat very near that of Mr Wordsworth, *there being only one between it and the one we were in*. We were rather disappointed in this gentlemans appearance especially as he appeared asleep the greatest part of the time He seemed about 60 This gentleman possesses a long face and a large nose with a moderate assortment of grey hairs and 2 small eyes grey not filled with fury wrapt inspired with a mouth of moderate dimensions that is quite large enough to let in a sufficient quantity of beef or mutton & to let out a sufficient quantity of poetry.

A window at the E end of the S wall commemorates the Arnolds; next to it is a lovely, exuberant window by Henry Holiday in memory of Jemima and Rotha Quillinan, Edward Quillinan's daughters and Dora Wordsworth's stepdaughters. The beautiful faces of the child-angels are typical of work by Holiday (1839–1927), a Pre-Raphaelite who was England's most prolific designer of stained glass (he also drew the weird, dreamlike illustrations for Lewis Carroll's *The Hunting of the Snark*.)

From the churchyard a gate opens into **Dora's Field** (*NT*). In 1826, when there was a risk of the Wordsworths being turned out of Rydal Mount to make way for their landlady's aunt, Wordsworth deterred Lady Le Fleming by buying this field and threatening to build a house there. Later he gave the field to his daughter. Wordsworth himself drained it and built a terrace at the upper end. 'A Wren's Nest' (1833) describes a nest built here in a low branch of a pollard oak, sheltered by primrose leaves. The field is still wooded and full of wild flowers.

Return to the main road and continue W for 100yds. On the corner is the **Glen Rothay Hotel**, formerly Ivy Cottage. This was the home of Captain Thomas Hamilton (1789–1842), author of *Annals of the Peninsular Campaign* and a once-famous autobiographical novel, *Cyril Thornton* (1827), and a prolific contributor to *Blackwood's Magazine* in its early days. Later Edward Quillinan lived here with his first wife Jemima, who died here by fire in an accident in 1822. For a literary walk from here to 'Grassmere' loaded with sentiment and facetious humour, see John Wilson's 1842 *Recreations of Christopher North* (Volume III), which gives a good picture of the area in the early Victorian period.

Rydal Water

To quote Thomas West, the road 'serpentizes' (his favourite word) from Rydal 'upwards round a bulging rock, fringed with trees, and brings you soon in sight of **Rydal-Water**'. Coleridge first saw this small but beautiful lake, with its two islands, in 1799 and jotted a verbal sketch:

> The Rydale Lake glittering & rippled all over/only on the Rydale side of the ovel Island of Trees that lies athwart the Lake a long round-pointed wedge of black glossy calm – Rocky Island across the narrow, like the fragment of some huge bridge, now over grown with moss & Trees –

The lake was deeply loved by the Wordsworths, and Dorothy often mentions it in her *Journals*. 'I always love to walk that way,' she wrote of the road that passes along the N side, 'because it is the way I first came to

Rydale and Grasmere, and because dear Coleridge did also'. Visiting the Lake District with William in 1794, she had reached the lake 'just at sunset. There was a rich yellow light on the waters, and the Islands were reflected there.' On November 7 1805 she noted:

> The trees on the larger island on Rydale Lake were of the most gorgeous colours; the whole Island reflected in the water … the rocky shore, spotted and streaked with purplish brown heath, and its image in the water were indistinguishably blended, like an immense caterpillar, such as, when we were children, we used to call *Woolly Boys*, from their hairy coats.

Wordsworth's poem 'The Wild Duck's Nest' (1817) describes a 'beautiful nest' seen by him on the large island. He seems to have been especially fascinated by the variety of birdsong to be heard here. In June 1806 he composed 'Yes, it was the Mountain Echo' on the S shore, hearing the cuckoo's call echoing from the rocks of Nab Scar; 'By the Side of Rydal Mere' (1834) celebrates 'liquid music's equipoise' as birds sing their evening songs by the lake, and 'The leaves that rustled on this oak-crowned hill' addresses the owl, whose 'unexpected shriek' echoes across the 'inverted mountains' reflected in the water.

'Written with a Slate Pencil upon a Stone, the Largest of a Heap lying near a Deserted Quarry, upon One of the Islands at Rydal' (1800) describes a 'hillock of mis-shapen stones' on the large island as

> nothing more
> Than the rude embryo of a little Dome
> Or pleasure-house, once destined to be built
> Among the birch-trees of this rocky isle

– by Sir William Le Fleming of Rydal Hall in the early eighteenth century. The project (which Wordsworth calls an 'outrage') was abandoned and Wordsworth saw the story as a salutary warning to people impatient to build themselves 'trim Mansion[s]' in the Lake District, advising them to

> think again; and, taught
> By old Sir William and his quarry, leave
> Thy fragments to the bramble and the rose;
> There let the vernal slow-worm sun himself,
> And let the redbreast hop from stone to stone.

Facing the lake across the road is **Nab Cottage**, a fine farmhouse dated 1702. In the early nineteenth century it was the home of the statesman John Simpson, whose daughter Margaret was courted (despite the Wordsworths' disapproval) by Thomas De Quincey and bore his son in 1816. As Dorothy Wordsworth wrote somewhat maliciously:

> At the up-rouzing of the Bats and Owls he regularly went thither – and the consequence was that Peggy Simpson, the eldest daughter of the house presented him with a son …

They married in 1817. When John Simpson fell into debt in 1829, De Quincey took on the mortage, became nominal owner and lived in the house from time to time but had to sell it in 1833. Later Hartley Coleridge rented the house and died here in 1849.

At the head of Rydal Water is the White Moss Car Park, occupying the old **White Moss Quarry**. Wordsworth's 'Beggars' (1802) describes a picturesque family of roguish beggars whom Dorothy recorded in her *Journal* on May 27 1800: she saw the father 'beside the bridge at Rydal ... sitting at the roadside, his two asses standing beside him, and the two young children at play upon the grass.' Wordsworth placed the beggars 'near the quarry at the head of Rydal Lake, a place still a chosen resort of vagrants travelling with their families.'

The small unsigned turning uphill immediately after the quarry is the old road over White Moss Common. The present road continues on the level, on a causeway built about 1831. A third route to Grasmere is by the bridle-path reached by the gate behind Rydal Mount (Wordsworth calls it 'the upper path'; we shall explore it later). Dr Thomas Arnold, as progressive in his views on road building as in his politics, used to tease Wordsworth by referring to the picturesque Upper Path as 'Old Corruption', the road over the Common as 'Bit by bit Reform', and the new level road as 'Radical Reform.' Wordsworth was never reconciled to the latter, for the new road cut brutally through Bainriggs wood and destroyed the lonely peace of the lakeshore. We take it nonetheless.

'Brothers Wood' and Dove Cottage

By the sign announcing 'Grasmere' a grove of trees slopes uphill from the road. This is all that remains of **'Brothers Wood'**, so called by Wordsworth and his family because the poet composed 'The Brothers' whilst walking there in 1799. The wood was, Wordsworth said, 'in a great measure destroyed by turning the high road along the side of the water. The few trees that are left were spared at my intercession'.

On the E side of A591 (opposite Prince of Wales Hotel) at the N edge of Grasmere is the main car park for **Dove Cottage and the Wordsworth Museum** *(open daily 9.30–5.30; closed mid-January to mid-February and Christmas Day; admission charge)*, home of William and Dororthy Wordsworth (and at times of their brother John) from 1799 to 1808, and from 1802 of the poet's wife Mary. From 1809 to 1820 it was the home of Thomas De Quincey, who continued to rent it and store books there until 1835.

To reach the cottage, from car park walk past front of restaurant and take small lane on R. At L you will see the 3° W Gallery, formerly a village shop known as **Island View**, now a gallery for contemporary art related to Lakeland and literary themes. The lane leads up to Dove Cottage.

Originally an inn, the Dove and Olive Branch, in Wordsworth's time the cottage had no name of its own and was simply considered part of Town End, the hamlet at the S end of Grasmere township. The name 'Dove Cottage' has been in common use only since the Wordsworth Trust acquired the cottage in 1890. William and Dorothy Wordsworth must have passed the cottage on their 1794 walk from Kendal to Keswick, but there is no sign that they took special notice of it. In November 1799 William revisited Grasmere with his brother John and Coleridge, and wrote to Dorothy of 'a small house … empty which perhaps we may take and purchase furniture'; on December 17, after a three-days' journey on foot and horseback in bitter cold from Sockburn-on-Tees, they moved in. The cottage, built sometime before 1617, had only just ceased to be used as an inn. There

DOVE COTTAGE
John M'Whirter, 1882

was little furniture and only 'a dying spark in the grate of the gloomy parlour', according to Dorothy, but 'we were young and healthy and had attained our object long desired, we had returned to our native mountains, there to live.'

The Wordsworths repaired and decorated the cottage themselves, put up a slate fence between the front garden and the road 'to make it more our own', and had a door made from the half-landing of the staircase into the garden.

Here, between 1800 and 1803, Dorothy kept her journal, an almost daily record of household doings, local excursions and the changing detail of the nearby landscape. Here too Wordsworth wrote many of his finest poems, including 'Michael', 'The Brothers', 'Resolution and Independence', 'Ode: Intimations of Immortality', the 1805 *Prelude* and most of the 1807 *Poems in Two Volumes*. The 'Preface' to the second edition of *Lyrical Ballads* was also written here.

The cottage is furnished much as it would have been in Wordsworth's time. The study contains his writing-chair and a painting of the poet dictating to his wife Mary. Notice the cuckoo-clock over the stairs: it comes from a later phase of Wordsworth's life, when he lived at Rydal Mount. His poem 'The Cuckoo-Clock', written in 1840 soon after the clock was given to him, conveys straightforward pleasure in it.

In the Wordsworths' time the cottage had an uninterrupted view across the lake to Silver How – now blocked by the houses of Lake Terrace, built in 1860. Dorothy Wordsworth's journal notes (December 12 1801):

> We played at cards – sat up late. The moon shone upon the water below Silver-How, and above it hung, combining with Silver-How on one side, a bowl-shaped moon, the curve downwards; the white fields, glittering roof of Thomas Ashburner's house, the dark yew tree, the white fields gay and beautiful. Wm lay with his curtains open that he might see it.

On March 8 1802 the moon

> hung over the northern side of the highest point of Silver How, like a gold ring snapped in two, and shaven off at the ends, it was so narrow. Within this ring lay the circle of the round moon, as *distinctly* to be seen as ever the enlightened moon is.

Visitors included Walter Scott and Humphry Davy (both in 1805) and Coleridge, who often came between 1800 (when he revised the *Ancient Mariner* here) and 1804. Dorothy's *Journal* records his arrival at the cottage after his moonlight walk over Helvellyn in August 1800 with Part Two of *Christabel* in his pocket.

There was also much hospitality to neighbours: at Christmas 1805, a fiddler came and 'all the children of the neighbouring houses' came into the kitchen to dance.

Not many of Wordsworth's poems explicitly mention the cottage. The most detailed reference is in 'A Farewell', written in May 1802, shortly before Wordsworth married Mary Hutchinson. The poem, addressed to the cottage, describes its future mistress as one who will prize the 'Dear spot' and its 'happy Garden':

> Farewell, thou little nook of mountain-ground,
> Thou rocky corner in the lowest stair
> Of that magnificent temple which doth bound
> One side of our whole vale with grandeur rare;
> Sweet garden-orchard, eminently fair,
> The loveliest spot that man hath ever found.

A curious fragment (also from 1802) celebrates Wordsworth's quiet joy in the sheer physical solidity and calmness of the house:

> These Chairs they have no words to utter,
> No fire is in the grate to stir or flutter,
> The ceiling and floor are mute as a stone,
> My chamber is hushed and still,
> And I am alone,
> Happy and alone.

In 'The Waggoner' (1806) the hero passes the cottage (after labouring over the 'craggy hill' of White Moss Common) and the poet comments

> Where once the DOVE and OLIVE-BOUGH
> Offered a greeting of good ale
> To all who entered Grasmere Vale
> And called on him who must depart
> To leave it with a jovial heart;
> There, where the DOVE and OLIVE-BOUGH

Once hung, a Poet harbours now,
A simple water-drinking bard.

The garden (open in good weather only) is a steep nook of land at the foot of the crags and woodland which run up the fell behind the cottage. Dorothy filled it with flowering plants taken from the wild or given by neighbours – snowdrops, pansies, wild columbine, foxgloves, honeysuckle, strawberries and scarlet runner-beans – and it is kept much as she would have known it, with the right balance between the wild and the cultivated.

On June 9 1800, according to Dorothy,

> In the morning W cut down the winter cherry tree. I sowed French beans and weeded. A coronetted Landau went by, when we were sitting upon the sodded wall. The ladies (evidently Tourists) turned an eye of interest upon our little garden and cottage.

The present summer-house stands on the site of a 'moss hut' or 'bower' built in the spring of 1804 by William and Dorothy (but demolished by De Quincey in 1811). According to Wordsworth it was circular, 'lined with moss, like a wren's nest, and coated on the outside with heath'. Here they read to one another, and William worked at his poems (so much composition was done in the garden that at one time Wordsworth considered using *The Orchard Pathway* as the title for a group of his poems).

Dorothy too liked to sit here and could hear, on a May morning,

> The small birds ... singing, lambs bleating, cuckow calling, the thrush singing by fits, Thomas Ashburner's axe ... going quietly (without passion) in the orchard, hens ... cackling, flies humming, the women talking together at their doors.

Poems written here and referring to the garden include 'To a Butterfly', 'The Kitten and Falling Leaves', 'Stanzas Written in my Pocket Copy of Thomson's Castle of Indolence', parts of the 'Ode: Intimations of Immortality', and 'The Green Linnet' (1802), which shows Wordsworth in the orchard:

> Beneath these fruit-tree boughs that shed
> Their snow-white blossoms on my head,
> With brightest sunshine round me spread
> Of spring's unclouded weather,
> In this sequestered nook how sweet
> To sit upon my orchard-seat!
> And birds and flowers once more to greet,
> My last year's friends together.

De Quincey took over the cottage in 1809. He had first come to stay with the Wordsworths for a few days in 1807 and his *Recollections of the Lakes and the Lake Poets* record the impact of his first glimpse of his hero, Wordsworth, at the door:

> Through the little gate I pressed forward; ten steps beyond it lay the

principal door of the house. To this, no longer clearly conscious of my own feelings, I passed on rapidly; I heard a step, a voice, and, like a flash of lightning, I saw the figure emerge of a tallish man, who held out his hand, and saluted me with the most cordial manner, and the warmest expression of friendly welcome that it is possible to imagine…The owner of this noble countenance was Wordsworth.

His description of the cottage shows it much as it is today:

A little semi-vestibule between two doors prefaced the entrance into what might be considered the principal room of the cottage … very prettily wainscotted from the floor to the ceiling with dark polished oak … One window there was – a perfect and unpretending cottage window, with little diamond panes, embowered, at almost every season of the year, with roses; and, in the summer and autumn, with a profusion of jessamine and other fragrant shrubs.

When he returned in 1809, he lived at first on a small private income and then in 1818–19 edited the *Westmorland Gazette*. After 1813 he was heavily addicted to opium and his *Confessions of an English Opium-Eater* show him relaxing in the cottage with 'a book of German metaphysics and … a quart of ruby-coloured laudanum'. The *Confessions* also describe the sublimely horrific opium-dreams De Quincey experienced here.

Finding the cottage too small for his library and his family, he moved to Fox Ghyll in 1820: 'Mr de Quinceys Books have literally turned their master and his whole family out of doors', commented Sara Hutchinson.

Since the cottage was opened as a showplace in 1890, sightseeing visits have generated a literature of their own. Inevitably, the best modern poems on the house take a sceptical stance: Geoffrey Hill's 'Elegiac Stanzas On a Visit to Dove Cottage' (1959) acknowledges the power of Wordsworth's language but questions the

Customs through which many come
To sink their eyes into a room
Filled with the unused and unworn.

Tony Harrison's 'Remains' commemorates a stoical message left in pencil by a Victorian paperhanger, briefly uncovered during modern restoration work: 'Our heads will be happen cold when this is found.' In prose, Wordsworth-lovers with a sense of mischief will enjoy Sue Limb's *The Wordsmiths at Gorsemere* (1987, from the radio series).

Just N of the cottage, in a former barn, is the **Wordsworth Museum** (*opening times as for Dove Cottage*), housing a permanent exhibition on the early discovery of the Lake District by landscape artists, followed by displays on the life, work and times of Wordsworth. There is much visual material, and manuscripts displayed include *The Vale of Esthwaite* (1787), the 1798 *Prelude* and *Vaudracour and Julia*, as well as volumes of Dorothy Wordsworth's *Journal* and part of De Quincey's *Confessions of an English Opium-Eater*. Most of the best portraits of Wordsworth are here as well as important portraits of most of his associates, including Coleridge, Scott, Davy, John Wilson, Burns and Leigh Hunt.

Take the steps between Dove Cottage and the Museum to find the **Rock of Names** at R of the garden at the back of the Museum. Carved with the initials of William, Dorothy and John Wordsworth, Mary and Sara Hutchinson and Coleridge, it is now a patchwork of fragments. It was part of a rock face at the S end of Thirlmere, at the point where Coleridge and the Wordsworths often met midway between their homes at Grasmere and Keswick. Coleridge notes (April 20 1802) 'Cut out my name & Dorothy's over the S.H. at Sara's Rock –', but it is not clear whether he carved all the initials and if so when. For details of how the rock got here, see p 94.

The Rock is mentioned several times in Dorothy's *Journal* and is addressed by Wordsworth in an original draft for 'The Waggoner':

> We worked until the initials took
> Shapes that defied a scornful look. –
> Long as for us a genial feeling
> Survives, or one in need of healing,
> The power, dear Rock, around thee cast,
> Thy monumental power, shall last ...
> And fail not thou, loved Rock! to keep
> Thy charge when we are laid asleep.

N of the Museum is a modern stone building, the **Jerwood Centre**, open to researchers by prior arrangement. The centre houses ninety percent of Wordsworth's verse manuscripts, all of Dorothy's journals and many Wordsworth letters, as well as manuscripts by Coleridge, De Quincey and many others. There is also an archive of drawings, paintings and memorabilia concerned with Wordsworth and the Lake District. The round tower contains the Voice Box, a performance space for poetry readings and other events.

The staff car park at the side of the Jerwood Centre was formerly the site of **Sunny Bank**, an undistinguished prefabricated bungalow made of asbestos and erected c. 1934. This was rented in 1957 by the novelist Malcolm Lowry, author of *Under the Volcano*. He told a friend cheerfully,

> it's Grasmere where Wordsworth designed the chimney pots and you may see de Quincey's room (smoking prohibited) in de Quincey's house to which, on payment of 1/6 you may be admitted on all days save Sundays as Wordsworth's cottage, which it was for 5 years.

The bungalow was removed in 2002.

Town End

Dove Cottage and the neighbouring buildings make up the hamlet of **Town End**. On the corner S of Dove Cottage, between the road and a narrow lane, is **Sykeside Farm**. This was John and Agnes Fisher's house. John helped in the Dove Cottage garden and his sister Molly, a much-loved and valued servant, helped Dorothy about the house. Molly was a highly individual character, remembered not least for refusing to let Coleridge go beyond the kitchen when he turned up at Dove Cottage one wet day in August 1802 with muddy boots. Agnes Fisher, another strong personality, is described in *Excursion* VI. A quick learner in youth, when

> nothing could subdue
> Her keen desire of knowledge, nor efface
> Those brighter images by books imprest
> Upon her memory, faithfully as stars
> That occupy their places,

she came to be dominated by 'avaricious thrift'. Nursed through her final illness by Molly, she resented her sister-in-law and on her deathbed

> was heard to say
> In bitterness, 'and must she rule and reign,
> Sole Mistress of this house, when I am gone?
> Tend what I tended, calling it her own!'

Due W of Dove Cottage, the corner cottage with small lean-to building on the end wall (now used for educational purposes) is **Ashburner's Cottage**, home of Thomas Ashburner and his wife Peggy. Ashburner, who helped the Wordsworths with odd jobs, had been a 'statesman' but had mortgaged his land and, after a hard struggle to pay his debts, sold it. Wordsworth's poem 'Repentance', much of which was 'taken verbatim from the language' of Peggy Ashburner, bitterly attributes the financial disaster to discontent and a 'covetous spirit'.

Ashburner survived his wife and seems to be the widower described in *Excursion* VI, which also sketches the cottage garden with its honeysuckle, roses, pinks and beehives, the eldest daughter indoors busy at her spinning-wheel and the whole house full of a sober gaiety.

N of Ashburner's Cottage, on the corner between A591 and the road to Dove Cottage is **Rose Cottage**, home from 1829 to 1840 of Hartley Coleridge, who was looked after by Mrs Diana Le Fleming (an arrangement made for him by the Wordsworths). Every few months he would wander off drinking and rambling about the country, sleeping in barns or haystacks, leaving a trail of unpaid bills which the Wordsworths settled for him.

To reach the two old 'roads' over White Moss Common to Rydal, turn uphill past Dove Cottage. 50yds uphill from Sykeside Farm and adjoining Chestnut Cottage is **Sykeside Cottage**, a small house with a tall metal gate. Fleur Adcock's poem 'The Keepsake' (collected in *The Incident Book*, 1986) is an elegy for Pete Laver, the poet, illustrator and librarian of the Wordsworth Library who lived here and died on Scafell in 1983. The poem describes an evening spent in this cottage.

A little way uphill a gate leads down into the garden of **How Foot**, now a hotel, formerly the holiday home of the Rev. William Spooner (1844–1930), Warden of New College, Oxford, who gave his name to the

'Spoonerism'. The famous examples ('You have hissed my mystery lectures; you have tasted the whole worm ...') are apocryphal; but he did indeed make such slips. He was a keen walker in the area and is said to be buried in the small cemetery at the N end of Grasmere village, though I have not been able to find his grave.

Continue uphill to the corner of the road; opposite the duckpond is **How Top Farm**. Dorothy Wordsworth describes a funeral here in 1800:

> About 10 men and 4 women. Bread, cheese, and ale. They talked sensibly and cheerfully about common things ... The coffin was neatly lettered and painted black, and covered with a decent cloth. They set the corpse down at the door; and, while we stood within the threshold, the men with their hats off sang with decent and solemn countenances a verse of a funeral psalm ... When we got out of the dark house the sun was shining, and the prospect looked so divinely beautiful as I never saw it. It seemed more sacred than I had ever seen it, and yet more allied to human life.

Here the two old 'roads' to Rydal diverge. The road to R (S) signed 'Rydal' is the former carriage road over White Moss Common. That to L (E) uphill is the bridleway or 'Upper Path'.

We take the carriage road first.

John's Grove, the Wishing Gate and Glowworm Rock

Opposite How Top Farm is Wishing-Gate House, formerly **Dry Close**, once the home of Colonel John Danson, a bibliophile who built up a famous and historically important collection of erotica, bequeathed at his death in 1978 to Trinity College, Oxford.

After 150yds the wall moves away from the upper side of the road leaving an open area of grass and reeds. The small iron gate in the wall that runs downhill to rejoin the road leads into **John's Grove**, so-called because it was a favourite place of Wordsworth's brother John, described by the poet as 'Meek, affectionate, silently enthusiastic, loving all quiet things, and a Poet in everything but words.' The grove commands a good view over the lake and island, with Silver How in the background. Now mainly oak, beech and hazel, it was largely a 'fir-grove' in Wordsworth's day. There is a seat in the middle of the grove, and the path rejoins the road at the S end.

The grove is described in Wordsworth's poem 'When, to the attractions of the busy world', which relates how Wordsworth on his walks sheltered here from the bitter winter weather of 1799–1800; the following year he noticed for the first time a path through the wood and discovered that his brother John had worn it

> By pacing here, unwearied and alone,
> In that habitual restlessness of foot
> That haunts the Sailor measuring o'er and o'er
> His short domain upon the vessel's deck
> While she pursues her course through the dreary sea.

During John's absence at sea and after his death the family associated it especially with memories of him.

On April 28 1802 – 'a beautiful morning' – William and Dorothy lay in the grass

> in the trench under the fence, listening to the waterfalls and the birds. There was no one waterfall above another – it was a sound of waters in the air – the voice of the air … we both lay still, and unseen by one another; [William] thought that it would be as sweet thus to lie so in the grave, to hear the *peaceful* sounds of the earth, and just to know that our dear friends were near. The lake was still; there was a boat out. Silver How reflected with delicate purple and yellowish hues, as I have seen spar.

In the autumn of 1804 Wordsworth came here:

> my favourite grove [he wrote]
> Now tossing its dark boughs in sun and wind,
> Spreads through me a commotion like its own,
> Something that fits me for the Poet's task

– inspiring him to continue Book VII of *The Prelude*, which had lain untouched for six months.

150yds S past John's Grove is the **Wishing Gate**, a plain wooden gate overlooking the lake. According to Wordsworth local tradition promised that wishes made there would be granted. It was a favourite spot of Wordsworth's sister-in-law Sara Hutchinson, and was sometimes known in the family as 'Sara's Gate'.

On October 31 1801 Dorothy walked here with Mary Hutchinson; Dorothy was

> much affected when I stood upon the second bar of Sara's gate. The lake was perfectly still, the sun shone on hill and vale, the distant birch trees looked like large golden flowers. Nothing else in colour was distinct and separate, but all the beautiful colours seemed to be melted into one another, and joined together in one mass, so that there was no difference, though an endless variety, when one tried to find it out.

Wordsworth's 1802 poem 'The Sailor's Mother' describes a woman met by the gate on 'A foggy day in winter time'; she was begging and carried under her cloak a songbird in a cage, cherished because it had been her dead son's pet. His 1828 poem 'The Wishing-Gate' sees the gate as a symbol of human aspirations. In 1841, hearing, incorrectly, that the gate had been removed, he responded with a second poem, 'The Wishing-Gate Destroyed'. Happily the gate (or a much-renewed later version of it) is still there to offer its 'balm of expectation' to the passer-by.

At the highest point of the road note the drive entrance to **Ladywood**, a house built by Ernest De Selincourt (1870–1943), editor of the standard edition of Wordsworth's poems. Just after the Ladywood driveway, on S side of road is a small car park in a disused quarry. Take the grassy path near the car park entrance. It runs around the quarry's upper side and goes due S to a gate in a wall. 100yds S of the wall is one of a pair of rock outcrops described in Wordsworth's 1845 poem 'Forth from a jutting ridge, around whose base'. The other outcrop is 100yds to the R (W).

The poem tells of the 'two heath-clad Rocks' in the wood, and of how

Up-led with mutual help,
To one or other brow of those twin Peaks
Were two adventurous Sisters wont to climb,
And took no note of the hour while thence they gazed,
The blooming heath their couch, gazed, side by side,
In speechless admiration.

The sisters were Mary and Sara Hutchinson.

The 'twin Peaks' look down on to the A591 road some fifty feet below. They make pleasant perches, and though the view is now restricted by tree-growth, in winter Rydal Water can be seen from the E rock.

Return to the road and follow it down to the **Glow Worm Rock**, the overhanging outcrop of rock on the L (N) side of the road 100yds before it joins the A591 at the White Moss car park. Several of Wordsworth's poems mention the rock, in particular 'The Tuft of Primroses' (1808) and 'The Primrose of the Rock' (1831). He explained 'We have been in the habit of calling it the glow-worm rock from the number of glowworms we have often seen hanging on it as described. The tuft of primrose has, I fear, been washed away by the heavy rains.'

Walking past the rock on April 24 1802 ('a very wet day') William, Dorothy and Coleridge

all stopped to look at the Glow-worm Rock – a primrose that grew there, and just looked out on the road from its own sheltered bower. The clouds moved, as William observed, in one regular body like a multitude in motion – a sky all clouds over, not one cloud.

The moment seems to have been the origin of 'The Tuft of Primroses', in which Wordsworth addresses the flowers and hopes that they will be safe not only from sheep, goats and children, but from greedy adults who might pick them.

'The Pilgrim's Dream, or, The Star and the Glow-Worm' (1818) was also 'suggested … on the road between Rydal and Grasmere, where Glow-worms abound', when Wordsworth noticed 'a star … shining above the ridge of Loughrigg Fell, just opposite'. And 'Inscribed Upon a Rock' (1818) describes a 'monument of ice', formed apparently on the same 'dripping rock' by water running down its face. Primroses and glow worms have gone from the rock; the stream of water is still there.

The Upper Path, White Moss Common and Nab Scar

For Wordsworth's 'Upper path' to Rydal, walk uphill past Dove Cottage and at How Top take the road E (signed 'Path to Rydal') to reach **White Moss Tarn**, much frequented by herons. The encounter with the leech-gatherer described in 'Resolution and Independence' perhaps took place here: Dorothy's journal (3 October 1800) describes meeting the old man, bent 'almost double', near Dove Cottage; the 'pool bare to the eye of heaven' suggests White Moss Tarn (not then overhung by rhododendrons), though the landscape of the poem is a composite one.

Paths lead upward from the tarn to **White Moss Common**, an attractive miniature fell with several small peaks offering fine views over the Grasmere and Rydal Valleys (West, calling it 'Grasmere Hill', advised visitors in 1778 to climb the Common to 'have a view of as sweet a scene as travelled eye ever beheld', for 'Mr Gray's description of this peaceful happy vale, will raise a wish in every reader to see so primaeval a place').

In Dorothy Wordsworth's words, White Moss is

> a place made for all kinds of beautiful works of art and nature, woods and valleys, fairy valleys and fairy tarns, miniature mountains, alps above alps.

Having walked up here at twilight on February 8 1802, she wrote

> There was a strange mountain lightness, when we were at the top of the White Moss. I have often observed it there in the evenings, being between the two valleys. There is more of the sky there than any other place. It has a strange effect sometimes along with the obscurity of evening or night. It seems almost like a peculiar *sort* of light.

From White Moss Tarn take the upper path heading NE (not the one sloping steeply downhill SE). This is the bridleway between Grasmere and Rydal which was always a favourite walk of Wordsworth's. Since for fifty years he lived at one end of it or the other he was a frequent presence on it; many of his poems were first thought of or actually composed on the path and it has a good claim to being viewed as one of the essential locations of his genius.

A few poems were inspired by particular details on the path. ¼m E of White Moss Tarn is a pair of cottages called **Brockstone**. Wordsworth's 'The Waterfall and the Eglantine' was suggested in 1800 by an eglantine or sweet briar rose growing on the small stream that comes out under the cottages (which were not then built), just below the path.

Continue ¼m to a point where the path passes through an area of old woodland between two wooden gates. 100yds above the path is a massive outcrop of rock one of whose overhanging blocks suggested 'The Oak and the Broom', which tells of two plants growing from 'a crag, a lofty stone/As ever tempest beat'.

Also conceived on the path somewhere between this point and Rydal Mount was 'To the Clouds' (1808). 'The clouds,' wrote Wordsworth, 'were driving over the top of Nab Scar across the vale; they set my thoughts agoing, and the rest followed almost immediately.' The poem addresses the

> Army of clouds ...
> Ascending from behind the motionless brow
> Of that tall rock, as from a hidden world

– the 'tall rock' being Nab Scar, the crag under which runs the E half of the path itself –

> A little hoary line and faintly traced,
> Work, shall we call it, of the shepherd's foot
> Or of his flock? – joint vestige of them both.

William and Dorothy Wordsworth walked here below the Scar with Coleridge on April 23 1802. 'It was very grand when we looked up,' wrote Dorothy, 'very stony, here and there a budding tree.' She and Coleridge 'left William sitting on the stones, feasting with silence' and pushed on before, scrambling up to 'a rock seat – a couch it might be under the bower of William's eglantine, Andrew's broom.' William saw them from below; 'He came to us, and repeated his poems ['The Waterfall and the Eglantine' and 'The Oak and the Broom'] while we sate beside him on the ground.' Coleridge 'went to search for something new' and found

> a bower – the sweetest that was ever seen. The rock on one side is very high, and all covered with ivy, which hung loosely about, ... on the other side it was higher than my head. We looked down upon the Ambleside vale, that seemed to wind away from us, the village *lying* under the hill. The fir-tree island was reflected beautifully. We now first saw that the trees are planted in rows. About this bower there is mountain-ash, common-ash, yew-tree, ivy, holly, hawthorn, mosses, and flowers, and a carpet of moss.

The 'bower' seems to be mentioned in passing as the 'wild cave' of Wordsworth's 1817 poem 'To the Same ('Enough of climbing toil, . .')'.

Many people have tried to find Coleridge's bower; so far all have failed.

Continue ¾m to a small metal gate into the garden of Rydal Mount. About 10 yds W of the gate is a small spring which runs under the path into a rectangular stone trough, fringed with ferns. This is what remains of the **Nab Well**, the spring that supplied Rydal Mount with drinking water. Its water still appears drinkable. Wordsworth's 'Composed when a Probability existed of our being obliged to quit Rydal Mount as a Residence' (1825) thanks the 'pellucid Spring' for

> cheer[ing] a simple board
> With beverage pure as ever fixed the choice
> Of Hermit, dubious where to scoop his cell;

and hopes that after his departure the spring will keep its 'Chaplet of fresh flowers and fern'.

Pearson's Boathouse, Bainriggs, Grasmere Lake, Grasmere Vale

Opposite the Dove Cottage car park is the Prince of Wales Hotel. Just S of the hotel is a stone **boathouse** with the inscription WP 1843. It was originally built in the early 1800s by William Pearson, one of Wordsworth's schoolfellows at Hawkshead, who became an eminent mathematician. It was very ugly and a great cause of irritation to Wordsworth, who valued the solitude of this part of the shore – 'not 200 yards' from Dove Cottage. It fell down several times and was at last rebuilt in its present form, having grown less uncouth as time went by – like its owner, Wordsworth remarked. Perhaps in revenge, Wordsworth refers to Pearson as the man whose grave is dug ready for him in *The Excursion* Book VI.

The E shore of the lake hereabouts is described in a poem of 1800:

> A narrow girdle of rough stones and crags,
> A rude and natural causeway, interposed
> Between the water and a winding slope
> Of copse and thicket, leaves the eastern shore
> Of Grasmere safe in its own privacy.

The poem tells of how Wordsworth, Dorothy and Coleridge strolled here in harvest-time and were surprised to see, on 'a point of jutting land', a man 'in peasant's garb' fishing instead of helping to get in the harvest. The walkers judged him 'Improvident and reckless' for neglecting his work until, drawing nearer, they found him to be 'worn down/By sickness'. Struck with 'self-reproach' for their hasty moralising, they named the foreshore **Point Rash-Judgment**. Now that the lake's level is lower, the 'point' cannot be identified.

Follow the pavement S along the lakeside to its end, then take the footpath into **Bainriggs**, the wood at the S end of the lake. From here paths lead E, parallel to the road, towards Rydal; or S, to a footbridge over the Rothay and thence E to Rydal or W to circle Grasmere lake.

Despite much pounding by human feet Bainriggs in autumn may be seen as Dorothy Wordsworth describes it (October 12, 1800):

> We walked before tea by Bainriggs to observe the many-coloured foliage.
> The oaks dark green with yellow leaves, the birches generally still green,
> some near the water yellowish, the sycamore crimson and crimson-tufted,
> the mountain ash lemon-colour, but many ashes still fresh in their summer
> green. Those that were discoloured chiefly near the water.

The lake, properly called simply 'Grasmere' , makes its first fictional appearance in a wonderfully absurd sentimental-Gothic novel, *Ethelinde, or The Recluse of the Lake* (1789) by Charlotte Smith, set in a fictitious 'Grasmere Abbey', 'on the borders of the small but beautiful lake called Grasmere Water, in the county of Cumberland [*sic*]'. There is disappointingly little landscape-description, and one guesses that Mrs Smith had never been anywhere near Grasmere.

The lake's appearance has changed since Wordsworth's time. The building of the causeway and road along the E side in 1831 obliterated a peaceful wooded and ferny shore; and in 1950 rocks at the SE corner were blasted to lower the water level and prevent the lake from flooding the village. This produced small gravelly beaches on the W shore (much appreciated by paddling children) but explains why Pearson's boathouse no longer touches the water.

Dorothy Wordsworth provides the best description of the lake's general appearance two centuries ago: as she looked down from White Moss Common, it appeared 'a little round lake of nature's own, with never a house, never a green field, but the copses and the bare hills enclosing it, and the river flowing out of it.' Her journal is full of observations of the Lake – its sounds, movements and colours, its endlessly changing appearances through the transformations of light, mist and cloud. At the end of January 1802, she and William

> amused ourselves for a long time in watching the breezes, some as if they came from the bottom of the lake, spread in a circle, brushing along the surface of the water, and growing more delicate, as it were thinner, and of a *paler* colour till they died away. Others spread out like a peacock's tail, and some went right forward this way and that in all directions. The lake was still where these breezes were not, but they made it all alive.

Dorothy often notes the lake's reflections: on December 27 1801, for example, Grasmere was 'a beautiful image of stillness, clear as glass, reflecting all things,' although 'the wind was up, and the waters sounding.'

Wordsworth once saw 'a remarkable appearance of an island ... on Grasmere lake, produced by a reflection from the rocks and woods ... on a sheet of ice on the lake, which made it appear as if an island of about four or five acres stood out from the lake, covered with wood and variegated with rocks, &c.' He thought at first 'that part of the mountain had slidden down into the lake; but ... afterwards, by comparing and examining the image,' he and Dorothy 'found it an exact reflection of part of the sides of the lake'.

The hut on the island is the subject of Wordsworth's poem 'Written with a Pencil upon a Stone in the Wall of the House (an Out-House), on the Island of Grasmere' (1800):

> Thou see'st a homely Pile, yet to these walls
> The heifer comes in the snow-storm, and here
> The new-dropped lamb finds shelter from the wind.
> And hither does one Poet sometimes row
> His pinnace, a small vagrant barge, up-piled
> With plenteous store of heath and withered fern, ...
>   And beneath this roof
> He makes his summer couch.

There were also pleasure-trips to the island in borrowed boats. In July 1800 Coleridge and the Wordsworths enjoyed a picnic there, splendidly described in one of Coleridge's letters:

> We drank tea the night before I left Grasmere on the Island in that lovely lake, our kettle swung over the fire hanging from the branch of a Fir Tree, and I lay & saw the woods, & mountains, & lake all trembling, & as it were *idealized* thro' the subtle smoke which rose up from the clear red embers of the fir-apples which we had collected. Afterwards, we made a glorious Bonfire on the Margin, by some alder bushes, whose twigs heaved & sobbed in the uprushing column of smoke – & the Image of the Bonfire, & of us that danced round it – ruddy laughing faces in the twilight – the

Image of this in a Lake smooth as that sea, to whom the Son of God had
said, PEACE!

William and Dorothy both made many observations of the lake at night.
On July 30 1800 Dorothy and her brothers were boating on the lake in the
late evening and watched 'a rich reflection of the moon, the moonlight,
clouds and the hills, and from the Rays gap [ie Dunmail Raise] a huge rainbow pillar.' There is a powerful nocturnal meditation in Wordsworth's
1807 poem 'Composed by the Side of Grasmere Lake', where the waters,

> steeled
> By breezeless air to smoothest polish, yield
> A vivid repetition of the stars

and an oracular voice, mindful of the Napoleonic Wars then raging overseas, whispers

> 'Be thankful, thou; for, if unholy deeds
> Ravage the world, tranquillity is here!'

The lake had practical uses too: Wordsworth frequently caught pike,
and Dorothy's journal records many fishing-trips. On June 12 1800, for
example, 'William and I went upon the water to set pike floats ... We
returned to dinner, 2 pikes boiled and roasted.' Another common catch
was 'bass' – properly perch.

Before turning to the village, we consider the valley as a whole. It has
often struck visitors as paradisal: Thomas Gray, the first to write about it in
detail, saw it as he approached from Keswick in 1769 and thought it 'a little
unsuspected paradise'; to William Wilberforce in 1779 it embodied 'the
idea of Rasselas's happy Valley'. These perceptions owe much to the
enclosed character of the valley. Dominated by the pyramidal Helm Crag
to the N and by Loughrigg Fell to the S, it is almost completely surrounded
by fells. Northward also is the spectacular 'inverted arch' (as Coleridge
called it) of Dunmail Raise where the pass leaves for Keswick.

In an early fragment, 'Anacreon , Wordsworth describes how

> silvered by the morning beam
> The white mist curls on Grasmere's stream,
> Which, like a veil of flowing light,
> Hides half the landskip from the sight.

In *An Evening Walk*, he gives an affectionate sketch of the valley; while in
'Home at Grasmere' (c1800) he recalls his early resolve that 'here/ Must be
his Home, this Valley be his World' and gives thanks that

> now ... perchance for life, dear Vale,
> Beloved Grasmere (let the Wandering Streams
> Take up, the cloud-capt hills repeat, the Name),
> One of thy lowly Dwellings is my Home.

The same poem celebrates the harmonious diversity of the valley's landscape, natural and man-made:

> Thou art pleased,
> Pleased with thy crags, and woody steeps, thy Lake,
> Its one green Island and its winding shores;
> The multitude of little rocky hills,
> Thy Church and Cottages of mountain stone
> Clustered like stars some few, but single most,
> And lurking dimly in their shy retreats,
> Or glancing at each other cheerful looks,
> Like separated stars with clouds between.

The landscape of the valley was used as the scene for *Excursion* V, although Wordsworth shifted its nominal location to 'the lower part of Little Langdale' to make a composite setting.

Changes in the valley are lamented in the first part of 'The Tuft of Primroses' (1808): on their recent return from Yorkshire the Wordsworths had been saddened to see that

> the aerial grove, no more
> Right in the centre of the lovely Vale
> Suspended like a stationary cloud,
> Had vanished like a cloud

together with other trees, leaving a barer landscape behind.

The principal change Wordsworth would notice now is the much greater density of building. Surprisingly, however, the character of the landscape as a whole has not been damaged, partly because there are now more trees so that groups of houses are screened and broken up.

Grasmere Village and St Oswald's Church

From the Dove Cottage car park follow A591 200yds and take the turning L (NW) to the village. This is Stock Lane (B5287). There is a large car park on the lane, and another at the village centre near the church.

At the corner of the main road and Stock Lane is the **Sports Field**. Grasmere Sports have been held here since 1861 on the Thursday nearest August 20. They attract huge crowds and include the famous Guides' Race (up and down Butter Crags near Greenhead Gill) as well as Cumberland- and Westmorland-style wrestling and Hound Trails.

Beatrix Potter attended the Sports in 1895 and noted 'We went late, and had difficulty in finding friends among the crowd of carriages' – an experience familiar to modern visitors. She watched hound trails:

> About nineteen dogs were thrown off, but two young hounds turned back at once, puzzling about the meadow. The spectators on the tarred wall received them with execrations and shouts of 'any price agin yon doug!' Rattler won, a lean, black and white hound from Ambleside ... Rattler's victory appeared popular, Mr. Wilkinson danced on the box, slapping his thigh ... Indeed, Mr Wilkinson raced so alarmingly on his own account with a wagonette that we began to wonder whether he was, to quote aunt

Booth's expressive phrase, 'boozy', the lower-orders were so extensively, but the weather was some excuse.

The village is picturesque from a distance and still nestles inconspicuously in the valley amongst its many trees. The painter Paul Nash stayed here in July 1914 and thought it 'a very Sammy Palmer village at even' – high praise from an admirer of Samuel Palmer's visionary twilight landscapes.

E.M. Forster stayed in Grasmere in July 1907: 'It rains all night and every day, but not always all day … I like Grasmere,' he told a correspondent. 'I have seldom enjoyed a sight more than Dove Cottage … Between the rain we row on the Lake pick Welsh Poppies and buy gingerbread.' The following day he was off on a trip 'round Thirlmere for 3/6', and he asked plaintively, '*Where* is Joanna's Rock?' (For an answer of sorts, see p 77.) Later he used Grasmere as a symbol of comfortable Englishness in *A Passage to India*:

> 'Ah, dearest Grasmere!' [exclaims Mrs Moore as the train winds across a scorching plain towards the Marabar Hills.] Its little lakes and mountains were beloved by them all. Romantic yet manageable, it sprang from a kindlier planet.

The Parish Church of St Oswald is easily found. W of the church and facing it across the road is **The Rectory**. The Wordsworths rented this house (built 1690; much enlarged in the late nineteenth century) from May 1811 to May 1813. In 1811, according to Dorothy's *Journal*,

> We had the finest Christmas day ever remembered, a cloudless sky and glittering Lake; the tops of the higher mountains covered with snow. The day was kept as usual with roast beef and plumb pudding.

On December 27 'The fiddlers are in the kitchen and D[ora] is dancing – I must go and join in the dance … William is at work on his great poem' – *The Excursion*, completed in 1812. In summer the children could play in the grassy churchyard. The house, however, was damp from the nearby river and the tenancy was a sad one, for in 1812 three-year-old Catharine and six-year-old Thomas both died and were buried in the churchyard. The Wordsworths left for Rydal Mount in 1813. (The house receives a fictionalised treatment in *The Excursion* Book VII, where Wordsworth gives it a holly-hedge and a gravel path through an avenue of ash-trees to the church. None of these features was really present.)

Opposite the church across the river is the Rowan Tree restaurant, formerly the site of the **Grasmere Tea Gardens**. The old Tea Gardens were a much-loved though distinctly down-market institution, embodying precisely the spirit of John Betjeman's poem 'Lake District', which gently satirises the interwar hiking boom:

> Spirit of Grasmere, bells of Ambleside,
> Sing you and ring you, water bells, for me;
> You water-colour waterfalls may foam;

GRASMERE FROM BUTTER CRAGS
Thomas Allom, 1832

Long hiking holidays will yet provide
Long stony lanes and back at six for tea
And Heinz's Ketchup on the tablecloth.

The Tea Gardens themselves serve as the poet's viewpoint in David Wright's sequence of 'Grasmere Sonnets' (collected in *To the Gods the Shades*, 1976):

In a tea-garden overhanging the Rotha
On whose clear surface cardboard packages
And other discards take their voyages
To the quiet lake, I wondered what he'd say,
Old mountain-trotter with a nose like Skiddaw
Safely asleep there where the river nudges
Its Coca-Cola can into the sedges,
Were his bleak eye to brood upon our day.

Enter the **churchyard** by the s gate (near the bridge). Until the late nineteenth century there was a stone seat fixed to the wall at L of this gate, and here the characters sit to talk in Book V of *The Excursion*:

The Vicar paused; and toward a seat advanced,
A long stone-seat, fixed in the Church-yard wall;
Part shaded by cool sycamore, and part
Offering a sunny resting-place to them
Who seek the House of Worship, while the bells
Yet ring with all their voices.

For much of Wordsworth's life most of the graves were unmarked, a practice which he praises in *The Excursion* Book VI.

St Oswald's Church is described in Book V of *The Excursion*:

> Not raised in nice proportion was the pile;
> But large and massy; for duration built;
> With pillars crowded, and the roof upheld
> By naked rafters intricately crossed,
> Like leafless underboughs in some thick wood ...
>   The floor
> Of nave and aisle, in unpretending guise,
> Was occupied by oaken benches ranged
> In seemly rows; ... An heraldic shield,
> Varying its tincture with the changeful light,
> Imbued the altar-window; fixed aloft
> A faded hatchment hung, and one by time
> Yet undiscoloured. A capacious pew
> Of sculptured oak stood here, with drapery lined.

This is mostly accurate. The building (medieval) is massive, heavily rendered and not picturesque outside. Inside it is more interesting, having an extraordinary row of shallow arches resting on square pillars: the result of enlarging the church by the simple method of adding a new aisle to the N, then cutting holes in the original N wall to leave 'pillars' which are simply the bits of the old wall that were not cut away. The 'thick wood' of 'intricately crossed' rafters was required to raise the roof after the N aisle was added.

The 'oaken benches', however, have been replaced by modern pews, and though there are several hatchments over the altar there was never a heraldic altar-window. Most of the other monuments described in the poem are fictitious. The 'capacious pew' of oak is a large square box-pew, filled with chairs, by the sanctuary at the S side of the nave.

John Stuart Mill was here in July 1831: it was the day of the Rushbearing procession, and he observed that

> the roof consists of naked slates, whitewashed internally, but shewing all the junctures; and nothing else except old bare rafters ... There are only one or two pews, and those of the simplest and most unpretending kind ... Every thing however that admitted of it was hung with bouquets and festoons of fresh flowers, intermixed with some quaint bunches of feathers; the rustic character of these ornaments harmonized as much as their gaudy colours contrasted, with the homely appearance of the building.

He looked into the tiny schoolhouse at the gate, but found 'nothing except two or three boys' hats, and sundry copies of Mrs. Trimmer's abridgment of the New Testament.'

On the S wall near the altar is a monument to Jemima Quillinan, first wife of Edward Quillinan, with an epitaph probably written by Wordsworth and Quillinan in collaboration:

> These vales were saddened with no common gloom
> When good Jemima perished in her bloom;
> When (such the awful will of heaven) she died
> By flames breathed on her from her own fireside ...

The lines have a certain doleful absurdity but record a real tragedy: Jemima Quillinan had become insane and died a lingering death after accidentally setting her clothes on fire. She was nursed by the poet's daughter Dora, later Quillinan's second wife.

On the N wall opposite Jemima's monument is one to Wordsworth, with an epitaph by Keble, translated from his original Latin.

An annual Rushbearing ceremony takes place on the Saturday nearest August 5; it is described by Wordsworth in 'Rural Ceremony':

> The village Children, while the sky is red
> With evening lights, advance in long array
> Through the still churchyard, each with garland gay,
> That, carried sceptre-like, o'ertops the head
> Of the proud bearer.

Leave the church and return to the path parallel to the river to reach the Wordsworth graves at the NE corner of the churchyard. The yew trees along this path were planted under Wordsworth's direction at the expense of Sir George Beaumont. Wordsworth thought the yews

> an ornament to a place which, during late years has lost much of its rustic
> simplicity by the introduction of iron palisades to fence off family
> burying-grounds, and by numerous monuments, some in very bad taste.

The planting may also have been an attempt to remedy earlier depredations, lamented in 'The Tuft of Primroses' (1808).

The graves can be identified as follows (L to R): *front row* the poet's son William ('Willie') and his wife Fanny; Dorothy Wordsworth; a memorial stone to the poet's brother John (drowned at sea and buried in Dorset); in front of his, Sara Hutchinson; William Wordsworth and his wife Mary; Dora Quillinan, the poet's daughter; Edward Quillinan, her husband; Jemima Quillinan, his first wife; Rotha Quillinan, daughter of Edward and Jemima; in front of this, Rotha's sister Jemima. *Second row* Reginald and Gordon Wordsworth, the poet's grandsons; Mary Louisa Mair, the poet's granddaughter; Catharine ('Kate'), the poet's daughter; Thomas, the poet's son; William, the poet's grandson and son of William ('Willie') and Fanny. Behind this last is the grave of Hartley Coleridge.

Wordsworth himself chose the spots for his own, Mary's and Hartley's graves immediately after Hartley's death in January 1849, standing to watch while the sexton measured out the ground.

The deaths of little Catharine, Thomas and his grandson William, all of whom died as young children, caused Wordsworth intense anguish. Catharine died in 1812, aged three; a comical and engaging child, she is described in Wordsworth's poem 'Characteristics of a Child Three Years Old' and in one of his saddest works, the sonnet 'Surprised by Joy – impatient as the Wind...'

Thomas De Quincey was also deeply attached to little Kate: distressed by her death, he claims that for more than two months he 'often passed the night upon her grave … in mere intensity of sick, frantic yearning after neighbourhood to the darling of my heart'. Depression following her death helped to increase his dependence upon opium. Six-year-old Thomas Wordsworth died six months after Catharine. His headstone carries a quiet but deeply-felt epitaph by Wordsworth, who spent nearly ten years perfecting it:

> Six months to six years added, he remained
> Upon this sinful earth, by sin unstained:
> O blessed Lord! whose mercy then removed
> A Child whom every eye that looked on loved;
> Support us, teach us calmly to resign
> What we possessed, and now is wholly thine!

The presence of Kate's and Thomas's graves within view of the Rectory was a factor in Wordsworth's decision to move to Rydal Mount in 1813.

Thomas Hardy visited the graves on his Lakeland holiday of June 1911, noting tartly:

> Wordsworth's grave and headstone are looking very trim and new. A group of tourists who have never read a line of him sit near, addressing and sending off picture postcards … Wrote some verses.

To R of the Wordsworth graves note the elaborate monument to one Louisa Lewes, with its mysterious inscription around the plinth under the urn: ERECTED BY T.D. OF LANCASTER, HER UNKNOWN FRIEND, MAY 1847. A few yds due W of Jemima Quillinan's grave is a memorial stone to the poet Arthur Hugh Clough (buried in Florence, where he died in 1861), flat in front of his mother's headstone. 10ft due W of Louisa Lewes's monument are the graves of the Sympsons of High Broadrayne, friends of the Wordsworths described at length in *The Excursion*.

Take the path from the Church to the lychgate. The Green family of Pavement End are buried in a long row of graves along the W side of the path. A well-known Grasmere family, they are described in *The Excursion* Book VII, where their house is fictionally renamed 'Gold-rill side', and Wordsworth tells the story of the seven brothers, and their sister Margaret who died in infancy. Margaret is mentioned on the third stone (counting from the yew tree) as having died aged one in 1802.

The Excursion's Book VII also describes, from Wordsworth's own observation, the funeral here of a young militiaman named Dawson, a hardy youth who dreamed of fighting Napoleon but died of natural causes and was buried with 'A volley, thrice repeated' from the rifles of his fellow-volunteers. His grave is unknown.

Leave the churchyard by the lychgate at the N side. Adjoining the gate is the **Gingerbread Shop**, formerly the village schoolhouse, built in 1660. Wordsworth's children attended school in this tiny building when the family lived at the Rectory in 1811–13. Until some time in the nineteenth century the children used the nearby part of the churchyard (which was largely free from graves) as their playground. In Book VII of *The Excursion* Wordsworth refers to

> Five graves, and only five, that rise together
> Unsociably sequestered, and encroaching
> On the smooth playground of the village-school

– which indicates that in 1812 the area was only just beginning to be used for burials.

The building ceased to be a school in 1855 and was taken by Sarah Nelson, formerly a cook at Patterdale, who quickly made her name as a gingerbread specialist. The present-day product, made to her recipe, is outstanding. Gingerbread is a long-established Grasmere delicacy, and was well known to Wordsworth: on January 16 1803, according to Dorothy's journal, 'Wm. had a fancy for some ginger bread' – so she went to the small village shop kept by Matthew Newton, a blind man, and 'bought 6 pennyworth'.

NW of the church is a long pink-rendered cottage, **Church Stile**, now housing the National Trust shop and a gallery. In the eighteenth century this was 'Robert Newton's Inn'. Joseph Budworth describes it as it was in 1792:

> I must first tell you, that this public-house was not distinguished by prints expressing rules for drinking, but by 'King Charles's good rules;' – a picture of the pursuit under the royal oak, and a large one explaining the twelve months, with instructive verses under each of them. Behind his cottage [the landlord] had dammed-in a small stream ... a receptacle for trout, pike, and perch, to be ready whenever he wanted them; and he had the precaution to slant some large flagstones, for the fish to retire under in hot weather.

Budworth set out to climb Helm Crag,

> after as good and well-dressed a dinner ... as man could wish; but the dinner was so cheap, I must mention what it consisted of:
>
> Roast pike, stuffed,
> A boiled fowl,
> Veal-cutlets and ham,
> Beans and bacon,
> Cabbage,
> Pease and potatoes,
> Anchovy sauce,
> Parsley and butter,
> Plain butter,
> Butter and cheese,
> Wheat bread and oat cake,
> Three cups of preserved gooseberries, with a bowl of rich cream in the centre:
> For two people, at ten-pence a head.

Budworth found the climb up Helm Crag 'formidable; and not less so, to speak in plain English, from having a complete belly-full.'

William and Dorothy Wordsworth probably spent a night at the inn on their 1794 walk through the Lakes; William and his brother John (and Coleridge) certainly stayed for five days on their 1799 tour of the Lakes, William noting Dove Cottage as a possible future home. About 1800 Robert Newton left and opened the Red Lion.

Just N of the Gingerbread Shop is the **Wordsworth Hotel** (no connection with Wordsworth), formerly the Hotel Rothay. In 1950 C. Day-Lewis, who enjoyed pretending to dislike the Lakes, stayed here for the Wordsworth Centenary celebrations, and told his daughter:

> The Mountains are … as revolting as ever: their lower slopes are dotted with sodden sheep and lumbering lady hikers in sensible skirts with humps on their backs and great big red bulging calves (I speak of the hikers not the sheep) … It has, I need not say, been raining all day.

Continue to the **Red Lion**. Basil Montague (friend of Wordsworth and Coleridge) and George Dyer (minor poet and friend of Charles Lamb) stayed here in October 1804. 'It is an old-fashioned little place,' wrote Harriet Martineau in 1854, 'where the traveller's choice is usually between ham and eggs and eggs and ham; with the addition, however, of cheese and oat cake.'

Lakeshore, Silver How, Loughrigg Terrace

To make a circuit of the lake, go W from the church past the garden centre (signed Langdale and Coniston). Just after the Goldrill Hotel on the S side of the road is the barn and white farmhouse of **Pavement End Farm**, home of the Green family, and the 'Gold-rill side' of *The Excursion*.

Dorothy describes a walk out of the village past Pavement End in her *Journal* for November 24 1801:

> John Green's House looked pretty under Silver How. As we were going along we were stopped at once, at the distance of perhaps fifty yards from our favourite birch tree. It was yielding to the gusty wind with all its tender twigs, the sun shone upon it, and it glanced in the wind like a flying sunshiny shower. It was a tree in shape, with stem and branches, but it was like a Spirit of water. The sun went in, and it resumed its purplish appearance, the twigs still yielding to the wind, but not so visibly to us. The other birch trees that were near it looked bright and chearful, but it was a creature by its own self among them.

(In *Judith Paris* Hugh Walpole quotes this passage and refers to 'John Greens house', quite wrongly, as if it were at Watendlath.)

Continue 300yds to a gateway marked 'Kelbarrow' and beside it a footpath (signed Chapel Stile and Great Langdale). Beatrix Potter made sketches on this hillside path in August 1899; later they served as a basis for the illustration of Mrs Tiggy-Winkle's door into the hillside in *The Tale of Mrs Tiggy-Winkle* (1905), though the location was changed to Catbells. To circle the lake, continue along the road; to climb Silver How follow the

Chapel Stile path along the hill for ¾m until a clear path crosses it at right angles to run NW up a gully between two crags to the summit.

Silver How opens to the eye wonderful views (to the Langdale Pikes westward, to Windermere southward) and wonderful skies: memories of them colour C. Day-Lewis's 'Transitional Poem' (1929):

> Chiefly to mind appears
> That hour on Silverhowe
> When evening's lid hung low
> And the sky was about our ears.
> Buoyed between fear and love
> We watched in eastward form
> The armadas of the storm
> And sail superbly above.

100yds S of the drive-entrance to 'Kelbarrow' is the gate to **Silverhowe**, a splendid early nineteenth-century mansion set in elaborately land-scaped grounds. This house stands on the site of an older house ('Gell's Cottage') built in the late eighteenth century by William Gell, landscape painter, pioneer of Greek archaeology and friend of the Wordsworths, who often borrowed his boat to fish for pike and perch on the lake. The attrac-tive asymmetrical front elevation of the present house, all dormer windows, inconsequent gables and bargeboarding, with a round tower at one corner, is best seen from the gateway to 'Silver Fell', the next house to the S.

½m further S is **The Wyke**, a very old and picturesque stone cottage with a round chimney, set a little back from the road. It was the home of the Mackereths, a well-known Grasmere family who were friends of Words-worth and inspired several of his poems. A Mackereth was landlord of the Swan Inn mentioned in 'The Waggoner'; another, George Mackereth, parish clerk of Grasmere, told him the story which became 'The Blind Highland Boy'. The Mackereths are also probably mentioned briefly in *The Excursion* Book V as 'The family who dwell within yon house/Fenced round with glittering laurel'. Sarah Mackereth is the ten-year-old 'cot-tage-maiden' heroine of 'The Westmoreland Girl' (1845), which describes her dangerous rescue of a lamb which had fallen into the Wyke Gill beck, the stream which enters Grasmere lake near the boat-hire yard.

100yds S of The Wyke the road forks. The upper road (signed 'Public footpath: Great Langdale'), for walkers only, leads to Hammerscar. The lower road leads to the lakeside, Dale End and Loughrigg Terrace. A permissive path leaves the lower road 50yds S of the fork and goes round the water's edge to Bainriggs. In the spring of 1800 Dorothy Wordsworth noted the woods here as 'extremely beautiful ... The primrose still pre-eminent among the later flowers of the spring. Foxgloves very tall, with their heads budding.' She was

> much amused with the business of a pair of stone-chats; their restless
> voices as they skimmed along the water following each other, their
> shadows under them, and their returning back to the stones on the shore,
> chirping with the same unwearied voice.

For **Loughrigg Terrace**, a far more spectacular walk of almost the same distance, continue S ¼m along the road to **Dale End Farm**, once the house of Mr Benson, the Wordsworths' landlord at Dove Cottage. After 300yds the roads enters a wood and starts to climb steeply. This is Red Bank. Take the gate by the cottage on the corner and follow the path uphill past the front of the cottage for Loughrigg Terrace, a beautiful raised footpath which traverses the slope of Loughrigg Fell some 150ft above the lake. The views over Grasmere Vale are fine and there are several seats. In Book IX of *The Excursion* the Terrace seems to be 'the grassy mountain's open side' where the Pastor stands to speak to his companions, summing up the philosophy of the poem at its end. The Lady offers a verbal land-scape-sketch of part of the scene:

> Behold the shades of afternoon have fallen
> Upon this flowery slope; and see – beyond –
> The silvery lake is streaked with placid blue;
> As if preparing for the peace of evening.
> How temptingly the landscape shines! The air
> Breathes invitation; easy is the walk
> To the lake's margin, where a boat lies moored
> Under a sheltering tree.

The Terrace was a favourite walk of the Wordsworths, who would make a circuit of Grasmere or, more ambitiously, of Grasmere and Rydal Water, crossing the Rothay by the stepping stones just S of Rydal. The walk could be extended by climbing Loughrigg Fell above the Terrace: from the Fell, Dorothy noted on the evening of May 18 1800, 'the prospect exceedingly beautiful … It was so green that no eye could be weary of reposing upon it.' On May 29 she was there again:

> I lay upon the steep of Loughrigg, my heart dissolved in what I saw, when I was not startled but re-called from my reverie by a noise as of a child paddling without shoes.

It turned out to be a lamb, 'seeking its mother.'

The lakeside at Loughrigg was a paradise of wild flowers: on June 27 1800 the Wordsworths 'rowed down to Loughrigg Fell, visited the white foxglove, gathered wild strawberries'.

From the E end of the Terrace, paths continue E to Rydal and Ambleside, or zigzag down to the lakeside and Bainriggs.

Hammerscar

For **Hammerscar**, 100yds S of The Wyke take the upper road (signed 'Great Langdale') which soon becomes unmetalled. After ¾m, take the wooden gate 15yds uphill from an iron kissing-gate. Follow the path uphill 250yds then go through an ungated gap in the wall at L (E) and ascend knoll. (The gap is 120yds below wooden gate at top of pass.) This is Hammerscar, and it commands a stunning view over Grasmere. West (1784) recommends this, or a spot near it (his directions are not clear) as a viewpoint, for Grasmere; Wordsworth rambled to this point as a schoolboy from Hawkshead, and recalled the moment later in 'Home at Grasmere' (1800):

> Once to the verge of yon steep barrier came
> A roving School-boy; what the Adventurer's age
> Hath now escaped his memory – but the hour
> One of a golden summer holiday,
> He well remembers, though the year be gone.
> Alone and devious from afar he came;
> And, with a sudden influx overpowered
> At sight of this seclusion, he forgot
> His haste ... and, sighing said,
> 'What happy fortune were it here to live! ...'
> The Station whence he looked was soft and green,
> Not giddy yet aerial, with a depth
> Of Vale below, a height of hills above.
> For rest of body perfect was the Spot,
> All that luxurious nature could desire,
> But stirring to the Spirit;

and he resolved that 'here/Must be his Home, this Valley be his World' – a wish fulfilled in 1799 when he moved into Dove Cottage. The cottage would have been visible then: now it is hidden by the Prince of Wales Hotel.

To this spot also Thomas De Quincey came in 1806, a timid nineteen-year-old admirer of Wordsworth longing to visit his hero but too shy:

> Once I absolutely went forward from Coniston to the very gorge of
> Hammerscar, from which the whole vale of Grasmere suddenly breaks
> upon the view in a style of almost theatrical surprise, with its lovely valley
> stretching in the distance, the lake lying immediately below, with its
> solemn boat-like island of five acres in size, seemingly floating on its
> surface; its exquisite outline on the opposite shore, revealing all its little
> bays and wild sylvan margin, feathered to the edge with wild flowers and
> ferns. In one quarter, a little wood, stretching for about half a mile towards
> the outlet of the lake, more directly in opposition to the spectator; a few
> green fields; and beyond them, just two bowshots from the water, a little
> white cottage gleaming from the midst of trees ... That little cottage was
> Wordsworth's ... Catching one hasty glimpse of this loveliest of
> landscapes, I retreated like a guilty thing, for fear I might be surprised by
> Wordsworth, and then returned faint-heartedly to Coniston and so to
> Oxford, *re infecta* ['with my task undone'].

Allan Bank, Easedale, Sourmilk Gill and Easedale Tarn

Leave the Red Lion Hotel heading NW and take the small road signed 'Public footpath: Score Crag, Silver How'. It leads straight to **Allan Bank**, a large mansion rendered in pinkish ochre, at the top of a knoll with a commanding view over lake and valley. This was the home of William Wordsworth from 1808 to 1811 (when he moved to Grasmere Rectory). Ironically, he had been outraged when the house was built in 1805 by John Crump, a Liverpool merchant, and had told a friend:

> A wretched creature, wretched in name and Nature, ... goaded on by his still more wretched Wife ... has at last begun to put his long impending threats in execution; and when you next enter the sweet paradise of Grasmere you will see staring you in the face ... a temple of abomination, in which are to be enshrined Mr and Mrs Crump. Seriously this is a great vexation to us, as this House will stare you in the face from every part of the Vale, and entirely destroy its character of simplicity and seclusion.

From the Dove Cottage garden, Allan Bank was right in the middle of the view of Easedale – hence the fury. Dorothy declared it 'a publick sorrow'. (De Quincey claims that when first built the house fell down, to the delight of locals, whilst the builders were celebrating in the Red Lion!)

However, with a fourth child expected, the Wordsworths found Dove Cottage too small; they swallowed their pride and moved into 'Crump's temple of abomination' in May 1808, becoming the house's first tenants. The owner allowed Wordsworth to lay out the grounds below the house with trees, many of which are still there, so that as we look at the house from the lake we are seeing a landscape shaped by Wordsworth himself.

Coleridge spent the winter of 1808–9 here, a troublesome guest, struggling with illness, opium-addiction, marital problems (Mrs Coleridge was there for part of the time, though they were supposed to have separated) and editing his philosophical-political paper *The Friend*. At the same time De Quincey stayed, and he and Coleridge helped Wordsworth write his pamphlet on the *Convention of Cintra*, denouncing British handling of the Peninsular War. Other prose works written here include the *Reply to Mathetes* (1809), the *Essays upon Epitaphs* (1809-12) and the earliest parts of the *Guide to the Lakes*.

Dr Thomas Arnold rented Allan Bank for the summer of 1832 and lived here (often playing host to the Wordsworths) whilst his house at Fox How was being built. Return to the village; or take N fork in drive below house then footpath NE towards white buildings for Easedale Road.

Between the Red Lion and the Grasmere end of Easedale Road, the **Heaton Cooper Studio** exhibits work by three generations of a family of Lakeland and mountain artists. A. Heaton Cooper (1864-1929) painted extensively in Norway as well as Britain (the Log House which he brought back still stands in Ambleside); his son W. Heaton Cooper (1903-95), a topographical watercolourist, illustrated guides for the Fell and Rock Climbing Club, as well as writing and illustrating several books on the Lakeland landscape including, *TheHills of Lakeland* (1938) and *The Tarns of Lakeland* (1960). *His* son Julian Cooper (b. 1947) has worked in the Andes and Himalayas as well as in Cumbria.

Facing Sam Read's bookshop across a field is **Dockwray Cottage**, the farm of Dorothy Wordsworth's friend Jenny Dockeray. On May 28 1800 Dorothy records that she walked up to the rocks above Jenny Dockeray's, sate a long time upon the grass, the prospect divinely beautiful. If I had three hundred pounds, and could afford to have a bad interest for my money, I would buy that estate, and we would build a cottage there to end our days in. I went into her garden and got white and yellow lilies, periwinkle, etc.,

– which she took back to Dove Cottage and planted.

Continue W along Easedale Road and after ½m cross Goody Bridge over Easedale Beck and 100yds later turn L (S) through the gate to Goody Bridge Farm and over the field to the beck (crossed by stepping stones). Words-worth reckoned in old age that he had composed 'thousands of lines' whilst walking beside Easedale Beck, and his poem 'It was an April morn-ing: fresh and clear' gives a detailed description of a walk up the beck and identifies a 'dell' with a waterfall and

> the natural foliage of the rocks – the birch,
> The yew, the holly, and the bright green thorn,
> With hanging islands of resplendent furze:
> And, on a summit, distant a short space,
> By any who should look beyond the dell,
> A single mountain-cottage might be seen.

In the poem the place is named 'Emma's Dell', 'Emma being Wordsworth's poeticism for Dorothy. **Emma's Dell** is on private land at the sharp bend in the beck 120yds downstream of the stepping-stones; there is a tiny water-fall where a small gill joins the beck. The 'single mountain-cottage' is Goody Bridge Farm, enlarged since but still picturesque.

Return to Goody Bridge Farm and the road. 50yds W of the farm, on the N side of the road, is **Easedale Lodge**. C. Day-Lewis frequently stayed here in the 1920s and '30s, walking, working on his early poems, and some-times driving up to Threlkeld to see W.H. Auden.

100yds beyond Easedale Lodge the road reaches the gate to **Lancrigg**, now a hotel. This was the home after 1840 of Mrs Eliza Fletcher, a lady of strong intellectual interests, who had been a radical and a feminist in Edin-burgh at the turn of the century, holding an informal salon which was much frequented by the founders of the *Edinburgh Review*. She retired here to be close to her daughter, who was married to Dr Davy and was especially friendly with the Wordsworths, Southey and Hartley Coleridge. Her *Autobi-ography* (1875) gives a good picture of Lake District society at the time.

Opposite the Lancrigg gate take the **footbridge** (signed Easedale Tarn) into a small wood. It is mentioned in Dorothy Wordsworth's *Journal* (December 9 1801):

> At the little footbridge we stopped to look at the company of rivers, which came hurrying down the vale this way and that; it [Easedale?] was a valley of streams and islands, with that great waterfall [Sourmilk Gill] at the head, and lesser falls in different parts of the mountains, coming down to these rivers.

THE TERRACE WALK, LANCRIGG
John M'Whirter, 1882

We are now entering Easedale. De Quincey wrote in 1839:

> I have often thought, whilst looking with silent admiration upon this
> exquisite composition of landscape, with its miniature fields, running up
> like forest glades into miniature woods; its little columns of smoke,
> breathing up like incense to the household gods, from the hearths of two or
> three picturesque cottages – abodes of simple primitive manners, and what,
> from personal knowledge, I will call humble virtue – … I have thought
> that, if a scene on this earth could deserve to be sealed up, like the valley
> of Rasselas, against the intrusions of the world – if there were one to which
> a man would willingly surrender himself a prisoner for the years of a long
> life – this it is – this Easedale – which would justify the choice and
> recompense the sacrifice.

The valley, a long shallow dale dominated by Helm Crag to the N, was one
of the Wordsworths' favourite haunts during their Dove Cottage years.
During their first months there, not knowing its real name, they called it
'The Black Quarter' because of the way it tends, viewed from Dove Cottage,
to fall into shadow late in the day.

Walks in the valley often included a stroll on the lower slopes of Helm
Crag, from where the village and church could be seen. In December 1801
Dorothy walked below Helm Crag, observing

> The birches on the crags beautiful, red brown and glittering. The ashes

beautiful spears with their upright stems. The hips very beautiful, and so good!! and, dear Coleridge! I ate twenty for thee, when I was by myself.

Coleridge too gives a fine impression of the valley in a brief notebook entry of 1801:

> Scenes in Easedale, rocks & woods, & trees starting up around Rocks & out of Rocks – where under the boughs & through the Boughs you have the glimmering Lake, & Church tower – places wherein
>
> To wander & wander for ever & ever –

It was probably also here that he found

> A Hollow place in the Rock like a Coffin – a Sycamore Bush at the head, enough to give a shadow for my Face, & just at the Foot one tall Foxglove – exactly my own Length – there I lay & slept It was quite soft. June 18. 1801. Thursday.

He was here with William and Dorothy on April 22 1802, and 'talked of his plan for sowing laburnum in the woods'. Dorothy was tired and sat down to rest by 'the single holly behind that single rock in the field', listening to the sound of the waterfall and of 'William flinging stones into the river'. The poet returned 'repeating the poem "I have thoughts that are fed by the sun"', which 'had been called to his mind by the dying away of the stunning of the waterfall when he came behind a stone.' On October 11 1802 the Wordsworths 'walked to the Easedale Hills to hunt waterfalls'.

Follow the clearly-marked stony path for ¼m, then turn L (W) through gate signed 'Blindtarn Moss'. The path leads straight to **Blindtarn (or Blentarn) Gill**, a house, Wordsworth said, which 'looked as if it had grown out of the mountain, an indigenous Dwelling, for indigenous inhabitants' but since enlarged. It was the home of George and Sarah Green, 'the poorest people in the valley', who had a small mortgaged estate and who died on the fells in 1808 leaving eight children. The Wordsworths helped raise a subscription for the benefit of the children, one of whom, Sally Green, already worked for them at Allan Bank.

Moving accounts of the tragedy were written by Dorothy Wordsworth and (less accurately) by De Quincey (*Recollections of Grasmere*, 1839). It was also the subject of Wordsworth's 'Elegiac Stanzas Composed in the Churchyard at Grasmere'. The parents had walked to Langdale over the pass immediately behind the cottage; returning in a blizzard they failed to find the pass and fell from a precipice. The children were left alone (though not, as De Quincey claims, snowed up in the cottage for three or four days) and at length raised the alarm. The parents were buried in Grasmere churchyard.

Return to the main path, which leads directly to **Sourmilk Gill** (formerly also Churn Milk or White-churn Gill) and its 'Force' or waterfall, named because of the water's thick, white appearance as it boils down the rocks after rain. Coleridge visited it with Wordsworth on their 1799 tour, and jotted in his notebook:

> Churnmilk Force – appearing over the Copse/the steaming air rising above it – the water full – the rock that stands up & intercepts all but the marges & rims of the lower half – the Copse, whose trees sometimes yielding & parting in the wind make the waterfall beneath the rock visible –

It became a favourite Wordsworth spot: on November 15 1801 Dorothy walked 'to Churnmilk Force nearly, and went upon Heifer Crags' (now unidentifiable, though Calf Crags is on the OS map).

The path climbs the side of the force – 'a knotted string of cascades', Eliza Lynn Linton calls it – and leads on to **Easedale Tarn**. The tarn, which fills a bleak, cupshaped valley, is – as De Quincey says – 'the most gloomily sublime of its class'. Apparently its solitude tends to inspire religious feelings. At any rate James Murray, first editor of the *Oxford English Dictionary*, had what he counted the most important religious experience of his life here in 1875: benighted after a long walk and without a map, he fell on his knees and prayed for guidance back to Ambleside. He set off along the N side of the tarn but suddenly 'a pure, irrational impulse' sent him running back along the S side, where he struck a path, met a guide from Easedale and was soon safely on his way.

C. Day-Lewis's 'Transitional Poem' (1929) suggests that he too was spiritually moved:

> By Easedale Tarn, where I sought a comforter,
> I found a gospel sterner than repentance.
> Prophetic earth, you need no lumber of logic
> Who point your arguments alike with a primrose
> And a sick sheep coughing among the stones …

The path continues to Blea Tarn and Great Langdale. Alternatively return to the footbridge for Grasmere or Far Easedale.

Far Easedale, Lancrigg, Helm Crag

From the corner by the footbridge 250yds W of Goody Bridge follow the metalled road ½m NW until it divides. Take the fork signed to Far Easedale. After the cottages take the small gate up stone steps for path through wood to **Lancrigg**. After 100yds the path enters the grounds of Lancrigg house, elaborately laid out in the nineteenth century but now decayed. Continue E, keeping upper path at fork, until the path skirts a mound with a stone carrying a Latin inscription: HOC IN SUPERCILIO SEDEBAT DOROTHEA WORDSWORTH DUM EX ORE FRATRIS PROPE INAMBULANTIS CARMINA DESCRIBIT ('On this brow Dorothy Wordsworth sat writing down poems from the lips of her brother walking nearby'). The poems probably included large portions of the 1805 *Prelude*.

The mound, topped with a rounded, glacier-smoothed boulder, is the subject of Wordsworth's sonnet 'Mark the concentred hazels that enclose …' which describes an 'old grey Stone, protected from the ray/Of noontide suns' and resembling the tomb of 'some ancient Chieftain'. The stone surface at the summit is now deeply covered with leafmould and other

GOODY BRIDGE
William Green, 1814

debris from the trees, planted since Wordsworth's day, so that only odd outcrops can be seen. It is still, though, a strange, beautiful and tranquil spot.

From the stone with the inscription, the path (known as **Lancrigg Terrace**) continues to Lancrigg House and so back to Grasmere. We, however, return to the gate and the Far Easedale path.

25yds after the gate is the turning (signed) to **Helm Crag**. A clear stony path leads to the summit, a short, stiff but satisfying climb rewarded by good views. On December 12 1801 – 'a fine frosty morning' – Dorothy Wordsworth walked by the lake and noted, 'Helm Crag rose very bold and craggy, a Being by itself, and behind it was the large ridge of mountains, smooth as marble and snow white.' Somewhere around the E side of the Crag *should* be 'Joanna's Rock'. Celebrated in 'To Joanna', one of Wordsworth's 1800 'Poems on the Naming of Places', the rock is said to be on the banks of the Rothay, where Joanna Hutchinson and Wordsworth one morning walked together

And when we came in front of that tall rock
Which looks towards the East, I there stopped short,
And traced the lofty barrier with my eye
From base to summit; such delight I found
To note in shrub and tree, in stone and flower,
That intermixture of delicious hues,
Along so vast a surface.

Joanna laughed at his expression, whereupon

> The rock, like something starting from a sleep,
> Took up the Lady's voice, and laughed again

– rousing a train of echoes, all the way (the poet claims) to Skiddaw and back. The 'tall rock/That looks towards the East' could be part of Helm Crag; other details in the poem cannot be factual.

The summit of the Crag is extremely rugged and several of the rocks have popular names. At the S end of the ridge are 'the Lion and the Lamb', best seen from near Dove Cottage. At the N end are the rocks described by Wordsworth in 'The Waggoner':

> The ASTROLOGER, sage Sidrophel
> Where at his desk and book he sits,
> Puzzling aloft his curious wits;
> He whose domain is held in common
> With no-one but the ANCIENT WOMAN,
> Cowering beside her rifted cell,
> As if intent on magic spell; -
> Dread pair that, spite of wind and weather,
> Still sit upon Helm-crag together!

These figures are best seen from the lay-by on the A591 at Dunmail Raise and will be discussed there. From the Crag's summit a steep path leads down to the Raise.

Otherwise return to the Far Easedale path. Continuing NW, note the large smooth rock outcrop in the centre of gently rising grassy ground to the L of the path as it runs above the buildings of Brimmer Head Farm (just before reaching a monkey-puzzle tree). On December 6 1800 Dorothy and William were there,

> and walked backwards and forwards in that flat field, which makes the second circle of Easedale, with that beautiful rock in the field beside us, and all the rocks and the woods and the mountains enclosing us round. The sun was shining among them, the snow thinly scattered upon the tops of the mountains.

The outcrop is probably Dorothy's 'beautiful rock'. Just below it the Easedale Beck is joined by Far Easedale Gill; 100yds up Far Easedale Gill from the junction is a tiny packhorse bridge mentioned in Coleridge's note-book:

> the first bridge from the water fall, one-arched – ferny – its parapet or ledge of single stones not unmorter'd yet cemented more by moss and mould –

The rock and bridge are on private land; there is no footpath. The path continues to the head of Far Easedale and on over Greenup Edge to Borrowdale.

The Swan and Greenhead Gill

Half a mile N of the Grasmere turnoff on the A591 is **The Hollins**, a heavy Victorian mansion incorporating the original house of the Wordsworths' friend John Olliff. William and Dorothy often used to walk in the wood and field attached to the house. On February 22 1802 Dorothy noted that the little 'syke' (streamlet) 'above Mr Olliff's house was very impressive. A ghostly white serpent line, it made a sound most distinctly heard of itself.'

Now that we are on the A591 again, we may note two literary journeys which follow its course hereabouts. Chapters XX to XXVII of William Black's novel *The Strange Adventures of a Phaeton*, a thinly disguised account of his own carriage-driving tour from London to Edinburgh, presents a cheerful view of the route as it was in 1883; and John Masefield drove down this road in 1936, recording his impressions in a poem, 'The Long Drive: Edinburgh to Boar's Hill'. The poem as a whole has some interest as a record of prewar car travel (no motorways, and frequent stops to clean the plugs), but the passage on Grasmere is disappointing.

100yds N of The Hollins' driveway turn E beside the small Catholic Church. On the L (N) side of the road is **Ben Place**, a substantial house with Victorian enlargements which was the home of the Dawsons, family of the young militiaman whose funeral in Grasmere churchyard Wordsworth describes in *The Excursion* Book VII. At the corner of the road is the gateway to the car park of Forest Side, a hotel. The original **Forest Side** is the small N wing of the L-shaped house at N side of the car park. This is the house identified by Wordsworth in 'Michael' as Michael's home. In the poem Michael's hardworking wife spins late into the night, hanging a lamp over the fireplace, and

> as it chanced
> Their cottage on a plot of rising ground
> Stood single, with large prospect, north and south,
> High into Easedale, up to Dunmail-Raise,
> And westward to the village near the lake;
> … from this constant light, so regular
> And so far seen, the House itself, by all
> Who dwelt within the limits of the vale,
> Both old and young, was named THE EVENING STAR.

The house has been blocked from view of the valley by later building. Dorothy Wordsworth noted (on the night of November 22 1801)

> the moon and the moonlight seen through hurrying driving clouds immediately behind the Stone-Man upon the top of the hill on the Forest Side. Every tooth and every edge of rock was visible, and the Man stood like a Giant watching from the roof of a lofty castle. The hill seemed perpendicular from the darkness below it. It was a sight I could call to mind at any time, it was so distinct.

Continue N to the **Swan Inn**, mentioned in Wordsworth's 'The Waggoner' – though it is the sign that is stressed, rather than the inn itself:

> Who does not know the famous SWAN?
> Object uncouth, and yet our boast,
> For it was painted by the Host;
> His own conceit the figure planned,
> 'Twas coloured all by his own hand;
> And that frail Child of thirsty clay,
> Of whom I sing this rustic lay,
> Could tell with self-dissatisfaction
> Quaint stories of the bird's attraction!

– for thirsty Benjamin the Waggoner has difficulty in forcing himself to pass the door. The inn now has a modern sign (colourful but not unduly sophisticated) carrying the first line of the quotation. Harriet Martineau used to spread a story that whilst staying with Wordsworth in 1805 Walter Scott, finding the diet at Dove Cottage limited, used to slip out here daily for a 'cold cut' and a glass of porter; the secret came out when the two men passed the Swan on a walk one morning and met the landlord, who exclaimed that Scott was early for his drink that day.

For the spot associated most closely with Wordsworth's 'Michael', take the lane alongside the Swan and take the second turning R (signed), following **Greenhead Gill** first on a tarmac lane, then up a stony track. When the gill bends L (N) continue to follow it; you will come to a small group of square stone ruins. These are traditionally supposed to be the remains of the sheepfold which inspired the poem. They do not look like a sheepfold at all, but in other ways the spot suits the place described in the opening lines:

> If from the public way you turn your steps
> Up the tumultuous brook of Green-head Ghyll,
> You will suppose that with an upright path
> Your feet must struggle; in such bold ascent
> The pastoral mountains front you, face to face.
> But, courage! for around that boisterous brook
> The mountains have all opened out themselves,
> And made a hidden valley of their own.
> No habitation can be seen, but they
> Who journey thither find themselves alone
> With a few sheep, with rocks and stones, and kites
> That overhead are sailing in the sky.
> It is in truth an utter solitude ...

The Wordsworths walked here many times in late 1800, and Wordsworth conceived 'Michael' near a sheepfold beside the Gill. After a walk there, Dorothy notes (on October 11), with curiously poignant appropriateness, that 'The sheepfold is falling away. It is built nearly in the form of a heart unequally divided.' The poem, finished on December 9, is one of Wordsworth's finest, and he continued to associate it with this place: he came here with Coleridge on New Year's Eve 1803 and read the poem aloud, an occasion described in a splendid passage from Coleridge's note-book:

> – the foot path so even on the steep breast, of the Mountain, with such a precipice beneath & the tumultuous Brook at the bottom/but as you turn round & come out upon the vale, O my God! the whole white vale, from Steel Fell this way, from the Force on Easedale the River with the Mountain Islanding the half almost of the vale, including Butterlip How, the Church/& o! just in sight close down beneath me that House with dark slates & dingy white walls! – O remember it –
>
> The eye – let it be a spectrum in my feverous brain! The connection by Intakes of the smooth bowling Green Vale with the steep Mountain, & of the sides of the mountain with its craggy castle-ruin-like Top/ – Road between Walls – the Lake with three walls rising each above the other – the Bridge with 2 arches -/- the smoke a perfect pillar/ – the whole River from the Force to the quiet Lake/ – On this blessed calming Day – sitting on the very Sheepfold dear William read to me his divine Poem, Michael. – The last day of the year.

In 1832, by contrast, Wordsworth walked here with Dr Arnold, who recalled that 'We had a good fight about the Reform Bill during a walk up Greenhead Ghyll'.

Return to the main road. 100yds N of the Swan turn E to **Knott Houses**, a white cottage under the fellside just before the lane turns R (S), mentioned in *The Excursion* as sole survivor of a group built from the mansion of a local gentleman:

> As a tree
> That falls and disappears, that house is gone; ...
> One ivied arch
> Myself have seen, a gateway, last remains
> Of that foundation in domestic care
> Raised by his hands. And now no trace is left
> [But] ... his family name
> Borne by yon clustering cottages, that sprang
> From out the ruins of his stately lodge.

The outcrop of rock on the skyline immediately above Knott Houses is **Stone Arthur**, described in Wordsworth's 'There is an Eminence', one of the 'Poems on the Naming of Places', where it is said that Mary Hutchinson named the rock – 'in truth/The loneliest place we have among the clouds' – after Wordsworth himself.

Grisedale Tarn and Helvellyn

Continue N ¼m to the Traveller's Rest, then watch for a small road coming up from L (W). Opposite this take the bridleway (signed Patterdale), which runs straight up NNE to **Grisedale Tarn**. It was apparently on the way up here, on 4 January 1804, that Wordsworth for the first time read aloud Book II of *The Prelude* to Coleridge – to whom the poem was dedicated.

120yds NNE of the outlet from the tarn is the Brothers' Parting Stone, a large rock outcrop (marked by a metal plate on a rod fixed to its top) with an inscription on its E face. It marks the place where William and Dorothy parted with their brother John 'in sight of Ulswater' on September 29 1800.

> It was a fine day [wrote Dorothy], showery, but with sunshine and fine clouds. Poor fellow, my heart was right sad. I could not help thinking we should see him again, because he was only going to Penrith.

In fact from Penrith he would go to take command of his ship, the *Earl of Abergavenny*, and though they saw him in London in 1802 he never came again to Grasmere: he was drowned when his ship sank off the Dorset coast in 1805.

William and Dorothy revisited the spot in June 1805 and here William wrote his 'Elegiac Verses in Memory of My Brother', from which eight lines are carved on the stone. Their attractive freehand lettering is now largely illegible, but they should read:

> Here did we stop; and here looked round
> While each into himself descends,
> For that last thought of parting Friends
> That is not to be found.
> Brother and friend, if verse of mine
> Have power to make thy virtues known,
> Then let a monumental Stone
> Stand – sacred as a Shrine;

– the poem's lines 21–4 and 61–4. In 1882 the indefatigable Canon Rawnsley took the poet at his word and arranged for the carving to be placed here.

Immediately SE above the tarn is **Fairfield**. Ellen Weeton's *Journal* gives an account of an excursion to the summit (from Ambleside) in July 1810. The party set out with their provisions on a donkey.

> Mr. Partridge, junior, by way of announcing our arrival at the foot of the mountain, blew a horn he had brought with him. He is a very conceited, pedantic, though clever young man, and appeared to fancy he blew the horn with so *much* grace! though he made it sound as like the braying of an ass as ever I heard. The ass mistook the sound as proceeding from a fellow creature in reality, and set up such a tremendous bray that every echo in the mountains resounded.

On reaching the summit the party found a sheltered spot out of 'the bitter cold wind', where they

> sat down upon the ground, and enjoyed a hearty meal of veal, ham, chicken, gooseberry pies, bread, cheese, butter, hung leg of mutton, wine, porter, rum, brandy, and bitters. When our hunger was appeased, we began to stroll about and enjoy the extensive prospect. We had several prospect glasses, and the air was very clear. I was much pleased, though awed by the tremendous rocks and precipices in various directions.

You can reach Fairfield by going E from Grisedale Tarn; or you can continue NE to Patterdale; or thirdly, as we shall do, go up the desperately steep slope at the tarn's N side to ascend Helvellyn. The slope is **Dollywaggon Pike** (the site, unexpectedly, of recalled adventure in John Betjeman's 'Shattered Image', where Rex's treacherous friend reminisces,

> Remember how we went to Ambleside
> And spent the night on Dollywagon Pike?
> I wouldn't have dared do it on my own.)

The ridge leads N to the summit of **Helvellyn** (3115ft), magnificently bare and (in the right weather, which is difficult to catch) commanding superb views over the whole of central Lakeland. Almost as much ink has been spilt over Helvellyn as over Skiddaw. Looking up at it from the valley, Gilpin in 1772 noted its 'superior grandeur; stretching, near a league and a half, in one vast concave ridge':

> Of all the rude scenery we had yet visited, none equalled this in *desolation*. The whole is one immensity of barrenness. The mountains are universally overspread with craggs, and stones, which are sometimes scattered carelessly over their surfaces; and sometimes appear in shivering cascades of crumbling fragments down their sides. Helvellin, through all it's space, is one intire pavement … These vast regions, whose parts are thus absorbed in the immensity of a whole, have the strongest effect on the imagination. They distend the mind, and fix it in a kind of stupor …

Climbers started coming up here quite early. The irrepressible Joseph Budworth was here in 1792, and celebrated **Brownrigg Well**, a spring down the slope some 200yds from the summit, in verse:

> Helvellyn's height at last we gain'd,
> And, panting for relief, remained
> To mark th'extension round;
> Then down with lighter pace we bent;
> A SPRING! the clearest Heav'n e'er sent –
> I kiss'd the moisten'd ground.

(The spring was popular with guides, who had their own way of making it palatable; as Jonathan Otley says, 'When mixed with a little brandy it makes a grateful beverage.') Wordsworth and Coleridge climbed Helvellyn on their November 1799 tour, and Coleridge compresses the views from the climb (*via* Grisedale Tarn) into a notebook entry:

> First the Lake of Grasmere like a sullen Tarn/then the black ridge of mountain – then as upborne among the other mountains the luminous Cunneston Lake – & far away in the Distance & far to the Lake the glooming Shadow, Wynandermere with its Island – Pass on – the Tairn – & view of the gloomy Ulswater & mountains behind, one black, one blue, & the last one dun/

He returned alone in August 1800, and climbed the peak by moonlight. Dorothy's journal placidly records his arrival at Dove Cottage:

At 11 o'clock Coleridge came, when I was walking in the still clear
moonshine in the garden. He came over Helvellyn. We sate and chatted till
½ past three, W. in his dressing gown. Coleridge read us a part of
Christabel. Talked much about the mountains, etc. etc.

Sometime before 1805 Thomas Wilkinson declined an invitation to
climb it in early spring with the Smith sisters of Coniston, for fear of meeting 'wreaths of snow and sheets of ice'; the young ladies 'ridiculed my
effeminacy [*sic*], telling me that they had all three made the summit of
Helvellyn without a guide.' At last he made the climb, only to meet yet
another fearless young lady,

> a mountain-maid, conducting a hurdle of peats into the valley. She set a
> foot on each corner of the sledge behind the hurdle, which she steadied
> with one hand, and with the other held the reins that guided her horse.
> Thus stationed, with the bloom of health on her countenance, she drove
> with as much agility and spirit down the mountain as the fair citizen does
> her curricle along the level streets of London.

Helvellyn was the nearest really high peak to the Wordsworth dwell-
ings at Grasmere and Rydal, and they all came here many times. Dorothy's
first known ascent was made from Legberthwaite on October 25 1801. It
was a fine day and she recorded

> glorious glorious sights. The sea at Cartmel. The Scotch mountains beyond
> the sea to the right. Whiteside large, and round, and very soft, and green,
> behind us. Mists above and below, and close to us, with the Sun amongst
> them. They shot down to the coves.

Wordsworth used Helvellyn as the viewpoint for the opening of *The
Prelude* Book VIII, where a village fair in one of the valleys is shown as
from the summit. 'To – on her first ascent to the summit of Helvellyn'
(1816), addressed to a Miss Blackett, describes the view 'from the watch-
towers of Helvellyn' and its geological

> record of commotion
> Which a thousand ridges yield;
> Ridge, and gulf, and distant ocean
> Gleaming like a silver shield!

His best description is hidden away in 'Musings Near Aquapendente', one
of the *Memorials of a Tour in Italy, 1837*, which gives a visionary sketch of
the view from Helvellyn's summit:

> hills multitudinous,
> (Not Appenine can boast of fairer) hills
> Pride of two nations, wood and lake and plains,
> And prospect right below of deep coves shaped
> By skeleton arms, that, from the mountain's trunk
> Extended, clasp the winds, with mutual moan
> Struggling for liberty, while undismayed
> The shepherd struggles with them. Onward thence
> And downward by the skirt of Greenside fell,

And by Glenridding-screes, and low Glencoign,
Places forsaken now, though loving still
The Muses, as they loved them in the days
Of the old minstrels and the border bards. –

and he reflects on how Sir Walter Scott, who had died in 1832, would have liked to fly with him in spirit to

old Helvellyn's brow,
Where once together, in his day of strength,
We stood rejoicing, as if earth were free
From sorrow, like the sky above our heads.

John Cowper Powys records in his autobiography how in 1894 he set out from Patterdale

with the intention of climbing alone to the top of Helvellyn; but about a mile from the top fear seized me and I came pelting down like a frightened beast. All the way home, to the shores of the lake where our cottage was, my oak stick, my magic stick 'Sacred', seemed to utter speech, as I grasped it by its curved handle. It kept repeating at every step I took 'Recreant ... recreant ... recreant!'

From the summit the dominant features of the view are the 'skeleton arms' Wordsworth mentions: two jagged, knife-edge ridges which curve E from the summit, enclosing Red Tarn. The N one is **Swirral Edge**, the S **Striding Edge**. It is possible, with care, to make a circuit of the two; there is no great danger except in ice or high winds.

Nonetheless plenty of people have fallen off, the best-known being Charles Gough of Kendal, a young man who fell from Swirral Edge (on the outer side, away from the tarn) on or about April 18 1805 and was not discovered until July 20, when his skeleton was found, still guarded by his faithful terrier bitch Foxey, who had somehow survived (and born a litter of puppies) beside him.

Wordsworth brought Scott and Humphry Davy up here in August of the same year and told them the story: afterwards both poets wrote poems about it, unaware of the coincidence. Wordsworth's is 'Fidelity'; Scott's, 'Helvellyn' . Extracts from both are on a monument 100yds SE of the summit placed in 1890 by Canon Rawnsley. (He is also said to have placed a memorial stone where Gough fell, and to have carved the letter O on a boulder at the spot where Scott stood to look down at Gough's landing-place: I have hunted in vain for both.)

Scott's 'Helvellyn' gives a sentimental treatment but opens with a certain panache:

I climbed the dark brow of the mighty Helvellyn,
  Lakes and mountains beneath me gleam'd misty and wide;
All was still, save by fits, when the eagle was yelling,
  And starting around me the echoes replied.
On the right, Striden-edge round the Red-tarn was bending,
And Catchedicam its left verge was defending,

One huge nameless rock in the front was ascending,
  When I mark'd the sad spot where the wanderer died.

Wordsworth's poem gives a superb description of Red Tarn:

It was a cove, a huge recess,
That keeps, till June, December's snow;
A lofty precipice in front,
A silent tarn below! ...
Thither the rainbow comes – the cloud –
And mists that spread the flying shroud;
And sunbeams; and the sounding blast,
That, if it could, would hurry past;
But that enormous barrier holds it fast.

Poor Gough's fame did not end there: his death is described by Thomas Wilkinson in his poem 'Emont Vale' and by De Quincey in his *Recollections* (1839). John Wilson in *Blackwood's* (November 1826) offered readers a choice of two contrasted treatments of Gough's fate: one, full of macabre comedy, imagines the body being dined on ceremoniously by a 'Red Tarn Club' of ravens; the other is a pathetic lament for a 'true Lover of Nature ... shrouded suddenly in a winding-sheet wreathed of snow by the midnight tempest!' A recent echo occurs in a frightening passage of Richard Adams's novel *The Plague Dogs*, where Snitter meets Foxey's ghost beside Red Tarn.

Quite apart from Gough, the Edges have been much described. From many Victorian accounts we may single out two for contrast. First that of Professor John Tyndall, equally well-known in his time as atheist, physicist and mountaineer, who marched along 'Swirl Edge' (as he calls it) in a blizzard in the 1850s: 'Here was surely the antithesis to the heavy air of a London laboratory', he reflected cheerfully as flying snow battered him in the face. The wind, he thought, had in it 'something suggestive of madness ... – a wild unreasoning fury, like that of a woman with strong feelings, and little intellect to guard them.' To represent the less impetuous, Mary Elizabeth Braddon (the sensational novelist, best remembered for *Lady Audley's Secret*, 1862) portrays herself at the summit with modest irony:

I sit and shiver on the topmost point of the mountain. I look feebly at the Striding Edge, a narrow and precipitous spur which juts out from the main bulk of Helvellyn, and try to note the points from which divers aspiring souls have been hurled to eternity, and above all the white tablet, which marks the spot where the dead youth was found, watched by his faithful dog, to live for ever in deathless verse.

The 'tablet' must be Rawnsley's now-elusive memorial stone.

Dunmail Raise

You will probably not want to descend Helvellyn the same way you came up. We, however, are going to resume our route from the A591 where we left it, just N of the Traveller's Rest. Continue 250yds N to **High Broadrayne**, home of the Rev. Joseph Sympson, Vicar of Wythburn, a

STRIDING EDGE, HELVELLYN
W.J. Linton, 1864

close friend of the Wordsworths. He and Wordsworth often went 'a fishing to the Tarns on the hill-tops' and his daughter Margaret often walked with Dorothy. The house is portrayed in Book VII of *The Excursion*, which describes Sympson's arrival 'With store of household goods, in panniers slung/On sturdy horses graced with jingling bells' and tells of how he and his wife improved the 'bleak and bare' cottage and faithfully undertook their duties to poor parishioners. The house is still recognisable, with its small windows 'By shutters weather-fended, which at once/Repelled the storm and deadened its loud roar' and the 'covert' of trees planted by Sympson.

Sadly, as *The Excursion* tells us, Sympson's wife, son, daughter and grandson all died within a two-year period; Sympson himself died peacefully in his garden (across the road from the cottage) in 1807, aged 92. The family is buried in Grasmere Churchyard.

The lay-by 100yds N of High Broadrayne gives a good view of the summit-rocks of Helm Crag mentioned in 'The Waggoner'. The 'Astrologer' is at the N end, supposedly a figure sitting at a desk, or possibly a huge propped-up book. Confusingly, the same rock is nowadays called 'the Old Woman at the Organ'. (Otley thought rather that 'a mortar elevated for throwing shells into the valley would be no unapt comparison'. Ann Radcliffe wrote of the Crag's 'strange fantastic summit, round, yet jagged and splintered, like the wheel of a water-mill'). Wordsworth's 'Ancient Woman', at the other end of the crag, is the figure nowadays known as 'The Lion and the Lamb', best seen from the S end of Grasmere Lake.

At **Dunmail Raise** the road temporarily becomes a dual carriageway. The pass is named after Dunmail, last King of Cumberland, who was defeated in battle here by King Edmund of Northumbria in AD945. The battle is commemorated by the large cairn of stones between the two carriageways at the crest of the rise, and Dunmail is sometimes said to be buried there. In fact he seems to have lived for several more years and died at Rome. The cairn is the highest point of the pass and marks the ancient border between England and Scotland, which is perhaps why a local proverb states ominously that 'Nowt good comes o'er t'Raise'. More recently it marked the boundary between Westmorland (S) and Cumberland (N).

Early visitors were most impressed by the dreariness of the scene to the N. Gilpin in 1772 wrote:

> The whole view is entirely of the horrid kind. Not a tree appeared to add the least chearfulness to it. With regard to the adorning of such a scene with figures, nothing could suit it better than a group of banditti. Of all the scenes I ever saw, this was the most adapted to the perpetration of some dreadful deed. The imagination can hardly avoid conceiving a band of robbers lurking under the shelter of some projecting rock; and expecting the traveller, as he approaches the valley below.

Coleridge 'pass[ed] over the inverted Arch' of the Raise with Wordsworth on their 1799 tour, and was startled by the bleakness of the view (it was November):

> Saddleback White & streaked – thought a cloud for a long time – Passed the Cherry [i.e. the Cherry Tree Inn] – the foam in furrows – behind the inverted arch, before in the narrowing & end of the view that rude wrinkled beetling forehead of rock – all between on both sides savage & hopeless – obstinate Sansculottism

– for the landscape suggested to him the sullen extremism of the French revolutionaries. Looking S, on the other hand, the prospect from the Raise can be idyllic. On 8 October 1769 Thomas Gray came this way from Keswick; the view inspired him to write the first memorable description of Grasmere Vale:

> I passed by the little chapel of Wiborn, out of which the Sunday congregation were then issuing; soon after a beck near Dunmail raise, when I entered Westmoreland a second time; and now began to see Holm-crag, distinguished from its rugged neighbours, not so much by its height as by the strange broken outlines of its top, like some gigantic building demolished, and the stones that composed it flung across each other in wild confusion. Just beyond it opens one of the sweetest landscapes that art ever attempted to imitate. The bosom of the mountains spreading here into a broad basin discovers in the midst Grasmerewater; its margin is hollowed into small bays, with bold eminences; some of rock, some of soft turf, that half conceal, and vary the little figure of the lake they command: from the shore a low promontory pushes itself far into the water, and on it stands a white village with the parish church rising in the midst of it: hanging inclosures, corn-fields, and meadows green as an emerald, with their trees and hedges, and cattle, fill up the whole space from the edge of the water: and just opposite to you is a large farm-house at the bottom of a steep smooth lawn, embosomed in old woods, which climb half way up the mountain's side, and discover above them a broken line of crags that crown the scene. Not a single red tile, no flaring gentleman's house, or garden-walls, break in upon the repose of this little unsuspected paradise; but all is peace, rusticity, and happy poverty in its neatest, most becoming attire.

Wordsworth gives a glimpse of the Raise itself in one of his earliest poems, *An Evening Walk*, and in 'The Waggoner' he describes Benjamin passing the cairn

> Heaped over brave King Dunmail's bones,
> He who had once supreme command,
> Last king of rocky Cumberland;
> His bones, and those of all his Power,
> Slain here in a disastrous hour!

De Quincey records a memorable moment here (probably in 1809):

> One night, as often enough happened, during the Peninsular War, [Wordsworth] and I had walked up Dunmail Raise from Grasmere, about midnight, in order to meet the carrier who brought the London newspapers, by a circuitous course from Keswick ... Upon one of these occasions, when some great crisis in Spain was daily apprehended, we had waited for an hour or more ... At intervals, Wordsworth ... stretched himself at length on the high road, applying his ear to the ground, so as to catch any sound of wheels that might be groaning along at a distance. Once, when he was slowly rising from this effort, his eye caught a bright star that was glittering between the brow of Seat Sandal and of the mighty Helvellyn.

Wordsworth stood gazing at the star, and then explained,

> I have remarked, from my earliest days, that, if ... the attention is braced up to an act of steady observation, or of steady expectation, then, if this intense condition of vigilance should suddenly relax, at that moment any beautiful, any impressive visual object ... falling upon the eye, is carried to the heart with a power not known under other circumstances.

The star, he said, unexpectedly seen at such a moment of relaxing attention, 'penetrated my capacity of apprehension with a pathos and a sense of the infinite, that would not have arrested me under other circumstances' – and he went on to illustrate the same idea with his own poem, 'There was a boy'.

It was hereabouts too that Sir Edward Baines met, in 1829, the Unknown Poet:

> His countenance was rather wild, and expressed a childish admiration and delight: he ... stood with eyes and mouth open, as if inhaling inspiration, and feeding, like the chameleon, on air ... All his pastoral and picturesque descriptions, had hitherto, as he said, been worked up by his own imagination, under the dun smoke of a manufacturing town ... At length the liberality of his patrons and friends – a liberality which he hinted was by no means equal to his deserts – had enabled him to make this tour, and he intended to publish a description of it, which should eclipse all that Goldsmith, Gilpin or Scott had done in that line.

'I never', concludes Baines, 'conversed with a man so full of egotism and vanity ... I had much ado to escape a deluge of his verses', and 'as I entered the carriage, he begged for my address and my subscription to his next volume of poems, which I could not refuse him.'

Thirlmere and Wythburn

½m N of the Raise the road enters conifer woods and a small road goes off L (W) to run round the far bank of the lake; for here we reach the shore of **Thirlmere**. The modern lake is a reservoir, very different from the Thirl- mere of old. It formerly had several names; West (1778) gives Leathes-Water, Wythburn-Water and Thirlmere-Water. Clarke (1789) calls it 'Thyrill-mere'. Eliza Lynn Linton (1864) adds 'Brackmere'. The original lake was hourglass-shaped, with a series of stone causeways linked by wooden bridges at the narrowest point. Gilpin gives a view of it in 1772:

> No tufted verdure graces it's banks, nor hanging woods throw rich reflections on it's surface: but every form, which it suggests, is savage, and desolate. It is about two miles in length, and half as much in breadth, surrounded by barren mountains, and precipices, shelving into it in all directions ... And to impress still more the characteristic idea of the place, the road hanging over it, ran along the edge of a precipice.

But the finest description of the lake as it used to be is an ecstatic jotting in Coleridge's notebook, made on October 23 1803:

> O Thirlmere! – let me some how or other celebrate the world in thy mirror. – Conceive all possible varieties of Form, Fields, & Trees, and naked or ferny Crags – ravines, behaired with Birches – Cottages, smoking chimneys, dazzling *wet places* of small rock-precipices – dazzling castle windows in the reflection – all these, within a divine outline in a mirror of 3 miles distinct vision! – and the distance closed in by the Reflection of Raven Crag, which at every bemisting of the mirror by gentle motion became a perfect Castle Tower, the corners rounded & pillar'd or fluted – /each corner ending in [received into] a round pillar, round save that slice off by which it lies flat on [& connects] the two sides. All this in bright lightest yellow, yellow-green, green, crimson, and orange! – The single Birch Trees hung like Tresses of SeaWeed – the Cliffs like organ pipes! – and when a little Breath of Air spread a delicious Network over the Lake, all these colours seemed then to float on, like the reflections of the rising or setting Sun. –

All this is now gone. Possibly the last glimpse of the old Thirlmere bridge is given by John Barrow, almost on the eve of the engineering work for the reservoir:

> We crossed the remarkable bridges, constructed about midway across the lake. They consist of five or six broad stone piers, with continuous wooden bridges resting upon them, with a handrail on one side, and are only a few feet above the water. Without this handrail I should have been sorry to have ventured across in such a high wind as was blowing. A fine avenue leads to the bridges, which will also disappear, as it is intended to raise the level of the lake by some fifty feet.

THIRLMERE BRIDGE
Thomas Allom, 1832

After long and bitter controversy the lake was enlarged by damming, flooding much of the valley to serve as a reservoir for Manchester. The water supply began to flow S on October 12 1894. The flooding of the valley and the village of Wythburn at its S end was painful to many who loved the area. According to W.G. Collingwood,

> The old charm of its shores has quite vanished, and the sites of its old legends are hopelessly altered, so that the walk along either side is a mere sorrow to any one who cared for it before; the sham castles are an outrage, and the formality of the roads, beloved of car-drivers and cyclists, deforms the hillsides like a scar on a face.

To the modern visitor there are some compensations. Dense afforestation has produced a strange atmosphere, a fairytale sense of the brooding dominance of trees. The slopes just above the lake are little visited outside the busiest seasons and it is possible to feel as alone here as anywhere in the Lakes.

You can travel along the lakeshores on either the E or W bank. Drivers simply passing the lake should stick to the A591 (E bank). Walkers and cyclists should heed Wordsworth:

> the beautiful features of the lake are known only to those who, travelling between Grasmere and Keswick, have quitted the main road in the vale of Wythburn and, crossing over to the opposite side of the lake, have proceeded with it on the right hand.

We shall deal with the **W bank** first, then return to the main road on the E. After 1m the car park has a signed footpath to Harrop Tarn and Watendlath. This is the route taken by Coleridge on his way from

Grasmere to Keswick in July 1802: he noted that 'The Torrent ... out of Harrop Tarn, ... I have repeatedly observed, is *the loudest* in the whole country.' Further up the path, he

> enquired of an old Woman the way to Watendlatter. – She was carrying in hay into a barn with vigor – four Grandchildren – sitting on the hay lazily helping her. Which way to W? – Up the gap – a canny road – How far – Two miles & more? – Is there much to climb beyond the highest point we see? as much again before we get on a level – Tis a gay canny climb ... She was eighty three – her son had 9 children those we saw were the 4 youngest –

The same route was taken in July 1833 by the eleven-year-old Matthew Arnold, with his father (Dr Arnold of Rugby), Captain Hamilton (of *Cyril Thornton* fame), his sister Jane and his brother Thomas. Arnold recalls the walk in his poem 'Resignation', where he sadly retraces the path ten years later.

Continue N 3m to the Armboth Car Park. Just downhill from here was formerly **Armboth House** (now submerged). According to Harriet Martineau, this was

> a haunted house. Lights are seen there at night, the people say; and the bells ring; and just as the bells all set off ringing, a large dog is seen swimming across the lake. The plates and dishes clatter; and the table is spread by unseen hands. That is the preparation for the ghostly wedding feast of a murdered bride, who comes up from her watery bed in the lake to keep her terrible nuptials. There is really something remarkable, and like witchery, about the house. On a bright moonlight night, the spectator who looks towards it from a distance of two or three miles, sees the light reflected from its windows into the lake; and, when a slight fog gives a reddish hue to the light, the whole might be taken for an illumination of a great mansion. And this mansion seems to vanish as you approach – being no mansion, but a small house lying in a nook, and overshadowed by a hill.

Continue to the N end of the lake, where the road turns to go over the dam to rejoin A591.

If, on the other hand, you keep to the **E bank**, staying on A591 , watch as you reach the lake's S end for the sign to the **Wythburn Church** car park. This beautifully simple little chapel, seventeenth-century with a late-Victorian E end which harmonises perfectly, is all that remains accessible of the village of **Wythburn** (pronounced Wyburn), now mostly submerged. Wordsworth's friend the Rev. Joseph Sympson of High Broadrayne was Vicar here, and in 'The Waggoner' Wordsworth mentions 'Wythburn's modest house of prayer,/As lowly as the lowliest dwelling'. Before the 1870s the church was extremely dilapidated. Collingwood tells a story about

> an ancient Wythburn clergyman who had only two sermons, and kept them in a crack in the wainscot behind his pulpit. Some wag pushed them down one day out of his reach, and the people smiled while he fumbled. At

last he turned, and began, 'My brethren, the sermons are down the grike [crack], but I'll read ye a chapter in Job worth the pair of them.'

Immediately across the road, inaccessible among trees and thick undergrowth, are the ruins of the **Nag's Head** (or Horse Head) **Inn**. Keats slept there on June 27 1818 and wrote a letter to his brother George. His companion Brown adds that 'many fleas were in the beds'. They 'could not mount Helvellyn for the mist so gave it up with hopes of Skiddaw which we shall try tomorrow if it be fine'.

It was from the Nag's Head that Matthew Arnold set out in 1833 for the walk to Watendlath described in 'Resignation':

We left, just ten years since, you say,
That wayside inn we left today.
Our jovial host, as forth we fare,
Shouts greeting from his easy chair.
High on a bank our leader stands,
Reviews and ranks his motley bands,
Makes clear our goal to every eye –
The valley's western boundary ...
And now, in front, behold outspread
Those upper regions we must tread!
Mild hollows, and clear heathy swells,
The cheerful silence of the fells.

Walk along the roadside 50yds N of the church and by the telephone box you will see a stone placed by Canon Rawnsley as 'A record of two walks over the Armboth Fells July 1833–43 which inspired Matthew Arnold's "Resignation" and in reverent memory of the poet'.

½m N was the Horse Head's great rival, the Cherry-Tree Inn. Joseph Budworth stayed there in 1792 and recalled that

they gave us a breakfast fit for labouring men. We had mutton-ham, eggs, butter-milk, whey, tea, bread-and-butter, and they asked us if we chose to have any cheese, all for seven pence a piece.

Budworth chatted in the kitchen with an old woman of 'between eighty and ninety' who

had seen sixteen landlords out ... She told us she had been a pretty shepherdess in her time, and that she had been too often upon Skiddow in her youth to be ill in her old age.

The Inn is given a splendidly riotous description in Wordsworth's 'The Waggoner', where the village 'Merry-Night' tempts the hero to forget his work with the 'Blithe souls and lightsome hearts ... Feasting at the Cherry Tree!' Wordsworth himself is said to have stopped here ('spouting his poems grandly') with Scott, Lockhart and Wilson on August 23 1823.

Roughly 1¼m from the point where the road first touches the lakeside, you may be able to spot a bronze plaque above the road at the edge of the wood. This commemorates the resting place (1886–1984) of the fragments of the **Rock of Names**, now in Grasmere. The story is somewhat complex. The Rock (on which see page 51) was in the way of the new road which was being built during construction of the dam. Canon Rawnsley made desperate efforts to save it, even bringing a stonemason to see if the face of the rock could be moved intact with the initials on it. It could not be done, and the engineers blew the rock up, planning to use the fragments for road chippings. Rawnsley collected the bits with the lettering, and made them into a cairn, directly up the slope from their original position. Here they stayed until removed to Dove Cottage and fixed together in 1984.

The Rock originally marked a point where Coleridge and the Wordsworths often met, roughly midway between Keswick and Grasmere. On May 4 1802 they were here, met the Rev Sympson fishing in the beck and 'saw Coleridge on the Wytheburn side of the water; he crossed the beck to us.' They went on up to 'the great waterfall' – possibly the one from Harrop Tarn – 'a glorious wild solitude under that lofty purple crag' – then descended and 'rested upon a moss-covered rock, rising out of the bed of the river.' Wordsworth and Coleridge 'repeated and read verses', whilst Dorothy herself 'drank a little brandy and water, and was in Heaven.'

They parted from Coleridge, who was going back to Keswick, at the Rock of Names, 'after having looked at the letters which C carved in the morning'. Coleridge 'parted from us chearfully, hopping upon the side stones'; the Wordsworths 'sate afterwards on the wall, seeing the sun go down, and the reflections in the still water.'

Just below the plaque there was formerly a rocky promontory, **Clarke's Leap**, from which a henpecked husband was said to have drowned himself. He consulted his wife about possible ways of killing himself. She advised against shooting, hanging or poison as too painful and uncertain, and suggested drowning. They went together to find a suitable place and decided on this rock. The wife pointed out the risk of hitting the rocks below and suggested he take a running jump to be sure of getting well out into the water. He did so, and duly drowned. James Clarke (no relation) claimed in 1789 to have checked the story with the wife: 'I had the curiosity (for she is still alive) to ask it from her own mouth.'

Fisher Place, High Bridge End and Naddle

After 1m you pass the Swirls Car Park; continue N 1m to a small sideroad leading to a long terrace of white houses. This is **Fisher Place**; in the middle, at number 3 (the old Post Office), in the autumn of 1881, the PreRaphaelite poet and painter Dante Gabriel Rossetti came with his model and mistress Fanny Cornforth and his secretary, the young writer Hall Caine. Rossetti was seriously ill and addicted to chloral hydrate, a sleep-inducing drug; the holiday was an attempt at getting some rest and controlling his addiction. He had ideas of painting again, and of writing a 'romantic ballad' using Lakeland scenery, but instead became steadily weaker and more depressed. Fanny lost patience and left; Caine kept Rossetti occupied by reading eighteenth-century novels aloud:

> I remember those evenings [wrote Caine] with gratitude and some pain –
> the little, oblong sitting-room, the dull thud of the waterfall like distant
> thunder overhead, the crackle of the wood fire, myself reading aloud, and
> Rossetti in his long sack-coat, his hands thrust deep in his upright pockets,
> walking with his heavy and uncertain step to and fro, to and fro, laughing
> sometimes his big, deep laugh, and sometimes sitting down to wipe his
> moist spectacles and clear his dim eyes. Not rarely the dead white gleams
> of the early dawn before the coming of the sun met the yellow light of our
> candles as we passed on the staircase, going to bed, a little window that
> looked up to the mountains and over them to the east.

After a few weeks they admitted defeat and returned to London, where Rossetti died the following year. Later Caine used the valley as setting for his first novel, *The Shadow of a Crime* (1885), which must rank as one of the worst novels ever written about the Lake District.

Rossetti's one feat of physical exercise in the district – performed the morning after his arrival, when things still looked promising – was to climb **Great How**, the small pudding-shaped fell directly opposite Fisher Place at the N end of Thirlmere. Great How is mentioned in Wordsworth's 'Rural Architecture' (1800), which tells of three local schoolboys who climbed

> to the top of GREAT HOW ...
> And there they built up, without mortar or lime,
> A Man on the peak of the crag.

A storm blew away their giant figure, but the poet offers to climb up and rebuild it with them. Great How is now covered with trees, but there is still a path to the top; it makes a pleasant and not very strenuous walk.

⅓m further N at fork go L (signed Keswick) then take road signed 'public road round lake'; a few yds up on R (N) is **High Bridge End Farm**, probably the house where Wordsworth and De Quincey called one summer day in 1813, hungry and thirsty after a long day's rambling, to ask for food. They were ushered into a 'comfortable parlour' and royally entertained, but could not tell whether they were in a private house or an inn: their host was a formidable 'man-mountain' whom they feared to offend, and

> To err, in either direction, was damnable: to go off without paying, if he
> *were* an inn-keeper, made us swindlers; to offer payment if he were not, ...
> made us the most unfeeling of mercenary ruffians. In the latter case we
> might expect a duel; in the former, of course, the treadmill.

Luckily they were able to question the servant, who told them her master acted out of pure hospitality 'and would have "brained us both" if we had insulted him with the offer of money.'

Two or three years later De Quincey passed the house on a cloudy moonlight night:

> Nine o'clock it was – and deadly cold as ever March night was made by the
> keenest of black frosts, and by the bitterest of north winds ... A little
> garden there was before the house; and in the centre of this garden was
> placed an armchair, upon which arm-chair was sitting composedly – but I
> rubbed my eyes, doubting the very evidence of my own eyesight – a or *the*
> huge man in his shirt-sleeves; yes, positively not sunning but *mooning*
> himself – apricating himself in the occasional moonbeams.

De Quincey never learned the reason for this eccentric behaviour.

Return to A591 and continue N. After a short stretch of dual carriageway turn R at Naddle (signed St John's Church). Follow the road past Dale
Bottom Farm for ¾m where there is a gate. Just after the gate is a long white
farmhouse, now divided into two houses, **Stone Cottage** and **Piper House**.
(The road is impassible to cars beyond this point; walkers can go on to St
John's Church.) The house name is said to commemorate a Scottish piper
who was snowed up there and played the bagpipes to pass the time. This
was the birthplace of John Richardson (1817–86), dialect poet and stonemason. He was the author of *Cumberland Talk* (1871–6) and built several
houses in Keswick as well as the St John's Vale parsonage, School and
Chapel. His witty and ingenious dialect poetry has lasted better than any
other Cumbrian dialect work; in particular, many people still know his
'Nobbut Me'. Return to A591 and either continue N into Keswick or return,
as we shall do, S to the junction and follow signs for Threlkeld and Penrith.

St John's in the Vale

Immediately above the road as you enter the Vale, and overhanging the
King's Head Inn, is **Castle Rock of Triermaine**, a great humped crag rising
steeply from the valley floor. William Hutchinson's *Excursion to the Lakes*
(1774) gives a fanciful account of the rock:

> In the widest part of the dale you are struck with the appearance of an
> ancient ruined castle, which seems to stand upon the summit of a little
> mount ... The massive bulwark shows a front of various towers, and makes
> an awful, rude, and Gothic appearance, with its lofty turrets and ragged
> battlements; we traced the galleries, the bending arches, the buttresses ...
> The traveller [is] assured, that, if he advances, certain genii who govern the
> place, by virtue of their supernatural art and necromancy, will strip it of all
> its beauties ... We were soon convinced of [the report's] truth; for this
> piece of antiquity, so venerable and noble in its aspect, as we drew near,
> changed its figure, and proved no other than a shaken massive pile of
> rocks.

Scott visited the area in 1797, and again walked here with Wordsworth
during his 1805 visit to Grasmere. The rock, and the passage in Hutchinson, inspired Scott's poem *The Bridal of Triermaine* (1805), a tale of how
King Arthur comes to the 'castle', finds it deserted and blows the bugle
hanging outside. The castle comes to life with 'torches, flashing bright' and
'A band of damsels fair' who hold Arthur enthralled. When at last he tears
himself away,

The Monarch, breathless and amazed,
Back on the fatal castle gazed –
Nor tower nor donjon could he spy,
Darkening against the morning sky;
But, on the spot where once they frown'd,
The lonely streamlet brawl'd around
A tufted knoll, where dimly shone
Fragments of rocks and rifted stone.

Formerly just 'Castle Rock', the crag acquired its present grand name in Victorian times from Scott's poem.

Continue N up **St John's in the Vale**, which is, curiously enough, the name of the valley as well as of the church. This is a delightful dale of lush pastoral scenery backed by steep crags and screes. Gilpin, visiting in 1772, was disappointed by the Vale, which, he wrote,

> is esteemed one of the most celebrated scenes of beauty in the country: but it did not answer our expectation. The ground, consisting of patches of fenced meadow, adorned with farm-houses, and clumps of trees, was beautifully tumbled about in many parts: but the whole was rather rich, than picturesque: and on this account, I suppose, it hath obtained it's celebrity. It's circular form, every where within the scope of the eye, wanted that variety, which the *winding* vale affords.

Modern visitors are unlikely to be so discontented.

After 2m watch for sign on L (W) for St John's in the Vale Church: take turning, then watch for a second similar sign. At the end of a long steep road is **St John's Church**. The present building is only 1845 but looks much older. It was rebuilt virtually single-handed by the poet John Richardson, who was master of the school (now the Youth Centre next to the church), which he also repaired. His grave is in the churchyard, 10yds from the E end of the church. For walkers, the bridleway continues down to join the Keswick road at Naddle.

Downhill, E of the church, is Richardson's home, **Bridge House**, reached by a footpath which leads up a side road, rejoining the Threlkeld road near Hill Top Farm. The road then continues N to join the A66 at Threlkeld. Go R (E) for Penrith or L (W) for Keswick.

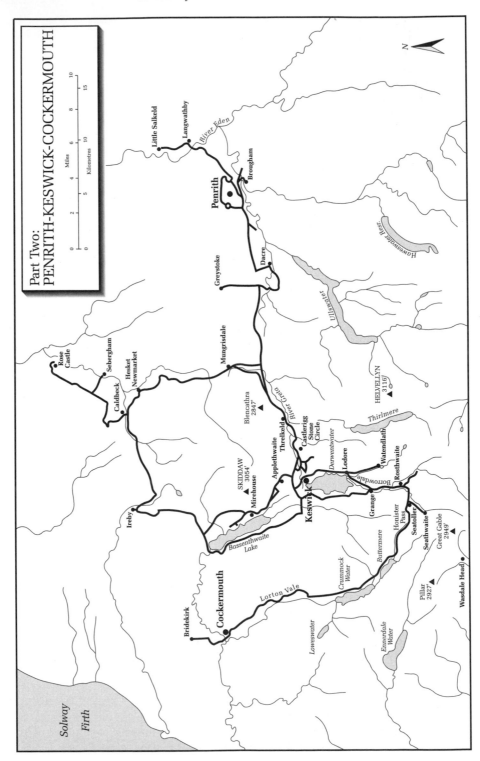

Part Two:
PENRITH-KESWICK-COCKERMOUTH

Miles

Kilometres

Little Salkeld

Langwathby

River Eden

Brougham

Penrith

Dacre

Greystoke

Ullswater

HAWESWATER Resr.

Sebergham

Rose
Castle

Hesket
Newmarket

Caldbeck

Mungrisdale

HELVELLYN
3116'

Blencathra
2847'

River Greta

Thirlmere

Castlerigg
Stone
Circle

Applethwaite

Threlkeld

Derwentwater

Watendlath

SKIDDAW
3054'

Lodore

Mirehouse

Rosthwaite

Ireby

Keswick

Borrowdale

Grange

Honister
Pass

Seatoller

*Bassenthwaite
Lake*

Seathwaite

Great Gable
2949'

Buttermere

*Crummock
Water*

Pillar
2927'

Cockermouth

Bridekirk

Lorton Vale

Loweswater

Wasdale Head

*Ennerdale
Water*

*Solway
Firth*

N

PART TWO
Penrith – Keswick –
Cockermouth

Penrith and Beacon Pike

Despite discouraging outskirts – light industry, superstores, grey hous-ing-estates – **Penrith** (*several well-signed car parks*) keeps much of its old centre, the homely but highly individual buildings made of local dark red sandstone. The winding streets and the 'yards' running off them offer intriguing vistas, mixing Tudor stonework, crowded cottage gardens and glimpses of seedy dilapidation – a historic environment left in peace and unselfconsciously lived with.

A small market and manufacturing town, Penrith was formerly a defen-sive bastion of the Borders. It was hotly disputed between England and Scotland throughout the middle ages, until the castle was enlarged and garrisoned by the English around 1400. In the 1470s Richard Duke of Glou-cester (later King Richard III) was Warden of the Western Borders, and had his headquarters at Dockray Hall – now the Gloucester Arms Inn near the town centre.

Celia Fiennes visited 'Peroth', as she calls it – her spelling probably reflecting local pronunciation – on her 'Great Journey' of 1698, and records:

> The stones and slatt about Peroth look's so red that at my entrance into the town thought its buildings were all of brick, but after found it to be the coullour of the stone which I saw in the Quarrys look very red, their slatt is the same which cover their houses; its a pretty large town a good market for cloth that they spinn in the country, hempe and also woollen; its a great market for all sorts of cattle meate corn etc.

Thomas Gray was here on 18 October 1769, and

> dined at three o'clock with Mrs Buchanan ... on trout and partridge. In the afternoon walked up Beacon-Hill, a mile to the top, and could see Ullswater through an opening in the bosom of that cluster of broken mountains ... and the craggy tops of a hundred nameless hills. To the east, Crossfell, just visible through mists and vapours hovering around it.

Mrs Buchanan apparently kept an inn: Ann Radcliffe stayed at 'Old Buchanan's inn' (whereabouts unknown) on her 1794 tour. 'The town', she wrote, 'consisting chiefly of old houses, straggles along two sides of the high north road, and is built upon the side of a mountain [Beacon Pike],

that towers to a great height above it.' Despite 'its many symptoms of antiq-
uity', she conceded, rather grudgingly, that Penrith was

> not deficient of neatness. The houses are chiefly white, with door and
> window cases of the red stone found in the neighbourhood. Some of the
> smaller have over their doors dates of the latter end of the sixteenth
> century.

Most streets lead readily to the Market Square, the best place to begin a
tour. At the N end **Arnison's** (delightful Victorian shop-front) stands on the
site of the house and draper's shop of Wordsworth's maternal grandparents William and Ann Cookson and his uncles William and Christopher.
William and Dorothy Wordsworth spent much time here in childhood,
and disliked it intensely. Wordsworth, staying here after his mother's
death in 1778, contemplated suicide to escape the oppressive household
and once attacked a Cookson family portrait with a whip. Dorothy
returned to live here in adolescence (1787–8) and was treated as a poor
relation, complaining of 'the cold insensibility' of her grandparents but
consoling herself with the friendship of Mary and Peggy Hutchinson who
lived nearby. They

> used to steal to each other's houses, and when we had had our talk over
> the kitchen fire, to delay the moment of parting, paced up one street and
> down another by moon or starlight.

An occasional visitor in the 1770s was William Wilberforce, a college
friend of William Cookson the younger.

Next door to Arnison's is the **George Hotel**. Arthur Young stayed here in
1768 and found it

> Exceeding good, reasonable, and very civil. The dinner was roast beef,
> apple pudding, potatoes, celery, potted trout, and sturgeon, 1s. a head.

Dorothy Wordsworth and Joanna Hutchinson were here in 1822; Dorothy
was

> Surprized with the beauty of the view from bed-room at the top of the
> house. The Castle, though in itself so little, interesting as a ruin, a fine
> object at that time; and when, after tea, I came again in twilight, I was
> reminded of Liège – towers (diminutive though they be) rising, as there,
> upon the hill.

Leave the Market Square at its SE corner for **St Andrew's Church**, which
has a twelfth-century tower and a sumptuous eighteenth-century interior,
possibly by Nicholas Hawksmoor. Just NE of the tower is the badly-weath-
ered blue slate gravestone of Mary and John Hutchinson (d 1783 and
1785), parents of Dorothy Wordsworth's friends, the Hutchinson sisters:
Mary (who became Wordsworth's wife), Sara (friend and companion of
Coleridge), Joanna and Peggy. Wordsworth's mother Ann is also buried
here in an unknown grave.

N of the church is the **Giant's Grave**, a grouping of two stone crosses

THE GIANT'S GRAVE, PENRITH
William Hutchinson, 1793

and four 'hogback' tombstones (c AD1000), which has one of Cumbria's most unexpected literary associations. In September 1926 James Joyce's patron, Harriet Weaver, on holiday near Penrith, sent him a photograph of the Grave and commissioned him to write something about it. Joyce, already at work on *Finnegans Wake*, set to, and

> The configuration of the giant's grave, with vertical stones at head and toe and four horizontal stones between, suggested at once to Joyce the configuration of his hero Earwicker in his topographical aspect, his head at Howth, his toes at Castle Knock in the Phoenix Park, and also suggested the barrel of whiskey at the head and the barrel of Guinness at the feet of Finnegan, whose modern incarnation Earwicker was to be. He decided to put the passage in 'the place of honour' at the beginning of the book to set the half-mythological, half-realistic scene.

After Joyce's linguistic transformations the visitor is unlikely to recognise much of the Giant's Grave in his account of 'Finnegan, erse solid man, [whose] humptyhillhead of humself promptly sends an unquiring one well to the west in search of his tumptytumtoes', though the grave is indeed oriented E-W and the stones bear some traces of intertwined Celtic ornament, appropriate for the grave/bed of the Irish hero.

Defoe visited the 'grave' in 1724 to measure it and record that it was

> the monument of Sir Owen Caesar, ... a champion of mighty strength, and of gygantick stature ... They relate nothing but good of him, and that he exerted his mighty strength to kill robbers, such as infested the borders much in those days.

Tradition adds that the 'hogbacks' are four boars killed by Sir Owen in nearby Inglewood Forest.

Sir Walter Scott was fascinated by the monument and Lockhart notes that on his way to London in 1831, he insisted on stopping to revisit it, though he had seen it 'dozens of times before'.

Just SW of the churchyard is a stone gable-end with RB 1563 carved on the sill of the top window. This was once Mrs Birkett's dame school, attended by William and Dorothy Wordsworth when they stayed at Penrith in early childhood. Here they first met, as fellow pupils, Mary and Sara Hutchinson.

Return to Market Square and go S along King Street to the **Robin Hood Inn**. Wordsworth and his friend Raisley Calvert stayed here on October 9 1794: they had walked from Calvert's house at Windy Brow near Keswick and intended to set off for a tour of Portugal but Calvert, who had tuberculosis, felt so ill that they gave up the tour here and returned to Keswick the next day.

Return N through Market Square past Arnison's and along to the end of Middlegate, then NE into Corney Square, dominated by **Wordsworth House**, now housing the Public Library and part of the Town Hall. This was the home of Captain John Wordsworth, cousin of the poet; he worked for the East India Company and commanded the *Earl of Abergavenny* (later captained by the poet's brother, also called John). Thomas De Quincey stayed here briefly in 1807. The building was originally two ornate red and white sandstone town houses designed (1791) by Robert Adam. The left half (with plaque) was Captain Wordsworth's. Conversion to the Town Hall in 1909 added a porch which, though scrupulously in the Adam style, makes it impossible to imagine the building as a pair of private houses.

From L end of Wordsworth House go NW along Portland Street, which becomes **Wordsworth Street**, a sloping road of sandstone Victorian terrace houses. At number 49a, Michael Roberts (poet and editor of those landmarks of 1930s literature, the anthologies *New Country* and *The Faber Book of Modern Verse*) and his wife, the critic and biographer Janet Adam Smith, shared their home in the early years of the Second World War with the poet Kathleen Raine, a period recalled in her autobiographical *The Land Unknown*. As winter came on coal was short and the pipes froze; they were consoled by records of Beethoven's quartets, by 'friendship of the mind, the best of talk, and the shared tasks of the day.' Roberts worked at his poems and his political-critical book *The Recovery of the West* and at weekends they went walking and climbing on Fairfield, Blencathra and Helvellyn.

Continue N up Wordsworth Street and turn R (E) at the T-junction for 200yds to the footpath for **Beacon Pike**. Hardly the towering 'mountain' mentioned by Ann Radcliffe, the Pike is climbed by a gently-sloping stroll of roughly 1m. The summit tower (built 1719) is on the site of earlier signal fires that warned of attack from Scotland. The beacon was last seriously used during a Napoleonic invasion scare.

As a child, Wordsworth climbed the Pike for the traditional Easter 'pace-egging' games – rolling eggs down from the summit. Later (in 1787 and 1788) Dorothy Wordsworth and Mary Hutchinson often walked here and were joined for the summer holidays by William, who fell in love with Mary. They walked widely in the surrounding countryside, and

> O'er paths and fields
> In all that neighbourhood, through narrow lanes
> Of eglantine, and through the shady woods,
> And o'er the Border Beacon, and the waste
> Of naked pools, and common crags that lay
> Exposed on the bare fell, were scattered love,
> The spirit of pleasure, and youth's golden gleam.

Red Hill, the Pike's E shoulder, is the scene of an eerie episode recalled in Book XII of Wordsworth's *Prelude*. Whilst staying at Penrith in 1775 the five-year-old Wordsworth (whose 'inexperienced hand/Could scarcely hold a bridle') came here to ride with a servant. The boy became separated from his guide

> and, through fear
> Dismounting, down the rough and stony moor
> I led my horse, and, stumbling on, at length
> Came to a bottom, where in former times
> A murderer had been hung in iron chains.
> The gibbet-mast had mouldered down, the bones
> And iron case were gone; but on the turf,
> Hard by, soon after that fell deed was wrought,
> Some unknown hand had carved the murderer's name.

The letters were still 'fresh and visible', and in terror the boy fled,

> Faltering and faint, and ignorant of the road:
> Then, reascending the bare common, saw
> A naked pool that lay beneath the hills,
> The beacon on the summit, and, more near,
> A girl, who bore a pitcher on her head,
> And seemed with difficult steps to force her way
> Against the blowing wind. It was, in truth,
> An ordinary sight; but I should need
> Colours and words that are unknown to man,
> To paint the visionary dreariness
> Which, while I looked all round for my lost guide,
> Invested moorland waste, and naked pool,
> The beacon crowning the lone eminence,
> The female and her garments vexed and tossed
> By the strong wind.

Owing to enclosure and tree-planting the spot can no longer be reached directly from the summit of the Pike. Return to the road at the foot of the

Pike (Beacon Edge), and go E 2m to T-junction with A686. About 200yds NE along the A686 Thomas Nicholson robbed and murdered Thomas Parker in 1767. Nicholson was hanged in chains on the hillock at the NW side of the road. The gibbet lay by the roadside for many years. Wordsworth is inaccurate, though, in recalling a murderer's name cut in the turf. There do seem to have been lettered stones at the spot but the letters – apparently 'T.P.M.' – did not stand (as some have thought) for 'Thomas Parker Murdered'. They probably marked a boundary between the Musgrave and Portland estates. (Lettered boundary stones were common: for another set, see p 291.) Wordsworth would have turned NW towards the Beacon summit to meet the girl with the pitcher.

Go SW down A686 to the **Cross Keys Inn**. Thomas Parker had a drink here just before he was murdered. It is claimed that the wooden beam visible over the blocked coach entrance to the barn behind the inn is part of the gallows salvaged from the roadside. This seems unlikely.

From the Cross Keys go ¼m uphill and turn L (N) up a small road. The entrance on R 200yds from junction leads to **Carletonhill**, a large house built about 1840 by Frances Trollope, novelist, author of *Domestic Manners of the Americans* (1832), and mother of the now better-known novelist, Anthony Trollope, who visited her here several times before she sold the house in 1843. Her other son, Thomas Adolphus Trollope, gives an account of its construction in his autobiography *What I Remember* (1887). In making the drive, the Trollopes changed the course of 'a tiny little spring' that rose there. Their neighbour Sir George Musgrave of Edenhall

> was dismayed. We had moved, he said, a holy well, and the consequence would surely be that we should never succeed in establishing ourselves in the spot.
>
> And surely enough we never did so ... for, after having built a very nice little house, and lived in it one winter and half a summer, we ... made up our minds that 'the sun yoked his horses too far from Penrith town,' and that we had had enough of it. Sir George ... said that he knew perfectly well that it must be so, from the time that we recklessly meddled with the holy well.

Either return to the town centre; or rejoin A686 for the Giant's Cave (see p 106).

Penrith Castle and Station

From the Market Square follow signs to **Penrith Castle**, of which only the central keep, a large pele tower of scarlet sandstone, remains. Much more was standing in the eighteenth century, and William Gilpin, that expert on picturesque landscape, gave it full marks for a fine display of lighting-effects when he passed in 1772 on his way N at sunset:

> A grand broken arch presented itself first in deep shadow. Through the aperture appeared a part of the internal structure, thrown into perspective

PENRITH CASTLE
William Hutchinson, 1793

to great advantage; and illumined by the departing ray. Other fragments of the shattered towers, and battlements were just touched with the splendid tint: but the body of light rested on those parts, which were seen through the shadowed arch.

In the offskip, beyond the castle, arose a hill, in shadow likewise; on the top of which stood a lonely beacon. The windows answering each other, we could just discern the glowing horizon through them – a circumstance, which however trivial in description, has a beautiful effect in landscape.

The arch Gilpin mentions, and much else, has since fallen or been demolished for building stone. Most was already gone by 1794, when Ann Radcliffe reported that

The venerable ruins ... crest a round green hill ... but have little that is picturesque in their appearance, time having spared neither tower, nor gateway, and not a single tree giving shade, or force, to the shattered walls.

Like other eighteenth-century visitors, she records one highly picturesque detail: there is supposed to be a secret passage from the castle ruins to the Gloucester Arms Inn. If the passage exists, it has never been found.

Opposite the Castle and, it has to be admitted, the reverse of picturesque, is **Penrith Railway Station**, which carries a surprising weight of literary association. In the days when most people travelled by train it was a gateway to the Lakes and as such had a certain magic about it. For Auden, exiled in America, it held a potent nostalgia, expressed in his 'Bucolics':

> Am I
> To see in the Lake District, then,
> Another bourgeois invention like the piano?

Well, I won't. How can I, when
I wish I stood now on a platform at Penrith
... at which you leave the express
For a local that swerves off soon into a cutting? Soon
Tunnels begin, red farms disappear,
Hedges turn to walls,
Cows become sheep, you smell peat or pinewood, you hear
Your first waterfalls.

And Kathleen Raine recalls arriving here from London in 1939 with her small children, escaping personal unhappiness as well as the expected bombing, on one of the first nights of the blackout:

> From the pitch-black night beyond the dim platform came the scent of wet fells, and sheep, and the North; and I knew that after long exile I had come back to my own.

On a less positive note, let us record that Wilfred Owen lost his luggage here on his way to Keswick in July 1912: 'Some blighter of a porter put it in the wrong coach', he explained with uncharacteristic spleen.

The Giant's Cave, Edenhall, Long Meg

From the roundabout at the S side of Penrith take the A686 and follow it 2½m NE to a lane on R (SE) (signed Whins Pond, Honeypot). This is a private road. Track runs past pond to farm; ask permission to visit cave (no right of way). Follow track to end, then through paddock and over small stile at E end. Struggle as best you can along steep and overgrown riverbank E to **The Giant's Cave**, an almost spherical hollow cut out of red sandstone. This is said to be one of two caves; the further and deeper, a tunnel which formerly had doors, now seems to be inaccessible owing to erosion and rockfalls. Perhaps this has been the case for a long time, for Defoe regretted not being able to visit

> the grotto on the bank of the River Eden ... the people telling us, the passage is block'd up with earth, so I must be content with telling you, that it seems to have been a lurking place, or retreat of some robbers in old time; ... it had certainly been worth seeing, if it had been possible, the entry is long and dark, but whether strait or crooked, I cannot say, the iron gates leading to it are gone, nor is there any sign of them, or what they were hung to.

Wordsworth and Coleridge were here in 1799, and Coleridge notes

> The Giant's Cave in the Banks of the Emont – ... Torquin lived here – a maiden (one of his Prisoners) escaped – leaped over a chasm, with a torrent underneath her, called the Maiden's Leap –

Torquin (or Tarquin) is another name for Owen Cesarius, the giant supposedly buried in Penrith Churchyard. According to Clarke's *Survey* (1789) he was killed by Sir Lancelot. I have not been able to identify the 'Maiden's Leap', though there are various high ledges in the rock.

Barbara Hoole (later Hofland) published in 1805 a 'Sonnet, composed in a cell (commonly called the Giant's Cave) on the banks of the Eimont, in Cumberland':

> Hail holy glooms! and thou mysterious cell,
> Wash'd by the gurgling Eimont's wildest flood,
> Where for unnumber'd ages thou hast stood
> A hermit-cavern in the rocky dell,
> Shelter'd amid the close embowering wood
> And shaded by the dimly distant fell ...

The cave bears many visitors' initials, some (which look authentic) dating back to the mid-eighteenth century. Return to A686.

200yds NE of the turning to Whins Pond turn R (E) (signed Edenhall Village). After ½m the road makes a zig-zag at large stone gateposts. This private drive leads ¾m NE to the former site of **Edenhall**. The Hall was demolished in the twentieth century. Bits of its fabric – stone blocks, columns, capitals, and even a broken chimney, all green with lichen – are still stacked against the wall inside. The old stable-block with a fine octagonal clock-tower can be seen from the road.

The hall is remembered chiefly for Longfellow's poem 'The Luck of Edenhall' (1840), a translation of 'Das Gluck von Edenhall' (1834) by the German poet J.L. Ühland. The hall formerly possessed a goblet said to have been left behind by fairy revellers surprised in the grounds by the butler. As the fairies fled, they chanted:

> If this glass should break or fall,
> Farewell the luck of Edenhall.

Ühland found the story in a book of English fairy-tales. In the poem the 'youthful lord' recklessly strikes the glass, crying

> 'The fragile goblet of crystal tall ...
> Has lasted longer than is right;
> Kling! klang! with a harder blow than all
> Will I try the luck of Edenhall!'
> As the ringing goblet flies apart,
> Suddenly cracks the vaulted hall;
> And through the rift, the wild flames start;
> The guests in dust are scattered all,
> With breaking the Luck of Edenhall.

T.A. Trollope gives an entertaining account of the mid-Victorian owner, Sir George Musgrave: he was 'the most hospitable man in the world ... but his hospitality was of quite the old world school.' Finding Trollope too eager one evening to leave his after-dinner port and rejoin the ladies,

> 'Come back!' he roared, before I could get to the door, 'we won't have any of your d—d forineering habits here! Come back and stick to your wine, or by the Lord I'll have the door locked.'

He attached great value to the famous 'Luck' of the Hall,

But instead of simply locking it up, where he might feel sure it could neither break nor fall, he would show it to all visitors, and not content with that, would insist on their taking it into their hands to examine and handle it. He maintained that otherwise there was no fair submission to the test of luck, which was intended by the inscription. It would have been mere cowardly prevarication to lock it away.

In June 1868 Sir George invited Longfellow, on his English tour, to lunch at the Hall, and the poet drank from the famous cup. Ironically, the glass has outlived the Hall, and is now in the Victoria and Albert Museum.

Continue N to rejoin A686, following it N to cross the **River Eden** at Langwathby. The river is addressed (by a wood-nymph, representing Mallerstang forest) in Drayton's *Poly-Olbion*:

> O my bright lovely Brooke, whose name doth beare the sound
> Of Gods forst garden-plot, th'imparadized ground,
> Wherein he placed Man, from whence by sinne he fell.
> O little blessed Brooke, how doth my bosome swell,
> With love I beare to thee, the day cannot suffice
> For *Malerstang* to gaze upon thy beautious eyes.

The local militia, raised during the Napoleonic wars in case of a French invasion, are celebrated in 'Edenside Volunteers' (1804), a rollicking song by 'the Blind Bard' John Stagg who also took the river as the setting for his sentimental ballad 'The Unfortunate Lovers': Ella, miserable at Edwin's long absence at the wars, drowns herself in the Eden; meanwhile, Edwin has returned and is already knocking at her cottage door. Discovering her 'floating corps' on the river, he too 'plunged into the fatal flood'.

Wordsworth has an 1833 sonnet to 'The River Eden, Cumberland', whose banks he explored on a holiday that year.

From Langwathby follow signs to Little Salkeld; then after ¾m signs to Long Meg for **Long Meg and her Daughters**, the third largest prehistoric stone circle in Britain. Meg herself is a fifteen-foot pillar of local sandstone; her daughters are 69 boulders (or thereabouts: tradition says they are a coven of witches turned to stone; if you count them twice and get the same number they will return to life).

Drayton celebrated the stones in *Poly-Olbion*:

> At the lesse *Salkeld*, neere
> To *Edans* Bank, the like is scarcely any where,
> Stones seventie seven stand, in manner of a Ring,
> Each full ten foot in height, but yet the strangest thing,
> Their equall distance is, the circle that compose,
> Within which other stones lye flat, which doe inclose
> The bones of men long dead (as there the people say).

John Aubrey quotes a description by a contemporary which suggests that it has changed since the seventeenth century: he calls it

> a circle of stones of about two hundred in number, of several tons. The diameter of this circle is about the diameter … of the Thames from the

Heralds' Office … In the middle are two tumuli, or barrows of cobble-stones, nine or ten foot high.

And he adds a memorandum to enquire about 'the giant's bone and body found there. The body is in the midst of the orbicular stones' – a matter about which one would like to know more.

Celia Fiennes in 1698 noted

A mile [*sic*] from Peroth in a low bottom a moorish place stands Great Mag and her Sisters, the story is that these soliciting her to an unlawfull love by an enchantment are turned with her into stone; the stone in the middle which is called Mag is much bigger and have some form like a statue or figure of a body but the rest are but soe many craggy stones, but they affirme they cannot be counted twice alike as is the story of Stonidge [Stonehenge], but the number of these are not above 30; however what the first design of placeing them there either as a marke of that sort of moorish ground or what else, the thing is not so wonderfull as that of Stonidge.

Wordsworth came on the stones by chance, while walking here in early 1821, and addressed the 'Giant-mother' in a sombrely impressive sonnet, 'The Monument Commonly Called Long Meg':

A weight of awe, not easy to be borne,
Fell suddenly upon my Spirit – cast
From the dread bosom of the unknown past,
When first I saw that family forlorn …

There is also an eerie poem by Andrew Young, 'Long Meg and her Daughters' (1936), in which

Viewing her daughters Long Meg said,
'Come, stranger, make your choice of one;
All are my children, stone of my stone,
And none of them yet wed.'

The poet declines the offer, but

Meg frowned, 'You should be dead
To take instead a young tombstone to bed.'

Brougham Castle and Countess' Pillar

From the roundabout at S edge of Penrith take A66 (signed Appleby) then first R (S), following signs to **Brougham Castle** (*open Good Friday or 1 April, whichever is earlier, to 30 September, daily 10–6; 1 October to Maundy Thursday or 31 March, whichever is earlier, Tuesday-Sunday 10–4; admission charge*). In 1540 Leland wrote:

At Burgham is an old castel that the commune people ther sayeth doth synke.

About this Burgham plowghmen fynd in the feldes many square stones tokens of old buildinges. The castel is set in a stronge place by reasons of ryvers enclosing the cuntery thereabowt.

Ann Radcliffe was here in 1794 and describes Brougham as if it were a setting for one her own novels:

> Dungeons, secret passages and heavy iron rings remain to hint of unhappy wretches, who were, perhaps, rescued only by death from these horrible engines of a tyrant's will.

> We were tempted to enter a ruinous passage below, formed in the great thickness of the walls; but it was soon lost in darkness, and we were told that no person had ventured to explore the end of this, or of many similar passages among the ruins, now the dens of serpents and other venomous reptiles.

She also noted 'large iron rings, fastened to the carved heads of animals', and guessed that they were used to secure prisoners. Clarke in 1789 also mentioned 'what is called the Sweating Pillar, from its being continually covered with moisture or dew.' All this sounds very exciting, but secret passages, iron rings, dungeons, sweating pillars and venomous reptiles, if they ever existed, have now disappeared.

Ann Radcliffe thought the Castle

> rendered more interesting by having been occasionally the residence of the humane and generous Sir Philip Sidney; who had only to look from the windows of this once noble edifice to see his own 'Arcadia' spreading on every side. The landscape probably awakened his imagination, for it was during a visit here, that the greatest part of the work was written.

This was a mistake (started by Clarke's 1789 *Survey of the Lakes*). Sidney was never at Brougham, though Wordsworth believed the tale and wrote of Brougham Castle in *The Prelude* as

> A mansion visited (as fame reports)
> By Sidney, where, in sight of our Helvellyn,
> Or stormy Cross-fell, snatches he might pen
> Of his Arcadia.

The woods near Brougham were a favourite walk of Dorothy Words-worth and the Hutchinson sisters. In September 1788 they were joined by Dorothy's brother William, who would later marry Mary. Wordsworth recalled in *The Prelude* Book VI these walks by 'The varied banks/Of Emont',

> And that monastic Castle, 'mid tall trees,
> Low-standing by the margin of the stream,

and how he and Dorothy

> having clomb
> The darksome windings of a broken stair,
> And crept along a ridge of fractured wall,
> Not without trembling, ... in safety looked
> Forth, through some Gothic window's open space,
> And gathered with one mind a rich reward
> From the far-stretching landscape, by the light

Of morning beautified, or purple eve.

Wordsworth's 'Song at the Feast of Brougham Castle' recounts a local tradition of how, after the Yorkist victory at Towton during the Wars of the Roses, Henry Lord Clifford, a Lancastrian, had to flee his estates at Brougham and spent twenty-four years living as a shepherd on the Caldbeck Fells, until Henry VII's accession in 1485 enabled him to come out of hiding and claim his property.

The castle is also the setting of John Stagg's Gothic poem 'The Sword' (1821), which tells the tale of Lady Eleanor, who uses magic to win a sight of her husband Lord Herbert, absent at the Crusades. He appears to her at night and vanishes at cockcrow, dropping his sword. On his return two years later he tells her that in the thick of battle he felt his soul snatched away by witchcraft and lost consciousness. He has vowed to kill the culprit; finding the lost sword in his wife's room, he kills her.

To reach **Countess' Pillar**, which requires a scramble and good shoes, from castle gate walk S along road then L at crossroads for 250yds. As you reach 'Give Way' signs for the A66 dual carriageway, you will see a short unmarked stretch of road running off diagonally R. This soon becomes a footpath; follow it for a few yards, then leave it and bear R through farm gate beside A66 and follow path (now simply a stretch of derelict roadway) for some 300 yds. Don't be discouraged: you will have to clamber over some rubble and the wooden fence at the end. Here you will find the pillar, a splendid decorative monument erected (1656) by Lady Ann Clifford to mark the place where she last parted from her mother, with a stone table for gifts of money to the poor of Brough (a charity still carried on). Defoe admired it as 'the best and most beautiful piece of its kind in Britain', and Wordsworth's sonnet 'Countess Pillar' celebrates the 'bright flower of Charity' represented by the monument. Unexpectedly it also figures in Samuel Rogers's *The Pleasures of Memory* (1792) as

> That modest stone which pious Pembroke reared;
> Which still records, beyond the pencil's power
> The silent sorrows of a parting hour;
> Still to the musing pilgrim points the place
> Her sainted spirit most delights to trace.

Two miles further E along A66 formerly stood the **Hartshorn Tree**, an ancient oak mounted with deer's antlers, said to be those of a 'hart-of-grease' (eight-year-old stag) chased by Hercules, a deer-hound, from this tree to Red-Kirk in Scotland and back, a total of over eighty miles, in one day in 1333. Returning to the tree the hart leapt the park fence and fell dead inside; the hound fell dead outside. A popular verse recorded that

> Hercules killed Hart-o-Grease,
> And Hart-o-Grease killed Hercules.

The horns remained until 1658. The tree was visited by Wordsworth and Coleridge on their 1799 tour, when Coleridge jotted in his notebook '*The*

Hartshorn – Oak – there seen from all the country –'. In 1833 Wordsworth described it in a sonnet, 'Hart's-Horn Tree, Near Penrith'.

Return to Brougham Castle. For **Brougham Hall** (*open 9-5 all year; opening times of individual shops and craft workshops vary*), follow the signed road SW from the castle gate. The Hall resembles another full-scale castle: it was rebuilt from a pele tower early in the nineteenth century in the Gothic revival style and was the home of the lawyer and politician Henry Brougham. It was gutted by fire in 1956 and is now being gradually rebuilt as a craft centre.

Dacre, Hutton John and Greystoke

Leave Penrith by A66 (signed Keswick). 1m after crossing M6 at round-about is a smaller roundabout; take A692 (signed Ullswater) and after 250yds park in small road signed Redhills. Walk a few yards SW along A692 to public footpath (signed Sockbridge). Follow path to end of ridge. On January 22 1802 William and Dorothy Wordsworth walked here with Mary Hutchinson, Wordsworth's future wife, who was staying nearby at Sockbridge. They sat for a while

> under a wall in the sun near a cottage above Stainton Bridge. The field in which we sate sloped downwards to a nearly level meadow, round which the Emont flowed in a small half-circle … The opposite bank is woody, steep as a wall, but not high, and above that bank the fields slope gently and irregularly down to it. These fields are surrounded by tall hedges, with trees among them, and there are clumps or grovelets of tall trees here and there. Sheep and cattle were in the fields. Dear Mary! there we parted from her. I daresay, as often as she passes that road she will turn in at the gate to look at this sweet prospect. There was a barn and I think two or three cottages to be seen among the trees, and slips of lawn and irregular fields.

The view is still much the same. The cottage has disappeared but must have been near the two stone gateposts which survive in isolation.

Return to A66 and after 3m turn L (S) to Dacre. **Dacre Castle** (mid-four-teenth-century) is highly picturesque, as is the whole village. An amusing account of the castle's renovation, and of daily life there, is given in *Pawn Takes Castle* (1971) by Bunty Kinsman, who bought it in 1961. The castle's solar (upstairs), known as the King's Chamber, is traditionally said to be the room where five kings met in 927 to swear peace: according to the *Anglo-Saxon Chronicle*

> King Aethelstan received the kingdom of Northumbria, and all the kings on this island were brought under his rule: first Hywel, king of the West Welsh; Constantine, king of the Scots, Uwen, king of the people of Gwent, and Ealdred, son of Ealdulf, from Bamburgh. With pledges and oaths they fastened a peace, in the place called Eamont Bridge, on July 12th, and renounced all idol-worship, and from there turned away in peace.

In reality the meeting probably took place at the large monastery which once stood where the parish church is now.

DACRE CASTLE
William Hutchinson, 1793

Bede tells of a miraculous cure at the monastery in about 698:

> In that monastery was a youth whose eyelid had a great swelling on it,
> which growing daily, threatened the loss of the eye. He touched it with a
> lock of [Saint] Cuthbert's hair; [and after four hours] touching his eye, on a
> sudden, found it as sound with the lid, as if there had never been any
> swelling or deformity on it.

To recreate a Wordsworth walk, from Dacre follow the road W (signed
Sparket, Thackthwaite); after 1m walkers should turn R up drive to Hesket
Farm and follow track through farmyard and NW to **Hutton John**. Other-
wise drive past Hesket Farm and at crossroads go R (N) to Hutton John.

After 'a melancholy parting' from the depressed Coleridge in July 1802
at the beginning of their Scottish tour, William and Dorothy Wordsworth

> turned aside to explore the country near Hutton-John, and had a new and
> delightful walk. The valley, which is subject to the decaying mansion that
> stands at its head, seems to join its testimony to that of the house to the
> falling away of the family greatness. The hedges are in bad condition, the
> land wants draining, and is overrun with brackens, yet there is a
> something everywhere that tells of its former possessors. The trees are left
> scattered about as if they were intended to be like a park, and these are
> very interesting, standing as they do upon the sides of the steep hills that
> slope down to the bed of the river, a little stony-bedded stream that spreads
> out to a considerable breadth at the village of Dacre.

The tale told in Wordsworth's 'The Horn of Egremont Castle' (of a younger
son who has his elder brother murdered for his estate) was actually told of
Hutton John; Wordsworth for some reason transferred it to Egremont.

Hutton John itself, a medieval pele-tower with many additions up to
1860, is now in good repair. Return to A66, cross it and continue 2½m N to
Greystoke. The village green is dominated by the imposing gates of

Greystoke Castle. Shelley and his wife Harriet stayed here with the Duke of Norfolk from 1 to 8 December, 1811. Shelley grumbled about being 'fatigued with aristocratical insipidity' but seems to have been in no hurry to leave.

Admirers of Edgar Rice Burroughs's *Tarzan of the Apes* (1912), recalling the hero's true identity as Lord Greystoke, may like to consider that these are the gates of his ancestral home. Burroughs, a native of Chicago, never visited England and says nothing of Tarzan's birthplace, but Philip José Farmer (in *Tarzan Alive: A Definitive Biography of Lord Greystoke*, 1972) traces his descent from the de Greystockes of 'Greystoke Manor, Cumberland'.

Threlkeld

Return to A66 and continue W. We are going to circle the Skiddaw massif clockwise, so for the moment we pass turnings to Caldbeck and Mungrisdale. 2 ½m after the Mungrisdale turn off, watch for small sign to Keswick Golf Club. 200yds down the drive (a public bridleway) is a large farm with traces of very old masonry in the outbuildings. This is **Threlkeld Hall**, formerly a fortified manor house. Wordsworth mentions it in 'Benjamin the Waggoner', referring to the legend of how, during the Wars of the Roses, the young Lord Clifford was hidden in its grounds disguised as a shepherd:

> And see, beyond that hamlet small,
> The ruined towers of Threlkeld-hall
> Lurking in a double shade,
> By trees and lingering twilight made!
> There, at Blencathra's rugged feet,
> Sir Lancelot gave a safe retreat
> To noble Clifford; from annoy
> Concealed the persecuted boy,
> Well pleased in rustic garb to feed
> His flock, and pipe on shepherd's reed
> Among this multitude of hills,
> Crags, woodlands, waterfalls, and rills.

A quarter of a mile further W on the A66 is the signed turning to **Threlkeld**, a small village at the foot of Blencathra. Near the E end of the village is the **Horse and Farrier**, where Ann Radcliffe stayed during her 1794 tour. It was

> a very humble inn, at which those, who have passed the bleak sides of Saddleback, ... may rejoice to rest. We had been blown about, for some hours, in an open chaise, and hoped for more refreshment than could be obtained; but had the satisfaction ... of observing the good intentions, amounting almost to kindness, of the cottagers towards their guests.

Wordsworth and Coleridge came to Threlkeld (and probably stayed at the inn) on their 1799 walking tour of the Lakes, and collected from local people the story of Lord Clifford, which became the basis for Wordsworth's 'Song at the Feast of Brougham Castle'. Coleridge noted down a garbled version of the tale:

> In the Civil Wars between York & Lancaster a Clifford, Earl of Cumberland, wandered about under Sattleback & deemed by the Shepherds an astronomic mysterious man.

At village centre, turn up Blease Road and follow it 1m to the National Park Authority's **Blencathra Centre**, which inspired Scarfe Hall, where Rose Clenell is trapped by the deranged Colonel Fawcus in Hugh Walpole's novel *A Prayer for My Son* (1936).

Return to Threlkeld and follow main street SW; at junction turn uphill (signed **Wescoe**). Continue 1m, passing Wescoe Farm. At next group of farm buildings, the white cottage opposite the post box, adjoining 'Far Wescoe', was formerly a holiday cottage belonging to W.H. Auden's parents. During the 1920s and 30s Auden and his friends spent much time here. In 1929 he stayed at the cottage to work on some of his finest early poems including 'It was Easter as I walked in the public gardens', which retains traces of the local landscape:

> In month of August to a cottage coming ...
> Being alone, the frightened soul
> Returns to this life of sheep and hay
> No longer his ...

In July 1932 he was here writing a 'choral ballet' about Orpheus for the Group Theatre; in the afternoons he would explore derelict mineworkings on the fells. And in March 1937, immediately on his return from Spain, he stayed here with Christopher Isherwood and wrote his famous poem about the Spanish Civil War, 'Spain 1937'. Return to the A66 and continue W. For Keswick, follow signs and turn to page 164. Our route will now circle the Skiddaw massif.

Ormathwaite, Applethwaite and Mirehouse

At the large roundabout just N of Keswick take exit signed Mirehouse, then immediately turn R (N) (signed Ormathwaite). After ½m lane leads NW past farm buildings to **Ormathwaite Hall**, a pair of elegant Georgian houses with a lawn and walled garden. This was the home of William Brownrigg (1711–1800), physician and chemist, one of the leading scientists of his day. He had a laboratory at Whitehaven supplied with firedamp (methane) on tap through tubes from the coalmines and conducted experiments with gases and coal-derived chemicals.

He had many scientific visitors. Benjamin Franklin visited in 1772; he and Brownrigg experimented on Derwentwater and proved that stormy water could be calmed by pouring oil on to it: 'The water, which had been in great agitation before, was instantly calmed, upon pouring in only a very small quantity of oil.' The results were sent to the Royal Society. Later the house was the home of the artist Joseph Wilkinson, for whose landscape engravings Wordsworth wrote the commentary which became his *Guide to the Lakes*.

Return to road. After 250yds is a sign 'Skiddaw via Public Footpath'; pass it 100yds NW to gate (signed Public Footpath) into wood. This is **Applethwaite**, and the path leads along a slope above a picturesque slate cottage built by Wordsworth's descendants on a plot of land given to the poet in 1803 by Sir George Beaumont, who hoped that it would enable him to live near Coleridge, then at Greta Hall. Wordsworth never lived here, but the land gave him a vote as 'a freeholder of the County of Cumberland', allowing him to take a part in local politics. His sonnet 'At Applethwaite, near Keswick' commemorates Beaumont's 'wish that I should rear/A seemly Cottage in this sunny Dell' and hopes that the Muses will love the spot even though the plan has not been fulfilled. In his *Guide* he calls it 'a rare and almost singular combination of minute and sequestered beauty, with splendid and extensive prospects.'

The cottage is a charming oddity: a perfect Victorian recreation of Lakeland architecture, but the architecture of the South Lakes. It looks as if magically transported from Rydal.

Continue W to rejoin A591. The car park for Dodd Wood and Mirehouse soon appears. From here there are forest walks on **Dodd**, a round foothill of Skiddaw. In the 1860s it was the home of the 'Dodd Man', also known more elegantly as the 'Skiddaw Hermit', a Scottish wanderer named George Smith who built himself a huge tepee-like dwelling of branches and bracken on the hillside. He drank in the Keswick pubs and paid his way by painting portraits. He also composed verse, but apparently none survives.

Opposite the car park is **Mirehouse** *(grounds open April-October 10-5.30; house open April-October Sundays, Wednesdays (and Fridays in August only) 2-5; admission charge).* James Clarke in 1789 wrote:

> I cannot paint to the reader all the advantages of view *Mirehouse* has, unless I were determined to dedicate a whole volume to that purpose. Let the traveller, however, be witness to the beauties of the place, and the hospitality of its worthy owner.

The house was built in 1666 and extended in 1790 with Gothic bays at each end and a handsome red sandstone porch whose pillars invite the hand to stroke them. Its setting is visually striking, with Bassenthwaite in front and Dodd and Skiddaw towering behind. There are fine grounds with many activities for children.

Mirehouse was the home of John Spedding, Wordsworth's schoolfellow at Hawkshead, and his son James Spedding (1808–81), who devoted himself to studying the Renaissance philosopher and politician Francis Bacon, Lord Verulam, whose biography he wrote in fourteen volumes.

Tennyson, a Cambridge friend of James's, came to stay in April 1835, and here met Edward Fitzgerald, later famous as translator of the *Rubaiyyat* of Omar Khayyam. Tennyson, his sister reported, admires the country near the lakes very much, but could dispense with the deluges of sapping rains. I understand the demon of vapours descends there in a perpetual drizzle.

He wore a huge cloak everywhere, indoors and out, and spent much time reading with his feet warming on the library fender. He read his poems to Fitzgerald and James Spedding and they discussed the early draft of the 'Morte d'Arthur'. (He also worked here on 'The Daydream', 'The Lord of Burleigh' and 'The Gardener's Daughter'.) James's father, a down-to-earth country squire, was puzzled by their activities. 'Well, Mr. F,' he asked Fitzgerald, 'and what is it? Mr. Tennyson reads, and Jem criticizes – is that it?'

SKIDDAW FROM APPLETHWAITE
Thomas Allom, 1832

Tennyson returned in 1850 with his wife Emily, on a honeymoon tour. Thomas Carlyle, another family friend, visited in 1818 and again in 1865, when he was on holiday recovering from the strain of writing *Frederick the Great*. Other visitors included the poet and politician Richard Monckton Milnes and the historian J.A. Froude (a cousin of the Speddings).

The house has a pleasantly lived-in feel, yet its rooms are elegant and its treasures so rich that it is hard to know what to mention. Items on display include James Spedding's huge collection of manuscripts and first editions of Francis Bacon; first editions of Bacon's pupil Thomas Hobbes; letters and manuscripts by Carlyle, Froude, Southey and Hartley Coleridge; and many drawings of Tennyson, Fitzgerald and Arthur Hallam by James Spedding (who knew them as a member of the Cambridge Apostles). Charles Lyell, the founder of modern geology, was a friend of James's elder brother Tom, and on display is his letter to Tom describing his first reactions on reading Darwin's *Origin of Species*.

For good measure there are small paintings by Turner, Constable, Girtin

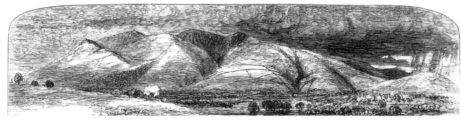

SKIDDAW
W.J. Linton, 1864

and Beatrix Potter, and when the house is open there is live music in the music room throughout the afternoon.

NW of the house is **St Bega's Church** (tenth or eleventh-century, restored 1874). It has been suggested that its dramatic setting between Skiddaw and the lake helped to inspire the landscape of 'Morte d'Arthur'. The stone cross outside the churchyard is modern: in the nineteenth century only its base remained, and perhaps the scene suggested the 'broken chancel with a broken cross' to which Sir Bedivere carries King Arthur, the lake itself inspiring Bedivere's

> 'I heard the ripple washing in the reeds,
> And the wild water lapping on the crag.'

Bassenthwaite Lake, Ruthwaite and Ireby

¾m N of Mirehouse gates, take the road W (signed Scarness) for two of West's 'stations' for viewing **Bassenthwaite**. Our first (actually West's third) is on private land at Broadness Farm, 1m from the junction. Walk up the drive towards the farm (private road; no parking). Just before gate to house (where permission should be sought) a track runs W into wood. After 100yds gate above track opens into field. West's station, giving an attractive view down the lake, is the crown of the knoll in this field.

The other 'station' (West's second) is at Scarness. Park near Bassenthwaite Lakeside Lodges entrance. Private road leads to gate marked 'The Dower House'. Ask permission to continue: the station is at the tip of the attractive wooded promontory due W of the house.

'Not one tourist in a hundred' wrote Eliza Lynn Linton, 'knows anything of the real beauty of Bassenthwaite.' She may be right: the lake's landscape is a gentle one, and has tended to be missed. It is worth looking at, despite the busy A66 roaring up its W bank, especially in misty autumn or winter weather when its melancholy beauty is enhanced by the many wildfowl which take refuge there.

Gray was here on October 6 1769:

> Went in a chaise eight miles along the east-side of Bassingthwaite-water to Ousebridge ... opposite to Widhope-brows, clothed to the very top with wood, a very beautiful view opens down to the lake, which is narrower and longer than that of Keswick, less broken into bays, and without islands. At

the foot of it ... stands Armathwaite in a thick grove of Scotch firs, commanding a noble view directly up the lake: at a small distance behind the house is a large extent of wood, and still behind this a ridge of cultivated hills, on which, according to the Keswick proverb, *the sun always shines*. The inhabitants here, on the contrary, call the vale of Derwentwater, *the Devil's* Chamber-pot, and pronounce the name of *Skiddaw*-fell, which terminates here, with a sort of terror and aversion.

Bassenthwaite was the scene of the first regatta on a Cumbrian lake, on 24 August 1780; regattas, with decorated boats, races and mock battles, soon became a craze which lasted well into the nineteenth century.

From Scarness return to the road; follow sign to Bassenthwaite to rejoin A591, then go NW to Castle Inn Hotel. Take the road NE opposite the Hotel. After 2¼m at junction go N (signed Ireby) and after 1m take small turning R (E) signed Ruthwaite.

On N side of road 50yds down is **John Peel Cottage**. This thoroughly restored cottage, with the barn (now a separate house), was the farm of John Peel, the huntsman celebrated in the famous song. Peel died here in 1854.

From Ruthwaite go W uphill ½m to **High Ireby**. There is no sign: the hamlet (home of the novelist and broadcaster Melvyn Bragg) is just a group of farms and cottages with a telephone box. Near the telephone box a large white wooden gate leads to the ruins of **The Grange**, a Victorian mansion, which inspired Walter Herries's house, 'The Fortress', in Hugh Walpole's novel of that name. Walpole came here in January 1931 looking for a suitable site and was astonished to find the ruin of exactly the house he had imagined for his novel, 'uncurtained, hens roosting on the windows, and Uldale all befrosted in the valley below, while the sun on Blencathra's snow was fiercely blazing.' The house was rebuilt a few years later, but destroyed by fire in about 1950.

In his novel Walpole moved the site to the hill ¼m NE, above the old lime kilns, so that Herries could overlook and intimidate his cousins at Uldale, clearly visible (note the white church) below in the valley.

Take the road opposite Manor Farm NE (1¼m) into Ireby. From crossroads in village go W along main street 200yds to the **Sun Inn**. On 29 June 1818 Keats and Brown, who had just climbed Skiddaw, walked to Ireby,

> where we were greatly amused by a country dancing school, holden at the [Sun], it was indeed 'no new cotillon fresh from France.' No they kickit & jumpit with mettle extraordinary, & whiskit, & fleckit, & toe'd it, & go'd it, & twirld it, & wheel'd it, & stampt it, & sweated it, tatooing the floor like mad; The differenc[e] between our country dances & these scotch figures, is about the same as leisurely stirring a cup o' Tea & [b]eating up a batter pudding ... there was as fine a row of boys & girls as you ever saw, some beautiful faces, & one exquisite mouth. I never felt so near the glory of Patriotism, the glory of making by any means a country happier. This [concluded Keats] is what I like better than scenery.

Return to the crossroads and go S (signed Uldale) ¼m to **Uldale Mill**

Farm, which stands on the site where Hugh Walpole placed David Herries' redbrick eighteenth-century farmhouse, Fell House, in *Rogue Herriess*. Here Deborah had her fine 'Chinese parlour' and on the lawn David suffered a fatal stroke at the shock of his son Francis's support for the French Revolution. Like several 'Herries' buildings, it was 'destroyed' to avoid conflict with real topography – Walpole had it burnt to the ground in Chapter 5 of *Vanessa*. The real farm bears no resemblance to Fell House.

Beside the farm is **St John's Church**. Just S of the church is the urn-topped monument of the Reverend Jonathan Cape FRS (1793–1868), whose mathematics textbooks and trigonometrical tables were once widely used. Appropriately, the monument is triangular.

Caldbeck and the Howk

Continue SE to Uldale village and follow signs for Caldbeck. After 4m the house called **Parkend** stands next to the birthplace of the famous huntsman John Peel (1777-1854), commemorated in the song 'D'ye ken John Peel?'. Peel was born in the building which is now the milking parlour of the farm.

Continue 1m; as you enter Caldbeck look for **Todcrofts**, a large farmhouse on the L (N) side of the road. This was the home after her marriage of Mary Harrison (née Robinson), the 'Maid of Buttermere' (for her story see p 170). Notice barn gable, with its ventilation-eye in a stone carved RH 1852 – the initials of Mary's husband Richard. From the stile by the barn a path runs NW across field to the Howk (see below).

Caldbeck (*large car park by bridge*) was once an important place: in the seventeenth century it was a mining town and in the eighteenth century industrial development came with mills for paper, corn, wool and bobbins, driven by the fast-flowing River Caldew. Perhaps for this reason an old proverb declares that

> Caldbeck and Caldbeck Fells
> Are worth all England else.

The village, whose limestone buildings include several of the old mills, has strong associations with the huntsman John Peel (1776–1854) and John Woodcock Graves (1795–1886), a Wigton man who owned a carding mill in Caldbeck and wrote the song 'D'ye ken John Peel with his coat so grey?'.

At the village centre is the **Oddfellows' Arms**, which displays a portrait of Graves. There is some doubt about its age (it appears to be a copy of a surviving daguerreotype) but it has a strong 'presence'.

According to Graves, the song was composed in 1824 'in a snug parlour' at his house 25yds SW of the inn (whitish house with 'BTB 1718' over door). Peel and Graves, both keen hunters, had spent a snowy evening 'by the fireside hunting over again many a good run, and recalling the feats of each particular hound'. When Graves's daughter happened to come in and ask him for the words of the tune her grandmother was using to sing the baby to sleep – 'a very old rant called *Bonnie* (or *Cannie*) *Annie*' – it occurred to Graves to write a new song to the old air.

> The pen and ink for hunting appointments being on the table, ... thus was produced, impromptu, *D'ye ken John Peel with his coat so gray*. Graves sang the song to Peel on the spot, and concluded, 'By Jove, Peel, you'll be sung when we're both run to earth.'

Graves adds that Peel himself was

> of very limited education beyond hunting. But no wile of a fox or hare could evade his scrutiny; and business of any shape was utterly neglected ... Indeed this neglect extended to the paternal duties in his family. I believe he would not have left the drag of a fox on the impending death of a child, or any other earthly event.

Peel maintained a pack of hounds at his own expense for 55 years.

Graves survived his friend, to write two more poems about him ('Monody on John Peel' and 'At the Grave of John Peel'). He emigrated to Hobart Town, Tasmania in 1833.

John Peel's brother Askew also lived at Caldbeck and was commemorated in song. Askew Peel was famed for driving a hard bargain and had a running argument with a local horse-dealer, one 'Pigtail' Armstrong, about the value of their horses. One day Askew offered to exchange his mare for Armstrong's. Unexpectedly, Armstrong agreed. As it turned out, both mares had just died – hence the sudden readiness to get rid of them – but Peel got the better bargain, for he had already taken off the hide and shoes from his own horse and sold them elsewhere. A local wit composed a song, concluding

> A'tween twea deed hosses theer not much t'choose,
> An Askew bet [beat] Pigtail be t'hide an fower shoes.

In **St Kentigern's churchyard** (200yds E of the Inn) is John Peel's grave, near the W wall of the churchyard not far from the church door. The whitewashed sandstone headstone, richly carved with hunting horns, a hound, roses and figs, makes an interesting contrast with the austere grey slate headstone of Mary Harrison ('The Maid of Buttermere') and her husband Richard (15yds W of point where a small side path branches off) which carries emblems of a rose ('Life how short') and an eye ('Eternity how long').

To reach **Caldbeck Howk** or the **Fairykirk** return to car park and leave it by exit at W corner, take road L (S) 50yds to stone barn and follow sign on corner of former barn (now a house) through wooden gate, and take paved path to second gate and boggy footpath through woods to ruined mill buildings, then a limestone gorge with a series of picturesque foaming waterfalls and strange recesses eroded from the rock. 'Howk' is Cumbrian dialect for 'scoop out', eloquently describing what the river has done in eroding the limestone hereabouts.

Coleridge explored it in October 1800 and noted

> Before you stand Fairies' parlors and fine Cathedral seats overhung by the rock – in the parlour two window-holes, one at the top, … re-ascend – go again into the Cavern, and see another Chamber, crawl into it – at the end one round Hole, thro which I glimpse another Waterfall. Shut my eyes/the noise of Water, like that when you are in a Mill, a room off the Great Wheel – climb out thro the Window hole.

In August 1803 he was here again with the Wordsworths. Dorothy thought the Howk

> a delicious spot in which to breathe out a summer's day – limestone rocks, hanging trees, pools, and waterbreaks – caves and caldrons which have been honoured with fairy names, and no doubt continue in the fancy of the neighbourhood to resound with fairy revels.

After viewing the falls you can return to the wooden bridge, cross it and take path over field SE to Todcrofts and back to the village.

Sebergham, Rose Castle and Hesket Newmarket

From Caldbeck go N on B5299 for 3½m to the String of Horses, then R (SE) 1m to **Sebergham**, a small village with an elegant two-arched bridge over the **Caldew**. John Stagg's ballad 'Lord Baldwin' (1810) is set on the banks of this river, in the forests of 'Warnell's tow'ring heights' (Warnell Fell is 1m W of Sebergham, and the woods run at its foot between Warnell Hall and the river). Here the wicked lord is tormented by the ghosts of two women whom he has betrayed and murdered.

Walkers can reach **St Mary's Church** by signed bridleway starting just uphill from E end of bridge (drivers go SE into village and take first L). The church has an outstanding collection of memorial tablets. The marvellous marble plaque on the N wall by the sculptor Musgrave Lewthwaite Watson (1804–47) to his father, Thomas Watson Esquire of Bogg Hall, looks thoroughly pagan and its three ferocious ladies, presumably the Fates, seem inspired by Fuseli's painting of *Macbeth*'s three witches (Watson was a pupil of Fuseli). The S wall has a tablet to Thomas Denton (1724–77), parson and poet, author of *The House of Superstition: A Poem (1762) and Religious Retirement for One Day in Every Month: freed from the peculiarities of the Romish superstition, and fitted for the use of Protestants* (1768). On the N wall of the sanctuary is a tablet to Sebergham's most famous son, Josiah Relph (1712–43), curate and schoolmaster here and well known in his day as a Cumberland dialect poet. His poems were collected in 1747, and again, with engravings by Thomas Bewick, in 1798. The elaborate Latin inscription celebrates his poetic talents as 'another Theocritus' and laments his early death. Finally, notice the marble and mosaic plaque near the door to five-year-old Ruth Pain (d 1931); garish at first sight, it has its own charms (note hydrangea bushes and snail).

Return to the String of Horses. Follow B5299 2½m N, then turn R (SE) following sign to **Rose Castle**, residence of the Bishop of Carlisle. In 1662 Fuller wrote that

> Rose-castle, the bishop's best seat, hath lately the rose therein withered; and the prickles, in the ruins thereof, only remain.

It was partly restored soon afterwards and in 1803 Coleridge and the Wordsworths found it in what must have been ideally picturesque condition. Coleridge noted:

> We are delighted with Rose Castle, the thickset green Fence to the garden, the two walls, the lower making a terrace/the House, the Orchard crowding round it – The Chestnuts – the masses of Ivy over the gateway, from one great root. This stands on the other side of the wall to my left as I face the gateway – Go in, the ivy over the Coach-House, belonging to the same mass – the horns of the dark old mulberry Tree among it – the Swallows & their Shadows on the Castle-House walls – the green shaven Bank, like the roof of a House between the main Building & the Castle, properly so called/the great Nets on this Castle, to cover the fruit Trees/ – all, all perfect – Cottage Comfort & ancestral Dignity!

The Castle was heavily restored again about 1830. Though still beautiful, it cannot quite live up to such a description.

Rose Castle is the most northerly point reached in this Guide: we are now only 7m from Carlisle. Some will want to follow Coleridge and his friends there, and on to the Borders and Scotland. Meanwhile, we turn S, returning to Caldbeck. Go E past Caldbeck church and continue 1m to **Hesket Newmarket**.

At the top of the N side of the main street is **Dickens House**, formerly the Queen's Head Inn. On August 14 1803, Coleridge and the Wordsworths were here and, says Dorothy, 'Slept at Mr. Younghusband's publick-house, Hesket Newmarket. In the evening walked to Caldbeck Falls'. The village was then more crowded, with a row of houses standing where the 'green' now runs down the middle of the street. Coleridge noted:

> Out of the little parlour window looking across the market place & over the market House ...
>
> The sanded stone floor with the spitting Pot full of Sand Dust, two pictures of young Master & Miss with their round Birds' Eyes & parlour Dress, he with a paroquet on his hand ... she with a rose in her uplifted perpend[icular] hand ... The whole Room struck me as Cleanliness quarreling with Tobacco Ghosts –

It was here too that Dickens and Wilkie Collins stayed in September 1857. They describe the village in *The Lazy Tour of Two Idle Apprentices*:

> Black, coarse-stoned, rough-windowed houses; some with outer staircases, like Swiss houses; a sinuous and stony gutter winding up hill and round the corner, by way of street. Old Carrock gloomed down upon it all in a very ill-tempered state; and rain was beginning.

They also devote an exuberant paragraph (far too long to quote entire) to the upstairs parlour where they stayed:

> The ceiling of this drawing-room was so crossed and recrossed by beams of unequal lengths, radiating from a centre, in a corner, that it looked like a broken star-fish. The room ... had a snug fireside, and a couple of well-curtained windows, looking out upon the wild country behind the house. What it most developed was, an unexpected taste for little ornaments and nick-nacks, of which it contained a most surprising number ... It was so very pleasant to see these things in such a lonesome by-place – ... so fanciful to imagine what a wonder [this] room must be to the little children born in the gloomy village – what grand impressions of it those who became wanderers over the earth would carry away; and how, at distant ends of the world, some old voyagers would die, cherishing the belief that the finest apartment known to men was once in the Hesket Newmarket Inn, in rare old Cumberland ...

From here they set out up Carrock Fell, Collins returning with a sprained ankle. They soon left (by carriage) for Wigton.

Mungrisdale, Carrock and Blencathra

Leave Hesket Newmarket heading E by the upper road (*not* the one signed Newlands and Carlisle) and after ½m at fork go R uphill, following signs for Mungrisdale. After 5m the road makes a right-angled bend at **Mosedale**, which has no road sign, then crosses the Caldew by a small bridge, reaching **Mungrisdale** after 1m. We are taking, in the opposite direction, the route followed by Coleridge and the Wordsworths on their August 1803 Scottish tour. They passed here, 'under the foot of Carrock, a mountain covered with stones on the lower part', along by

> the foot of Grisedale [i.e. Mungrisdale] and Mosedale, both pastoral vallies, narrow and soon terminating in the mountains – green, with scattered trees and houses, and each a beautiful stream ... At Grisedale our horse backed upon a steep bank where the road was not fenced, just above a pretty mill at the foot of the valley; and we had a second threatening of a disaster in crossing a narrow bridge between the two dales; but this was not the fault of either man or horse.

The dangerous bridge was the one at Mosedale, now greatly enlarged. Coleridge also came here for a short walking-tour in August 1800 and noted a tale about the exploits of local Quakers Isaac Ritson and John Slee, who lived in Mungrisdale:

> Isaac Ritson with Slee & others carried off the Bell of Grisdale Chapel & buried it among some stones in woody Park – They took it down on a ladder, it made a Hole in the Earth/ weighed 14 Stone hummed [i.e. fooled] the folks & sent them to seek for it in strange places –

Slee later taught mathematics in Kendal; Ritson, his pupil, was a poet and wrote the *Borrowdale Letter*, an early piece of comic dialect literature.

Above Mosedale looms the rocky head of **Carrock Fell**. Coleridge many times climbed this small but rugged peak, whose summit has the remains of a pre-Roman fortress. He describes one especially stormy occasion in a letter (1800) to Humphry Davy – the quotation is a mere fragment of a breathless epic –

> On this mountain Carrock, at the summit of which are the remains of a vast Druid Circle of Stones, I was wandering –; when a thick cloud came on, and wrapped me in such Darkness that I could not see ten yards before me – and with the cloud a storm of Wind & Hail, the like of which I had never before seen & felt. At the very summit is a cone of Stones, built by the Shepherds ... but the winds became so fearful & tyrranous that I was apprehensive, some of the stones might topple down upon me. So I groped my way further down, and came to 3 rocks, placed ... like a Child's House of Cards, & in the Hollow & Screen which they made I sate for a long while sheltered as if I had been in my own Study, in which I am now writing – Here I sate, with a total feeling worshipping the power & 'eternal Link' of Energy. – The Darkness vanished, as by enchantment – : far off, far far off, to the South the mountains of Glaramara & Great Gavel, and their Family, appeared distinct, in deepest sablest *Blue* – I rose, & behind me was a rainbow bright as the brightest ...

Dickens and Wilkie Collins climbed the fell (despite discouragement from the locals – 'No visitors went up Carrock. No visitors came there at all. Aa' the world ganged awa' yon' -) on a wet day in September 1857:

> The sides of Carrock looked fearfully steep, and the top of Carrock was hidden in mist. The rain was falling faster and faster ... Up and up, and then down a little, and then up and then along a strip of level ground and then up again. The wind, a wind unknown in the happy valley, blows keen and strong; the rain-mist gets impenetrable; a dreary little cairn of stones appears ... [Collins], drenched and panting, stands up with his back to the wind, ascertains distinctly that this is the top at last, looks round with all the little curiosity that is left in him, and gets, in return, a magnificent view of – Nothing!

The party got lost, Dickens broke his compass, Collins fell down a ravine and sprained his ankle. At last they found their way to safety, Dickens carrying Collins down the mountain whilst impersonating the hero of Collins's play *The Frozen Deep*.

At the group of buildings ½m S of Mosedale, a path leads 2m W along the fellside, climbing steeply for the last ½m, to the lonely **Bowscale Tarn**. Wordsworth's 'Song at the Feast of Brougham Castle' recalls the local tradition of two immortal fish that live in the tarn: during Lord Clifford's wanderings, says Wordsworth,

> ... both the undying fish that swim
> Through Bowscale-tarn did wait on him.

Eliza Lynn Linton says they 'used to be called "Adam and Eve." We never knew of any one who had seen them, but they are nonetheless there.'

According to Bishop Nicolson in 1703, however, the tarn is 'So cold, yt nothing lives in it. Fish have been put in: But they presently dy.'

From Mungrisdale walkers should either stay on the W bank of the river and follow the gated road from the Mill Inn round to Scales or take the path upstream along the Glenderamackin towards Mousethwaite Combe. Drivers should take the larger road on the E bank of the river to join the A66 then head W and after 2m take small turning R at sign for White Horse Inn (there is no sign for Scales).

All these routes take us along the foot of **Souther Fell**, famous for a series of appartions seen during the eighteenth century. On Midsummer Eve 1735 a servant 'saw the eastern side of the summit covered with troops, which pursued their onward march for an hour [and] disappeared in a niche in the summit'. In 1737, again on Midsummer Eve, a large army was seen, marching across the summit and disappearing, and on the same day in 1745 troops were seen in a 'multitude beyond imagining', this time with carriages amongst them. The sight was witnessed by twenty-six people; no carriages, however, could possibly get up there, and investigation revealed no marks on the turf. Other smaller groups of phantom figures have been seen on the fell from time to time, always on the E side and travelling from N to S. The 1745 apparition was explained by the fact that Bonnie Prince Charlie's rebel troops had at the time been 'exercising on the western coast of Scotland, whose movements had been reflected by some transparent vapour'. The phenomena on the Fell are discussed in detail by Sir David Brewster in his *Letters on Natural Magic* (1832).

To reach **Scales Tarn** either leave the A66 at Scales and drive ¾m past

SCALES TARN ('THRELKELD TARN')
William Westall, 1829

inn to car park; or leave gated road 2¼m S of Mungrisdale. Then follow footpath (near bridge and small car park) signed Mungrisdale Common. After ¾m above steep gulley path forks; go NW. Soon it forks again. The L (southerly) path runs along Scales Fell ridge to Blencathra summit; the R (more northerly) fork runs above River Glenderamackin to Scales Tarn (formerly also Threlkeld Tarn). 'Here, the saying is, the sun never shines and the stars are visible at noonday'. This is not true, but the tarn, at the foot of precipitous crags, does have a surface like polished black stone and is strangely impressive.

John Stuart Mill came here in July 1831, drawn partly by Southey's description in the *Colloquies*, and found himself almost poetically inspired:

> we descended to its brink: it was the first genuine tarn that we had seen in these mountains … and we could not take our eyes off it. The water, which is of the deepest blue, seems hid, out of the reach of man; no trees or shrubs, nor even the smallest herb, overshadow it, yet one wonders at having found it, and deems it a prodigy that it should not have been overlooked.

From the tarn, paths run up to the summit of Blencathra. For the adventurous, there is a fairly frightening walk round the N side of the tarn via Sharp Edge. Stout footwear and nerves of steel essential.

Blencathra, with its jagged crags and weird flat summit like a dented anvil (whence its other name, Saddleback) has caught the imagination of many writers.

Wordsworth's 'Song at the Feast of Brougham Castle' depicts the exiled Henry, Lord Clifford wandering disguised as a shepherd-boy among

> Blencathra's rugged coves,
> And … the flowers that summer brings
> To Glenderamakin's lofty springs.

Another wanderer here was the legendary 'Student of St Bees', who is supposed to have killed himself on Blencathra. (For details, see p 195). Coleridge's 'A Thought Suggested by a View' elaborates some lines by Ritson to sketch the mountain, counterpoising turmoil with massive stability:

> On stern Blencartha's perilous height
> The winds are tyrannous and strong;
> And flashing forth unsteady light
> From stern Blencartha's skiey height,
> As loud the torrents throng!
> Beneath the moon, in gentle weather,
> They bind the earth and sky together.
> But oh! the sky and all its forms, how quiet!
> The things that seek the earth, how full of noise and riot!

Thomas Wilkinson has a cautionary tale to tell: he took a blind scientist (could it have been Gough the botanist?) to the summit, where

I attempted a description of the fearful precipices beneath us; ... – when I saw him fall on the ground with dizziness, and cling to the earth, and scream out, with the apprehension of tumbling down the rocks into the abyss below. Till then I thought the idea of giddiness must be received at the eye; certainly it was as vivid in the mind of our learned and accomplished companion, as if he had seen the terrors around him. But we now moderated our descriptions, and only talked of extent and the appearance of distant objects.

Most people are delighted by both the rocks and the views. Ruskin in 1867 called Blencathra

the finest thing I've yet seen [in Cumberland], there being several bits of real crag-work, and a fine view at the top over the great plain of Penrith on one side, and the Cumberland hills, as a chain, on the other. Fine fresh wind blowing, and plenty of crows ... There were some of the biggest and hoarsest-voiced ones about the cliff that I've ever had sympathetic croaks from.

In Walpole's Elizabethan novel *The Bright Pavilions* (1939) Frau Hostetter (whose persecutors must have been exceptionally strenuous) is burnt as a witch on the summit of Blencathra at night; Gilbert Armstrong saves her daughter Catherine from the crowd by claiming to be her fiancé – whereupon he and Catherine are dragged downhill to Crosthwaite Church and married on the spot. Return to the A66.

Keswick

All roads hereabouts lead to **Keswick** (*several large, well-signed car parks*). 'Where as the water of the Darguent risith,' wrote Leland in 1540, 'is a lytle poore market town cawled Keswike, and it is a mile fro S. Hereberts isle that Bede speketh of'. In 1564 the little market town became a centre of copper mining, when German miners were brought over by a company partly owned by Queen Elizabeth. She hoped they would find gold, but instead they established a copper industry which continued in a small way until 1648, when it was ruined by the Civil War. As Thomas Fuller (whose whole account of the coppermines is delightful) put it in 1662,

Sad, that the industry of our age could not keep what the ingenuity of the former found out. And I would willingly put it on another account, that the burial of so much steel in the bowels of men, during our civil wars, hath hindered their digging of copper out of the entrails of the earth; hoping that these peaceable times will encourage to the resuming thereof.

Metal mining was resumed, and continued until the twentieth century. By 1800 Keswick was an industrial town. Leaving after a visit to Coleridge at 4 o'clock on a December afternoon in that year, Dorothy Wordsworth noted 'It was a little of the dusk when we set off. Cotton mills lighted up.' But Keswick's main industry, dating from the 1560s, concerned 'a material' as Wordsworth says, 'which the Reader is daily holding in his hand in the familiar shape of a Pencil', for nearby Bcrrowdale was the first known source of graphite. It is said to have been discovered in the early sixteenth century, when an ash tree uprooted by a gale was found to have a black mineral clinging to its roots. The stuff turned out to be useful for marking sheep, then as a lubricant and for making metal castings. By 1660 a writing instrument – a wooden stick with a splinter of graphite fitted into the tip – had been devised, probably in Italy. Keswick became the world centre of the graphite and pencil industries.

Next came tourism. The scenery of the vale of Keswick was among the first areas of intensely 'picturesque' scenery to be discovered in Britain. John Brown's *Description of the Vale and Lake of Keswick* (1753, published 1767), Dr John Dalton's *Descriptive Poem* (1755) and finally Thomas Gray's letters to Thomas Wharton, written on his 1769 tour and published in 1775, drew educated travellers and artists here.

From the beginning, superlatives were employed with indiscriminate enthusiasm; as early as 1770 Arthur Young contrasted the area favourably with Versailles: 'What are the effects of Louis's magnificence to the sportive play of nature in the vale of *Keswick*! How trifling the labours of art to the mere pranks of nature!' He felt, however, that nature needed a little help:

> it is much to be regretted that art does not lend more of her assistance ... There are a vast many edges of precipices, bold projections of rock, pendent cliffs, and wild romantic spots, which command the most delicious scenes, but which cannot be reached without the most perilous difficulty: to such points of view, winding paths should be cut in the rock, and resting-places made for the weary traveller.

By the end of the eighteenth century Keswick had become the first Lakeland tourist resort. Coleridge, newly arrived to make Keswick his home, described the situation in 1800:

> It is no small advantage here that for two thirds of the year we are in complete retirement – the other third is alive & swarms with Tourists of all shapes & sizes, & characters – it is the very place I would recomend to a novellist or farce writer.

Hester Lynch Piozzi (better known by her first married name as Mrs Thrale, Dr Johnson's friend) came here on her north-country tour in 1789, and her *Journey Book* shows how self-consciously contemporary vistors strove to say the right things. She may get her placenames garbled, but her deployment of the fashionable phrases is a *tour de force*:

> This lovely lake from the jaws of Botterdale fortified with rising Rocks, yt abruptly hinder your examination of its Limits, & look like Avernus in Fenelon's elegant & moral Romance – down to the sweet Garden Scenes exhibited at the other End, where Woods & Walks & Gentlemen's Seats variously disposed draw your Eyes from Skiddaw, & make them follow on to another Mere called Basswater is deliciously picturesque: but the Black Lead Mine exists no longer, & who now shall make Designs of Places where Claude Cuyp & Salvator might entertain themselves with Views of such

exquisite mutability as should be admired in every Nation who would then surely hasten hither & enjoy the charming Originals ...

One sees why the fashion for visiting Keswick had its opponents. The aesthete Richard Payne Knight, in *The Landscape: A Didactic Poem* (1794), found Derwentwater painfully unsubtle:

> Keswick's favoured pool
> Is made the theme of ev'ry wand'ring fool,
> With bogs and barrenness here compass'd round,
> With square inclosures there, and fallow'd ground;
> O'er its deep waves no promontories tower,
> No lofty trees, high over-arch'd, imbower;
> No winding creek, or solitary bay,
> 'Midst pendant rocks or woods is seen to stray:
> But small prim islands, with blue fir-trees crown'd,
> Spread their cold shadows regularly round,
> Whilst over all vast crumbling mountains rise,
> Mean in their forms, though of gigantic size.

One 'wand'ring fool' who found his way to Keswick was the naïve Dr Syntax, hero of William Combe's *Dr Syntax's Tour in Search of the Picturesque* (1810), whose faithful steed Grizzle celebrates his arrival by throwing him into the lake. Otherwise his visit is disappointingly lacking in detail, perhaps because Combe had never been here.

More local knowledge is shown in James Plumtre's delightful 'Comic Opera' (really just a play with songs), *The Lakers* (1798), where the novelist Veronica gives us a lesson in the use of local colour:

> You must know, Sir Charles, I have always several works in hand at the same time; and, as I always introduce a great deal of description of scenery in my romances, I keep that in my eye while I am travelling, and write a romance at the same time with my tour ... I think I shall lay the scene of my next upon Derwent-water, make St. Herbert to have murdered a pilgrim, who shall turn out to be his brother, and I shall call it 'The Horrors of the Hermitage.' I can introduce a mysterious monk of Borrowdale, and shall have fine opportunities of describing luxuriant groves and bowery lanes, in all the pomp of foliage of beech, birch, mountainash, and holly. It shall be a romance of the fourteenth century; the castle upon Lord's Island shall be haunted by an armed head: and, I believe, Lydia, I shall draw my heroine from either you or myself, and make her passionately fond of drawing and botany; she shall be mistress of the Linnaean system, and then, if I should make her stop, in the midst of her distresses, to admire the scenery, or gather a plant, it will be perfectly natural.

Certainly some of Keswick's tourist-traps were farcical enough: William Gell in his 1797 *Tour* mentions the museum-keeper Peter Crosthwaite (1735–1800), who used to sit in his Museum in Main Street with mirrors placed so that he could see every carriage as it arrived. On the approach of any stranger he would start a barrel-organ and bang a drum to attract attention and the stranger would be inveigled into the building.

Other kinds of Keswick entertainment are described by Joseph Budworth, who visited in 1792:

> In the evening we went to see *The Merchant of Venice* in an unroofed house ... The walls were decorated, or rather hid, with cast-off scenes, which shewed in many places a rough unplastered wall ... Some of the actors performed very well, others rather middling ... I found it so extremely hot, and I felt some knees press so hard upon my back, against a piece of curtain which composed the separation of pit and gallery, that I took my departure, and enjoyed a walk to the head of Derwentwater lake.

Keats and Charles Brown were here on their June 1818 walking tour. Keats thought

> The approach to Derwent Water surpassed Winandermere – it is richly wooded & shut in with rich-toned Mountains ... We took a complete circuit of the Lake going about ten miles, & seeing on our way the Fall of Low-dore.

William Hazlitt was here in 1803, seeking commissions for portraits (he was then trying to live as painter rather than writer). He was forced to leave in undignified haste, after getting into some scrape involving a local girl. No-one knows what really happened; according to Wordsworth's perhaps malicious account, Hazlitt made a sexual proposition to the girl, who called him 'a black-faced rascal';

> Hazlitt enraged pushed her down, '& because, Sir,' said Wordsworth, 'she refused to gratify his abominable & devilish propensities,' he lifted up her petticoats & *smote* her on *the bottom*.

He was chased out of town by a mob and fortunately met Coleridge, who lent him the money to take the first coach south.

A dark side of Keswick also appears in Chapter 13 of the modern poet Thomas Blackburn's harrowing 1969 autobiography *A Clip of Steel*, a nightmarish episode where the young poet, in the grip of alcoholism and a nervous breakdown, wanders the town helplessly at night.

To complete a trio of diasters, Dante Gabriel Rossetti arrived here, seriously ill and addicted to chloral, in September 1881, under the supervision of the young novelist Hall Caine. Caine was trying to control his dosage but at Keswick railway station Rossetti found a bottle hidden in Caine's luggage and drank the lot. Their visit, not a happy one, was spent mainly at Legburthwaite.

Keswick's most important fictional appearances are probably in the Victorian Edna Lyall's *Hope the Hermit*, and in Hugh Walpole's *A Prayer for My Son* and his *Herries* series.

For a tour of Keswick, begin from the **Market Place** at the town centre. At the E side of the street, the passage alongside Young's antique shop is **King's Head Court**. The cottage on L up stone steps was the home of Jonathan Otley (1766–1856). An eminent self-taught scientist, Otley gave the first clear understanding of Lakeland geology in *Remarks on the Succes-*

sion of the Rocks in the District of the Lakes (1820), made the first accurate map of the Keswick area, kept records of local climate and lake levels and wrote a good solid guidebook, *A Concise Description of the English Lakes and Adjacent Mountains* (1823). He also liked to plant flower seeds on his scientific excursions around the fells.

20yds downhill from King's Head Court is the **Queen's Hotel** (formerly the Queen's Head). In 1802 John Hatfield, the impostor who married the 'Maid of Buttermere', established himself here to begin his charade as an 'Honourable' and Member of Parliament; the inn, before its Victorian refurbishment, is richly portrayed in Melvyn Bragg's novel *The Maid of Buttermere*.

Just S of the Moot Hall used to be Storm's Café, now an outdoor clothing shop. This, according to Hugh Walpole, used to be 'the meeting-place for the Keswick gossipers of a morning, and on a fine day it is one of the most cheerful places in the universe.' The tribute comes from his novel *A Prayer for My Son*, where Colonel Fawcus celebrates his birthday at Storm's with coffee and ice creams. The nearest approximation now is the Keswickian Tea Room at the S end of the square, where you can still sit to watch the goings-on in the square and 'the visitor from the outside world who lingers from shop to shop,' though sheep are no longer driven 'wandering-fashion from point to point' along the High Street as they still were in the 1930s.

Leave the Square at its SE corner and go along St John's Street 250yds to **St John's Church**, a pleasant red sandstone building of 1838. Hugh Walpole's grave, marked by a Celtic cross, is at the corner of the terrace S of the church, a place he chose for himself after a springtime visit of which he wrote

> The view from the churchyard was superb … In front, the hills, just touched with rose; behind, the little grey street, quite silent, thin spirals of smoke coming from the chimneys. The churchyard scattered with snowdrops.

By the gate at the E side of the churchyard are the graves of Frederick Myers (1811–51), first incumbent of the parish and a minor author, and his better-known son F.W.H. Myers (1843–1901), now forgotten as a poet (*St Paul*, 1867; *The Renewal of Youth*, 1882) but remembered as founder of the Society for Psychical Research.

Opposite the church is **Derwentwater Place**. The terrace, now incorporating the Cumbria Hotel, was built by John Richardson, the stonemason poet of St John's Vale. At Number 3, now engulfed by the hotel, William Smith (1808–72), essayist and mystic, used to rent rooms. Here in 1856 he finished his first philosophical dialogue, *Thorndale, or the Conflict of Opinions*, and also met his future wife, the German translator Lucy Cumming, when he went upstairs to complain about Lucy's niece practising the piano while he was trying to write. They married in 1861.

Continue E along Ambleside Road; this becomes Manor Brow. On R (E) you pass a small road called Rogersfield. Here, at **Windrush**, a modern house with a superb view over Derwentwater and Catbells, lived the naturalist Enid J. Wilson, whose *Country Diary*, a rich day-to-day picture of Lakeland wildlife, appeared in the *Guardian* from 1950 until 1988, when it was published in book form.

Continue up Manor Brow and at A591 junction go L (signed Motorway, Penrith). ¼m after junction, on corner as road descends Chestnut Hill, is **Shelley Cottage**, where Shelley and his wife Harriet lived from November 1811 to February 1812, renting it furnished for £1.10s a week – expensive for those days.

Shelley responded to the landscape in characteristic style; though different in political tone, his observations rival Coleridge's in spontaneous intensity:

> I have taken a long *solitary* ramble today. These gigantic mountains piled on each other, these waterfalls, these million shaped clouds tinted by the varying colors of innumerable rainbows hanging between yourself and a lake as smooth and dark as a plain of polished jet, – oh! these are sights admirable to the contemplative.

He told Elizabeth Hitchener,

> Oh! how you will delight in this scenery. These mountains are now capped with snow. The lake as I see it hence is glassy & calm. Snow vapours tinted by the loveliest colours of refraction pass far below the summits of these giant rocks. The scene even in a winter sunset is inexpressibly lovely. The clouds assume shapes which seem peculiar to these regions; ... Oh! give me a little cottage in that scene, let all live in peaceful little houses, let temples and palaces rot with their perishing masters ... I think the Christian Heaven (with its Hell) would be to us no paradise, but such a scene as this! – How my pen runs away with me!

His writings whilst here included the poems 'Mother and Son' and 'The Devil's Walk', and the pamphlet *An Address to the Irish People*. Mary remembered the area too: Cumbrian settings turn up briefly in both *Frankenstein* and *The Last Man*.

Continue N, then R (E) at junction (signed Penrith) and immediately first R for ½m to **Castlerigg Stone Circle** (*NT, some parking in layby*), a Bronze Age monument on the brow of a rounded hill with fine views E over St John's in the Vale and W over Keswick. Almost every eighteenth-century visitor recorded some impression of the stones. Thomas Gray (in 1769) says that they were then in a corn field, and notes:

> a Druid circle of large stones, one hundred and eight feet in diameter, the biggest not eight feet high, but most of them still erect: they are fifty in number ... the sun breaking out, discovered the most enchanting view I have yet seen of the whole valley behind me, the two lakes, the river, the mountains in all their glory.

Coleridge came here with Wordsworth in 1799, and Keats and Brown visited in June 1818. They had already walked from Legburthwaite to Keswick, then all round Derwentwater:

CASTLERIGG STONE CIRCLE
C.W. Dymond, 1877

We had a fag up hill, rather too near dinner time, which was rendered void, by the gratification of seeing those aged stones, on a gentle rise in the midst of Mountains, which at that time darkened all round, except at the fresh opening of the Vale of St John.

The visit probably inspired the simile in *Hyperion* of

a dismal cirque
Of Druid stones upon a forlorn moor,
When the chill rain begins at shut of eve
In dull November.

Southey uses the spot in his *Colloquies* (1829) as the setting for a debate on whether people have improved morally since the days of human sacrifice.

Return to the main road, and continue W into Keswick. Where the road draws alongside the River Greta, walkers may cross the picturesque Calvert Bridge and follow the path NE up to Old Windebrowe. Otherwise continue to the next junction and go R (NE) up Station Road to the **Keswick Museum and Art Gallery**. (*Reliable information about opening times, admission charges, displays etc. cannot be given, since at the time of writing a renovation programme is about to start which will continue for several years. Check with Tourist Information Offices.*) Currently the museum displays letters by Wordsworth, Hugh Walpole and Southey, the manuscripts of many of Walpole's novels, and many books from Southey's library. There is also the only authentic portrait of Jonathan Otley, together with his barometer and other scientific instruments. Its main joy, however, is a marvellous miscellany of oddities – an 1834 scale model of the Lake District, the 'Bell, Rock and Steel Band', the Five Hundred Year Old Cat.

Continue up Station Road and turn R opposite the Leisure Pool into Brundholme Road, then R into Briar Rigg. Follow it ½m to **Old Windebrowe**, now the Calvert Trust Riding Centre for the Disabled. This was formerly Windy Brow, home of Wordsworth's friend and benefactor Raisley Calvert (1773–1795).

William and Dorothy stayed here after their walk through the Lake District in April 1794, and here Wordsworth wrote most of his early poem 'Adventures on Salisbury Plain'. (The 'Wordsworth Rooms' where he lived and wrote are no longer open to the public.)

Two months later Wordsworth returned to act as companion and nurse to Calvert, who was dying of consumption. He remained until Calvert's death in January 1795. Calvert, believing in Wordsworth's future greatness, left him a legacy of £900 which enabled William and Dorothy to live independently at Grasmere, generosity commemorated in a fine sonnet, 'To the Memory of Raisley Calvert'.

During their first visit the Wordsworths made a seat somewhere on the wooded slope between the house and Calvert Bridge. Both Wordsworth and Coleridge wrote poetic 'inscriptions' for it: Wordsworth's is 'Inscription for a Seat by the Pathway Side Ascending to Windy Brow' (1794); Coleridge's is 'Inscription for a Seat by the Road Side Half-way up a Steep Hill Facing South' (1800). The poems are different in wording but so similar in import that one suspects a game or collaboration.

When the Wordsworths settled at Grasmere Windy Brow remained a favourite place: on August 9 1800 Dorothy notes 'I walked with Coleridge in the Windy Brow woods', and on August 13, 'Made [ie repaired] the Windy Brow seat.'

After Raisley's death his brother Robert rebuilt the house and invited the Wordsworths to share it with him; he even proposed adding a laboratory so that they, Coleridge and Humphry Davy could study chemistry here. These plans came to nothing.

Later residents at Windy Brow are glimpsed in Eliza Lynn Linton's autobiographical novel *Christopher Kirkland* (1885). Called in the novel 'Dalrymple', the wife a passionate sentimentalist, the husband an eccentric aesthete, they had an emotionally and intellectually stimulating effect on the young Eliza. Mr Dalrymple

> had a passion for little dogs ... he had exactly twenty; all of rare kinds and of perfect breeds. It was one of the sights of the place to see this elegant, aristocratic-looking man, dressed in the latest fashion – light trousers buttoned round his ankles, light kid gloves, ... hair and whiskers artificially curled and highly perfumed, scented handkerchief and superb jewellery, as if he were in Bond Street, not among the Cumberland mountains – daintily picking his way on the rough roads, with his twenty little dogs, all in pairs, streaming behind him.

From here you may climb Latrigg and/or Skiddaw (see p 143). Otherwise return to Keswick and go NW up the Market Place and along Main Street. From Main Street turn R (NE) into Stanger Street. As you reach the crest of the hill, you will see the entrance to the private car park of Greta Hamlet on your left. Notice the attractive houses and beautiful gardens of Greta Hamlet, a model estate built in 1910 in attractive arts-and-crafts style and reflecting the radical 'garden city' experiments of the time at Welwyn and Letchworth. The Hamlet is still run as a co-operative. Pedestrians may be forgiven for walking into the car park for the best available view of **Greta Hall**, now a private house, home of Samuel Taylor Coleridge from July

SOUTHEY'S STUDY, GRETA HALL
Caroline Southey, 1862

1800 to December 1803, and of Robert Southey from 1803 until his death in 1843.

The house belonged to William Jackson (a carrier, and the original of Benjamin's employer in Wordsworth's 'The Waggoner'), who remodelled it 1799–1800. It has an elegant frontage with curious rounded bays at the sides and a beautiful pillared porch. Coleridge liked to sit on the flat part of the roof and wrote several letters there: one from July 1800 is dated

> From the leads on the housetop of Greta Hall, Keswick, Cumberland, at the present time in the occupancy and usufruct-possession of S.T. Coleridge, Esq, Gentleman-poet and Philosopher in a mist.

Here Coleridge underwent his first serious period of opium addiction (1801) but also worked at political essays for the *Morning Post* and wrote a number of major poems, including Part Two of *Christabel* (1800), 'The Keepsake' (a marvellous sketch of a wet Lakeland summer), 'The Picture' (his most vivid poetic recreation of his impetuous fell-walking), and 'Dejection: An Ode', composed as a verse-letter to Sara Hutchinson in 1802. 'Dejection' shows him watching the night sky from his study-windows and hearing the wind howl outside whilst he philosophically analyses his own loneliness and depression.

Many of his notebook entries describe the views from his study windows at the Hall, often interblended with his own emotions, as in this symphonic passage (which must stand for countless others equally wonderful):

> October 20th – 1802. My 30th birthday – a windy, showery Day – with

great columns of misty Sunshine travelling along the lake toward Borrodale. the Heavens, a confusion of white Clouds in masses, & bright blue Sky – Sunshine on the Bassanthwaite Window, while Rain & Hail was scourging the Newlands window – the whole vale shadow & sunshine, in broad masses. No clouds on the tops of the mountains – I meditating on Switzerland, & writing the Letters to Mr Fox – Eleven in the morning – The crescent moon waning in the Sky – the Sun not far below it. -

½ past one – the whole of Newlands full of a shower-mist drunk & dazzling with Sunshine in one part transparent, & Great Robinson, & The Green Ridge & hollow below or seen thro it. It passed off – & floated across the Lake toward Lodore in flossy silk. The Birches, auburn & gold, shew themselves among the Oak grove – the white flossy Sun-mist floats along, & now Borrodale looks thro it. The upper segment of the arch of the Sky is all blue, bright blue – and the descent on all sides white massy clouds, thrusting their heads into the blue, in mountain shapes.

In 1800 he told Humphry Davy, 'My dear fellow, I would that I could wrap up the view from my House in a pill of opium, & send it to you!'

His visitors included Samuel Rogers (1801), the Wordsworths (many times) and Mary and Charles Lamb (1802), who reported:

Coleridge had got a blazing fire in his study, which is a large antique ill-shaped room, with an old-fashioned organ, never play'd upon, big enough for a church, Shelves of scattered folios, an Eolian Harp, & an old sofa, half bed &c. And all looking out upon the last fading view of Skiddaw & his broad-breasted brethren: what a night!

From here Coleridge set out on the famous walk of August 1800 over Helvellyn by moonlight to the Wordsworths at Grasmere:

The next morning, it being Sunday, Aug. 31, 1800, left my house, crossed the Greta, passed Window brow, went on thro the wood by Wescote and kept the road till it joins the great Turnpike a little above Threlkeld, then got into a field, crossed the Glendaratara, then scaling stone fences wound up along the stony knot at the foot of the green fells/under the White-pike, a hot cloudy Day ...

and so made his way along the whole ridge via Great Dod, Stybarrow Dod, Raise, Helvellyn, Dollywaggon Pike, Grisedale Tarn and down to Grasmere. In August 1802 he set out on an equally memorable walk in the opposite direction, anticlockwise around the western Lakes by way of St Bees, Gosforth, Wasdale, Scafell Pike, Eskdale and Coniston.

After his period in Malta Coleridge, estranged from his wife, rarely visited, the last occasion being in 1812. From 1804 Southey supported Coleridge's family as well as his own wife and seven children.

De Quincey describes his first (1807) visit to Southey in *Recollections of the Lakes and the Lake Poets* (1839). Wordsworth arrived and the two poets made subversive jokes about the royal family. Southey's study, says De Quincey, contained a magnificent library in English, Spanish and Portuguese, 'decorated externally with reasonable elegance':

This effect was aided by the horizontal arrangement upon brackets of many rare manuscripts – Spanish or Portuguese. Made thus gay within, this room stood in little need of attractions from without. Yet, even upon the gloomiest day of winter, the landscape from the different windows was too permanently commanding in its grandeur, ... to fail in fascinating the gaze of the coldest and dullest of spectators.

Here Southey wrote many of his poems (including 'My days among the dead are past,' 'The Cataract of Lodore', and the epics *Madoc* (1805), *The Curse of Kehama* (1810) and *Roderick* (1814)), and his many essays and historical works.

Shelley sought out Southey (whose early radical works he admired) here in December 1811. It was an odd encounter: the fiery youth went to accuse the now-conservative Southey of political treachery, but found a gentle, modest man whom he could not dislike. Southey told Shelley 'Ah! when you are as old as I am you will think with me' – a suggestion which worried Shelley a good deal. For his part, Southey said that Shelley 'acts upon me as my own ghost would do. He is just what I was in 1794'. Another, though milder, visitor with radical views was John Stuart Mill, who stayed here for some days during his 1831 tour.

Coleridge's daughter, Sara, the essayist, children's writer and editor of her father's works, was born here in 1802 and her autobiography gives a vivid description of

dear Greta Hall [with its] orchard of not very productive apple trees and plum trees [below which] a wood stretched down to the river side ... Oh that rough path beside the Greta! How much of my childhood, of my girlhood, of my youth, was spent there!

She recalls the study 'where my Uncle [Southey] sate all day occupied with literary labours & researches'; downstairs were the kitchen and the pantry where

clogs and pattens were ranged in a row for out of door roamings ... ranged in a row from the biggest to the least & curiously emblem[ing] the various stages of life.

Sara's life nearly ended abruptly, for at the age of two she fell 'between the rails of the high wooden bridge that crossed the Greta' whilst playing. She was saved by the local blacksmith. To see the bridge (now replaced with a safer metal one), return to Stanger Street and continue L (NE) to the end, where it joins a footpath running alongside the river.

Coleridge found the **River Greta** itself a source of inspiration at times. He often sat at his window watching the moon on the Greta, and Wordsworth wrote a sonnet 'To the River Greta, near Keswick' in 1833:

Greta, what fearful listening! when huge stones
Rumble along thy bed, block after block:
Or, whirling with reiterated shock,
Combat, while darkness aggravates the groans ...

The weird noise made by the river is noted by Coleridge too:

> By the bye, Greta, or rather Grieta, is exactly the Cocytus of the Greeks –
> the word litterally rendered in modern English is 'The loud Lamenter' – to
> Griet in the Cumbrian Dialect signifying to roar aloud for grief or pain -:
> and it does roar with a vengeance!

The boulders which produced the sound have since been removed for
building.

Return to Main Street. Turn R by the bridge to the **Cumberland Pencil
Museum** (*open 9.30–4 every day except Christmas, Boxing Day and New
Year's Day; car park; admission charge*). Attached to the buildings of the
only surviving Keswick pencil factory, the museum has displays on the
history of graphite mining and pencil making, and a vast collection of early
and unusual pencils. There are also videos connected with the industry
(the animated film of Raymond Briggs's *The Snowman* was drawn with
Cumberland coloured pencils).

Return to the main road. By the bridge are two monuments to the 'Arts
and Crafts' movement of the turn of the century. The Italian restaurant at
the bridge's NW side was the **School of Industrial Arts**, founded by Canon
Rawnsley to teach woodwork, metalwork and other crafts; it ran until the
1984. Its frontage carries the motto

> The Loving Eye And Patient Hand
> Shall Work With Joy And Bless The Land.

200yds further N is the seventeenth-century **Porch Cottage**, home of
Marian Twelves, a teacher of spinning formerly living in Langdale. A disciple of Ruskin, she came to Keswick in 1889 to encourage spinning and set
up looms to weave flax as part of the School of Industrial Arts. The
Keswick Linen Industry continued for many years and had widespread
influence: Gandhi heard of it and made hand-spinning part of his vision of
a new India.

Crosthwaite

Continue N ¼m along High Hill and at the corner go R along Church Lane to
St Kentigern's Church, Crosthwaite. This is probably the church whose
origin (about 550AD) is described by Jocelin of Furness, who says that
Kentigern

> heard that many among the mountains were given to idolatry ... Thither he
> turned aside, and, God helping him, ... remained some time in a thickly
> planted place, ... where he erected a cross as a sign of the faith; whence it
> took the name, in English, of Crosfeld ... In which very locality a basilica,
> recently erected, is dedicated to the name of blessed Kentigern.

The church is famous not only for its early foundation but for its association with the remarkable Canon H.D. Rawnsley (1851–1920), (vicar here
1883–1917). Rawnsley's accomplishments were many: minor poet, disciple of Ruskin, patron of arts and handicrafts, conservationist, fighter for
public access to the countryside, biographer, topographer and local histo-

rian, placer of monuments and inscriptions, indefatigable lecturer, joint founder of the National Trust, a generous, devout and socially-concerned clergyman who seems to have enjoyed every moment of his incredibly full life, he must often have seemed absurd or irritating but he pioneered values – social, aesthetic and ecological – which most of us now take for granted.

We meet his influence at once, for he designed the salmon, bell and other Celtic motifs on the churchyard gate, and the fact that the church is full of good woodcarving, metalwork, mosiac and stained glass is his doing, or the result of his example.

An earlier vicar (1820–1855) was James Lynn, father of the novelist Eliza Lynn Linton. She recalls the church's then condition in her autobiographical *Christopher Kirkland* (1885): the structure was drab and dilapidated; 'the pews were the familiar old cattle-pens of every size and shape, wherein the congregation sat in all directions and went to sleep in the corners comfortably.' Southey was one of the congregation, but though he

> came regularly to church, as any other decent body might, when the prayers were over he ostentatiously folded his arms, shut his eyes, and sat during the sermon in a state of frigid indifferentism, like one no more interested in the proceedings. He had done his duty to God and the Establishment by saying his prayers and following the service; to the sermon, which was purely personal, he openly refused to give his attention.

Ruskin's *Iteriad* confirms the filthy condition of the church in 1830

> ... [we] were shown into a seat
> With everything, save what was wanted, replete;
> And so dirty, and greasy, though many times dusted,
> The ladies all thought it could never be trusted.

But he was consoled by seeing Southey, whose 'dark lightning-eye made him seem half-inspired'; his prose journal adds that the poet seemed 'extremely attentive & by what we saw of him we should think him very pious.'

Inside the church, note the baptistry, a monument to Rawnsley and his wife. In the ringing chamber under the tower is a set of 'Orders' for the bell-ringers, in verse, dated 1826:

> He who in ringing interrupts a Peal,
> For such offence shall pay a quart of Ale.
> In falling Bells one Penny must be paid,
> By him who stops before the Signal's made,
> And he who takes God's Holy Name in vain
> Shall pay one shilling and this place refrain ...

In the S aisle, just beside the sanctuary, is a tablet to William Brownrigg of Ormathwaite, and near it the memorial to Robert Southey, a stiff but elegant figure reclined on an enormous pile of cushions on a Gothic 'tomb'

CROSTHWAITE CHURCH
W.J. Linton, 1864

(though he is actually buried outside). The quiet but splendid verse epitaph is by Wordsworth, who fretted a great deal about the wording: one can see that the last line had to be recut.

The church makes a fictional appearance in Hugh Walpole's novel *The Bright Pavilions*, where Gilbert Armstrong and Catherine Hostetter are dragged and forcibly married here by the mob which has just burnt Frau Hostetter on top of Blencathra.

In the churchyard Southey's grave is clearly signed near the N side of the church. A yard away, under a tree, is the grave of Jonathan Otley, and further N, close to a large conifer, that of William Knight (1836-1916), the pioneer editor of Wordsworth. The graves of Canon Rawnsley and his wife Eleanor are by the path at the N end of the churchyard. Under the church wall, by the most easterly window of the N side, is a memorial tablet (beside her father's tomb) to Eliza Lynn Linton, whose ashes were scattered here.

Return S along Church Lane and turn L up Vicarage Hill. Go past entrance to new vicarage; at the top of hill opposite Lairbeck Hotel is the original **Crosthwaite Vicarage**, now a private house with no public access. Thomas Gray stayed here on October 4 1769, and wrote to his friend Thomas Wharton,

> I got to the Parsonage a little before sunset, and saw in my glass a picture, that if I could transmit to you, and fix it in all the softness of its living colours, would fairly sell for a thousand pounds. This is the sweetest scene I can yet discover in point of pastoral beauty; the rest are in a sublimer style.

The terrace commands a fine view S over Derwentwater, and is West's eighth Derwentwater 'Station': he identifies the 'horsing-block' (now gone) as the exact place to stand. Canon Rawnsley had the passage from Gray's letters inscribed on the stone parapet of the terrace, where it can still be seen.

Eliza Lynn Linton (1822–90) was born in the vicarage, daughter of the Reverend James Lynn, and spent her childhood here. She describes it in *The Autobiography of Christopher Kirkland* (1885), a novel which (despite its male protagonist) is a disguised autobiography.

Her mother died when Eliza was five months old, and her upbringing was chaotic: she had no schooling, and when her father was asked by the bishop of Carlisle what he intended to do for his children, his reply was 'Sit in the study, my Lord, smoke my pipe, and commit them to the care of Providence.' Parental discipline took the form of occasional floggings, and Eliza was sometimes locked in a dark cupboard under the stairs for punishment.

On the other hand,

> we had a hay-field, a farm-yard, and two cows – 'Cushie' and 'Hornie' – which in the summer evenings we used to go with the cook to bring home from the field to the milking-byre. I think I could replace every dock and ragwort and plot of nettles and mayweed in that ragged bit of pasture-land, sloping down to the little brook where the minnows were.

Most of the field is now built over.

Eliza largely educated herself, and left home in 1845 to live as a writer in London, becoming the first successful English woman journalist, a prominent novelist and (paradoxically) both a pioneer of female emancipation and an attacker of feminism. Her most famous work was her essay 'The Girl of the Period' (1868), an attack on the modern woman as

> a creature who dyes her hair and paints her face ... a creature whose sole idea of life is fun; whose sole aim is unbounded luxury ... She lives to please herself, and does not care if she displeases everyone else.

She returned to visit the vicarage in 1889, when she was 67:

> I went through the Limepots to the vicarage; asked the servant to go into the garden, and made her take me through the hall into the kitchen; ... went into the study and touched the old book-shelves and cupboards; looked into the pantry and the larder place where we had the flour-bin; and then went over the garden. The gardener gave me a bunch of flowers, and I gave him a shilling ... I feel half in a dream here. It is Keswick and yet not Keswick, as I am Eliza Lynn and yet not Eliza Lynn.

Her host on this visit was the then Vicar, Canon Rawnsley.

Somewhere in the fields beyond Crosthwaite Church was the campsite where Wilfred Owen stayed in July 1912 when he attended the **Keswick Convention**, an Evangelical Christian gathering which still meets in Keswick each July. The headquarters are now in Skiddaw Street. Owen's letters describe the camp, 'about a mile and a half from the Town' and his tent with three beds, each equipped with 'one blanket (of stuff like sack-cloth!)'. He found the food 'very ordinary indeed' and the tea 'horrid';

nor was he much impressed by the preaching. More significant was his meeting with

> a Northumberland lad who works in the pits, whose soul-life and Christianity is altogether beyond my understanding. He has absolute peace of mind; [and] faith before which mountains not only sink, but never become visible.

Owen's admiration for the boy helped to inspire his 1918 poem 'Miners'. He also found time to climb Latrigg and enjoy the views from Castle Head and Friar's Crag, but did not write about 'mountains or lakes or streams ... Surely if Wordsworth, Coleridge, Southey, Shelley, and Ruskin made it a matter of years to describe them, I cannot do so now'. It rained for most of his visit.

Latrigg and Skiddaw

To reach **Latrigg**, go uphill past Old Windebrowe, cross small concrete bridge and take stile by gate. A permissive path runs N straight up the slope for a strenuous ½m to the top. The views S over Derwentwater, N to Bassenthwaite and Skiddaw, are marvellous and there is a well-positioned seat. This was West's seventh 'station' for viewing Derwentwater.

Coleridge walked here with his children soon after moving to Greta Hall in 1800 and recorded a splendid skyscape:

> August 24 – Sunday Evening, walked to Latterrigg with Sara & Hartley – the Sun set with slant columns of misty light slanted from him/the light a bright Buff – /Walla Crag purple red, the lake a deep dingy purple blue – that Torrent Crag opposite Elder seat a Marone – /but the Clouds – that great Egg – almost 1/20 of the whole Heaven in appearance – a fine *smoke-flame*/ ... As we turned round on our return, we see a moving pillar of clouds, flame & smoke, rising, bending, arching, and in swift motion – from what God's chimney doth it issue?

And in the autumn he was up here thinking about his poem on the 'Windy Brow Seat'; his notebook records a wonderful stream-ofconsciousness:

> The Sopha of Sods – whole life – sliding down Lattrig – Snow-tree – planting & sowing – poem hid in a tin box – stooping from sublime Thoughts to reckon how many Lines the poem would make/

From the summit a path leads N to the foot of the fell and then E beside the wood to the car park. From here you can take the road W to Applethwaite and Keswick, or follow the bridleway NE for Skiddaw. At the fork after 200yds the R path runs 200yds up Whit Beck then turns E and follows the contour 2½m to Skiddaw House. The L path runs NW 2½m to Skiddaw summit.

Skiddaw House, a former shooting lodge, later a shepherd's bothy and now the highest Youth Hostel in Britain, is a mysterious and dramatically remote building. It appears as the scene of the duel between Uhland and John Herries in Hugh Walpole's *The Fortress* – one of Walpole's most

SKIDDAW HOUSE
A. Wainwright, 1962

successful and frightening episodes. It is also the model for 'Green House' in Walpole's later 'Elizabethan' novel *The Bright Pavilions*, where Robin Herries attends a secret celebration of the Mass.

From Skiddaw House follow the track NW 2m for **Whitewater Dash**, a steep waterfall. Coleridge was here in 1800 and noted its 'variety & complexity – parts rushing in wheels, other parts perpendicular, some in white horse-tails ... they are the finest Water furies, I ever beheld'. From the fall the track continues NW to join the Keswick road.

The main routes up **Skiddaw** are from Millbeck near Applethwaite and from the N side of Latrigg. It is the easiest of the high Lakeland mountains to ascend, but the most often clouded.

Skiddaw has been more written about than any other British mountain. Conspicuous from all roads into Keswick, it was a famous tourist attraction (and wrongly regarded as England's highest mountain) long before its rivals, Helvellyn and the more remote Scafells, were much thought of. Camden (c 1580) quotes a proverb that

> Skiddaw, Lanvedin, and Casticand
> Are the highest mountains in all England.

('Casticand' is Catstycam, 'Lanvedin' Helvellyn).

It was even famous enough to be the one Lakeland place mentioned by that inveterate Londoner, William Blake: it appears in *Jerusalem* (1804–20) as a sinister setting where Hand, one of the Sons of Albion, is betrayed by his consort Cambel:

Hand slept on Skiddaw's top, drawn by the love of the beautiful
Cambel, his bright beaming Counterpart, divided from him;
And her delusive light beam'd fierce above the Mountain,
Soft, invisible, drinking his sighs in sweet intoxication.

Dr John Dalton in 1755 found its height almost too alarming to contemplate, and ends with apologies to the ladies addressed in his 'Descriptive Poem':

Supreme of mountains, Skiddow, hail!
To whom all Britain sinks a vale! ...
'Twere glorious now his side to climb,
Boldly to scale his top sublime,
And thence – My muse, these flights forbear,
Nor with wild raptures tire the fair.

Having a kind of double summit (the so-called Little Man, 1m SE of the true summit, is only about 200ft lower), it was early seen by poets as an English equivalent of Mount Parnassus, classical source of poetic inspiration and famously 'two-headed' in Greek poetry. Thus Drayton's *Poly-Olbion* (1619) hails

Of the Cambrian Hills, proud *Skiddo* that doth show
The high'st, respecting whome, the other be but low, ...
And of the Mountain kind, as of all other he,
Most like *Pernassus* selfe that is suppos'd to be,
Having a double head, as hath that sacred Mount,
Which those nine sacred Nymphs held in so hie account.

And Wordsworth asked (in 'Pelion and Ossa flourish side by side'), 'What was the great Parnassus' self to Thee/Mount Skiddaw?' Even Ellen Weeton in 1810 sensed the mountain's quality of literary dominance, noting in her journal that 'The great and noble Skiddaw ... is among mountains what Dr. Johnson was amongst authors'.

Perhaps the oddest compliment paid to the mountain was Edward Lear's, who after his 1836 tour boasted to a friend 'I know every corner in Westmoreland; Scawfell Pikes is my cousin, and Skiddaw is my mother in law.' Since both mountains are in Cumberland, his geography is as odd as everything else in this statement from the master of nonsense.

Skiddaw even has its own Christmas carol, the early twentieth-century 'Carol of the Skiddaw Yows' by Edmund Casson, hauntingly set to music by Ivor Gurney.

Recorded ascents of Skiddaw (normally by pony) began surprisingly early. Bishop Nicolson went up for the view in 1684; in 1689 John Adams, surveying for what he hoped would be the first accurate map of England and Wales, built a hut near the summit

to contain his telescopes and optic glasses, whereby he was enabled to give a better description of the two counties; but being arrested by his engraver, and death soon following, his labours were lost.

William Stukeley (1724) writes:

> The ascent of this hill (Skiddaw) is from the east, for the west side of it is
> exceeding steep, and drawn down into frightful ribs, like the roots of a tree
> ... Cnut-berries grow a-top of it, a delicious fruit.

William Wilberforce climbed it in September 1779 and found it less daunting than he expected. Indeed, from a distance, with its many steep spurs it
'look'd like the hundred-handed Giant Briareus'; once climbed, however,
'Its Top is perfectly green & has a beautiful appearance; compare it to a
Woman or a green Cushion.'

Coleridge addressed Skiddaw in 'A Stranger Minstrel' (1800). He also
records a curious experience at the summit:

> I was standing on the very top of Skiddaw, by a little shed of Slate-stones
> on which I had scribbled with a bit of slate my name among the other
> names – a lean expressive-faced Man came up the Hill, stood beside me, a
> little while, then running over the names, exclaimed, *Coleridge*! I lay my
> life, that is the *Poet Coleridge*.

The most often-quoted account of the summit-view is Charles Lamb's
(he and Mary came up whilst staying with Coleridge in August 1802):

> O its fine black head & the bleak air a top of it, with a prospect of
> mountains all about & about, making you giddy, & then Scotland afar off &
> the border countries so famous in song & ballad -. It was a day that will
> stand out, like a mountain, I am sure, in my life.

Keats and Brown got up at four in the morning to climb Skiddaw on their
June 1818 walking tour.

The alarmingly precocious twelve-year-old Ruskin, in *Iteriad*, gives a
picture of a typical early Victorian ascent of Skiddaw *via* Latrigg: a fussy,
bustling affair of guides, ponies, spare riding skirts for the ladies, cloaks,
mantles, tied-on hats, sips of brandy and huge quantities of food.

It was left to Henry Alford, in his sonnet 'Summit of Skiddaw, July 7,
1838', to celebrate in verse the all-too-common experience of getting to the
top and being unable to see a thing:

> At length here stand we, wrapt as in the cloud
> In which light dwelt before the sun was born ...
>
> ...Alone and in a shroud
> Of dazzling mist, while the wind whistling loud
> Buffets thy streaming locks:- result forlorn
> For us who up yon steep our way have worn,
> Elate with hope, and of our daring proud.

Macaulay imagined an Elizabethan warning-beacon on the summit,
and fixed the image with two resounding lines in 'The Armada' (1832):

> Skiddaw saw the fire that burned on Gaunt's embattled pile
> And the red glare on Skiddaw roused the burghers of Carlisle

– the 'pile' being Lancaster Castle. But there was no beacon on Skiddaw until Peter Crosthwaite built one in 1796. Since then, many celebratory fires have been lit.

On August 21 1815 Wordsworth and Southey joined a crowd to celebrate the Battle of Waterloo, eating roast beef and plum pudding around a bonfire of blazing tar barrels. Wordsworth enlivened the festivities by accidentally kicking over the kettle that held water to dilute the gentry's rum punch. Bravely, the company drank it undiluted.

Derwentwater and its islands

For a circular walk or drive round the lake, turn to p 151. For the moment we contemplate the lake from the point nearest Keswick. Follow signs through Keswick to Lakeside and the Lake Road car park. Opposite the car park is **Crow Park** (*NT*), a meadow sloping gently down to the shore of the lake. Gray was here in 1769, admiring the long shades of the sunset and noting that 'At a distance were heard the murmurs of many water-falls, not audible in the day-time'. Next day he was back, observing that the Park, 'now a rough pasture', was

> once a glade of ancient oaks, whose large roots still remain on the ground, but nothing has sprung from them. If one single tree had remained, this would have been an unparalleled spot ... for it is a gentle eminence, not too high, on the very margin of the water, and commanding it from end to end, looking full into the gorge of Borrowdale.

The felling of the oaks was the end of a larger tragedy, for Crow Park had belonged to the last Earl of Derwentwater, who rashly joined the Jacobite rebellion in 1715. When the rebellion failed he was executed for treason and his estate was given to the commissioners of Greenwich Hospital. The commissioners sold the oaks and they were cut down in 1751. There was much local opposition, partly on aesthetic grounds – perhaps the first occasion on which there was public protest over damage to the environment, and an indication that picturesque taste had established itself in educated public opinion. Following Gray, West listed the meadow as his second Derwentwater 'station'.

Early writers were more interested in copper than in the view. Typical is Drayton's *Poly-Olbion* (which seems to assume that the mines are on an island, and that Thirlmere is linked to Derwentwater):

> Where *Darwent* her cleere Fount from Borodale that brings,
> Doth quickly cast her selfe into an ample Lake,
> And with *Thurls* mighty Mere, betweene them two doe make
> An Island, which the name from *Darwent* doth derive,
> Within whose secret breast nice Nature doth contrive,
> That mighty Copper Myne, which not without its Vaines,
> Of Gold and Silver found, it happily obtaines
> Of Royaltie the name, the richest of them all
> That *Britan* bringeth forth, which Royall she doth call.

Eighteenth-century writers were fascinated by the view s down the lake to Borrowdale, and liked to contrast the rugged 'sublimity' of the craggy Borrowdale end of the valley with the milder 'beauty' of the lake's northern shores. Thus Thomas Pennant in 1774:

> The two extremities of the lake afford most discordant prospects: the southern is a composition of all that is horrible; an immense chaos opens in the midst, whose entrance is divided by a rude conic hill, once topt with a castle, the habitation of the tyrant of the rocks; beyond, a series of broken mountainous crags, now patched with snow, soar one above the other, overshadowing the dark winding deeps of *Borrowdale*. In these black recesses are lodged variety of minerals, the origin of evil by their abuse, and placed by nature, not remote from the fountain of it ...

> But the opposite or northern view is in all respects a strong and beautiful contrast: *Skiddaw* shews its vast base, and bounding all that part of the vale, rises gently to a height that sinks the neighbouring hills; opens a pleasing front, smooth and verdant, smiling over the country like a gentle generous lord, while the *fells* of *Borrowdale* frown on it like a hardened tyrant.

Gilpin, who visited in 1772, records the judgement of 'an ingenious person who, on seeing the lake for the first time, 'cryed out, *"Here is beauty indeed – Beauty lying in the lap of Horrour!"*'. For, says Gilpin, 'Nothing conveys an idea of beauty more strongly, than the lake; nor of *horrour*, than the mountains'. Exaggerated descriptions became the norm, so that later visitors were often disappointed.

Twelve-year-old John Ruskin records a visit to the lake in *Iteriad* (1830–31): more interesting than his conventional praise of the picturesque is this glimpse of women doing their laundry near Crow Park:

> But there on the beach – and with shame be it said –
> Some women were washing, – oh, women indeed! –
> Disfiguring the Derwent, their linen were washing,
> And tubbing, and wetting, and splashing, and dashing.
> They hung them all out on the boughs to be dried,
> And clothed with a margin of linen the tide!

The lake's three largest islands, and the only ones of significant size, are all towards the N end. They have a rich past. The northernmost is **Derwent Island**. In the 1560s German miners were quartered here, partly for their own protection against suspicious natives. Hugh Walpole's novel *The Bright Pavilions* gives a fictional (and wholly improbable) picture of the island at this time flourishing under 'proper German tidiness':

> There was a brewery with living-rooms adjoining it. There was a pigeon-house painted a bright green; a windmill painted crimson, and a smooth lawn running to the Lake edge, box hedges and flowers – now all the flowers of the spring – in lines and pools of colour under the open sky.

Something like this regimented neatness was in fact created in the late eighteenth century by 'Squire' Joseph Pocklington, a retired banker who bought it, briskly changed its name to 'Pocklington's Island' and built a house there, 'a tall square habitation' – to quote Wordsworth – 'with four sides exposed, like an astronomer's observatory, or a warren-house' surrounded with 'platoons of firs', a mock church, a 'Druid' circle and a miniature fort. Coleridge in 1799 catalogued several further enormities, including the landscaped waterfall at Barrow House which we shall pass shortly:

> Pocklington shaved off the Branches of an Oak, Whitewashed & shaped it into an Obelisk – Art beats Nature – ... Commonplace Cascade at King Pocky's.

According to the architect's grandson, when the island house was built

> they took the materials up on a ladder; and, when nearly finished, it was found he had forgot the staircase, which had to be put in the best corner they could find.

Pocklington also organised a series of regattas on the lake during the 1780s. Typically the entertainment included a mock naval battle with plenty of cannon, boat races, running races and a firework display, all rather vulgar and thoroughly enjoyable. Walpole recreates one such evening in Chapter V of *Judith Paris*. West's *Guide* (1784) gives an account of the 1782 regatta, including a mock-attack on Pocklington's Island, and James Clarke wrote a not-very-good poem 'On the Regatta at Keswick, 1786'.

St Herbert's Island is traditionally the site of the Saint's hermitage. According to Bede,

> There was a priest of praiseworthy life named Herebert, who ... lived the life of a hermit on an island in the great lake which is the source of the river Derwent.

Herbert's friendship with St Cuthbert (whom he used to visit at his hermitage on Farne Island) was so close that when he heard Cuthbert was dying he prayed that he might die at the same time. His prayer was granted; both saints are said to have died on the same day in 688. Traces of the foundations of a small building are still just visible on the island – not the Saint's cell but the chapel raised there for pilgrims who came after his death: around 1374 there was an annual pilgrimage to the island on April 13, and in modern times Canon Rawnsley revived the custom with an annual sermon on the island, the congregation going over in boats. The event is no longer annual, but still happens from time to time.

Wordsworth tells the Saint's story in 'For the Spot Where the Hermitage Stood on St Herbert's Island'.

Samuel Rogers, who must have passed here on one of his tours to Scotland, uses the island, and the S end of the lake, as setting for an episode in *The Pleasures of Memory* (1792), in the slightly absurd tale of Florio, 'a blithe and blooming forester' and his sweetheart Julia:

The rapt youth, recoiling from the roar,
Gazed on the tumbling tide of dread Lodore;
And thro' the rifted cliffs, that scal'd the sky,
Derwent's clear mirror charmed his dazzled eye.
Each osier isle, inverted on the wave,
Thro' morn's grey mist its melting colours gave:
And, o'er the cygnet's haunt, the mantling grove
Its emerald arch with wild luxuriance wove.

He takes his betrothed for a trip on the lake, but a squall overturns the boat and she is drowned.

When Beatrix Potter sketched lake views in 1901 as backgrounds for *The Tale of Squirrel Nutkin*, she based 'Owl Island' on St Herbert's Island (though Old Brown's Oak was drawn from a tree at Fawe Park).

Paradoxically, Derwentwater's most famous island is rarely seen, and some visitors refuse to believe that it exists. This is the **Floating Island**, a curiosity which fascinated the Victorians. Not really floating at all but simply a temporary bulge in the bed of the lake, it appears above the surface for a few days or weeks at a time in hot summers and (according to Jonathan Otley) is

> situated in the south-east corner of the lake, not far from Lowdore, about 150 yards from the shore, where the depth of the water does not exceed six feet in a mean state of the lake ... it generally rises after an interval of a few years, and towards the conclusion of a warm summer. Its figure and dimensions are variable; it has sometimes contained about half an acre of ground, at other times only a few perches.

It was prodded and analysed by several leading nineteenth-century scientists including John Dalton, Adam Sedgwick and Otley himself, all of whom came to the same conclusion – that decaying vegetable matter, probably peat, was somehow trapped under layers of mud and clay at the shallow end of the lake. When summer heat increased the rate of decay the gases collected and pushed up a 'blister' in the lake bottom. Dalton identified the gases as 'carburetted hydrogen and azotic gases, and some carbonic acid' (in modern terms methane, nitrogen and carbon dioxide). John Stuart Mill saw it in July 1831 and noted its unimpressive appearance:

> it seems a kind of bog, barely above the level of the water and covered with the vegetation that grows in the shallow part of the lake.

Probably its most recent literary appearance is in 'The Floating Island', a puzzling poem (c 1940) by Drummond Allison, where the poet's imagination is compared to 'the Floating Island which each summer/Swells up submerges out on Derwentwater'. The 'island' still appears in most hot summers, generally during August, though it is smaller than it used to be: really no more than a large flattish area of vegetable matter.

A circuit of Derwentwater

From Crow Park walk S along the shore past the landing stages to **Friar's Crag** (*NT*). This famous beauty-spot (West's second Derwentwater 'station') is the 'Darien' of Arthur Ransome's *Swallows and Amazons*, the promontory which 'dropped, like a cliff, into the lake' and where the children camp (though Ransome moves it to a composite Coniston-Windermere landscape). At the top of the knoll is a memorial to John Ruskin, who first visited the spot with his parents at the age of five and wrote:

> The first thing which I remember, as an event in life, was being taken by my nurse to the brow of Friar's Crag on Derwent Water; the intense joy mingled with awe, that I had in looking through the hollows in the mossy roots, over the crag into the dark lake, has ever associated itself more or less with all twining roots of trees ever since.

Later he described the view from the Crag as 'one of the three most beautiful scenes in Europe'. The Memorial, placed here in 1900, is of Borrowdale Stone, with lettering drawn by W.G. Collingwood and cut by a local mason. It was also a favourite spot of Southey's, who wrote that 'In the field adjoining Friar's Crag ... if I had Aladdin's lamp, or Fortunatus' purse, ... I would build myself a house.' Mercifully, he had neither.

Return to the landing stages and thence to the lakeside road (B5289). The first patch of woodland adjoining the road is Castlehead Wood. Where pavement stops take path into wood and up slope of **Castle Head** (*NT*) (West's third 'station'), which gives a lovely view over the town and lake. Another station is reached by continuing S along the road until it runs close to the water once more at **Calfclose Bay**. We are following in the foot-

DERWENTWATER BY MOONLIGHT
W.J. Linton, 1864

steps of Thomas Gray, who describes delightfully his walk from Keswick to Borrowdale in 1769:

> Oct. 3. A heavenly day; rose at seven and walked out under the conduct of my landlord to Borrowdale; the grass covered with a hoar-frost, which soon melted and exhaled in a thin bluish smoke; crossed the meadows, obliquely catching a diversity of views among the hills over the lake and islands, and changing prospect at every ten paces ... to the left the jaws of Borrowdale, with that turbulent chaos of mountain behind mountain, rolled in confusion; beneath you, and stretching far away to the right, the shining purity of the lake reflecting rocks, woods, fields, and inverted tops of hills, just ruffled by the breeze, enough to show it is alive.

Gray was looking – Claude glass in hand – from Calfclose Bay:

> here [he says] the glass played its part divinely, the place is called Carf-close-reeds; and I chose to set down these barbarous names, that any body may inquire on the place, and easily find the particular station that I mean.

Notice the split boulder on the shore, carved with a delicate web-like pattern by sculptor Peter Randall-Page to commemorate the centenary of the National Trust.

Just before the S edge of the wood the road passes close to **Cat Gill**, a small vivid waterfall with a large boulder across it. From a stile just above the road a footpath leads up the gill, emerging at the top on to **Walla Crag**. This was a favourite route of Southey's, who in his *Colloquies* describes a walk up the Gill with his children. 'The walk', he says, 'has just that degree of difficulty and enterprise wherein children delight and may safely be indulged.' It is possible to follow the path along the top of the crag NE 1m to Rakefoot and so back to Keswick.

Near the middle of the crag is a steep cleft or gulley known as **Lady's Rake**, traditionally said to be the route by which Lady Derwentwater escaped after her husband's execution, fleeing the local people who blamed her for her husband's illfated involvement in the 1715 rebellion. Until well into the nineteenth century a white stone up here used to be pointed out as 'Lady Derwentwater's handkerchief', supposedly dropped during her escape.

Return to the road. ¼m S of Cat Gill a road runs uphill to Ashness Bridge and Watendlath. If you want to take it, turn to p 161. We go past it 200yds to **Barrow House** (now Derwentwater Youth Hostel), built (1787–97) as 'Cascade House' by Joseph Pocklington. King Pocky (as Coleridge called him) also altered the course of the waterfall behind the house to give a better view from the interior. 'What a possession for a dining-room window! – an outlook right into the heart of a waterfall, not a hundred yards away!' exclaimed Eliza Lynn Linton. The waterfall is spectacular, though the dining-room view is now somewhat obscured by bushes.

If you intend to visit the Lodore Falls, after passing Barrow House you should look out for the Kettlewell Car Park. There is no suitable car park

SOUTHEY ABOVE CAT GILL
William Westall, 1829

nearer to Lodore, though the Falls can pleasantly be reached by launch from the Keswick boat-landings, so if you are driving you should park at Kettlewell and take the signed footpath to Lodore.

Half a mile further S and impossible to miss is the **Lodore Hotel**. In 1789 this was still what Clarke calls 'Low-low-Door, a neat and commodious little Inn.' It has followed the usual process of hypertrophy whereby successful Lakeland inns grow over the centuries into enormous hotels, and is now a vast Victorian building with late twentieth-century additions. Behind the hotel, reached by a signed path, are the famous **Lodore Falls** (*minuscule admission charge*). In 1854 Harriet Martineau advised visitors that

> To visit the fall, the way is through the gay little garden, and the orchard, (where the fish-preserves are terrible temptations to waste of time) and over a foot bridge, and up into the wood, where the path leads to the front of the mighty chasm.

The path and footbridge are still there, though the back of the hotel is now a barren waste of loading bays and ventilation-ducts, and in place of the fishponds visitors find themselves admiring the hotel swimming-pool through the curved plate glass windows. But at least the hotel no longer keeps a cannon on the lakeshore to 'awaken an uproar from the surrounding crags' as it did until late-Victorian days. 'Don Espriella', Southey's Spanish mouthpiece in his satirical *Letters from England* (1807), paid for

> a cannon to display the echo; it was discharged for us, and we heard the sound rolling from hill to hill, – but for this we paid four shillings ... So that English echoes appear to be the most expensive luxuries in which a traveller can indulge. It is true there was an inferior one which would have

cost only two shillings and sixpence; but when one buys an echo, who would be content for the sake of saving eighteen pence, to put up with second best, instead of ordering at once the extra-double-superfine?

Beatrix Potter's journal reveals that in the 1880s the Hotel had 'a very bad name. Keswick roughs have a regular habit of getting drunk there every Sunday, and Saturday too.' On August 16 1885, when she was staying nearby,

> five Keswick men and one from Penrith went to Lodore Hotel to drink, and coming back at 8 o'clock, dusk, began fighting, upset the boat, and they were drowned ... They belonged to the lowest set in the town, and will not be missed.

She adds that 'There have been many drownings on this lake, but invariably caused by drink ... Bodies are always upright, on their head or feet' – recalling Wordsworth's account of the drowned man 'bolt upright' in Esthwaite Water.

The falls, descending in a wooded cleft between the towering portals of Gowder Crag (NE) and Shepherd's Crag (SW), were early celebrated as an example of 'sublime' landscape. The first poet to describe them at length was Dr John Dalton, whose *Descriptive Poem* (1755) is full of excited ambivalence:

> Horrors like these at first alarm,
> But soon with savage grandeur charm
> And raise to noblest thought the mind:
> Thus by thy fall, Lodore reclin'd,
> The craggy cliff, impendent wood,
> Whose shadows mix o'er half the flood,
> The gloomy clouds, which solemn sail,
> Scarce lifted by the languid gale
> O'er the caped hill, and darken'd vale; ...
> I view with wonder, and delight,
> A pleasing, tho' an awful sight.

Arthur Young, visiting in 1768, takes the same overwrought tone in prose:

> You look up to two dreadful pointed rocks, of a vast height, which almost hang over your head, partly scattered with shrubby wood, in the wildest taste of nature. Between them is a dreadful precipice of broken craggy rock, over which a raging torrrent foams down in one vast sheet of water, several yards wide ... Nothing can be fancied more grand, more beautiful, or romantic.

Thomas West in 1778 called it 'the Niagara of the lake', to which his editor William Cockin added a footnote:

> I do not know that the height of this cataract has ever been estimated, but when viewing it, the reader may like to have it recalled to his mind, that Carver says, the fall of Niagara does not exceed 140 feet.

Surprisingly enough, Cockin is not far out: the drop at Niagara is 162 feet, only some twelve feet more than at Lodore. There, however, the similarity ends.

Keats, in June 1818, took a more down-to-earth view, and noted – what has often disappointed visitors – the lack of water in the falls. They are high but only thunder down impressively after extremely heavy rain; and (despite many eighteenth-century drawings) they *never* give a single unbroken billow of water:

> I had an easy climb among the streams, about the fragments of rock & should have got I think to the summit, but unfortunately I was damped by slipping one leg into a squashy hole. There is no great body of water, but the accompaniment is delightful; for it ooses out from a cleft in perpendicular Rocks, all fledged with Ash & other beautiful trees. It is a strange thing how they got there.

The most famous verse about the falls is Southey's doggerel-poem 'The Cataract of Lodore' (1820) which tries to answer the question 'How does the water/Come down at Lodore?' The gradually-widening poem imitates the shape of the falls as well as their sound, as

> From its sources which well
>   In the Tarn on the fell;
>   From its fountains
>   In the mountains,
>   Its rills and its gills;
>   Through moss and through brake,
>   It runs and it creeps

until

> Collecting, projecting,
> Receding and speeding,
> And shocking and rocking,
> And darting and parting,
> And threading and spreading,
> And whizzing and hissing ...
> All at once and all o'er, with a mighty uproar,
> ... This way the Water comes down at Lodore.

The exiled artist and poet Chiang Yee, visiting the Falls in 1936, thought them very Chinese: 'As I listened to the roar of the tumbling water I easily imagined myself back in my native land, visiting the 'Yellow-Dragon Falls' of Lu Mountain'. In the evening he rowed on Derwentwater with a Chinese friend, expecting to see the full moon. It failed to put in an appearance, but he had his reward: he dreamed that night of the full moon shining over the pine-forests of his native Lu Mountain.

A path of sorts leads up beside the falls, more a scramble over boulders and scree than a walkway. With good shoes and plenty of energy it can be fun.

¼m S of Lodore, opposite the Borrowdale Hotel, is a curious, tall little house with a battlemented porch. This is **Newton Place**, probably the house built by Dorothy Wordsworth's friend Mary Barker (1774-c.1853), 'an active climber of the hills' (Dorothy climbed Scafell with her in 1818) as well as 'a painter, [who] labours hard in depicting the beauties of her favourite Vale'. The expense of building it landed her in debt and at the end of 1818 she had to flee to Boulogne. She was the author of 'Lines Addressed to a Noble Lord', a poem urging Lord Byron to come and live in the Lake District.

Here in the 1860s William Smith and Lucy Cumming spent part of each year, Smith writing countless articles for *Blackwood's Magazine* and his philosphical dialogue *Gravenhurst, or Thoughts on Good and Evil.*

Continue ½m to the road junction and bridge. For Borrowdale, continue S on main road and turn to p 163. To complete the circuit of Derwentwater, cross the bridge.

We are now at **Grange**, so-called because it was the monastic 'grange' or granary in medieval times when Borrowdale belonged to Furness Abbey (the other main grain-store was at Grange-over-Sands). The bridge features in a horrifying episode of Walpole's *Rogue Herries*, where old Mrs Wilson is thrown from the bridge and drowned as a witch.

Gray came to the village in 1769:

> Here [he wrote] we met a civil young farmer overseeing his reapers (for it is now oat harvest) who conducted us to a neat white house in the village of Grange ... [The farmer's] mother and he brought us butter that Siserah would have jumped at, though not in a lordly dish, bowls of milk, thin oaten-cakes, and ale; and we had carried a cold tongue thither with us. Our farmer was himself the man, that last year plundered the eagle's eyrie; all the dale are up in arms on such an occasion, for they lose abundance of lambs yearly, ... He was let down in ropes to the shelf of the rock on which the nest was built, the people above shouting and hilloaing to fright the old birds, which flew screaming round, but did not dare to attack him. He brought off the eaglet (for there is rarely more than one) and an addle egg.

Caleb Fisher, the young farmer who received Gray so warmly, was still entertaining travellers in his old age (around 1815) with accounts of the poet's visit. Gray's report also made the assaults on the eagles' nests famous: in 1779 the young William Wilberforce asked about them and was told that Gray's account was 'strictly true', his informant adding for good measure that **Bull Crag** (1m W of the village) was so-called 'because the Eccho is there so great and so often repeated that a Bull can never be held there long, above two years old, without going mad from hearing the Returns of its own roarings.' One suspects a tall story.

The road soon passes the church. 100yds W of the church, on the other side of the road, is an ordinary, suburban-looking house, **Copperfield**, so-called because Hugh Walpole bought it in 1934 to house his domestic staff whilst he went to Hollywood to script *David Copperfield* for MGM. (This was the famous version with W.C. Fields as Mr Micawber; Walpole took a bit-part as the Vicar of Blunderstone and amazed the director by ad-libbing a different sermon for each of the eight 'takes' of his scene.)

Later the cottage became an annexe for Walpole's own home, Brackenburn, housing the overflow of guests, books and pictures.

After Grange the road turns N again. After about 1m it passes **Brackenburn**, Hugh Walpole's 'little paradise on Cat Bells', which he bought in November 1923. Originally little more than a bungalow, it was built of Cumberland stone in 1909. Walpole enlarged it and converted the upper storey of the detached garage below the house (now 'Brackenburn Lodge') into a library-cum-study, which eventually housed his library of 30,000 books and a collection of paintings by Cezanne, Renoir, Picasso, Gaugin, Klee and Utrillo.

The terraced garden in front of the house was designed by Walpole himself, who channelled a small beck to feed two fountains and a pool (in summer he enjoyed hearing its rippling as he lay in bed). He shared the house with his friend and chauffeur Harold Cheevers.

The young J.B. Priestley visited him here in 1927, and together they wrote a novel (Priestley's first), *Farthing Hall*. The American novelist Sinclair Lewis (who was exploring England by caravan and sending back a weekly article to the *New York Herald Tribune*) stayed here in 1928. Arthur Ransome was a fairly frequent caller in the 1930s and 40s, and in 1934 W.H. Auden turned up: Walpole found him 'very jolly, simple, honest, clear-headed ... We got on beautifully and he didn't make me feel a silly worn-out old man.' Another visitor, in September 1928, was the novelist Francis Brett Young. Walpole and Young walked together on Catbells debating their different ideas about fiction, and Young left determined to find a home in the Lake District, which he did almost at once, at Esthwaite Lodge. Walpole later added another storey to his library at Brackenburn, giving him a fine view over Derwentwater, to equal Young's view of Esthwaite Water.

Walpole alternated restlessly between Brackenburn and London, never staying here for more than five weeks at a time. Nonetheless he wrote a great deal at Brackenburn including most of *Harmer John, Wintersmoon, Jeremy at Crale, Hans Frost, Captain Nicholas, John Cornelius, The Joyful Delaneys* and *A Prayer for My Son*, as well as his Cumberland family saga *The Herries Chronicle* (*Rogue Herries*, 1930; *Judith Paris*, 1931; *The Fortress*, 1932; *Vanessa*, 1933) and its later-added prequels, *The Bright Pavilions* (1940) and *Katherine Christian* (unfinished, 1944). At Brackenburn he also wrote the fifteen volumes of his diaries.

Walpole placed the house of the writer Adam Paris in *The Fortress* on the site of his own house, 'so that much of the scenery could be described straight from his window'. He also introduced a joking reference to himself and the house into the last part of *Vanessa*, where Tom and Sally pass it: '"Who lives there now?" Sally asked, and Tom told her that it was a novelist, none of whose books Sally had ever read'; he adds, 'only I wish he hadn't painted his garage door blue.' At the time of writing the garage doors are still blue.

Immediately behind the house, on the grassy outcrop about 100ft above it, is a stone seat marking a favourite spot of Hugh Walpole's, who discovered it in 1933 and claimed to have seen 'the whole of my real life ... stretched in front of me' as he sat there for the first time. The seat was placed there by Harold Cheevers after Walpole's death.

From some 200yds W of Brackenburn, various paths slope down to the lakeside. The long wooded promontory running out into the lake is Brandelhow Point, and on the point is **Abbot's Bay House**, much enlarged since it was built in the early years of the twentieth century by Percy Withers, minor poet, art collector and biographer of A.E. Housman. Withers gives an account of its construction and his pleasure in living there in *In a Cumberland Dale* (1914). Withers's book, full of small pomposities and pleasant self-satisfactions, frequently recalls *The Diary of a Nobody*. Return to the road.

After 1m at junction follow sign to Skelgill. There is a small car park. After 200yds the road reaches the picturesque **Skelgill Farm**. We are in the territory of Beatrix Potter's Mrs Tiggy-Winkle (who, we recall, washed the 'woolly coats belonging to the little lambs at Skelghyl.') Although Beatrix Potter tells us that Lucie lived at Littletown, the illustrations to *The Tale of Mrs Tiggy-Winkle* unmistakably show the buildings of Skelgill. The geography of the story is imaginary and cannot entirely be matched to real locations.

The poet Stephen Spender, aged nine, stayed at Skelgill Farm in the summer of 1918. He enjoyed the 'rainy lakeside days' which brought out 'long black slugs on paths wrinkled by many torrential downpours ... and how on our walks we found rock crystals on the stones like lost enjewelled caskets.' The 'seed of poetry was planted in [him]' there when his father read him Wordsworth's 'We are Seven' and other poems, and he fell asleep to 'the murmuring of my father's voice as he read the Longer Poems of Wordsworth to my mother.' He decided to become a poet himself.

Take the path that runs S along the fellside above Skelgill. This is the path Lucie takes in *The Tale of Mrs Tiggy-Winkle* (1905) and Beatrix Potter's illustration clearly shows the S end of the valley ahead. Various smaller green paths run up towards the ridge of Catbells, any one of which may be imagined as leading to Mrs Tiggy-Winkle's door. After 1m the path curves W to rejoin the road at **Littletown Farm**, which has a claim to be the home of Beatrix Potter's Lucie (since Potter certainly says Lucie lives there) but which is not the farm shown in the pictures.

We are now in the **Newlands Valley**, at the top of which (according to West's 1778 *Guide*) there

> present themselves an arrangement of vast mountains, entirely new, both in form and colouring of rock; large hollow craters scooped in their bosoms, once the seeming seats of raging liquid fire, though at present overflowing with the purest water, that foams down the craggy brows.

The valley, whose steep sides mingle pointed crags and peaks with rich green pasture, is indeed a remarkable and beautiful place. Present-day residents include the novelist and biographer Molly Lefebure, perhaps best known for her books on local history and on Coleridge. Follow the road across the valley floor to a small stone bridge, below which is the old road with a ford across the **Rigg Beck** –

> Young as the grass that fringes where it sprays,
> Old as the clefts from whence it takes its flight

in Margot Adamson's 1925 poem 'Rigg Beck'.

Either drive N and follow signs for Keswick or take footpath E from gate near Rowling End Farm across valley and back to Skelgill. When you reach conifer plantations you will see the sign for the drive to **Lingholme**, a private house with, unfortunately, no public access. The gardens are fine, the house a somewhat funereal Victorian mansion of the kind Rupert Potter (Beatrix's father) delighted to rent for family holidays. Beatrix Potter stayed here several times in the 1890s and in the summer of 1903 painted backgrounds for *The Tale of Benjamin Bunny* here. Details used included the pear-tree, the lettuce bed and the red-brick garden wall. Views of Derwentwater from the gardens were also used in *The Tale of Squirrel Nutkin*.

Walkers may follow the Lingholme drive a short distance to the footpath which leads N to **Fawe Park**, if possible an even gloomier Potter holiday home. Beatrix Potter stayed here for the summer of 1885 (and spent short periods on many occasions up to 1912) and based details of Mr MacGregor's vegetable garden in *The Tale of Peter Rabbit* on a garden here. She warned, however, that 'it would be vain to look for it ... as a firm of landscape gardeners did away with it, and laid it out anew with paved walks etc.' A fine old oak in the grounds served as model for Old Brown's Oak in *The Tale of Squirrel Nutkin*. Here in 1901 she met Lucy Carr of Newlands, heroine of *The Tale of Mrs Tiggy-Winkle*. The lakeshore in front of the house is the sixth of West's 'stations' for the lake. He recommends it, in particular, as 'a sweet evening walk'.

Opposite the gates of Fawe Park is the wooded hill of **Swinside**, whose brow is West's fifth Derwentwater 'station', now private and inaccessible.

The road continues N to the village of **Portinscale** and joins the main road for Keswick. Somewhere hereabouts was the imagined site of 'Westaway', Pomfret Herries' ornate house in Walpole's *Rogue Herries*. With its lacy wrought ironwork, fluted columns and gardens 'which ran down to the weeds and rushes of the lake-end', one would like to believe in it, but it was wholly imaginary and to make his fiction match reality Walpole had it demolished later in the *Herries* saga.

Walkers should turn R (NE) in Portinscale and follow path over little suspension bridge then along riverbank to Keswick.

Bassenthwaite Lake, West Bank

The W bank of the lake is burdened with the A66, a major road. Nonetheless it holds some places of interest. It is also the shortest way to Cockermouth. Just after we pass Portinscale, the B5292 branches off L (W). This is **Whinlatter Pass** and offers a steeper, more wooded and more leisurely route to Cockermouth. In the hills overlooking the pass on its S side, 'in a hollow between Grisedale Pike and Hobcarton', Hugh Walpole (in *Vanessa*) placed Hatchett's Fosse, the (fictional) farm where Benjamin Herries fights Robert Endicott and sleeps with Marion Halliday, thus blighting his relationship with Vanessa.

It you want to explore the lakeshore take the L (NW) turning signed Thornthwaite. You are following the road taken in June 1828 by Dorothy Wordsworth, who admired 'the many cloudy summits and swelling breastworks of Skiddaw'. Viewing the scene as if it were a painting, she was 'particularly struck with the amplitude of style and objects – flat Italian foreground, large fields, and luxuriant hedges, – a perfect garden of Eden with immense rose bushes garlanded with flowers, the white elder rich with ivory and pearls.'

As the road comes level with the S end of the lake look up at the fellside. You will see a curious object like a misshapen snowman. This is **The Bishop** (or Bishop Rock), a knob of rock which for many years local people have kept painted white. The story goes that in 1783 the newly-appointed Bishop of Londonderry was staying at the nearby Swan Inn (now gone) on his way to Whitehaven, where he planned to take a boat to his new diocese. He foolishly accepted a wager that he could ride his pony to the top of the fell, known as Barf. At the point marked by this rock the pony tripped. The Bishop and his mount were both killed in the fall. (The only flaw in this story is that, historically, no Bishop of Londonderry died in 1783 or any date close to it, nor did any die in Cumbria. We are dealing with folklore, not fact.) If you want to reach the rock look for a tiny turning off the road just after Beckstones Farm. 100 yds up the lane take footpath through a small gate on R . It leads first to a smaller white-painted rock like a stunted gatepost, known as 'The Clerk', where the Bishop is said to be buried. The path continues up the fellside to the Bishop itself. A local army unit now gives the rocks their annual whitewash.

The Thornthwaite road has two car parks; the best for visiting the lakeshore is the second, Woodend Brow. From here, with extreme caution, walkers can cross the A66 to the lake and go ½m N to **Beck Wythop**, a picturesque promontory offering good views of Bassenthwaite Lake with Skiddaw and Dodd beyond. This is West's fourth station for the lake.

Continue N along A66 and turn off at Dubwath. Follow signs to Castle Inn. Near the attractive red stone **Ouse Bridge** at the foot of the lake Gray, on his 1769 tour, 'din[ed] at a public-house, which stands here near the bridge (that crosses the Derwent just where it issues from the lake)'. The public house is now gone. Just over the bridge is **Armathwaite Hall**, now a hotel, family home of the Speddings before they inherited Mirehouse in 1802. Camden stayed here (1774) at *'Mr Spedyn's* of *Armethwaite'*. The house was completely rebuilt in 1881 and after, in a rather slick style, but the terrace has a superb view of the lake and is West's first 'station' for viewing it. Continue to the Castle Inn, where you can either return to Keswick or take your choice of roads to Carlisle, Cockermouth or Caldbeck.

Ashness and Watendlath

From Keswick follow B5289 S past Calfclose Bay and turn uphill on road signed Ashness Bridge and Watendlath. After ½m the small stone pack-horse bridge is **Ashness Bridge**, a famous picturesque object. 1m further is the **Surprise View** (*several small car parks nearby*), a point where the road curves W at the top of a rise to reveal a panoramic view of Derwentwater. It has been a regular part of the picturesque itinerary since the eighteenth century, though its present name seems to be Victorian. The 'surprise' only really works when you are coming *from* Watendlath, when the spacious vista appears much more abruptly.

Another mile and a half brings us to **Watendlath** (*NT; car park*). 'A native of London or Bath, transported to Watinlath, might sicken for society,' wrote Thomas Wilkinson in 1824, but the solitude has not deterred visitors from this tiny village, bridge and tarn set in an isolated side-valley between Thirlmere and Derwentwater.

Gilpin visited in 1772, because 'the beauties of Watenlath had been so strongly represented to us', apparently taking the bridleway from Rosthwaite. '"Which way to Watenlath?" said one of our company to a peasant' – a question so often asked by eighteenth-century tourists that it became a standing joke and local proverb. The peasant's reply was 'That way' – pointing up 'a lofty mountain, steeper than the tiling of a house'; so Gilpin's party struggled up.

> And yet there is something unmanly [Gilpin thought ruefully] in conceiving difficulty in traversing a path, which, we were told, the women of the country would ascend on horseback, with their panniers of eggs, and butter, and return in the night. To move upwards, keeping a steady eye on the objects before us, was no great exercise to the brain: but it rather gave a rotation to look back on what was past – and to see our companions below *clinging*, as it appeared, to the mountain's side; and the rising breasts and bellies of their horses, straining up a path so steep, that, it seemed, as if the least false step would have carried them rolling many hundred yards to the bottom.

No Victorian holiday was complete without a visit, and Eliza Lynn Linton (with typical asperity) gives us a glimpse of the rituals expected of the tourist:

> The valley is very high, but the mountains are higher still, and there is no way back to the world again save by the hill tops to Borrowdale … so you

WATENDLATH BRIDGE
W.J. Linton, 1864

must sit for a short time in the porch of a farm cottage where every one sits, and, if you can, sketch that old woman in her scanty purple dress, with her blue-checked apron over her head, painfully gathering sticks. Some among you may think that more comfort and less picturesqueness would perhaps advance that poor flickering life a little; but others, if artists of a certain school, hold to the blue-checked apron and the scanty purple dress, stained by the weather to such a delicious tone.

At the N end of the hamlet is **Steps End Farm** (formerly Watendlath Farm), still recognisable as the house whose 'deep porch with stone steps led up to the thick oak door ... ', in which are set the first pages of Edna Lyall's Victorian Lakeland novel *Hope the Hermit*.

In July 1921 Lytton Strachey stayed here with a group of 'Bloomsbury' friends including Gerald Brennan, Ralph Partridge, Dora Carrington and several Stracheys. Lytton climbed the hills and got blisters, or enjoyed 'sitting ... rather comatose,' as he wrote to Virginia Woolf, 'green mountains out of the window, the stuffed head of a very old female sheep over the window.' Meanwhile James Strachey (future translator of Freud) studied Dr Varendonck on the pyschology of daydreams; and Partridge fished doggedly, catching nothing, while his wife Carrington conducted a passionate affair with Brennan on the riverbank or in a nearby barn.

Watendlath's strongest literary association is with Hugh Walpole, who visited it in September 1929 and decided to use **Fold Head Farm** (beside the car park, with plaque) as the main setting for his second (and best) *Herries* novel, *Judith Paris*. The farm, a fine example of the traditional 'long house' with domestic and farm buildings in a single block, is introduced as 'a queer little place indeed, crouched into the soil as though it feared a blow, its narrow windows peering blindly on to Armboth Fell that here was split to allow a beck to tumble down the hollow.'

The house also appears in Walpole's last novel *Katherine Christian*, and in *The Bright Pavilions*, Nicholas Herries is brought to Watendlath by his servant Gilbert to witness a witches' sabbath beside the Tarn.

Unless you are walking to Thirlmere or Rosthwaite, you will now have to turn round and return to the B5289.

Borrowdale and Honister Pass

Follow B5289 S past Lodore. After 2m the road enters oakwoods and draws close to the Derwent. This is **Borrowdale**, one of the most beautiful of Lakeland valleys. Attention was drawn to it first by Gray's 1769 journal; his account, though it now seems overwritten and concentrates mainly on the Lodore area rather than on the narrows of Borrowdale proper, shaped the perceptions of visitors for a century afterwards – perhaps still does:

> we entered Borrowdale: the crags named Lawdoor-banks begin now to impend terribly over your way, and more terribly when you hear that three years since an immense mass of rock tumbled at once from the brow and barred all access to the dale (for this is the only road) till they could work their way through it. The whole way down the road on both sides is strewn with piles of the fragments strangely thrown across each other, and of a dreadful bulk: the place reminds me of those passes on the Alps, where the guides tell you to move on with speed, and say nothing, lest the agitation of air should loosen the snows above, and bring down a mass that would overwhelm a caravan.
>
> *Non ragioniam di lor, ma guarda, e passa!*

Gray is quoting Dante's *Inferno*: 'Let us not speak of them, but look, and pass on!' It became fashionable to describe Borrowdale in horrific terms; thus, for example, Ann Radcliffe in 1794: 'Dark rocks yawn at its entrance, terrific as the wildness of a maniac'.

To add to the excitement, rumours circulated that the valley's inhabitants were exceptionally primitive. They were said to be so backward that the use of the wheel was not known (in reality sleds were used because of the poor roads: Ruskin's *Iteriad* indicates that as late as 1830 carriages could not pass and even riding 'sure-footed ponies' was difficult), and so stupid that they had once built a wall across the valley to keep the cuckoo in, hoping that spring would last for ever. This was a standing joke for centuries: according to Harriet Martineau in 1854,

> Only last year, when a Borrowdale man entered a country inn, a prior guest said simply 'cuckoo,' and was instantly knocked down; and a passionate fight ensued.

In the same tradition is one of the earliest published pieces of Lakeland dialect writing, the *Borrowdale Letter* by Isaac Ritson (1789), supposed to be the comical account by a Borrowdale shepherd of his sea-trip from Whitehaven to Dublin.

In 1883 the valley had a narrow escape from noise and suburban devel-

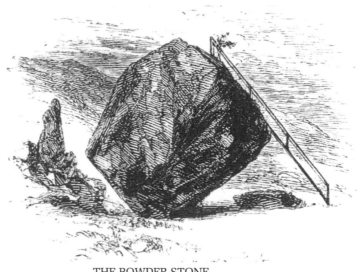

THE BOWDER STONE
W.J. Linton, 1864

opment, when a plan to build a railway from Keswick through Borrowdale to Buttermere was defeated by opposition led by Canon Rawnsley. *Punch* published a satirical comment in verse, 'Lakes and Locomotives':

> What ho my merry Philistines here's news and no mistake,
> They're going to run a railway round and spoil each pretty lake,
> And near the famous cataract that Southey sang of yore
> The locomotive's noise shall drown the murmur of Lodore ...

The controversy inspired the founding of the Lake District Defence Society, an ancestor of the National Trust.

¾m S of the Grange Bridge, on the E side of the road clearly signed and with a car park, is **The Bowder Stone** (*NT*), a huge boulder once thought to have been left by retreating glaciers after the ice age but now considered from its shape and texture more likely to have fallen from the crags above. It has been calculated to weigh about 2,000 tons and is a strange and splendid sight. William Gilpin recorded in 1772 that

> In the middle of one of the recesses of the valley lies an enormous stone; which is called in the country *Boother-stone*. Massy rocks of immense size, rent from the mountains, are every where found: but this stone appears to be of a different kind. It does not seem to have been the appendage of a mountain; but itself an independent creation. It lies in a sort of diagonal position; overshadowing a space, sufficient to shelter a troop of horse.

James Clarke, who calls it '*Bowder-Stone, Powder-Stone*, or Bounder Stone' claims it is 'said to be the largest *self-stone* in England.' Self-stones, he adds, are 'those which do not appear ever to have been connected with the general strata – stones somehow primevally formed in their independent roundness.

The little house beside the stone, and the hole under it, were 'improvements' made by the irrepressible Joseph Pocklington, and earned some forthright comments from Southey's 'Don Espriella':

> The same person who formerly disfigured the island in Keswick Lake with so many abominations, has been at work here also; has built a little mock hermitage, set up a new druidical stone, erected an ugly house for an old woman to live in who is to show the rock, for fear travellers should pass under it without seeing it, cleared away all the fragments round it, and as it rests upon a narrow base, like a ship on its keel, dug a hole underneath through which the curious may gratify themselves by shaking hands with the old woman.

It is still possible to shake hands under the stone, experiencing an eighteenth-century shudder of the sublime from the 'impending' mass of rock overhead.

Continue S 1m to the village of **Rosthwaite**. Gilpin, who visited in 1772, viewed the place as a pastoral paradise:

> Here the sons, and daughters of simplicity enjoy health, peace, and contentment, in the midst of what city-luxury would call the extreme of human necessity; Stealing their whole dominion from the waste; Repelling winter-blasts with mud and straw ... Their herds afford them milk; and their flocks, cloaths; the shepherd himself being often the manufacturer also. No dye is necessary to tinge their wool: it is naturally a russet-brown; and sheep and shepherds are cloathed alike; both in the simple livery of nature.

At the N edge of the village, on a grassy knoll 300yds E of the road, is the **Hazel Bank Hotel**, which stands on the site of the fictional 'Herries', the tumbledown house with its gabled roof, latticed windows and 'shaggy farm byres' belonging to the hero of Walpole's *Rogue Herries*. Here young David Herries arrives at the beginning of the novel, and here, in its sequel *Judith Paris*, the newly-born Judith is rescued amidst the snow from the freezing house by Tom Gauntry.

In *Vanessa* Walpole describes the house which really does stand on the site – a 'solid, comfortable little Victorian house with its sloping lawn, its trim garden' – supposedly replacing the original 'Herries'.

At the middle of the village is the **Royal Oak**, probably the 'Rosthwaite Inn' where Wordsworth stayed in 1812, and had to share a bed with 'a Scotch pedlar' ('which however,' a friend reported, 'he did not seem to mind.')

From the village centre follow the track to the riverside and cross the small bridge for a path that leads round NW then N to the spectacularly steep **Castle Crag** which is West's fourth 'station' for Derwentwater, giving 'a most astonishing view'.

Continue S ¾m to sign 'Public Footpath Longthwaite' by bridge. Follow path across field to **Folly Bridge**, a picturesque lopsided stone bridge. The slab at SE corner is inscribed with a verse (1781) by 'John Braithwaite of

Seatoller', who defends his apparent folly in building a bridge to join two parts of an estate for which he has no male heir:

> I count this Folly you have done.
> As You have neither Wife nor Son.
> Daughter I have. God give her grace.
> And Heaven for her Resting-place.

Either cross the bridge and walk ¼m W to Seatoller or return to the road and continue W to **Seatoller** (*large car park*).

Here the main literary landmark is **Seatoller House**, the large rambling farmhouse with a pleasant garden on the corner by the telephone box. It has been a famous setting for academic and literary gatherings since the mid-nineteenth century. At Easter 1895 the Cambridge Apostles and other student friends held a reading-party here. The group included the historian G.M. Trevelyan, the composer Ralph Vaughan-Williams and the philosopher G.E. Moore. The 'Wordsworthians of the party' walked over to visit Grasmere and Rydal Mount.

In the 1920s a frequent visitor was C.E. Montague, keen mountaineer, novelist and journalist on *The Manchester Guardian* in its great days, who called it 'Uncommon good ... one of the best remaining specimens of the old Cumberland "statesman's" house and wondrously comfortable'. Now almost forgotten, Montague deserves to be remembered as the author of two classic climbing stories, 'In Hanging Garden Gulley' (1923) and 'Action' (1928).

At the junction by Seatoller Bridge turn L following sign to **Seathwaite** (*car park at end of road*). From the car park, look W. The largest waterfall is Sour Milk Gill; to R of it is a squarish conifer plantation. To R of conifers and higher up slope are several spoil heaps. These mark the mouths of the old **graphite mines**, at the top of Newhouse Gill.

Graphite (also known as wadd, plumbago and blacklead) was discovered here, in exceptionally pure form, in the sixteenth century. Camden mentions that

> Here also is found in several places that metallic earth or hard glittering stone, which we call *Black Lead*, used by painters to draw lines and drawings in black and white. Whether it be Dioscorides' *Pnigitis*, or *Melanteria*, or ochre burnt black by the heat of the earth, or totally unknown to the antients, I cannot determine, but shall leave it to others.

It was also in demand for making metal castings and cannon balls, as a lubricant, and for 'blackleading' stoves.

Gilpin in 1772 saw the mines, and wrote

> I could not help feeling a friendly attachment to this place, which every lover of the pencil must feel, as deriving from this mineral one of the best instruments of his art; the freest and best expositor of his ideas. We saw the site of the mine at a distance, marked with a dingy yellow stain, from the ochery mixtures thrown from it's mouth, which shiver down the sides of the mountain.

In the seventeenth and eighteenth centuries graphite mining (and theft) brought quick money: a vein or 'sop' might contain twenty-eight tons of graphite, which could be sold at forty shillings a pound. The mines were guarded by armed men and the product was treated like gold: according to Otley (1823) over the mine's mouth 'a house is built, where the workmen are undressed and examined as they pass through it on leaving their work'. The industry's social impact was considerable: in the eighteenth century it was said that the poor of Keswick lived mainly by dealing in stolen graphite, and Wordsworth confided that

> The lover of truth will forgive me, though he may be startled, when he is informed that among the inhabitants of this deeply sequestered spot [Borrowdale] the agitations of gaming were prevalent in an extraordinary degree, that the book of Hoyle was a favourite study of the wealthier Yeomen, & that if 30 or 40 Guineas were won & lost in the course of one evening at whist, it was no unusual occurrence.

Still looking W from the Seathwaite car park, to the R again of the mines is a strip of woodland; at its lower edge is a clump of dark yew trees. These are the **Borrowdale Yews**, an ancient group of yew-trees celebrated in Wordsworth's 'Yew-Trees' as

> those fraternal Four of Borrowdale,
> Joined in one solemn and capacious grove;
> Huge trunks! and each particular trunk a growth
> Of intertwisted fibres serpentine
> Up-coiling, and inveterately convolved;
> … a natural temple scattered o'er
> With altars undisturbed of mossy stone.

The grove was badly damaged by a gale in 1883, an event which moved Canon H.D. Rawnsley to compose a melancholy 'Trilogy of Sonnets on the Yews of Borrowdale'. However the yews now look as impressive as ever.

Gray found the landscape around Seathwaite too intimidating to explore further, merely noting that

> all farther access is here barred to prying mortals, only there is a little path winding over the fells, and for some weeks in the year passable to the dalesmen; but the mountains know well that these innocent people will not reveal the mysteries of their ancient kingdom, 'the reign of Chaos and old Night:' only I learned that this dreadful road, dividing again, leads one branch to Ravenglass, and the other to Hawkshead.

The path he describes in such dramatic terms is simply the **Sty Head Pass**. To reach it walk S from the end of the road to a small and perfect stone bridge. This is **Stockley Bridge**, where young David Herries fished and met the pedlar with his 'sharp bright face' and curious silver box, who claimed to be the Devil, in *Rogue Herries*. Immediately up the slope E above the bridge is **Glaramara**. Michael Roberts's eerie poem 'On Glaramara: 1947' evokes a New Year's Eve spent at the summit under a full moon – an enterprise reminiscent of Coleridge:

HONISTER CRAG
Thomas Aspland, 1855

Midnight, and the pale snow
  Crisp underfoot,
A frost-encircled moon
  On Glaramara ...

A country of stone dreams
  The ghost of a hill,
A frozen tarn, the still
  Echo of bells ...

From Stockley Bridge one path runs due S up Grains Gill, passing above Sprinkling Tarn to join the path leading E over Esk Hause to Rossett Gill and Great Langdale.

The R (SW) branch is the Sty Head Pass proper, which runs up to Sty Head Tarn at the foot of Great Gable and Scafell, then W down into Wasdale. This was the route taken by Charles Dodgson ('Lewis Carroll') on his 1856 tour of the Lakes: he and some friends rowed from Keswick to Lodore, then

> walked down Borrowdale, and lunched at Seathwaite, where it is said more rain falls in the year than in any other place in England. The whole party ascended Great Gable but we got no view as it was entirely wrapped up in mists. At the foot the party divided, and Collyns and I walked on to Wasthead, where we got beds at a cottage.

Unless heading for one of these destinations, return to the road and retrace the ½m NE to the road junction and Seatoller.

Continue ¾m W from Seatoller. This is the **Honister Pass**, which runs through the midst of Lakeland's formerly most productive slate quarries. At the top of the Pass is the Youth Hostel and a car park; beside it you can see the buildings of the **Honister Slate Mine** (*daily tours all year except late December – mid-January, advance booking essential; car park, admisson charge*), now happily reopened after some years of closure. A path leads S up the slope to **Grey Knotts** and **Brandreth**, stony peaks where around 1900 G.M. Trevelyan, Geoffrey Winthrop Young and their friends (all scholarly Cambridge men and pioneers of rock-climbing) used to play Manhunt: one man was given a start, the rest pursued; a game not recommended except for seasoned climbers with – as Young claimed he had – exceptionally strong ankles. The game is still played hereabouts, the team setting out from Seatoller House.

The quarries make a dramatic sight on both sides of the road. Eliza Lynn Linton gives a vivid account of the industry here around 1860:

> This slate quarrying is awful to look at, both in the giddy height at which the men work, and in the terrible journies which they make when bringing down the slate in their 'sleds.' It is simply appalling to see that small moving speck on the high crag, passing noiselessly along a narrow grey line that looks like a mere thread, and to know that it is a man with the chances of his life dangling in his hand. As we look the speck moves; he first crosses the straight gallery leading out from the dark cavern where he emerged, and then he sets himself against the perpendicular descent, and comes down the face of the crag, carrying something behind him – at first slowly, and, as it were, cautiously; then with a swifter step, but still evidently holding back; but at last with a wild haste that seems as if he must be overtaken, and crushed to pieces by the heavy sled grinding behind him. The long steps seem almost to fly; the noise of the crashing slate comes nearer; now we see the man's eager face; and now we hear his panting breath; and now he draws up by the road-side – every muscle strained, every nerve alive, and every pulse throbbing with frightful force. It is a terrible trade – and the men employed in it look wan and worn, as if they were all consumptive or had heart disease. The average daily task is seven or eight of these journies, carrying about a quarter of a ton of slate each time.

Eliza Linton's observation is accurate: the workers' 'consumptive' look was the result of inhaling slate dust, which proved fatal to many of them.

The pass leads down to Buttermere. Just before it reaches the lake it passes the gate to **Lower Gatesgarth**, an unexpectedly beautiful stone house built in 1910 by the Cambridge economist Arthur Cecil Pigou, a founding theorist of the Welfare State and author of *The Economics of Welfare* (1920). A keen mountaineer, he climbed with many of the pioneers, including the legendary George Mallory. In 1953 Wilfred Noyce's mother, wife and baby daughter stayed here whilst Noyce, with Sir Edmund Hilary and others, made the first successful ascent of Mount Everest. When the news came through, Pigou 'was with difficulty restrained from giving the baby champagne'. Many climbing-parties were held here in the university vacations: guests were expected to take a swim in the lake before breakfast. During the Second World War Alan Turing, the melancholy genius who broke the German 'Enigma' code and was largely responsible for the invention of the computer, spent several holidays here.

Buttermere and Lorton Vale

Buttermere has had a good (and plentiful) press over the years. Melvyn Bragg describes the lake's 'pleasing shape – like an almond-stone sliced open'. The valley of Buttermere and Crummock Water is the 'Secret Valley' explored in Nicholas Size's historical romance of that name (1929). In another novel, *Shelagh of Eskdale*, Size describes the building by Norse settlers of what was probably the first water-powered corn mill in Britain: it operated until 1735, and was on the Sail Beck: the place where the rock was cut out to hold the water-wheel can be seen in the stony gorge behind the **Bridge Hotel** in the village.

'If you are fond of strong ale,' wrote Joseph Budworth, 'I must tell you, Buttermere is reckoned famous for it'. The Bridge Hotel and the more famous **Fish Inn** face each other at the village centre. Modern extension has left the Fish the less picturesque of the two, but it remains famous as the home of Mary Robinson, the 'Maid of Buttermere', whose story has been told in many plays, poems and novels, the most recent being Melvyn Bragg's 1987 novel *The Maid of Buttermere*.

The affair was precipitated by a guide-book: Joseph Budworth stayed here in 1792 and his popular *Fortnight's Ramble to the Lakes* included a description of 'Mary of Buttermere', the innkeeper's daughter:

> She brought in part of our dinner, and seemed to be about fifteen. Her hair was thick and long, of a dark brown, and, though unadorned with ringlets, did not seem to want them; her face was a fine oval, with full eyes and lips as red as vermilion; her cheeks had more of the lily than of the rose ...
> After she had got the better of her first fears, she looked an angel; and I doubt not but she is the reigning Lily of the Valley.
>
> Ye travellers of the Lakes, if you visit this obscure place, such you will find the fair MARY OF BUTTERMERE.

Thanks to Budworth's advertisement, Mary soon became a tourist attraction, and Budworth elaborated his account in subsequent editions of his book, seeming to revel in the embarrassment the publicity evidently caused her.

In 1802 a stranger toured the Lakes under the name of the Honourable Augustus Hope. Apparently drawn by Budworth's account, he visited the Fish Inn, and in short order proposed to Mary and married her. It soon emerged that the Honourable Augustus was a confidence trickster and bigamist, John Hatfield by name. He was taken to Carlisle, where he was tried and sentenced to death for forgery. The Wordsworths, on their way to tour Scotland, visited him in the condemned cell − he in turn had now become a tourist attraction − and he was hanged on September 13, 1803. Poor Mary returned to the Fish Inn, where she worked − still the centre of huge curiosity − until she married a farmer and moved to Caldbeck.

The story caught the popular imagination: novels and plays about it poured from the press. Coleridge reported on the affair in the *Morning Post*; De Quincey (who had seen her serving at the Fish) wrote an account of it in 1834:

> unquestionably she was what all the world have agreed to call 'good-looking.' But … I confess that I looked in vain for any *positive* qualities of any sort or degree. B*eautiful*, in any emphatic sense, she was not.

He records a claim that Mary, a day or two after Hatfield's execution, serving a large party at the Fish, 'threw upon the table, with an emphatic gesture, the Carlisle paper, containing an elaborate account of his execution.'

In *The Prelude* Wordsworth recalls visiting London and seeing a melodrama based on

> a story drawn
> From our own ground, − The Maid of Buttermere −
> And how, unfaithful to a virtuous wife,
> Deserted and deceived, the Spoiler came
> And wooed the artless daughter of the hills,
> And wedded her, in cruel mockery
> Of love and marriage bonds. These words to thee

− he tells Coleridge −

> Must needs bring back the moment when we first
> Ere the broad world rang with the maiden's name,
> Beheld her serving at the cottage inn;
> Both stricken, as she entered or withdrew,
> With admiration of her modest mien
> And carriage, marked by unexampled grace.

New versions of the story have continued to appear ever since.

Budworth remained impervious: it never struck him that he bore some responsibility for disrupting Mary's life. As he saw it, it was all her own fault, and in the third (1810) edition of his book he took

> this opportunity of deploring that he ever wrote in commendation of any young living creature, as vanity, alas, is the most intoxicating of human plants! and too apt to spread, when unfortunately introduced to public approval.

Somewhat inappropriately, in view of all this notoriety, the village features as the quietest and most secluded of rural backwaters in Henry Mayhew's Victorian satire *1851: or, The Adventures of Mr and Mrs Cursty*

Sandboys and Family, who came up to London to 'Enjoy Themselves' and to see the Great Exhibition:

> Here the knock of the dun never startles the hermit or the student – for (thrice blessed spot!) there are no knockers. Here are no bills ... for (oh earthly paradise!) there are no tradesmen! ... Burst your pantaloons – oh, mountain tourist! – and it is five miles to the nearest tailor.

Follow the road NW to **Crummock Water**. Immediately after the road runs under crags at the very edge of the lake, it reaches a small car park. From here walk back a few yards to **Hause Point**, a steep promontory with a miniature pass or 'hause' over its top. It features prominently in Edward Lear's 1836 watercolour of Crummock Water, and also in Melvyn Bragg's *The Maid of Buttermere*, where it becomes the schizophrenic John Hatfield's favourite spot, scene of his 'revelation' of God and Death.

Follow the road N. It leaves the lake and you may wish to take the signed turning for **Loweswater**, one of the most beautiful and little-visited of the lakes. Nearby is the home of notable Cumbrian writers Hunter Davies and Margaret Forster. Davies is known for his journalism and a range of books on quintessentially Northern subjects, from Wordsworth and the Beatles to footballer Paul Gascoyne; Forster for her broadcasting, novels (*Georgie Girl, Lady's Maid, Is There Anything You Want?* among others) and biographies of Daphne du Maurier, Elizabeth Barrett Browning *et al*. We return to the B 5289 and continue N towards Cockermouth. 2m N of Crummock Water, the road enters **Lorton Vale**, a beautiful pastoral valley. William Gilpin's description (1772) does it justice: the Vale, he says,

> is in general a rich, cultivated scene; tho in many parts the ground is beautifully broken, and abrupt. A bright stream, which might almost take the name of a river, pours along a rocky channel; and sparkles down numberless cascades. It's banks are adorned with wood; and varied with different objects; a bridge; a mill; a hamlet; a glade over-hung with wood; or some little sweet recess; or natural vista, through which the eye ranges, between irregular trees, along the windings of the stream.

> Except the mountains, nothing in all this scenery is *great*; but every part is filled with those sweet engaging passages of nature, which tend to sooth the mind, and instill tranquillity.

2m after entering the Vale, at Low Lorton, take turning R (E), signed Keswick. At next junction follow sign for High Lorton and Keswick. Watch out for Yew Tree Hall (long stone building on corner) and immediately after it turn R (S) into small road signed Boon Beck, Scales. The road at once crosses a bridge over Whit Beck. On R is a telephone box, and in a small enclosure beside it the **Lorton Yew**.

Wordsworth's poem 'Yew-Trees' describes

> a Yew-tree, pride of Lorton Vale,
> Which to this day stands single, in the midst
> Of its own darkness, as it stood of yore ...
> Of vast circumference and gloom profound

This solitary Tree! a living thing
Produced too slowly ever to decay;
Of form and aspect too magnificent
To be destroyed.

Returning over the bridge, you can get an even better view of the tree by taking the narrow way between the end of Yew Tree Hall and the white house (Yew Tree View) next to it, and looking across the beck. Despite Wordsworth's prediction that it could never 'decay' the Yew was severely damaged by a gale in about 1855 and much of its wood removed for cabinet-making. You can see the shattered edges of the trunk on the S side.

Return to B5289 and continue N ¼ to Lorton. Watch for the Wheatsheaf Inn. 75yds S of the Inn a path leads E over a field to **St Cuthbert's Church, Lorton**, an unusual early Gothic Revival Church (1809) replacing the dilapidated earlier building where the imposter John Hatfield married Mary Robinson on October 2 1802. Continue N 3m to Cockermouth.

Cockermouth

Cockermouth (*large, signed car park at centre, others scattered about; drive round and keep your eyes open*) is distinctly a Cumberland town rather than a 'Lakeland' one, and its solid, chunky sandstone buildings remind you that Scotland is not far away. John Leland, about 1540, noted carefully that

> The towne of Cokermuth stondeth on the ryver of Coker, the which thwarteth over the town, and Coker runneth yn Darwent hard at the point of the castel of Cokermuth.

At the W end of Main Street is **Wordsworth House** (*NT; open Mon-Fri late March to end May, Mon-Sat June to August, Mon-Fri September to early October (dates vary slightly year to year), 10.30-4.30; closed early October to late March; admission charge*), an elegant Georgian town house built in 1745. William and Dorothy Wordsworth (and their brothers Richard, John and Christopher) were born here. Their father John Wordsworth was legal and political agent to the Earl of Lowther, who owned the house. Here John Wordsworth introduced his son to poetry, encouraging him to learn by heart 'large portions of Shakespeare, Milton and Spenser' and giving him free access to his large library.

There is a pleasant walled garden with a terrace at its foot overlooking the River Derwent. In 'The Sparrow's Nest' Wordsworth recalls the nests which were built in the hedge at this end of the garden, and the anxious tenderness with which Dorothy had viewed 'The Sparrow's dwelling'.

The sound of the **River Derwent** is the first childhood memory recorded by Wordsworth in *The Prelude*, where he recalls how

> one, the fairest of all rivers, loved
> To blend his murmurs with my nurse's song,
> And, from his alder shades and rocky banks,

And from his fords and shallows, sent a voice
That flowed along my dreams.

In summer the Wordsworth children played in its shallow waters:

When, having left his mountains, to the towers
Of Cockermouth that beauteous river came,
Behind my father's house he passed, close by,
Along the margin of our terrace walk.
He was a playmate whom we dearly loved.
Oh, many a time have I, a five years' child,
A naked boy, in one delightful rill,
A little mill-race severed from the stream,
Made one long bathing of a summer's day ...

He also wrote a sonnet 'To the River Derwent'.

The Wordsworth children were sent away when their mother died in 1778. After their father's death in 1783 the house fell into decay: William and Dorothy revisited in 1794 and found

all ... in ruin, the terrace-walk buried and choked up with the old privot hedge which had formerly been most beautiful, roses and privot intermingled – the same hedge where the sparrows were used to build their nests.

Passing the house in 1828, Dorothy noted, with almost religious gravity, 'Life has gone from my Father's Court.'

At L of Wordsworth House is **Low Sand Lane**. The house at the corner (plaque), with the long multi-paned windows of a weaver's cottage, is the birthplace of Fearon Fallows, mathematician and astronomer (1787–1831). An infant mathematical prodigy, he taught himself Latin whilst working at the loom as a child, became an arithmetic teacher, won a scholarship to Cambridge and in 1826 went out to found the Cape Town Observatory, producing the southern hemisphere's first star catalogue. His papers were published in 1851.

Behind Wordsworth House and a few yards downstream is a footbridge over the Derwent giving a good view of the Castle, which seems to be shown in the background of Stevie Smith's illustration for her poem 'The Castle' (1950).

COCKERMOUTH CASTLE
Stevie Smith, 1950

Cockermouth Castle is a seat of the Earls of Egremont and is the scene (so far as any actual place is) of the poem:

> I married the Earl of Egremont,
> I never saw him by day,
> I had him in bed at night,
> And cuddled him tight ...
>
> Oh that was a romantic time,
> The castle had such a lonely look,
> The estate,
> Heavy with cockle and spurge,
> Lay desolate ...
>
> Oh I love the ramshackle castle,
> And the turret room
> Where our sons were born.

The outline of the castle is immediately recognisable, once one realises that the triangular object in the centre is the cupola of Jennings' brewery, which from the bridge appears in just that position.

Return to Main Street, at whose E end is the **Black Bull Hotel**. In the hotel's rear yard the pious Reuben Herries, in Hugh Walpole's novel *Judith Paris*, intervenes (with disastrous results) in a bear-baiting. Just E of the Black Bull is the Market Place. From here go S 200yds for **All Saints' Church**, on the hilltop, an imposing building almost like a cathedral, rebuilt 1852–4. Wordsworth was confirmed in the earlier church on this site, an occasion recalled in his sonnet 'Catechizing'. The E window is a memorial to Wordsworth himself.

The white sandstone headstone of 'Mr John Wordsworth' (1741–83), the poet's father, is by the path at the SE corner of the church. (Just across the path, incidentally, notice the gravestone of Ann Dunn, whose poor mason had terrible trouble spelling 'here' (?hear) and deciding which way round the figure 4 went, and left his uncertainties laboriously cut in stone.) By the path at the N side of the church is a memorial stone to Fearon Fallows and his parents.

In 1776–7 Wordsworth attended the Grammar School (now demolished), which stood in the churchyard. Another pupil was Fletcher Christian, who led the mutiny on HMS *Bounty* in 1789. He was six years older than Wordsworth and they probably never met.

To reach **Cockermouth Castle** return to the Market Place and go 300yds N. Stukeley says it

> was a stately building, and strong in the old manner; but now they daily pull it down for the sake of its materials. They report that the earth of the *vallum* on the outside the walls was fetched from Ireland, whence no venomous creature can pass over it.

The huge castle (a private residence and, tantalisingly, not open) is certainly 'ramshackle', as Stevie Smith puts it, and one of its towers leans perilously. The road round the base of its outer wall winds through the centre of Jennings' Brewery, a collection of weird and sombrely impressive buildings almost as interesting as the castle.

William and Dorothy Wordsworth as children played in the castle, then neglected and open, and in a late poem, 'Address from the Spirit of Cockermouth Castle', Wordsworth imagines the castle solemnly reminding him of times

> 'when thou, in boyish play,
> Entering my dungeon, didst become a prey
> To soul-appalling darkness. Not a blink
> Of light was there; – and thus did I, thy Tutor,
> Make thy young thoughts acquainted with the grave;
> While thou wert chasing the winged butterfly
> Through my green courts; or climbing, a bold suitor
> Up to the flowers whose golden progeny
> Still round my shattered brow in beauty wave.'

For **Bridekirk** (about 3m N of Cockermouth) leave Cockermouth following signs for A595 Carlisle through roundabouts until signs for Bridekirk appear. The ancient Church of St Bridget was restored with devastating vigour in 1868 and now resembles a Romanesque basilica. The jewel in this casket is a quite extraordinary and beautiful rectangular twelfth-century font, carved, as Collingwood says:

> with dragons and strange beasts, … the expulsion from Eden and the baptism of Christ, and on the fourth side a portrait of the artist with chisel and mallet and his autograph signature in runes of the twelfth century, 'Rikarth he me wrokte, and to this merthe gernr me brokte' – 'Richard me wrought, and to this beauty eagerly me brought.'

This is probably Richard of Durham, the greatest sculptor of Northern England in the period. The self-portrait and the sharp, wiry inscription in runes, are unique: no other artist of the period left such a personal trace.

Next to the church is the **vicarage**, a lovely old house with Georgian additions, birthplace of Joseph Williamson (1633–1701), an important

QUARRYMAN'S SLED
W.J. Linton, 1864

Restoration politician, President of the Royal Society from 1677–70 and founder of *The London Gazette* (now Britain's oldest surviving newspaper). He was the first editor to use foreign correspondents, an idea he invented.

Also born here, and also the son of a vicar, was Thomas Tickell (1686-1740), minor poet and editor of Addison's works. His main work was his poem 'Kensington Gardens' (1722), 'of which' (says Dr Johnson in *Lives of the Poets*) 'the versification is smooth and elegant, but the fiction unskilfully compounded of Grecian deities and Gothic fairies'. Wordsworth's comment was: 'Kensington gardens: strange choice for a Man ... whose birthplace was within a short walk of one of the most romantic rivers in the world, [the] Derwent.'

From Bridekirk, you may want to wander N through a maze of small roads to the Solway plain. Alternatively turn S for the Cockermouth -Carlisle road (A595) or W for A594 to Maryport and Allonby.

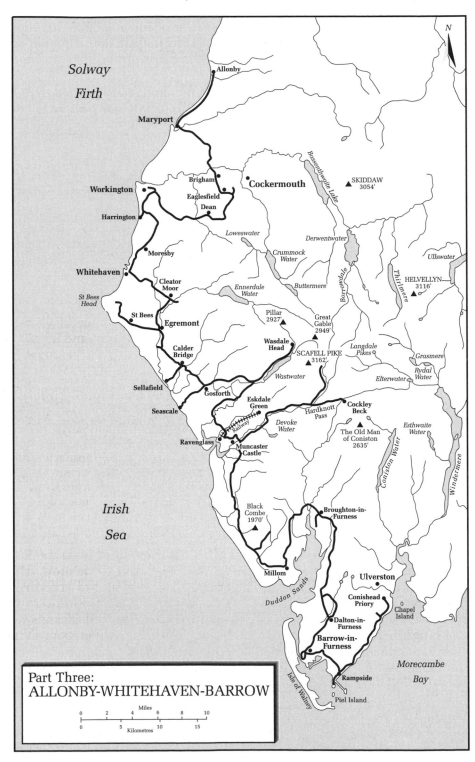

Solway Firth

Allonby

Maryport

Brigham

Workington

Cockermouth

Eaglesfield

Dean

Harrington

SKIDDAW
3054'

Loweswater

Derwentwater

Moresby

Crummock
Water

Ullswater

Whitehaven

Cleator
Moor

Ennerdale
Water

Buttermere

Borrowdale

HELVELLYN
3116'

St Bees
Head

St Bees

Egremont

Pillar
2927'

Great
Gable
2949'

Langdale
Pikes

Grasmere

Calder
Bridge

Wasdale
Head

SCAFELL PIKE
3162'

Elterwater

Rydal
Water

Sellafield

Gosforth

Wastwater

Thirlmere

Seascale

Eskdale
Green

Hardknott
Pass

Cockley
Beck

Esthwaite
Water

Ravenglass

Railway

Devoke
Water

The Old Man
of Coniston
2635'

Muncaster
Castle

Coniston Water

Windermere

Irish

Sea

Black
Combe
1970'

Broughton-in-
Furness

Millom

Ulverston

Duddon Sands

Conishead
Priory

Chapel
Island

Dalton-in-
Furness

**Barrow-in-
Furness**

**Morecambe
Bay**

Rampside

Isle of Walney

Piel Island

Part Three:
ALLONBY-WHITEHAVEN-BARROW

Miles
0   2   4   6   8   10

0   5   10   15
Kilometres

N

Allonby and Maryport

> Hail to you,
> Moors, mountains, headlands, and ye hollow vales,
> Ye long deep channels for the Atlantic's voice,
> Powers of my native region! Ye that seize
> The heart with firmer grasp! Your snows and streams
> Ungovernable, and your terrifying winds,
> That howl so dismally for him who treads
> Companionless your awful solitudes!

So Wordsworth (in *The Prelude* Book VIII) salutes the Cumberland coast, and the dales – Ennerdale, Wasdale, Eskdale – which run inland from it to the central mountains of the Scafell *massif*, exposed to all the powerful winds coming from the Irish Sea and the Atlantic beyond.

We begin modestly enough, however, with **Allonby**, a village which enjoyed a brief flowering as a seaside resort in the early nineteenth century. Writers have not been kind to it: 'The only house of entertainment suitable to the wants of visitors', wrote Sir George Head in 1836,

> is the Ship Inn, an ordinary country ale-house, in front of whose windows, and not exceeding a few yards in distance, a row of stepping stones, as if for the benefit of those who wear shoes and stockings, stretch across the principal drain of the village, where pigs and ducks dabble amicably together in the black stream.

Dickens and Wilkie Collins stayed here in September 1857. Collins had sprained his ankle badly on Carrock Fell, so he spent his days at the **Ship Inn** whilst Dickens walked strenuously in 'a twelve-mile circle' around the village. In the evenings they collaborated on a fictionalised account of their travels, *The Lazy Tour of Two Idle Apprentices* – Collins working with especial vigour because he was worried by the size of the bill Dickens was helping him run up. They stayed in a 'clean little bulk-headed room' at the top of a 'clean little bulk-headed staircase' in the inn.

Once settled at the inn, Collins ('Mr Idle') asked Dickens ('Mr Goodchild') what sort of place Allonby was:

> It was, Mr. Goodchild went on to say, in cross-examination, what you might call a primitive place. Large? No, it was not large. Who ever expected it would be large? Shape? What a question to ask! No shape. What sort of a street? Why, no street. Shops? Yes, of course (quite indignant). How many?

179

NEAR THE MOUTH OF THE DUDDON
W.J. Linton, 1868

Who ever went into a place to count the shops? Ever so many. Six?
Perhaps. A library? Why, of course (indignant again). Good collection of
books? Most likely – couldn't say – had seen nothing in it but a pair of
scales. Any reading-room? Of course, there was a reading-room. Where?
Where! why, over there. Where was over there? Why, *there*! Let Mr. Idle
carry his eye to that bit of waste ground above highwater mark, where the
rank grass and loose stones were most in a litter; and he would see a sort of
long, ruinous brick loft, next door to a ruinous brick out-house, which loft
had a ladder outside, to get up by. That was the reading-room, and if Mr.
Idle didn't like the idea of a weaver's shuttle throbbing under a
reading-room, that was his look out.

They sent for a doctor to see to Collins's ankle. The doctor's cadaverous
assistant – 'a startling object to look at, with his colourless face, his sunken
cheeks, his wild black eyes, and his long black hair' – made such an
impression on Collins that he at once wrote a story about him, incorporating it into the *Lazy Tour*, and later drew on him again for Ozias Midwinter
in *Armadale* and Ezra Jennings in *The Moonstone*.

After all this you may be surprised to find Allonby an attractive seaside
village, somewhat battered but architecturally fascinating. Shaggy fell
ponies wander about the streets at their ease and browse on the strip of
grass along the sea front. The Ship Hotel is easily found, and 200yds N of it
the **Library** mentioned by Dickens, an unattractive and dilapidated
redbrick building with tall windows and outside staircase, now empty and
almost derelict.

Take the coast road S (5m) to **Maryport**, a small port created for
coal-shipping in 1749 by Humphrey Senhouse, local landowner and
coal-mine proprietor, who named it after his wife. For a time it had a large
trade with America and exported iron as well as coal. But its attractive
harbour was too small, and it always remained a poor relation of
Whitehaven, declining catastrophically after 1899.

It has one poet of some significance, Jonathan Douglas, who was Gover-
nor of the workhouse (now demolished). Douglas was no Wordsworth, but

MARYPORT HARBOUR
1939

his *Miscellaneous Poems* (1836), mostly about Maryport, have freshness, disarming honesty and lively observation of social life, as in 'On Emigrants Sailing to America':

> On the quay piled with luggage, I wander alone
> 'Mong groups of the strangers, unheeded, unknown;
> The contrast of feelings, of passions combin'd,
> Depict in the features what preys on the mind ...
>
> How fondly they linger, and weeping, embark
> As lonely as those who were saved in the ark,
> To people new regions, when doomed to explore,
> A world of waters without any shore.

Douglas found writing poetry in the workhouse rather a tiresome business; in 'The Poor House' he grumbles about

> The sea-mews screaming 'mid the yeasty foam,
> The dash of waters, and the unceasing din
> Of noisy inmates in their parish home,
> In daily dole the thread of life to spin –
> Unfit retreat to woo the Muses in:

and he regards the 'noisy inmates' themselves with an odd mixture of compassion and disapproval:

> Here puling infancy, and helpless age,
> The lame, the lazy, blind, and spendthrift go;
> And those long hackney'd on the gilded stage
> Of worldly pleasures – here a veil I'll draw
> To hide their deeds unfit for public show;
> And all the motley crowd which it contains,
> From new-made widows in the weeds of wo,
> And ruin'd virgin, who repentance feigns,
> To Amos in his crib, and Charley in his chains.

But his cheerful ballad 'The Poor House Elopement' suggests that on the whole he could contemplate the plight of the pauper with equanimity. A far greater poet, though only here briefly, was Gerard Manley Hopkins, who as a Jesuit priest was sent here in 1882 to preach at a Mission – 'something like a Revival but without the hysteria and the heresy,' he explained. He must have preached powerfully to the sailors, dockers and miners, for he recalled 'it had the effect of bringing me out and making me speak very plainly and strongly (I enjoyed that, for I dearly like calling a spade a spade)'. But he does not tell us what he made of Maryport itself.

Dickens wandered about the town a good deal in September 1857 whilst waiting for Wilkie Collins's sprained ankle to recover. He records his impressions in the voice of the fictional 'Francis Goodchild':

> I go to a region which is a bit of water-side Bristol, with a slice of Wapping, a seasoning of Wolverhampton, and a garnish of Portsmouth, and I say, 'Will *you* come and be idle with me?' And it answers, 'No; for I am a great deal too vaporous and a great deal too rusty, and a great deal too muddy, and a great deal too dirty altogether; and I have ships to load, and pitch and tar to boil, and iron to hammer, and steam to get up, and smoke to make, and stone to quarry, and fifty other disagreeable things to do, and I can't be idle with you.'

Brigham, Eaglesfield and Dean

Leave by A594 and after 3m turn R (S) to **Little Broughton**, birthplace of Abraham Fletcher (1714–93), the self-educated son of a tobacco-pipe maker, who became a noted mathematician, botanist and astrologer; he was widely known as author of *The Universal Measurer* (1755), a technical manual for craftsmen, sailors and engineers. Follow signs for **Brigham** and you will see **St Bridget's Church**, a Norman building restored with colourful Victorian painted ceiling and beams by Butterfield. George Fox came here in 1653, on the preaching tour that led to the founding of the Society of Friends (Quakers):

> And when I came Into ye steeplehouse yarde I saw people comeinge as to a fayre: & abundans was already gathered in ye lanes & about ye steeplehouse.

He disliked the idea of preaching in a 'steeplehouse' or church but 'saw yt woulde bee ye convenierist place to speake unto ye people from' so went inside and preached from a pew for three hours, even the vicar listening to him.

A later vicar (from 1833) was Wordsworth's son John, who built a new **Parsonage** – the square house due E of the church. The poet wrote a sonnet, 'To a Friend: On the Banks of the Derwent' about the house, encouraging his son in his ministry:

> Pastor and Patriot! – at whose bidding rise
> These modest walls ...
>
> A welcome sacrifice
> Dost Thou prepare, whose sign will be the smoke
> Of thy new hearth.

Nonetheless it is sad that the poet's son deserted the **Old Parsonage** – the fine old farmhouse close to the N side of the church, said locally to be 'older than the church itself' – for this dull Victorian mansion.

Nearby (apparently somewhere under the present A66 road) was the **Nun's Well**, used by a convent that once stood close by. Wordsworth wrote a sonnet, 'Nun's Well, Brigham' about it:

> The cattle crowding round this beverage clear
> To slake their thirst, with reckless hoofs have trod
> The encircling turf into a barren clod; ...
> Yet, o'er the brink, and round the lime-stone cell
> Of the pure spring ...
> A tender spirit broods – the pensive shade
> Of ritual honours to this Fountain paid
> By hooded Votaresses with saintly cheer.

From Brigham follow signs to **Eaglesfield**, turning L by the sign announcing the village. Straight ahead you will see **John Dalton House**, the small cottage birthplace of John Dalton (1766–1844), Cumberland's most famous scientist, who first established the Atomic Theory in 1803 with a paper on 'the relative weights of the ultimate particles of bodies'. He also in 1794 published the first description of colour-blindness, from which he suffered. Dalton made an almanac when only ten, and at 13 opened a village school in a nearby barn – possibly the one at the end of this block. He left for Kendal in 1781 and moved to Manchester in 1793. Dalton, like so many early Cumbrian scientists, was a Quaker. He also wrote poetry.

Follow signs for Cockermouth on to A5086, then go L (N) for ½m to public bridleway (signed Eaglesfield). This leads to **Morland Close**, a large and in part very ancient farm which was the birthplace of Fletcher Christian, leader in 1789 of the mutiny on HMS *Bounty*. Return to A5086.

Continue 3m S and turn R (W) to **Dean**, birthplace (confusingly) of the *other* John Dalton. This one, always referred to as 'Dr' John Dalton (1709–63), was a clergyman and a poet. Today he is only remembered as the author of *A Descriptive Poem Addressed to Two Young Ladies at their*

Return from Viewing the Mines near Whitehaven (1755), the earliest poem to celebrate at length the beauties of Lakeland landscape. But in 1750 he was important enough to have his popular adaptation of Milton's *Comus* staged with David Garrick in the title role and a prologue by Samuel Johnson.

From Dean go W through Branthwaite and follow signs to Workington.

Workington, Harrington and Moresby

Leland in 1540 records 'a prety creke wher as shyppes cum to, wher as ys a lytle prety fyssher town cawled Wyrkenton'. Nowadays **Workington**'s best friends would hardly call it pretty, though it has improved in recent years and signs of industrial dereliction have been cleared away. Its architecturally varied and interesting centre is quite pleasant, and its eighteenth- and nineteenth-century waterfront interesting.

Until large-scale coalmining began in the wake of the Industrial Revolution, Workington's history was picturesque but minimal. In 1568, after her escape from Lochleven, Mary Queen of Scots landed here from a fishing boat and was escorted, under Queen Elizabeth's orders, to Carlisle; Wordsworth wrote a little-known sonnet, 'Mary Queen of Scots', commemorating the episode in 1833.

Defoe visited in about 1724, and noted that 'from Workington at the mouth of this river' – the Derwent –

> notwithstanding the great distance, they at this time carry salmon (fresh as they take it) quite to London. This is perform'd with horses, which, changing often, go night and day without intermission, and, as they say, very much out-go the post; so that the fish come very sweet and good to London, where the extraordinary price they yield, being often sold at two shillings and sixpence to four shillings per pound, pay very well for the carriage.

John Stagg (1770–1823), the 'Blind Bard of Cumberland', died here. Born near Carlisle, he lost his sight in early childhood but became an accomplished fiddler, poet and collector of folktales and folksongs. He published several books of poems and ballads, notably *The Minstrel of the North: or, Cumbrian Legends* (1810) and *The Cumbrian Minstrel* (1821).

By 1828 the town had already acquired a grim aspect: Dorothy Wordsworth passed through in that year, and her only comment is a sad one: 'Workington very dismal. Frightened in the streets.'

Take the main road S to **Harrington** and follow sign to station and marina for car park. There is a stony beach with attractive headlands jutting out to sea. Somewhere on this coast, according to the chronicler Simeon of Durham, in AD875 Bishop Eardulf and several monks, fleeing from the Danes, attempted to embark for Ireland, taking with them the body of St Cuthbert and various treasures from their monastery. As they put out to sea a terrible storm arose and a copy of the Gospels, bound in gold and jewels, was swept overboard and lost. The saint was thought to be displeased at the attempt to take him overseas and the voyage was abandoned. Soon Cuthbert appeared in a dream to one of the monks and told him where the book would be found. They came to the beach here at Harrington and found it, washed up by the tide undamaged. It was the Lindisfarne Gospels, one of the world's great works of book illumination and the masterpiece of the golden age of Northumbrian art. It is now on display in the British Museum.

This may also be as good a place as any to think of John Kirkby (1705–54), novelist and tutor to the historian Edward Gibbon, who mentions him in his autobiography. Kirkby was the author of a work on grammar and of a novel with the splendid title *The Capacity and Extent of the Human Understanding, exemplified in the extraordinary case of Automathes, a young nobleman ... accidentally left in his infancy upon a desert island* (1745). Gibbon takes the book's opening to be a personal plaint by Kirkby:

> During my abode in my native County of Cumberland, in quality of an indigent curate, I used, now and then in a summer, when the pleasantness of the season invited, to take a solitary walk to the sea-shore, which lies about two miles from the town where I lived ... One time, among the rest, taking such a journey in my head, I sat down upon the declivity of the beach, with my face towards the sea, ... when immediately the sad thoughts of the wretched condition of my family, and the unsuccessfulness of all endeavours to amend it, came crowding into my mind, which drove me into a deep melancholy, and ever and anon forced the tears from my eyes. I had not long continued in this pensive mood, ere I was diverted from it by the sight, as I imagined, of a small cylindrical trunk, about a foot long, rolling along with the tide, just below where I sat, with a key tied to the handle.

The trunk turns out to contain a manuscript which forms the main body of the novel.

Poor Kirkby must have been doomed to failure: he finally got preferment in the church, only to lose it when he offended his patron by accidentally missing out the King's name one day when he was reading morning prayers. Nobody knows where he was born, or which beach he sat on, or how he died, or even if he was really a Cumbrian. If he lived in a town two miles from the sea, perhaps it was Egremont. But let us imagine him here at Harrington, planning his novel and dreaming of that lucky 'cylindrical trunk' rolling up onto the pebbly beach.

Return to the road and follow it SE until it joins A595, then go R (S) 3m. Pass the turning to Distington, then turn R (W) at sign for Parton and Lowca. You will at once see **St Bridget's Church, Moresby**, where Wordsworth's son John was rector from 1829 to 1833. It was rebuilt in 1822 and a medieval arch from the old church stands outside.

Wordsworth visited in the spring of 1833, and heard

> from the brow of the steep Church field at Moresby, the waves chafing and

murmuring in a variety of tones below, as a kind of base of harmony to the shrill yet liquid music of the larks above.

The field is the one immediately W of the churchyard, overlooking the sea.

During the visit he wrote three of his fine but now neglected 'Evening Voluntaries': 'By the Sea-Side', 'Composed by the Sea-Shore' and 'On a High Part of the Coast of Cumberland', the latter 'composed on the road between Moresby and Whitehaven on Easter Sunday, April 7 1833.' Return to A595 and follow it S into **Whitehaven**.

Whitehaven

'And there is Whitehaven,' says Eliza Lynn Linton, 'for those who care to see a town given up to coals and fish'. This one was a tiny fishing-village until 1680, when the harbour was built and coal began to be dug by the Lowther family, local landowners. It is now a pleasant place, less grimy than many West Cumberland towns, and retains its elegant seven-teenth-century town plan – the first integrated plan for a new town since the middle ages.

In 1724 Defoe was already reporting that it was

> grown up from a small place to be very considerable by the coal trade, which is encreased so considerably of late, that it is now the most eminent port in England for shipping off coals, except Newcastle ... and 'tis frequent in time of war, or upon ordinary occasion of cross winds, to have two hundred sail of ships at a time go from this place for Dublin, loaden with coals.

Mining expanded steadily through the eighteenth and nineteenth centuries until the Whitehaven pits were among the largest in the country, running for more than a mile under the sea-bed, making the Lowthers fabulously wealthy.

In 1778, during the American War of Independence, Whitehaven was attacked by the American privateer John Paul Jones, who put into the harbour in the small hours of the night and planted incendiary devices in a number of ships at the quay. The fires were quenched and Jones was deterred with gunfire from the harbour batteries, but Whitehaven retains the honour of being the last English port to be attacked by an American warship.

Unexpectedly, the Whitehaven pits provide the setting for one of the earliest and most influential Lakeland landscape poems, Dr John Dalton's *A Descriptive Poem Addressed to Two Young Ladies at their Return from Viewing the Mines near Whitehaven* (1755). Dalton's poem is also one of the first serious attempts at a poetic description of the steam engine.

The ladies in question were members of the Lowther family, friends of Dalton's who had daringly taken a trip to see the subterranean sources of their family wealth:

> Agape the sooty collier stands,
> His axe suspended in his hands,
> His Aethiopian teeth the while
> "Grin horrible a ghastly smile,"
> To see two goddesses so fair
> Descend to him from fields of air.
> But on you move thro' ways less steep
> To loftier chambers of the deep ...
> Where cavern crossing cavern meets,
> (City of subterraneous streets!)
> Where in a triple story end
> Mines that o'er mines by flights ascend.

Dalton is eloquent about the prosperity the mines are bringing to his native town:

> Where late along the naked strand,
> The fisher's cot did lonely stand, ...
> Now lofty piers their arms extend,
> And with their strong embraces bend
> Round crowded fleets ...
> The peopl'd vale fair dwellings fill,
> And lengthening streets ascend the hill.

The mines became a regular attraction for genteel tourists, who found this industrial underworld a rich source of the exotic. Thomas Pennant went down in 1774 and

> could not help enquiring there after the imaginary inhabitant, the creation of the laborer's fancy,
>
> > The swart Fairy of the mine,
>
> and was seriously answered by a black fellow at my elbow, that he really had never met with any; but that his grandfather had found the little implements and tools belonging to this diminutive race of subterraneous spirits.

He claims that before recent improvements in ventilation, 'the men who worked in [the pit] inhaled inflammable air, and, if they breathed against a candle, puffed out a fiery stream.' William Stukeley followed him in 1776 and admired 'the famous fire-engine, which is a notable piece of machinery working itself entirely'.

In the 1770s William and Dorothy Wordsworth stayed here as children with their uncle Richard Wordsworth, who was Controller of Customs in the then-busy port. Wordsworth loved the area, and later recorded that

> With this coast I have been familiar from my earliest childhood, and remember being struck for the first time by the town and port of Whitehaven and the white waves breaking against its quays and piers, as the whole scene came into view from the top of the high ground down which the road (it has since been altered) then descended abruptly. My sister, when she first heard the voice of the sea from this point, and beheld

the scene before her, burst into tears. Our family then lived at
Cockermouth, and this fact was often mentioned among us as indicating
the sensibility for which she was so remarkable.

Possibly the road in question was the steep one (no longer the main
road) which still descends through Hafras from Hensingham: they could
well have come from Cockermouth *via* Cleator Moor. New building now
obscures the view.

Later Wordsworth many times visited **Whitehaven Castle**, Lord Lonsdale's town residence, still prominent at the E side of the town centre at the
top of Lowther Street, a large square crenellated mansion against a wooded
hill, recently converted into apartments. The lawns on the town side of the
Castle are now a public park.

Wordsworth also visited the town for 'hot sea-baths' to cure a sprained
arm in the autumn of 1835, and wrote 'To the Moon (Composed by the
Seaside)', another of his 'Evening Voluntaries'. Another occasional visitor
was the Scotsman Thomas Aird, a minor poet but a major insomniac, who
in 1856 complained that he had been driven from the town by the nocturnal crowing of cocks.

Whitehaven's strangest contribution to literary biography concerns
Jonathan Swift, who in 1667, when he was one year old, was kidnapped
and brought from his native Dublin to Whitehaven by his nurse, 'a woman
of Whitehaven', who,

> being under an absolute necessity of seeing one of her relations ... and
> being at the same time extremely fond of the infant, stole him on ship
> board unknown to his mother and uncles, and carried him with her to
> Whitehaven, where he continued for almost three years. For, when the
> matter was discovered, his mother sent orders by all means not to hazard a
> second voyage, till he could better be able to bear it.

He stayed here for three years, and for the rest of his life 'loved Whitehaven
as though he had been born there'. The house where he lived is on the
clifftop at the SW side of the harbour. If you look in this direction, you will
see a tall, solitary chimney with a square base, known locally as 'the
Candlestick Chimney'. Head for this by taking the road past the Beacon
Museum to the overflow car park and then following the tarmac coastal
path up to the chimney. **Jonathan Swift House** is over rough grass, 100 yds
SW of the chimney. A small, L-shaped, cement-rendered stone building
(currently with bright red-painted door and window-frames, and some
mobile homes parked alongside), it does not look in good condition. In the
eighteenth century it was an inn known as Bowling Green House; the
bowling green was the grassy area overlooking the sea. It was also at one
time known as The Red Flag (a flag was hoisted there when the militia were
engaged in target-practice). Local opinion suggests that memories of hours
spent looking down from this house on the busy port, swarming with tiny
figures, helped inspired the miniature kingdom of Lilliput in *Gulliver's
Travels*: a pleasant theory which no-one can disprove.

WHITEHAVEN
G. Pickering, 1832

Two little-known local authors deserve mention. One is John Roach, who around 1780 published his memoirs as *The Surprizing Adventures of John Roach, Mariner, of Whitehaven, Containing, A Genuine Account of his cruel Treatment during a long Captivity amongst the savage INDIANS, and Imprisonment by the SPANIARDS, in SOUTH-AMERICA. WITH His Miraculous Preservation and Deliverance by Divine Providence; and happy Return to the Place of his Nativity, after being thirteen Years amongst his inhuman Enemies.* The second is 'Putty Joe' (1810–95), real name Joseph Hodgson, a self-educated poet and chapbook author – he attended school for only one week – who tramped the roads as a pedlar before settling down at Whitehaven as a glazier (hence the putty). His fascinating autobiography, *Memoirs of Joseph Hodgson, Glazier, a Native of Whitehaven, Cumberland, Comprising his Various Itineraries Through the United Kingdom by Sea and Land to the Forty-First Year of his Age* (1850), is probably the only known life of an author of chapbooks, cheap pamphlets sold by pedlars to the just-literate poor.

Many of the town's literary connections simply take the form of sea-departures, with all the uncertainty and tedium that implies. Shelley stayed here on his way to Ireland in February 1812:

> We are now at Whitehaven, which is a miserable manufacturing seaport Town … We may be detained some days in the Island [of Man], if the weather is fine we shall not regret it. At all events we shall escape this filthy town and horrible Inn.

Dorothy Wordsworth passed through in 1828, before sailing for the Isle of Man. Her view of the town, hastily jotted, is a mixture of the squalid and the picturesque:

> streets often terminated prettily; a hall, a church; the sea, the castle; dirty women, ragged children and filthy; no shoes, no stockings. Fine view of cliffs and stone-quarry; pretty, smokeless, blue-roofed town; castle and trees a foreign aspect.

She 'Embarked at 10. Full moon – lighthouse – luminous sky.'

Thomas Carlyle, travelling towards London by coastal steamer, spent 'six weary hours' here in August 1831 whilst his ship lay at anchor. He wandered about the town with an old friend, talking mysticism, and

> re-embarked at last amid a tumult of human noises and the bellowing of cattle, above which rose the sound of a fiddle, like the fire that streaked the smoke spouting from the funnel.

At the N side of the town, at **7 High Street**, lived the pioneer meteorologist John Fletcher Miller (1816–56); he built an observatory here, 'a small circular building with a conical copper roof '(now demolished). From 1844 onwards Miller kept rain-gauges at many points throughout the Lake District (one was on top of Scafell) and regularly made marathon walks to read them. He kept records and diaries of the weather and it was the publication of data from his rain gauges that first inspired the notion of siting reservoirs in the Lake District to supply the needs of the growing cities.

Finally, a no doubt insoluble riddle. Coleridge's notebook for November 1799 contains a cryptic note: 'In the arms of Morpheus – Miss Potter of Whitehaven' . Who was Miss Potter? And why was her sleep of interest to Coleridge?

At the S side of Whitehaven the A595 passes through the suburb of **Hensingham**. Look for **St John's Church**, a solid Edwardian Gothic sandstone building with a square tower. The poet Thomas Blackburn (1916–77) was born in the Rectory (the Victorian house at S side of church); in the church there was a portrait photograph of his father – the terrifying Eliel of Blackburn's autobiography *A Clip of Steel* (1969), where Blackburn recalls revisiting Hensingham in his youth, on the verge of a nervous breakdown: 'I remember standing under Father's picture in Hensingham Church in a miasma of guilt and unworthiness. Then the unconscious took over' and he wandered off to Whitehaven and then Keswick, sinking into alcohol and amnesia. The only trace now of the Rev. Eliel Blackburn is the brass plate about the bells, on the wall at the SE corner of the church interior, where his name is listed.

Follow signs to Cleator Moor to B5295 and continue straight through Cleator Moor to T-junction by bridge. A small R-L zig-zag will allow you to follow the sign to the village of **Ennerdale Bridge**, and **St Mary's Church**. Wordsworth and Coleridge were here during their 1799 walking tour, and this is the 'Parish Chapel ... Girt round with a bare ring of mossy wall' which is the setting of Wordsworth's 1800 poem 'The Brothers', based on a story picked up further down the valley. Sadly wall and church were, like so many ancient Cumbrian churches, rebuilt in the 1870s; the priest's reference to 'those two bells of ours, which there you see – /Hanging in the open air' was rendered obsolete at the same time. The churchyard where Leonard found his brother's grave has not been so drastically changed: even in 1799 it was not really, as in the poem, full of unmarked graves.

Ennerdale and Egremont

There are several roads to Ennerdale Water. For the one that extends furthest, at junction ignore turning signed Ennerdale Lake and head for Croasdale. After ¾m you pass the entrance to **How Hall Farm**, birthplace of the twentieth-century poet Tom Rawling (1916-96), best remembered for two superb books of poems on nature and Cumbrian subjects, *Ghosts at My Back* (1982) and *The Names of the Sea Trout* (1993). After an unhappy childhood here and at Whitehaven (his schoolmaster father was too fond of the cane) Rawling left Cumbria, returning only in his poems and, occasionally, to fish the River Esk with his friend Hugh Falkus (on whom see p 214). From Croasdale follow signs to Ennerdale Water only. There is a car park.

Ennerdale is, paradoxically, one of the Lakeland valleys least touched by modern technology, and yet most changed in modern times. Until 1989 it had no electricity and there is still no public road. On the other hand its general appearance has altered utterly: formerly rocky but pastoral and not unlike Eskdale in looks, it was planted with conifers by the Forestry Commission in the 1930s. The action aroused an outcry, and but for these protests probably far more of the Lake District would now be under conifers. For one who never saw the valley in its unforested state, the old Ennerdale is now unimaginable.

This was not the only battle fought over Ennerdale. In 1883 there was a plan to run a railway through the valley; Canon Rawnsley and the Lake District Defence Society opposed it fiercely, and the *Pall Mall Gazette* published an ironic 'Poetical Lamentation on the Insufficiency of Steam Locomotion in the Lake District':

> Wake, England, wake! 'tis now the hour
> To sweep away this black disgrace –
> The want of locomotive power
> In so enjoyable a place.

> Nature has done her part, and why
> Is mightier man in his to fail?
> I want to hear the porter's cry,
> 'Change here for Ennerdale!'

The railway was abandoned. More recently there have been similar battles between conservationists and those wanting to open the valley to motor traffic.

Coleridge explored the shores of **Ennerdale Water** in 1799 with Wordsworth, and came here again alone in 1802; he was intrigued by the lake's

ENNERDALE WATER
Thomas Allom, 1832

shape ('Ennerdale ... compleatly fiddle shaped', he wrote) and collected
stories from local people:

> Iron Crag – back of this the wild Cat fell into the water, four Hounds & a
> Terrier with it – when they came up, they were all of a mat, each hold of
> the Cat – the Cat of all of them/5 minutes under the water/

Iron Crag is the outcrop at the summit of the slope immediately S of the
head of the lake. There is a footpath around the whole shore of the lake,
and it makes a good walk (some 10m by the shortest route).

For **Pillar** walk along the N shore then continue E past the Youth Hostel
for 2m. Take the path R (S; signed Pillar) and cross the footbridge. You will
reach a dirt-track road with another coming down to join it at a junction.
Go up the upper road a few yards: the path to Pillar runs straight up the fell.

The fell is named after **Pillar Rock**, the rocky needle just to the north
side of its summit, overlooking Ennerdale. The rock can be seen right
across the valley in good weather; in mist, on the other hand, it can be
impossible to locate – a grey object in a grey landscape on ground so rough
that paths are not clearly visible. If you want to get to it, choose your day
carefully and be prepared for some scrambling.

Somewhere near here on their 1799 tour Wordsworth and Coleridge
met a farmer who told them the tale of a young shepherd, James Bowman,
who

> broke his neck ... by falling off a Crag – supposed to have layed down &
> slept – but walked in his sleep, & so came to this crag, & fell off – This was
> at Proud Knott on the mountain caled Pillar up Ennerdale – his Pike staff
> stuck midway & stayed there till it rotted away –

EGREMONT FROM THE RAVENGLASS ROAD
G. Pickering, 1830

Wordsworth adapted the story for 'The Brothers', changing the location to Pillar Rock itself (a most unlikely place for anyone to sleep) and the shepherd's name to Ewbank.

It was here not long afterwards that true rock-climbing began. The 'Pillar Stone' was described in Otley's 1823 *Guide* as 'unclimbable'; a local shepherd, John Atkinson, took up the challenge and climbed it the next year. Gradually a trickle of others, mainly visitors, began to follow suit. In 1850 an English-educated Swiss, C.A. Baumgartner, established what is now known as the 'Old Wall Route'.

The tricky route, the North Climb which overhangs Ennerdale, was the achievement of W. Haskett-Smith in 1890. On his first attempt, in 1889, he succeeded only in dislodging a gigantic boulder which nearly took him with it as it thundered down into the valley, and left him hanging by his hands over empty space. Still in a state of shock when he found a foothold again, he was surprised to hear his own voice reciting '*autis epeita pedonde kulindeto laas anaides*' – (Homer, *Odyssey* XI 598: 'Then down again to the plain would come rolling the pitiless stone.') Nothing deterred, he returned and accomplished the climb in 1890. It is now a popular route.

Return to Cleator Moor and follow A5086 3m S to the small town of **Egremont** (*car parks on both sides of main street*). As so often, the best description is from Coleridge's notebooks:

> View, from Egremont Castle, of Houses & River & Hill. Fields beyond River, as impossible to describe to an other as a Dream/The Arch, the buildings before the Church, the Church, the Hills with the gap –...
> The fine noble Ash Tree in the Road between the Castle Hill & the Buildings – the Buildings, Wall, Garden with its various beds – so slovenly

in its tyrannically strait parallelogram inclosures, the Marygolds, yellow
Lillies, loftiest Peas in Blossom, Beans, Onions, Cabbages – then the
Houses – in such various outlines, all formal, yet the formality neutralized
by the variety of the formal & their incursions on each other/some
thatched, some slated, some meeting the eye with their broad fronts, some
with their corner Gavels – some spank new, some in ruins – Houses &c in
the River & dark Trees by their backs over the River – various Linen, blue,
crocus, & white, on the formal Hedges/ here the Hills & fields peeping over
the Town, here the higher Houses intercepting the Hills & Fields. The
Country itself banks in harmonious Irregularity – Egremont Castle, August
3. 1802.

Egremont is now a scruffy but pleasant town, somewhat marked by heavy
industry. The stumpy remains of **Egremont Castle** are at the S end of the
main street, in a park which seems to be open all daylight hours. It
commands a good view, though if you look out over the town and compare
what you see with Coleridge's description, you will reflect sadly on what
the last two centuries have done.

Just below the Castle is the **Horn of Egremont** pub, commemorating
Wordsworth's poem 'The Horn of Egremont Castle' (1806), which sets here
a medieval tale of brotherly treachery and credits the Castle with a magical
horn 'which none could sound … Save He who came as rightful Heir'.

St Bees and Gosforth

From Egremont follow signs to the delightful coastal village of **St Bees**,
built of red sandstone with many very old buildings. It is one of those
places which keeps a certain magic from having been, once, of great importance and being now almost forgotten. The **Priory**, of eroded red sandstone, is heavily restored from the original 1120 building but still feels very
ancient. It contains a particularly splendid organ, the masterpiece of
'Father' Henry Willis (1821–1901), greatest of Victorian organ builders.

The place is full of legends. The main one concerns St Bega herself, who
is said to have sailed here from Ireland in about AD 650. She and her nuns
begged the lord of the manor for a piece of land; he contemptuously told
them they might have as much ground as the snow covered at midsummer.
On Midsummer Day it duly snowed, and the land was given to found the
Priory. (Defoe, who visited in 1724, was sceptical of the legend: 'these, and
the like tales, I leave where I found them, (viz) among the rubbish of the old
women and the Romish priests', he snorted.)

Many poems have told the Saint's story, among them the Rev Richard
Parkinson's 'The Legend of St. Bega's Abbey' in his *Poems Sacred and
Miscellaneous* (Whitehaven 1832). Wordsworth, on his way to the Isle of
Man in 1833, wrote (at sea, as the title suggests) 'Stanzas Suggested in a
Steamboat off Saint Bees Head', about the Saint and the Abbey, including
good wishes for 'the new-born College of St Bees' – the theological college
established here in 1816. The poem is quite outstandingly dull, its only
point of interest being a technical freak whereby Wordsworth ends every

one of the *eighteen* stanzas with the words 'St Bees', and manages to rhyme the two preceding lines with it.

Eliza Lynn Linton mentions another legend, that somewhere hereabouts is 'the giant's grave – if you can find it':

> In the library of the Dean and Chapter of Carlisle is an account of the finding a giant at St Bees, in the year 1601, just before Christmas time: it is in Machell's MSS., and tells how that 'he the said Gyant was four yards and a half long, and was in complete armour; that his teeth were six inches long, and that he was buried four yards deep in the ground, which is now a cornfield. His armour, sword, battle-axe are at Mr. Sand's, of Redington (Rollington), and at Mr. Wyber's, at St. Bees.

Opposite the Priory is **St Bees School**, founded by Edmund Grindall, Archbishop of Canterbury. There is a characteristically eloquent account of him by Fuller, who says he lost favour with Queen Elizabeth I by

> keeping others from breaking two of God's commandments, 'Thou shalt not steal,' when he would not let the lord of Leicester have Lambeth-house; and 'Thou shalt not commit adultery,' when he would not permit Julio, the earl's Italian physician, to marry another man's wife.

His enemies tried to set the Queen against him; but though he 'was willing to undress before he went to bed' – ie to give up his Archbishopric during his lifetime – the Queen, 'commiserating his condition, was graciously pleased to say, that, as she had made him, so he should die an archbishop'.

> Worldly wealth he cared not for, desiring only to make both ends meet; and as for that little that lapped over, he gave it to pious uses in both universities, and the founding of a fair free-school at Saint Bees, the place of his nativity.

The school itself remained a small local grammar school until the early nineteenth century, when it was discovered that the Lowther coalfields went under land which formed part of the school's small endowment. The Lowthers put up a bitter fight in the courts but were forced to pay for the coal they were extracting and the school's fortunes suddenly changed.

It is now a large and well-known independent school, and provides us with yet another local legend, that of the early nineteenth-century 'Student of St Bees', told in De Quincey's *Recollections* and in a poem (1853) by James Payn. The student, a 'meditative young boy' who studied at the school, was ordered by his family to abandon his studies and go into business. Rather than submit to this fate he committed suicide in the 'cloudy wildernesses' of Blencathra, taking an overdose of opium and dying with his head pillowed on the works of his favourite classical authors. No-one seems to know if there is any truth in the tale.

To find **Archbishop Grindall's birthplace** go into the village and walk up the main street, then round the corner by the Manor House Inn. 30yds NE of the inn is the house, which has a plaque.

For **St Bees Head** from the Abbey go N (bearing L up steep hill) then L again at cottages just before chemical works. Where road forks at grassy triangle, park and walk along drive to lighthouse, then follow coastal path L (SW) to the headland, a spectacular point with sandstone cliffs and a deep chasm eroded by the sea. Besides being St Bega's landing-place, the Head is now well-known as the starting point for A. Wainwright's Coast-to-Coast walk.

Return to Egremont and follow A595 S 2m. After Thornhills turn R at lights (signed St Bees, Beckermet) then at once sharp R (signed St Bees) again. At bridge over river park, and walk ¼m S along riverbank to **Wotobank**, an attractive farmhouse rebuilt 1816 between the river Ehen and the Bank after which it is named, a green escarpment running behind the house. The weird name is traditionally explained by an unlikely story (told here by Eliza Lynn Linton):

> There was once a certain lord of Beckermet, who one day went out hunting wolves, accompanied by his lady and a lordly retinue. The 'ardour of the chase' separated him from his wife, who was soon missing from the cavalcade, but after a search was found lying dead on the side of a hill, with a wolf devouring her. In the agony of his sorrow the husband cried out, 'Woe to this bank!' and succeeding ages crystallized the cry, which at this day is the name of a pretty modern house built on the site of the poor lady's untimely deathbed.

Return to A595 and at roundabout just S of traffic lights, follow signs to Sellafield Visitor Centre for **Sellafield Nuclear Reprocessing Plant** (*open April-October, 10–6; November-March, 10–4; free admission, car park; shop, café*). There are in fact three closely-related nuclear installations here. **Windscale** (opened 1951, distinguishable by tall concrete chimney bulging at top) produced plutonium for the British atomic bomb; **Calder Hall** (opened 1956; distinguishable by cooling towers) is a nuclear power station; **Sellafield** is a plant for dealing with spent radioactive materials from various sources worldwide. The site has drawn the attention of distinguished modern poets.

In 1957 Windscale was the scene of Britain's worst-ever nuclear accident, when the reactor overheated and a meltdown was narrowly avoided. Investigations showed that for years radioactive particles had been leaking from the chimneys over the surrounding countryside (the full details were suppressed for decades). Local milk was poured down the drains and beef cattle slaughtered and burned to avoid spreading the contamination. Norman Nicholson's poem 'Windscale' reflects bitterly on the disaster, and the bland reassurances given to the public at the time:

> The toadstool towers infest the shore:
> Stink-horns that propagate and spore
> Wherever the wind blows ...
>
> This is a land ...
> Where sewers run with milk, and meat
> Is carved up for the fire to eat,
> And children suffocate in God's fresh air.

More recently Seamus Heaney, in 'A Paved Text', has reflected on the waste materials released into the Irish Sea:

> Now nuclear poisons re-anglicize a sea
>
> that is yours and mine as well,
> our saint-crossed, whitecapped, scouse-cursed
> swan-road and path of exile
> become a dump for waste.
>
> *Windscale*: it was pristine,
> imagined and self-cleansing ...

but not any more, in Heaney's opinion.

The visitor centre offers a dazzling display on nuclear energy and the processes used at Sellafield; there are also free coach tours of the site.

Return to A595, which leads directly into **Calder Bridge**. Coleridge was here on his August 1802 walking tour and was charmed, like most visitors, by the clustering of village, bridge and Abbey in a rocky, wooded dell. Harriet Martineau urges us to

> step into the inn garden at the bridge, and see how beautifully the brown waters swirl away under the red bridge and its ivied banks, while the waving ferns incessantly checker the sunshine. It is a mile to the Abbey, through the churchyard, and along the bank of the Calder, where again the most beautiful tricks of light are seen, with brown water and its white foam, red precipitous banks, and the greenest vegetation, with a wood crowning all ... The ruins are presently seen, springing sheer from the greenest turf ...
>
> The ruins should be approached from the front, so that the lofty pointed arches may best disclose the long perspective behind of grassy lawn and sombre woods.

This picturesque spot is still much as she describes it. The footpath runs along the N bank of the river from the churchyard; from it you can see **Calder Abbey** but not visit it, since the path is fenced off at the end and the Abbey is on private land. The building is quite extraordinary: ruins of the late twelfth-century Abbey (splendid sandstone transept arches and arcades), with a handsome late eighteenth-century house built on to the S end, with a massive and pretty tasteless Victorian mansion built in turn onto that: three completely incongruous buildings grafted together as if by some weird accident.

Return to the village and continue S on A595. After 2m you pass the **Red Admiral Inn**, formerly the Boonwood Hotel. Coleridge paused here for refreshment on his walking tour in August 1802, and as usual collected a story:

> Arrived at Bonewood, Wednesday 12 o'clock – a neat little public House kept by one Manson – on the top of the Hill – a nice view of the Sea with the Isle of Man on one side ... [The landlady] Lost her son, last new year's day 7 year, in Bassenthwaite, attempting to save Dr. Head of Cockermouth

CALDER ABBEY
W.J. Linton, 1864

& another Gentleman/they saved, & he lost/consoled the old Mother by contrasting his Fate with a Soldier's dying in attempting to kill his fellow creatures.

He then walked on another mile to Gosforth, where we shall follow him.

Gosforth (*car park at centre*), ('the reddest of villages' according to Harriet Martineau), is notable for the **Gosforth Cross**. Take turning opposite Methodist Church and go 200yds to **St Mary's Church**: the slender fourteen-foot Cross, by the S door, is of red sandstone. Dating from 1000AD, it is richly carved with scenes from the Norse Voluspa, an epic poem describing the creation and end of the world.

The church (heavily restored in the 1890s) contains several tenth-century monuments, including two impressive Norse 'hogback tombstones' found under the church during its restoration. One of these forms the basis for Nicholas Size's historical romance *Shelagh of Eskdale, or The Stone of Shame* (1932), which elaborates the theory that the curious carvings on the stone represent the army of the Saxon King Ethelred ('the Unready') surrendering the English standard to a Norse army which surrounded them on Wrynose Pass one Whitsunday in about 950AD.

On a window-sill at W end of church is the T'ang Dynasty bell which surprised and delighted the exiled Chinese poet, painter and calligrapher Chiang Yee when he visited in 1936. It was captured by a local naval commander at Canton in 1841. The huge crack commemorates an ill-fated attempt in 1896 to use it as a church bell: fitted with an iron clapper by the blacksmith, it was rung once and split. Chinese bells are meant to be beaten with padded hammers.

From Gosforth follow signs S across A595 to **Seascale**, formerly a fairly popular seaside resort, now quieter and hemmed in by battalions of grey council houses. The seafront is still pleasant. George Gissing spent child-hood holidays here and used it as a setting for several chapters of his novel *The Odd Women* (1893): 'Seascale has no street, no shops;' Gissing writes, 'only two or three short rows of houses irregularly placed on the rising ground above the beach'. The heroine, Rhoda Nunn, takes lodgings here for a holiday in 'uncertain weather':

> Over Wastdale hung a black canopy; from Scawfell came mutterings of thunder; and on the last night of the week ... Rhoda saw the rocky heights that frown upon Wastwater illuminated by lightning-flare.

As well as a view of Wasdale her sitting-room window overlooks the rail-way station (she must have been staying at the **Scawfell Hotel**, formerly a well-known hostelry next to the station, now demolished and replaced by a housing estate) and she watches anxiously for the arrival of the hero, Everard Barfoot. Later they take the Ravenglass and Eskdale Railway to Boot and walk over to Wasdale Head, returning for an ironically unroman-tic proposal scene on the Seascale beach at sunset. The **Seascale railway station** itself was well known to C.L. Dodgson ('Lewis Carroll'), who frequently alighted here, on his way to visit his cousins on the Lutwidge family estate at Holmrook.

At the dawn of the Industrial Revolution there were ironworks half a mile s down the coast at **Whitriggs**, giving a weird vision of industrial horrors to come. Thomas Pennant in 1774 made an excursion to

> the great iron mines at Whitriggs ... [where] ... the ore lies in vast heaps about the mines, so as to form perfect mountains; is of that species called by mineralogists *haematites* and kidney-ore; is red, very greasy and defiling. The iron race that inhabits the mining villages exhibit a strange appearance: men, women and children are perfectly dyed with it, and even innocent babes do quickly assume the bloody complexion of the soil.

From Gosforth follow signs for Nether Wasdale 1m; just over the crest of the hill is **Sowermyrr**, a grey pebbledashed farmhouse where Hugh Walpole (who calls it Sower Mire Farm) spent childhood summer holidays with his parents between 1893 and 1898 – a welcome respite from board-ing-school in Durham, and the beginning of his addiction to the Lake District:

> I stood on the pebbly path that bordered the garden ... and drank in the scene. That moment was my initiation. That little windy garden, smelling of cow-dung, carnations, snapdragons and – in some mysterious fashion – hens' feathers, looked straight out to sea. On clear days it was said that you could catch a vision of the Isle of Man.

Wasdale and the Scafells

Continue E 4½m to **Wastwater** with its extraordinary **Screes**, cascades of loose stones which pour down the steep south-eastern side of the valley to

WASTWATER – THE SCREES
W.J. Linton, 1864

the edge of the lake. 'When people go forth to see the world', wrote Thomas Wilkinson in 1824,

> they are sometimes in search of beauty. If beauty is the leading object of their search, they need not go to Wast Water. The prominent features round Wast Water are sternness and sterility ... The mountains of Wast Water are naked to their base: – their sides and their summits are uniform: their summits shoot up into lofty points, and end in the form of pyramids. We have heard of the pyramids of Egypt, built by the hand of man; but these are the Pyramids of the world, built by the Architect of the Universe.

As Wilkinson's grand passage suggests, the valley *does* have an austere beauty, though in the language of his day he would have called it sublimity, as Wordsworth does. The lake, says the poet, is 'long, narrow, stern and desolate' but also 'well worth the notice of the traveller who is not afraid of fatigue; no part of the country is more distinguished by sublimity.'

Coleridge's 1802 letter is eloquent:

> it is a marvellous sight / a sheet of water between three & four miles in length, the whole (or very nearly the whole) of it's right Bank formed by the Screes, ... consisting of fine red Streaks running in broad Stripes thro' a stone colour – slanting off from the Perpendicular, as steep as the meal newly ground from the Miller's Spout ... like a pointed Decanter in shape, or an outspread fan ... When I first came the Lake was a perfect Mirror; & what must have been the Glory of the reflections in it! This huge facing of Rock *said* to be half a mile in perpendicular height, with deep Ravins the whole *winded* & torrent-worn, except where the pink-striped Screes come in, as smooth as silk / all this reflected, turned into Pillars, dells, and a whole new-world of Images in the water!

At 260ft, Wastwater is the deepest lake in England and, though occasionally mirrorlike, its waters are more often dark green or inky black. Its sombre beauty was appreciated by Edward Lear, who painted it during his 1836 sketching tour.

The red or pink tinges in the Screes are caused by iron in the rocks. This was formerly a source of 'ruddle', which (according to Parkinson's *The Old Church Clock* (1843)) is

> a stone strongly mixed with iron, which, by wetting and rubbing, produces

a deep red paint which hardly any exposure to the weather can wash away, especially when stained upon an oily substance like wool.

It was used for marking sheep and local boys would gather it from the face of the screes to sell to farmers:

> steady step and firm nerve ... are required to descend the surface of the steep and loose declivity, and avoid any disturbance of their rolling mass, which, once commencing its movement, would to a certainty hurl the bold adventurer to the bottom.

In summer 1809 Wordsworth, De Quincey and others came here to camp and fish with John Wilson (essayist, editor of *Blackwood's Edinburgh Magazine* and minor 'Lake Poet'). One of Wilson's most ostentatious exploits, the party brought thirty-two pony-loads of baggage. 'Towards evening', wrote Wilson,

> the inhabitants of the valley, not exceeding half-a-dozen families ... drawn by the unusual appearance, came to visit the strangers in their tent ... At a late hour, their guests departed under a most refulgent moon that lighted them up the surrounding mountains, on which they turned to hail with long-continued shouts and songs the blazing of a huge fire, that was hastily kindled at the door of the tent to bid them a distant farewell.

Wilson's poem 'The Angler's Tent', describing the excursion and the lavish hospitality given to the visitors, includes a few lines contributed by Wordsworth about

> The placid lake that rested far below
> Softly embosoming another sky

– presenting Wastwater in unusually friendly aspect. The twentieth-century poet William Scammell captures a more ominous weirdness in 'The Screes' (from *Yes and No*, 1979):

> The screes are speeding down at perfect pitch
> before they tuck themselves in silences
> Wastwater seals and never means to post...
> A cormorant, wings unpacked, hung out to dry,
> stands phoenix-fixed upon a rock.

Coleridge's 1802 walk followed the road up the valley towards Wasdale Head, which offers a superb panorama of the lake and the Screes. **Wasdale Head** is a long, narrow strip of flat farming land enclosed between the towering slopes of Yewbarrow to the W, Kirk Fell to the N and Lingmell (a foothill of Scafell) to the E. It is best seen – a really astonishing view – from Great Gable. Wordsworth describes it nicely,

> with its little chapel and half a dozen neat dwellings scattered upon a plain of meadow and corn-ground intersected with stone walls apparently innumerable, like a large piece of lawless patch-work.

The crazy-quilt effect of the fields is beautifully clear from Great Gable, though some of the colour has vanished, for there are no 'corngrounds' now.

WASTWATER
Thomas Allom, 1832

Wasdale Head is traditionally the stronghold of Herdwick sheepfarming: according to Clarke's *Survey* (1785) 'the inhabitants of Nether Wasdale say' that the original flock of Herdwicks was 'taken from aboard a stranded ship' – perhaps a Norse ship – in the early middle ages. The sheep 'take the stormy side of the mountain, which saves them from being overblown with snow: 'this valuable instinct was first discovered by the people of Wasdalehead'.

Despite many tourists, the valley was still very primitive in the mid-nineteenth century. In 1854 Harriet Martineau noted that the local schoolmaster was still

> entertained on 'whittlegate' terms: that is, he boards at the farmhouses in turn. An old man told us that the plan answers. 'He gets them on very well,' said he; 'and particularly in the spelling. He thinks that if they can spell, they can do all the rest.' Such are the original conclusions arrived at in Wastdale Head. It struck us that the children were dirtier than even in other vales, though the houses are so clean that you might eat your dinner off the board or the floor. But the state of children's skin and hair is owing to superstition, in all these dales, ... A young lady who kindly undertook to wash and dress the infant of a sick woman, but who was not experienced in the process, exclaimed at the end 'O dear! I forgot its hands and arms. I must wash them.' The mother expressed great horror, and said that 'if the child's arms were washed before it was six months old, it would be a thief;' and, added she, pathetically, 'I would not like that.'

Wasdale Head's most distinctive landmark – visible for miles as a long, offwhite building – is the **Wasdale Head Inn**, one of the most famous hotels in the Lake District. Originally a farmhouse known as Rowfoot, it was the birthplace (in 1808) of Will Ritson, friend of De Quincey, John

Wilson and Wordsworth. Famous as huntsman, wrestler and raconteur, Ritson cultivated the role of the archetypal 'Cumberland Statesman', becoming the uncrowned 'King o' Wasdale' and, for much of the nineteenth century, a prominent tourist attraction in himself. His tales, laced with dry wit and sharpened by a judicious use of dialect, were (according to a Victorian guide-book)

> as varied as they were numerous ... The stories of the wrestling match with Professor Wilson, of the miserly Eskdale parson, and the famous pony-race down Sty Head, are only a few of a host of Cumbrian 'epics' which will, we hope, be preserved.

Ritson specialised in tall stories, and is said to have won a lying contest outright by declaring himself unable to enter because, like George Washington, he could not tell a lie. (This aspect of his character is commemorated by the 'World's Greatest Liar' competition, held annually at Santon Bridge.)

Having added a wing to his farmhouse to accommodate paying guests, Ritson in 1856 obtained a pack of hounds and a licence and turned his premises into 'The Huntsman's Inn'. It was a timely move: rock climbing had lately begun in the area, and though Ritson himself never climbed and even discouraged early climbers, in the 1860s the visitors' book at the Inn began to be used as a route book to record climbs.

Ritson retired in 1879 and died in 1890, but interest in climbing continued to grow and in the 1880s the pioneers of British climbing, W.P. Haskett-Smith, Owen Glynne Jones and the photographer-brothers George and Ashley Abraham used the Inn as the base from which they developed the classic routes up neighbouring crags such as Great Gable, Scafell and Pillar. Until the First World War the Inn was invaded every Christmas by the climbing fraternity, who would hope for a good freeze, when (as Geoffrey Winthrop Young put it) 'the sky stayed steel-blue and the rocks were all draped in dull ivory ice'.

These holidays developed their own traditions: the children of the village school would perform a pantomime for the party from the Inn, who would return the favour with a performance of their own the following night. A perennial joke was the 'Barn Door Traverse', where climbers had to make their way up and over the large barn door to R of the Inn, under the stone lintel still marked 'POST HORSES': in those days the stonework was unpointed, which made things easier.

In the 1910s and 20s literary mountaineers included I.A. Richards (later to write *Practical Criticism, Coleridge On Imagination* and other foundations of modern literary theory) and his wife, the climbing-writer Dorothy Pilley, whose *Climbing Days* gives a lively account of Lakeland mountaineering at this period. Besides being prominent in climbing memoirs, the Inn has made several fictional appearances, notably in A.E.W. Mason's grim Victorian thriller *A Romance of Wasdale* (1895), where the blackmailer Austin Hawke encounters the heroine in one of the Inn's bedrooms, and – less realistically – in *Rogue Herries* (1930), where Hugh Walpole (perhaps unaware that there was no inn here until the mid-nineteenth century) imagines the Inn's parlour as it might have been in about 1760: 'a small place, dim with the smoke from the fire, smelling of food, ale, dung, human unwashed bodies.'

The Inn has been many times enlarged and is now a very substantial building, but for once this has been done without seriously damaging its appearance and character. It keeps many nineteenth-century features, including the entrance hall shown strewn with climbing-boots in a famous Abraham Brothers photograph, and has a collection of climbing memorabilia (much of it on display in 'Ritson's Bar' at the N end of the building) and prints of many Abraham photographs.

Take the lane N alongside the Barn Door Shop for 50yds to **Rowhead**, a seventeenth-century building with garden and large barn. It was probably here, or at Rowfoot long before it became an inn, that the young William Wilberforce stayed in the spartan pre-tourist days of 1776 with his cousin Samuel Smith and 'slept, or rather pass'd the night, in the same Wooden Crib, after piercing thro' the Gorge of Borodale'.

In the later nineteenth century Rowhead, like the Inn, took climbing parties, often sharing them: 'Tyson's Farm' and the Inn were thought of almost as a unit, and like the Inn, Rowhead has made fictional appearances. The novelist and critic Arthur Quiller-Couch brought reading-parties of Oxford students here in the Easter holidays of 1885–7. They studied in the mornings and spent the afternoons climbing. In 1887 the students 'toiled over Aristotelian logic' whilst 'Q' 'sat at a table in the "Windy Parlour" of the farmhouse' writing *Dead Man's Rock*, the first of his series of Cornish adventure stories. Among the students that year was the future thriller-writer A.E.W. Mason. Mason's hero in *A Romance of Wasdale*, David Gordon, stays at this farmhouse and several melodramatic scenes take place here and on the crags of Scafell above.

Take the path signed Sty Head 200yds E from the Inn to a grove of yew trees, which hide **St Olaf's Church**, thought to be the third smallest church in England. The churchyard contains the graves of many climbers; note also those of Alexandrina Wilson, 'Last Schoolteacher of the Dale' (d 1947) and of the Shakespeare scholar A.P. Rossiter, whose finely lettered headstone says nothing of his books on Elizabethan drama or his work (with I.A. Richards) on Basic English, recording simply that he 'Climbed in these Hills'.

Continue N on the path to **Burnthwaite** (*NT*), a long, low farmhouse of local stone. Wordsworth and Coleridge stayed there on their 1799 walking tour before taking the Sty Head Pass to Rosthwaite and Coleridge returned alone in the course of his fellwalking excursion on August 1 1802. He was 'welcomed kindly' by the farmer, Thomas Tyson, 'had a good Bed, and left it after breakfast' heading for Scafell.

In 1877 the great Victorian lexicographer James Murray, editor of the

Oxford English Dictionary, stayed here with his two young sons after a marathon walk over Scafell from Chapel Stile in Langdale. Having 'secured a bed' and a meal, they set off to watch an eclipse of the moon from the gate opposite the Inn.

Wasdale is a convenient starting-point for Scafell, Scafell Pike and Great Gable. We shall follow Coleridge's 1802 route, which takes in the rest of literary Wasdale. From Burnthwaite he 'went down the Vale almost to the water head, & ascended the low Reach between Sca' Fell and the Screes'. To do likewise, take the road S towards the lake and turn E over bridge (signed Wasdale Head Hall Farm). Just beyond car park follow footpath (signed Eskdale). The path runs due S up the fellside and along the upper edge of a small wood.

Continue S up slope to **Burnmoor Tarn**, 'it's Tail towards Sca' Fell, at its head a gap forming an inverted arch with Black Coomb & a peep of the Sea seen thro' it' as Coleridge says. The Tarn is the scene of a picnic in George Gissing's *The Odd Women* (1893), an idyllic moment in an otherwise grim and urban novel, when Rhoda Nunn and Everard Barfoot pause here on their way to Wasdale Head:

> A wild spot, a hollow amid the rolling expanse of moorland, its little lake of black water glistening under the midday sun. And here stood a shepherd's cottage, the only habitation they had seen since leaving Boot. Somewhat uncertain about the course to be henceforth followed, they made inquiry at this cottage, and a woman who appeared to be quite alone gave them the needful direction. Thus at ease in mind they crossed the bridge at the foot of the tarn, and just beyond it found a spot suitable for repose. Everard brought forth his sandwiches and a flask of wine, moreover a wine-glass, which was for Rhoda's use. They ate and drank festively.

'An ideal realized for once in one's life. A perfect moment,' reflects the hero.

Ninety years earlier, it was from here that Coleridge began his ascent of Scafell. Looking N from the tarn, you will see two small watercourses flowing down on to the NE end of the plateau, where they join. Follow the L of these, Hardrigg Gill, uphill, keeping the stream on your R. After half a mile a tributary joins the gill from L (NW): do not cross this but keep it on your R; after it peters out the path turns eastward and is cairned to Scafell summit.

Coleridge's route here was slightly different but cannot be recommended because of the danger of erosion. He seems to have crossed the new tributary and headed due NE, straight up the slope. This strenuously direct route leads to steep and stony terrain – no wonder Coleridge 'climbed & rested, rested & climbed' – looking back to see the 'flounder-shaped' Burnmoor Tarn, the S end foreshortened into a fishtail, the little peninsular at N forming the mouth.

Once at the summit of **Scafell**, a short walk N brings us to the top of **Scafell Crag**, where we can share Coleridge's exaltation at the stupendous prospect (looking N):

> O my God! what enormous Mountains these are close by me, & yet below
> the Hill I stand on … But O! what a look down just under my Feet! The
> frightfullest Cove that might ever be seen / huge perpendicular Precipices,
> and one sheep upon it's only ledge … Tyson told me of this place, and
> called it Hollow Stones. Just by it & joining together, rise two huge Pillars
> of bare lead-colored stone – / I am no measurer / but their height & depth is
> terrible.

Nonetheless Coleridge kept enough self-possession to find 'a nice Stone
Table' and settle down in the sunshine to write Sara Hutchinson 'surely
the first Letter ever written from the top of Sca' Fell'. It was August 5 1802.

Notice the plaque recording the 'dedication' of the summit to the nation
by Gordon Wordsworth (the poet's grandson) and A.C. Benson
(1862–1925), Cambridge don, prolific essayist and critic, who was a keen
walker in the area. Wordsworth and Benson, early members of the
National Trust, bought the summit in 1924 from Lord Leconfield, who was
puzzled by their motives:

> I can't see why you should want to *buy* – you can go anywhere, do
> anything already. I have no rights but mineral and shooting rights; and
> there isn't an ounce of anything but soft stone, nor any sign of life … Still if
> you have money to throw away and like to buy rights which you already
> enjoy, well and good.

We return to 1802 and Coleridge, who having enjoyed the prospect
from Scafell now faced the problem of getting down. As all well-prepared
walkers know these days, there is no direct route from Scafell to Scafell
Pike. To get across to the Pike you must first descend by way of Green How,
Lord's Rake or Foxes Tarn. Coleridge, however, noted 'A Ridge of Hill' –
Mickledore – joining Scafell and the Pike like a 'hyphen' between two
words. He fell into the trap; he turned E where only serious climbers
should follow him, and – on the principle 'where it is first *possible* to
descend, there I go' – began to descend what is now known as **Broad Stand**:

> I slipped down, & went on for a while with tolerable ease – but now I came
> … to a smooth perpendicular Rock about seven feet high – this was
> nothing – I put my hands on the Ledge, and dropped down / in a few yards
> came just such another / I *dropped* that too / and yet another … but the
> stretching of the muscle of my hands & arms, & the jolt of the Fall on my
> Feet, put my whole Limbs in a *Tremble*.

Several more drops brought him to a point where only two more remained,

> but of these two the first was tremendous/ it was twice my own height, &
> the Ledge at the bottom was exceedingly narrow, that if I dropt down upon
> it I must of necessity have fallen backwards & of course killed myself. My
> Limbs were all in a tremble – I lay upon my back to rest myself, & was
> beginning according to my Custom to laugh at myself for a Madman, when
> the sight of the Crags above me on each side, & the impetuous Clouds just
> over them, posting so luridly and rapidly northward, overawed me / I lay in
> a state of almost prophetic Trance and Delight … O God, I exclaimed aloud

– how calm, how blessed am I now / I know not how to proceed, how to return / but I am calm & fearless & confident.

He then noticed a 'rent' in the rock: he got into it, 'slipped down as between two walls' and dropped on to safe ground. He had discovered the cleft (about 25yds down the scree E of Mickledore) still used by climbers as the first pitch in ascending Broad Stand. He was lucky to be alive. It was the completion of the first recorded ascent of Scafell. He had had enough climbing for the day and rather than ascend the Pike he descended into Eskdale, where we shall follow him in due course.

Meanwhile, some general considerations about the Scafell group. Owing to its remoteness, until the 1820s the massif was not generally recognised as containing the highest peak in England, that honour being given instead to Skiddaw. Local opinion in West Cumberland, however, knew better: in 1779 William Wilberforce recorded being shown 'a high Hill with a kind of crack in it … said by the People thereabouts to be higher than Skiddaw.' This was Scafell. Within twenty years of Coleridge's ascent Scafell had become a standard climb for the hardier Lakeland visitor, though usually with guides and ponies. Coleridge climbed it in August; now someone is there every day of the year.

The summit gives the views, but other impressive aspects, such as Scafell Crag and Broad Stand, should be seen from below, from the Wasdale-Eskdale footpath over Hollow Stones and Mickledore. The grim walls above the Mickledore ridge provide a suitably ferocious setting for the climax of A.E.W. Mason's *A Romance of Wastdale*: the hero, David Gordon, climbs Broad Stand whilst the villain, Austen Hawke, is making his way up the Chimney. They meet on the traverse between the two routes and Gordon murders Hawke on the small 'platform' between. It is a gruesome business: Gordon slashes Hawke's wrist, knocks him unconscious and leaves him to bleed to death.

For most walkers, the goal after Scafell will be its neighbour, **Scafell Pike**, the highest mountain in England. It was cairned in 1826 to distinguish it from Scafell and mark the highest point – an indication that by then visitors wanted this information.

The most famous lines of verse mentioning the Pike are actually a dismissal: in *Letter to Lord Byron*, W.H. Auden asserted (not altogether coherently) that 'Clearer than Scafell Pike, my heart has stamped on / The view from Birmingham to Wolverhampton', asserting his preference for an 'ideal scenery' of 'tramlines and slagheaps'.

Dorothy Wordsworth climbed the Pike in 1818 with Elizabeth Barker; her praise of the summit's solitude reads rather poignantly now, an echo of an age when mountain-walking was the recreation of a few eccentrics:

> not a blade of grass was to be seen – hardly a cushion of moss, and that was parched and brown and only growing rarely between the huge blocks and stones which cover the summit and lie in heaps all round to a great distance, like skeletons or bones of the earth not wanted at the creation,

and there left to be covered with never-dying lichen, which the clouds and dews nourish; and adorn with colours of the most vivid and exquisite beauty, and endless in variety. No gems or flowers can surpass in colouring the beauty of some of these masses of stone which no human eye beholds except the shepherd led thither by chance or traveller by curiosity; and how seldom this must happen!

(The lichen is no longer noticeable; has acid rain removed it, or is it the pressure of too many visitors?) Dorothy and Miss Barker enjoyed a picnic on the summit: 'There was not a breath of air to stir even the papers which we spread out containing our food ... and the stillness seemed to be not of this world.' To complete their happiness they 'each wrote a letter to our far-distant friend in S. Wales, Miss [Sara] Hutchinson'. Did they know that Coleridge had written to her from the neighbouring peak sixteen years before?

Rather surprisingly, the Pike's only significant fictional appearance seems to be in Hugh Walpole's *Vanessa*, where Tom Herries dies (from exposure following a fall) just below the summit.

Completing the trio of splendid peaks is **Great Gable**, 2m to N of the Scafell Pike summit and clearly visible from it. Wordsworth liked to place the centre of the Lake District exactly half way between the summits of Scafell and Great Gable. From this point, he said, the valleys diverge 'like spokes from the nave of a wheel'.

The mountain itself, a massive red pyramid, is immensely impressive, 'hollowed in the centre' says Eliza Lynn Linton

> and buttressed with grey pillars on each side – a whole cascade of immense boulders pouring from that sweeping curve to show what wind and rain have done, and the jewelled brightness of its sides shining many coloured and glorious if the sun lights on them – it is the most picturesque of the Wastdale mountains ... It is one of the finest mountains to ascend; giving some of the grandest views and most glorious effects; not to speak of the natural basin in a rock on the summit, always full of the purest water, and the garnets to be found embedded in the slate.

Wordsworth tells us more about the 'natural basin' at the summit:

> the shepherds say that it is never dry: certainly when I was there, during a season of drought, it was well supplied with water. Here the Traveller may slake his thirst plenteously with a pure and celestial beverage; for it appears that this cup or bason has no other feeder than the dews of heaven, the showers, the vapours, the hoar frost, and the spotless snow.

The basin, to quote Otley, is 'a triangular receptacle in the rock, six inches deep and capable of holding two gallons'. Alas, it is no longer there, perhaps displaced by the war memorial on the summit.

Thomas Blackburn has a fine poem on **Hell's Gate**, the 'cascade of boulders' mentioned by Mrs Linton, which pours down the mountain's S face:

> Where Great Gable
> Plunges down in carmine scree

Through rock pillars to Wastwater
And the heartbeat of the sea.
Once I'd only to remember
That sheer scree-shoot and the wind
Making silences more silent
To become both deaf and blind
To the beast roar of a city
Where I earned my daily bread;
Pillar Rock, Gimmer and Scafell,
Pavey Ark and its wreathed head
Plunged like ships of storm to leeward
From the pavement where I stood ...

At the foot of Great Gable and close to the most popular ascent (via Aaron's Slack) is **Sty Head**, marked by Sty Head Tarn and the top of the pass which descends into Borrowdale. The spot figures in Walpole's novel *A Prayer for My Son*, where Rose, Rackstraw, John and Janet, escaping from the deranged Colonel Fawcus, climb the pass by moonlight from Borrowdale and watch the dawn from the shores of the Tarn.

Take the path above S end of the Tarn and go SE for ½m to **Sprinkling Tarn** (formerly Sparkling Tarn). According to rain-gauge readings made in the nineteenth century by John Fletcher Miller, the neighbourhood of the Tarn is the wettest place in England, and as if to commemorate the fact there is currently a very old copper rain-gauge standing nearby. Readers of *Rogue Herries* may recall how David Herries, eloping with Sarah Denburn, fought here in the fog with Denburn and Captain Bann, wounding the Captain and finishing off Denburn by hurling him into the Tarn. A more tranquil episode occurs in Marjorie Lloyd's *Fell Farm Holiday* (1951), where the children camp at Sty Head and bathe in Sprinkling Tarn.

From Sprinkling Tarn continue SE 1m to **Esk Hause**, the top of the pass from Eskdale. Dorothy Wordsworth and Elizabeth Barker walked up here from Seathwaite on October 7 1818 with 'a statesman shepherd of the vale

STY HEAD
Marjorie Lloyd, 1951

as our companion and guide'. From the top of 'Ash Course' as she calls it, following local pronunciation, they saw 'magnificent scenes' -

> Below us, were the Langdale Pikes, then our own vale [of Ambleside] below them, Windermere, and far beyond Windermere, after a long distance, Ingleborough in Yorkshire. But how shall I speak of the peculiar deliciousness of the [other] prospect? ... The green Vale of Esk – deep and green, with its glittering serpent stream was below us; and on we looked to the mountains near the sea – Black Combe and others – and still beyond, to the sea itself in dazzling brightness. Turning round we saw the mountains of Wasdale in tumult; and Great Gavel, though the middle of the mountain was to us as its base, looked very grand.

They went on to ascend Scafell Pike. We, however, shall return to Wasdale.

Taking the road SE along the shore of Wastwater, turn L (S) 1m after leaving the lake. A picturesque winding road of 2m brings you to the **Bridge Inn** at Santon Bridge. A contest is held here annually in November to find 'The World's Greatest Liar'. The event commemorates Will Ritson (on whom see p 203), a notable teller of tall tales: as Ritson himself said, 'The lees Aa tell isn't malicious, they're nobbut gert big exaggerations'. Lying contests would traditionally have been spontaneous affairs, developing in the course of an evening's drinking. This one is said to have been 'revived' as an organised event in 1975.

From the Inn go W 2m to A595 then S to the **Lutwidge Arms**, a large hotel at the roadside, which stands on the site of the former home farm of Holmrook Hall, seat of the Lutwidge family. The Lutwidges were cousins of Charles Lutwidge Dodgson ('Lewis Carroll'), who frequently visited the Hall in the 1870s and mentions it in his diaries. The site of **Holmrook Hall**, demolished in recent times, is 200yds uphill (N) on the corner of the road, through a gate signed Public Footpath: Irton Church. Take the footpath and you will see the coach-house and an elegant archway, which are all that survive of the Hall buildings. After the demolition some of the furniture and fittings were transferred to the Ludwidge Arms. If you look into a mirror here or sit in an armchair, it's possible that the author of *Alice in Wonderland* was there before you.

Irton, Ravenglass and Eskdale

Continue along the footpath (a pleasant ¾m) for **St Paul's Church, Irton**. Coleridge came here on his 1802 tour, noting

> green Hazel Trees, with Hay-fields & Hay-makers to your right, beyond them the River with a beautiful single Stone arch thrown over it, & shadowed with Trees, & beyond the River Irton Fell, with a deep perpendicular Ravin, with a curious fretted Pillar, crosier-shaped, standing up in it/

The 'fretted pillar' is the famous **Irton Cross**, a tenth-century monument of weathered sandstone with elaborate interlace work and solar discs. The

Victorian church itself is pleasant, with a fine Burne-Jones window and a beautiful churchyard.

Return to A595 and continue S to **Ravenglass**, a tiny village consisting mainly of a single street which is a lovely jumble of traditional Cumberland architecture from a variety of periods. The rivers Irt, Mite and Esk all meet here, forming a 'trident' as Coleridge says, in a narrow channel cut off from the sea by dunes. There is also a legend that the shore here was once a pearl-fishery. Drayton's *Poly-Olbion* gives a suitably embroidered picture:

> As Eske her farth'st, so first, a coy bred *Cumbrian* Lasse,
> Who commeth to her Road, renowned *Ravenglasse*,
> By *Devock* driven along, (which from a large-brim'd lake,
> To hye her to the Sea, with greater haste doth make)
> Meets *Myte*, a nimble Brooke, their Rendezvous that keepe
> In *Ravenglasse*, when soone into the blewish Deepe
> Comes Irt, of all the rest, though small, the richest Girle,
> Her costly bosome strew'd with precious Orient Pearle,
> Bred in her shining Shels, which to the deaw doth yawne,
> Which deaw they sucking in, conceave that lusty Spawne,
> Of which when they grow great, and to their fulnesse swell,
> They cast, which those at hand there gathering, dearly sell.

Camden writes:

> Some will have it to have been called antiently *Aven glas* or the *blue river*, and tell many stories about King Eveling, who had a palace here ...

> Higher up the little river Irt runs into the sea, in which the shell-fish having by a kind of irregular motion taken in the dew, which they are extremely fond of, are impregnated, and produce berries, or, to use the poet's phrase, *baccae* concheae, shell-berries, which the inhabitants, when the tide is out, search for, and our jewellers buy of the poor for a trifle, and sell again at a very great price.

There is no reliable record of pearls being found here, and if it ever happened it must have been in Roman times or earlier. Defoe in 1724

> enquired much for the pearl fishery here ... which has made a kind of bubble lately: But the country people, nor even the fishermen, could give us no account of any such thing.

Gordon Bottomley's ballad 'Avelinglas' is based on the legend that the village was founded by 'King Avelin/Who built his palace here':

> Between the river and the tide
> Only one street may stand,
> But once the streets were seven and wide
> Before men came to the sand.

Avelin builds a palace but his daughter, longing for a lover from overseas, combs her golden hair at the window and calls up the sea-wind:

> The sea grew, the sky sank;
> Streets made the long waves fret;

The river ran without a bank;
The housewives' knees were wet.

Tower and town, pine-wood and willow
Melted as though by rain;
And once the trough of a piling billow
Was paved with a golden mane.

The town is submerged by the sea, leaving only the strange little single-street settlement which still stands.

Ravenglass appears prominently in Walpole's *Rogue Herries*: Harcourt Herries' house is here, a 'little square white-fronted house thrust back from the street in a small, walled garden' – not an actual building, but one that would fit well. David and his father row out from the harbour to the offshore sandbar, where they have their final confrontation and David breaks the cane his father has raised against him.

Ravenglass is also the starting-point for the **Ravenglass and Eskdale Railway**, its terminus prominent next to the British Rail station. The railway is well-described by George Gissing in his 1893 novel *The Odd Women*, and little changed since:

> The journey up Eskdale, from Ravenglass to Boot, is by a miniature railway, with the oddest little engine and a carriage or two of primitive simplicity. At each station on the upward winding track – stations represented only by a little wooden shed like a tool-house – the guard jumps down and acts as booking-clerk, if passengers there be desirous of booking. In a few miles the scenery changes from beauty to grandeur, and at the terminus no further steaming would be possible, for the great flank of Scawfell bars the way.

The railway was built in 1875 to carry iron ore from the mountains but soon found passengers more profitable. It provides an exhilarating ride through magnificent scenery.

Modern fictional appearances include Reginald Hill's 1971 detective novel *Fell of Dark* (the narrator travels on it in Chapter Four) and Richard Adams's *The Plague Dogs*, where Snitter and Rowf stow away on one of the trains to make their escape from the encircling paratroopers. They travel in the opposite direction – from Eskdale down to Ravenglass and the coast.

1m E of the station is **Muncaster Castle** (*car park opposite gates; grounds open daily 10.30-6, or dusk if earlier; castle open April to early November (exact dates vary from year to year) 12-5 except Saturdays; admission charge*.) The beautiful red sandstone castle, overlooking a panoramic view of Eskdale, with its gardens in the chasm below full of flowering shrubs, is an extraordinary sight. The estate has belonged to the Pennington family since 1208. From a fourteenth-century pele tower the house was enlarged in 1862 to designs by Anthony Salvin, whose embellishments include a lovely octagonal library.

King Henry VI was sheltered here after losing the Battle of Hexham in 1464: he is said to have been found by shepherds hiding in a hollow oak in

MUNCASTER CASTLE FROM BIRKBY FELL
G. Pickering, 1832

the park. Before leaving by sea he gave his gilded glass drinking bowl to his host, prophesying that

> So long as this cup shall stay unriven,
> Pennington from Muncaster shall ne'er be driven.

The cup, the 'Luck of Muncaster', is kept in the house.

The house has many other treasures, among them a superb portrait of the last household Fool, Thomas Skelton (active around 1600), who is shown with long lugubrious face in a blue and yellow chequered gown, his Last Will and Testament in doggerel verse on a scroll beside him.

The family has long held (and still holds) the 'right of shipwreck', entitling it to property washed ashore from wrecks at Drigg. In the past this was exercised with no qualms whatsoever: in 1648 some exotic gourds were washed up from a wreck, together with several passengers, among them a page boy with silver buttons on his tunic. Sir William Pennington thriftily had the buttons cut off and the gourds made into cups mounted with the silver, composing an urbane verse which can be seen engraved on the rim of one cup:

> By Neptune I was cast on Dreggs dry shore
> As was the silver sett mee thus before
> Both by the lord of the Mannour seized as wreck,
> I on a Rock, that in a doublets neck.

Two members of the family reluctantly became published authors under tragic circumstances. The first was the mid eighteenth-century Lady Sarah Pennington, who was cynically rejected by her husband Sir Joseph Pennington, Fourth Baron Muncaster, after she had born him eight children and watched him squander her fortune. She was forbidden to see her children but wrote to them; her letters were published in 1761 as *An Unfor-*

tunate Mother's Advice to her Absent Daughters. The book was popular and went through many editions.

The other was Josslyn, the fifth Baron, who, with his wife and several friends, was kidnapped by brigands whilst travelling in Greece in 1870. The party voted to send Josslyn out to raise a ransom and negotiate their release, but in his absence the Greek government sent in troops and the brigands killed all their prisoners. Muncaster was unjustly accused of deserting his friends and published part of his diary to clear his name. More recently a fuller selection from the journals was published as *Ransom and Murder in Greece* (1989).

Continue E on A595. If you want to stay on the coast road, a further three miles will bring you to the village of **Waberthwaite**, home of the crime novelist Reginald Hill, creator of the Dalziel and Pascoe detective novels. We, however, leave the A595 after 1m and turn L (E) for the road into Eskdale. After 1¾m, on the R (S) side of the road, near a footbridge over the Esk, is **Cragg Cottage**, home of Hugh Falkus (1917-96), classic fishing-writer and maker of wildlife films. In his autobiography *Some of It Was Fun* Falkus gives a fine description of a dawn on the Esk, and his first sight of the cottage:

> Ribbons of mist clinging to the water gradually dispersed and disappeared as sunlight spread above the hills. Shaking with the ripples of a leaping salmon, the surface of the pool below me reflected undulating ribs of red and yellow flame. In bankside hazel bushes a willow warbler sang. Slanting sunlight flashed suddenly on the windows of a small grey cottage. Instantly the thought occurred to me that any sportsman who found himself living in that cottage, with a stretch of water on the enchanted river I was fishing, would be the luckiest man alive.

He saw a girl come out of the cottage. In due course he was to marry her and live there from 1957 until his death, writing classic works on *Sea Trout Fishing*, *Salmon Fishing* and *Freshwater Fishing*.

After some 3m turn R (E, signed Ulpha) and after 2 ½ m watch for signpost to Stanley Ghyll. There is a little car parking space beside it. Walk ¾m W along track to **Devoke Water**, a picturesquely bleak tarn which features in Hugh Walpole's *The Bright Pavilions*: the villain Philip Irvine and his men are hunted here by local people through a snowstorm and killed beside the lake.

Return to the road and unless you are going to Ulpha, follow it N into **Eskdale**. Turn E along the valley, following signs to Boot. Eskdale is very dramatic, with its contrast of a lush, green valley-floor overlooked by precipitous, knobbed crags. Despite the railway it is not really overvisited: most people come on the train and go straight back to Ravenglass. It is peaceful and well worth exploring at leisure.

Follow the road through Boot and pass the Youth Hostel. About ½m after the latter watch out for a white house with tall conifer downhill from the road. This is Wa House Farm. Just after it a cart track (unsuitable for cars) goes off L (N): it leads to **Taw House**, an old white stone farmhouse with a large barn. Coleridge, on the recommendation of Mr Tyson at Wasdale Head, made for this house immediately on completing his perilous descent from Scafell on August 5 1802. (He called it 'Toes' – reflecting local pronunciation of 'Taw 'Us').

He stayed the night, and next morning his host, Vic Towers, gave him a tour of Upper Eskdale and the crags of its NW slopes – Brock Crag, Cat Crag, Heron Crag and the others. After lunch Coleridge set out again, heading for Devoke Water.

Follow the road 1m further up the valley to **Hardknott Castle** (small car park below cut into the hillside), a well-preserved Roman fort built to guard the pass and provide a base for military escorts bringing goods from Ambleside to the port at Ravenglass. This is presumably 'The fortress like a motionless eagle eyeing the valley' of W.H. Auden's 'Spain 1937'. It also features in the seventeenth of Wordsworth's *River Duddon* sonnets, where the poet imagines an eagle sailing over the ruins,

> shedding where he flew
> Loose fragments of wild wailing, that bestrew
> The clouds and thrill the chambers of the rocks;
> And into silence hush the timorous flocks,
> That, calmly couching while the nightly dew
> Moistened each fleece, beneath the twinkling stars
> Slept amid that lone Camp on Hardknott's height,
> Whose guardians bent the knee to Jove and Mars.

You will by this time have read the warning signs about the road, which is Hardknott Pass. It zigzags furiously at terrifying gradients over to join Wrynose Pass at Cockley Beck. It is a notorious place for breakdowns and in summer is frequently blocked by exhausted cars with steaming radiators. It was surfaced with tarmac only because of an administrative error in 1934 and should never have been opened to traffic. We shall leave it to the walkers and return to the coast road (A595), which we follow S until after 4m we find ourselves under the great shoulder of **Black Combe**.

There is an old proverb that 'Nowt good comes round Black Combe' – recalling Viking and Scottish raiders who up to 1322 used to sail S to loot the coastal settlements. The Combe is a huge dome-shaped fell, 2000ft high and the most southerly fell in the district. That pioneer fellwalker Thomas Wilkinson climbed it, around 1800, with his host, when he happened to be staying at Po-House near its foot; there is an account in his *Tours to the British Mountains*. Charles Farish's *The Minstrels of Winandermere* also has some pleasant lines about it:

> Close by the Sea, lone sentinel,
> Black-Comb his forward station keeps;
> He breaks the sea's tumultuous swell, –
> And ponders o'er the level deeps ...

Wordsworth described the 'View from the Top of Black Comb' (1811–13) – not one of his best poems, though correct in its claim that the Combe offers

BLACK COMBE
W.J. Linton, 1864

'the amplest range/Of unobstructed prospect ... That British ground commands', since it has no high neighbours and in clear weather gives tremendous views along the coast both N and S, from the 'Cambrian hills' to 'The hoary peaks of Scotland'.

Another Wordsworth poem of the same period, 'Written with a Slate pencil on a Stone, on the Side of the Mountain of Black Comb' typifies the black clouds which gave the Combe its name in an incident reported by one of the Ordnance Surveyors:

> On the summit whither thou art bound,
> A geographic Labourer pitched his tent,
> With books supplied and instruments of art,
> To measure height and distance; lonely task,
> Week after week pursued! ... He made report
> That once, while there he plied his studious work
> Within that canvas Dwelling, colours, lines,
> And the whole surface of the out-spread map,
> Became invisible: for all around
> Had darkness fallen – unthreatened, unproclaimed –
> As if the golden day itself had been
> Extinguished in a moment; total gloom,
> In which he sate alone, with unclosed eyes,
> Upon the blinded mountain's silent top!

To climb it, follow the coast road S and at the John Bull Inn turn E (signed Barrow) on A595. 200yds E of turning take signed footpath uphill beside large barn. The path runs N straight to the summit.

Millom and Barrow-in-Furness

Rejoin the coast road (A5093) and go 4m S to **Millom**, formerly an iron town dependent on the rich iron-ore deposits on the coast at Haverigg. The iron has now gone and the industry with it, leaving a pleasant, clean, undistinguished country town with no *raison d'être*. The important thing now about Millom is Norman Nicholson (1914–87), the finest Cumberland poet of the twentieth century, and perhaps the best in all Cumbria (though some would say the Westmorlander Margaret Cropper runs him close). Nicholson's poems (published, notably, in *Five Rivers* (1944), *Rock Face* (1948), *The Pot Geranium* (1954), and *A Local Habitation* (1973)) reflect on the life, characters and industrial decline of Millom with wry humour, acute observation and some philosophical depth. They are supplemented by two historical novels about the town (*The Green Shore* (1947) and *The Fire of the Lord* (1948)) and several excellent prose books, including an autobiography, *Wednesday Early Closing* (1975), and *Provincial Pleasures* (1959), an account of a year in the town in twelve delightful monthly essays. Nicholson's prose and verse at times deal also with the wider Lake District, and establish a friendly but not uncritical relationship with Wordsworth. His *Cumberland and Westmorland* (1949) and *The Lakers* (1955) are essential works. He also wrote several religious verse plays.

Nicholson spent his entire life (apart from a period of youthful ill-health in Hampshire) at **14 St George's Terrace**, which runs downhill from the E end of the Market Square. His father was a men's outfitter, and the building is still a shop. There is a plaque, poignant in the intensity of its local pride, commemorating Nicholson, 'Cumbrian poet ... Man of Millom'. Nicholson wrote in the attic bedroom he had used as a child: the dormer window may be seen from the street. Many of his poems mention the room, or his view from the window: in 'The Pot Geranium', for example,

> I turn from the window ...
> And lie on my bed. The ceiling
> Slopes over me like a tent, and white walls
> Wrap themselves round me, leaving only
> A flap for the light to blow through

– yet the room is also a watchtower from which the goings-on of the whole town, as well as the view of the mountains beyond, can be observed.

Nicholson is buried in **St George's Churchyard**. The church, at the S side of the Market Square, also has a splendid stained glass window in his memory. To find Nicholson's grave, walk up alongside the church and turn R into the new part of the churchyard, beyond a low stone wall. The grave is on your right, in the row nearest the church, twelfth from the upper end, facing a fence and wooden bench. Nicholson is buried with his wife Yvonne. The epitaph -

> Let my eyes at the last be blinded
> Not by the dark
> But by dazzle

MILLOM: BLACK COMBE BEYOND
B. Biro, 1959

– is adapted from the conclusion of his poem 'Sea to the West', where he reflects on the coastal view near Millom and foresees his own death.

250 yds W of the Square, the Tourist Information Office at the railway station incorporates the **Millom Folk Museum** (*open April to October, Mon-Fri 10-1 and 2-4.30; free admission*) which has a small display of books, photographs and personal effects relating to Nicholson, as well as displays on the history of Millom.

Millom's other literary connections are few. Arthur Ransome, unexpectedly, cherished a fondness for the town and, marooned in Stockholm as foreign correspondent for the *Daily News* in 1918, consoled himself by smoking black plug tobacco ('guaranteed to kill at ten yards') and dreaming nostalgically of being 'in a good old stinking Furness Railway third-class carriage with a lot of miners going oop Millom way'. He also mentions that there was a 'gipsy centre' at Millom, where the true Romanies of the district spent the winter – presumably the field at the N edge of the town called Gipsy Lonning; within living memory it was a favourite Gipsy camping place.

A final detail, and a mildly bizarre one, is that on the nearby shore at Haverigg the poet, climbing-writer and psychiatrist Menlove Edwards (1910–1958) landed after crossing overnight from the Isle of Man in a collapsible canoe in 1934. Edwards was given to extreme feats of endurance and eventually committed suicide.

From Millom take the A5093 (signed Barrow) N 4m to join the A595 at Hallthwaites. Continue N on A595 ¾m and watch for sign to Broadgate.

Follow it up a small road and after ¾m take signed bridleway to **Swinside Stone Circle**, also known locally by the splendid name of Sunkenkirk. This is a large and impressive monument, with a setting to rival that of Castlerigg. It was a favourite place of Wordsworth's, who describes it in *Duddon Sonnet* XVII as

> that mystic Round of Druid frame
> Tardily sinking by its proper weight
> Deep into patient Earth, from whose smooth breast it came!

It is probably also the 'famed temple where of yore/The Druids worshipped' in Book II of the 1850 *Prelude*: Wordsworth claims that the boys from Hawkshead used to ride here on holidays.

Return to A595 and continue 3m to **Broughton-in-Furness**, a small and attractive market town. Wordsworth stayed here in 1789 with his cousin Mary, and commemorates his walks with her in the meadows by the Duddon in *Duddon Sonnet* XXI. In the Market Square is the **Manor Arms**, the 'Manor Hotel' where Digby Driver pumped Mr Powell for information in Richard Adams's *The Plague Dogs*.

Lovers of Wordsworth's *The River Duddon* will be inspired by the sequence's magnificent conclusion with a desire to see the estuary. They should be warned that there is nothing much to see, certainly nothing to equal the superb swell of the last few sonnets ('*now* expands/ Majestic Duddon, over smooth flat sands/Gliding in silence with unfettered sweep! ...') For a view of the estuary, leave Broughton going S following signs for Foxfield. At junction go L (S) and continue ½m to Foxfield Station (small lay-by opposite). Cross railway line by gate at level crossing to look across the estuary. The view is not much, but you can create a sense of occasion (especially if you have walked here from the Three Shires Stone) by reciting the final sonnet:

> For, backward, Duddon! as I cast my eyes,
> I see what was, and is, and will abide;
> Still glides the stream, and shall for ever glide ...

Return to A595 and follow signs to Barrow.

As the name of Broughton-in-Furness implies, we are now in the **Furness Peninsula**, which until 1974 was part of Lancashire. The Duddon formed the W boundary with Cumberland; the E boundary, with Westmorland, was formed by the Winster, just E of Windermere, and then by Morecambe Bay, which cut it off completely from the rest of Lancashire. In the middle ages the peninsula was virtually an independent state, ruled by the monks of Furness Abbey, who had their own army and kept order in this inaccessible district.

The area had a wild reputation: in the Ballad of Flodden Field (1513) the English soldiers come

> From Silverdale and Kent sand side,
> Whose soil is sown with cockle shells;

From Cartmel eke and Connyside,
With fellows fierce from Furness Fells.

Camden (1586) picturesquely describes it as

> almost torn off by the sea ... For the shore here running out a great way to
> the west, the sea, as if enraged at it, lashes it more furiously, and, in high
> tides, has even devoured the shore, and made three large bays, viz.
> *Kentsand*, ... *Levensand*, ... and *Duddonsand*, between which the land
> projects in such a manner that it has its name thence; Foreness and
> Foreland signifying the same with us as *promontarium anterius* in Latin.
> This whole tract, except on the coast, rises in high hills and vast piles of
> rocks called Foreness Fels.

From prehistoric times the area was known to be rich in iron; in the middle
ages the monks worked it using the plentiful charcoal from nearby forests,
and later small enterprises led up to the massive iron and steel works of the
industrial age.

Traces of the more primitive, rural phase of iron working were still
evident in the Victorian period; Harriet Martineau (though more interested
in the charcoal-burners) mentions that all over the peninsula are

> specimens of roads and lanes which are locally called Ore Gates (ways,)
> from their being constructed from the slag and refuse of the iron-ore
> formerly brought into the peninsula to be smelted, on account of the
> abundance of charcoal there. There are few objects more picturesque, to
> this day, than the huts of the woodcutters, who remain on a particular spot
> until their work is done. Upon piled stems of trees heather is heaped, to
> make a shaggy thatch; and when the smoke is oozing out, thin and blue,
> from the hole in the centre, or the children are about the fire in front,
> where the great pot is boiling, the sketcher cannot but stop and dash down
> the scene in his book. The children will say he is 'spying fancies,' – as they
> say of every one who sketches, botanizes, or in any way explores; and
> perhaps someone may have the good taste to advise him to come at night,
> when the glow from the fires makes the thicket a scene of singular
> wildness and charm.

Continue S on the A595 towards Barrow. At Ireleth and Askham turn L
(SE) by the Bay Horse Inn. Watch for the Black Dog Inn, and after ¼m, by
stone cottage with decorative barge-boarding, is gate to private drive to
Tytup Hall, a large seventeenth-century house with extensive outbuildings and attractive gardens. This was the home of Father Thomas West
(1720–1779), Catholic priest and antiquary, author of two of the earliest
and most important works on Lakeland topography, *The Antiquities of
Furness* (1774) and the immensely popular *Guide to the Lakes* (1778), the
first book to offer systematic guidance to the best viewpoints in the Lakes,
and thus a pioneering work of landscape interpretation. We have already
visited many of his 'stations'. West was born in Scotland, but settled in
Furness in 1774 and devoted his life to the history and landscape of his
adopted home.

Continue S into **Dalton-in-Furness**, clearly once an attractive village but now grimy and battered, though retaining some pleasant parts. Take the A590 towards Barrow: **St Mary's Church** is on a rocky outcrop overlooking the road as it reaches the edge of the village. The grave of George Romney (1734–1802), who was born nearby, is by the path at the S side of the church. Romney (whose name was actually the familiar Lakeland one of Rumney, and was so pronounced) went to London in 1762 and came to rival Sir Joshua Reynolds as the most fashionable painter of the age.

Follow the A590 towards Barrow. As you enter the town, pass the modern red sandstone 'Abbey Lodge' (a nice piece of pastiche but nothing to do with the Abbey) and watch for signs to Furness Abbey on L (E) side of road. A small road leads down into the Abbey precincts beside the Abbey Tavern. The Tavern is the remains of the large Victorian hotel which served the many tourists brought by the railway, which used to stop beside it at a station now gone. The hotel in turn had been enlarged from the mansion of the landowners who obtained the Abbey lands when the monastery was suppressed in 1537 by Henry VIII.

Nathaniel Hawthorne, visiting in 1855, noted the incongruity of the railway station side-by-side with the Abbey:

> continually there is the shriek, the whiz, the rumble, the bellringing, denoting the arrival of the train, and passengers alight and step at once (as their choice may be) into the refreshment-room to get a glass of ale or cigar, or upon the gravelled paths of the lawn, leading to … the Abbey.

Furness Abbey (*open April – September daily 10-6; October – March daily except Tuesday and Wednesday, 10-4; closed 24-26 December and 1 January; car park; admission charge*), the centre of Furness life and government in the middle ages, is a beautiful and splendid place, well worth spending time on. It was the home of several notable literary monks, among them Jocelin of Furness, a compiler of saints's lives who wrote biographies of St Patrick and St Kentigern around 1180, and (according to Eliza Lynn Linton) 'one John Stell, a monk and poetical historian of the time of Henry VI' who composed verses about the Abbey:

> Haec vallis olim sibi nomen ab herba
> Bekan, qua viruit, dulcis nunc, tunc sed acerba;
> Inde domus nomen, Bekansgill, claruit ante.

'This valley formerly took its name from the herb Bekan (deadly nightshade), which flourished there, a sweet place now but then bitter; whence the name of the house, Bekansgill, was famous of old' – a story which subsequent writers (among them West and Wordsworth) loved to repeat. Deadly nightshade is not noticeable these days, however.

The Abbey's picturesque aspect appealed strongly to eighteenth-century writers: according to Ann Radcliffe, who was here in 1794,

> The finest view of the ruin is on the east side, where, beyond the vast, shattered frame that once contained a richly-painted window, is seen a perspective of the choir and of distant arches, remains of the nave of the abbey, closed by the woods.

NORTH-EAST VIEW OF THE RUINS OF FURNESS ABBEY
W. Close, 1774

She rested opposite the east window and imagined 'the midnight procession of monks, clothed in white and bearing lighted tapers'.

In his *Guide* Wordsworth quotes from an unpublished poem on the Abbey by an unknown poet:

> Tread softly, taste the consecrated brook
> That in meanders creeps along the Vale
> And in soft murmurs mourns the Abbey's fate ...
> The walls that glowed with tapestry, breathing life,
> Are bare, save where the circling ivy twines
> Around yon arches, nodding with the blasts ...

Alas, the rest of the poem has been lost and where Wordsworth found it remains a mystery.

Book II of *The Prelude* mentions boyhood visits by Wordsworth and his schoolfellows from Hawkshead, on hired ponies. He also wrote two sonnets called 'At Furness Abbey': the first, composed in 1840, views the ruins as evidence of the interplay of Time and Nature; the second, from 1845, includes a pleasantly unexpected vignette of workers on their lunch break from building the new railway.

Continue into **Barrow-in-Furness**, still the industrial heart of southern Cumbria but much less grim than it was between 1850 and 1950, the century of its greatest prosperity. In its heyday the town was dominated by heavy industry on a positively nightmarish scale: late nineteenth and early twentieth-century writers describe it in the sort of terms their eighteenth-century predecessors reserved for Borrowdale. It was horribly sublime. Thus W.G. Collingwood, for example, claimed that there was 'abundant poetry and picturesqueness, for anyone who does not travel in blinkers, at the ship-yards and steel-works, and even in the streets of Barrow.' He recalled one December night, wet and gloomy, when the working-folk, rough-coated men and lasses hooded in their shawls, were shopping after the day's work, under the gas-lamps that streamed their reflections down the pavement; and suddenly aloft from enormous towers, bulking on the darkness like some Babylonian architecture in a picture, there flared out great banners of fire, lighting up the cloud into a brown glow against interspaces of deep violet. It blazed and flickered and faded again, and the people in the streets were like ghosts hurrying to and fro.

In its prime, Barrow made its presence felt in the heart of the Lakes:

from Coniston Waterhead we see the flare on the clouds of a dark night, and on the finest day a soft south wind brings up the smoke that Barrow keeps not for its own consumption, but sends to soil the grass of the mountain-tops, to blacken the snow and scum the lake.

Today the dominant industry is still shipbuilding, though this is currently in decline; formerly there were also enormous steelworks, which have now been completely removed. Throughout the twentieth century, the shipyards were operated by the Vickers company. In 1997 this was taken over by BAe Systems (formerly British Aerospace), an armaments company which now makes and repairs submarines in Barrow.

The town features as 'Froswick' in Book Three of Mrs Humphry Ward's *Helbeck of Bannisdale* (1898), whose heroine, Laura Fountain, is not impressed with

the new buildings and streets, the brand new squares and statues of Froswick.

'How can people build and live in such ugly places?' she said at last ... making a little face at the very ample bronze gentleman in a frock coat who was standing in the centre of a great new-built empty square, haranguing a phantom crowd. 'Oh! how ugly it is to succeed – to have money!'

The kind of statue she has in mind is easily found: from the Town Hall go either L or R along Duke Street; at the NW end is a bronze statue (1872) of James Ramsden, complete with frock coat, and at the SE is one of H.W. Schneider. These were the two businessmen who created Barrow. Both are now marooned on traffic islands at the centre of their respective squares, and look vaguely foolish.

To find the shipyards leave the SE end of Duke Street and go S down Michaelson Road. You cross the Devonshire Dock by a bridge and can then turn R up Bridge Road to make a circuit back to the town centre. On the way you will pass between numerous vast buildings of BAe, formerly Vickers. In *Helbeck of Bannisdale* Laura and her friends visit the shipyards, though

Laura ... could hardly drag her feet up and down the sides of the great skeleton ships that lay building in the docks, or through the interminable 'fitting' sheds with their piles of mahogany and teak, their whirring lathes and saws, their heaps of shavings, their resinous wood-smell.

They also have a tour of the 'Froswick Steel and Hematite Works', which Mrs Ward preserves for us in vivid detail:

> A vast shed, much of it in darkness, and crowded with dim forms of iron
> and brick – at one end, and one side, openings, where the June day came
> through. Within – a grandiose mingling of fire and shadow – a vast glare of
> white or bluish flame from a huge furnace roaring against the inner wall of
> the shed – ingots of glowing steel, pillars of pure fire passing and
> repassing, so that the heat of them scorched the girl's shrinking cheek –
> and everywhere, dark against flame, the human movement answering to
> the elemental leap and rush of the fire, black forms of men in a constant
> activity, masters and ministers at once of this crackling terror round about
> them.

The scene leads up to a terrible accident in which a man is killed by the
molten steel. The episode gives a clear view of the appalling working
conditions in late-Victorian Barrow.

D.H. Lawrence and three friends ended a walking tour at Barrow in
August 1914 just as war was declared:

> I had been walking in Westmorland, rather happy, with water-lilies twisted
> round my hat – big, heavy, white and gold water-lilies that we found in a
> pool high up – and girls who had come out on a spree and who were
> having tea in the upper room of an inn, shrieked with laughter. And I
> remember also we crouched under the loose wall on the moors and the
> rain flew by in streams, and the wind came rushing through the chinks in
> the wall behind one's head, and we shouted songs, and I imitated
> music-hall turns ... Then we came down to Barrow-in-Furness, and saw
> that war was declared. And we all went mad. I can remember soldiers
> kissing on Barrow station, and a woman shouting defiantly to her
> sweetheart – 'When you get at 'em, Clem, let 'em have it,' as the train drew
> off ... Messrs Vickers-Maxim call in their workmen – and the great notices
> on Vickers' gateways – and the thousands of men streaming over the
> bridge. Then I went down the coast a few miles. And I think of the
> amazing sunsets over flat sands and the smoky sea ... and a French onion
> boat coming in with her sails set splendidly, in the morning sunshine –
> and the amazing, vivid, visionary beauty of everything, heightened by the
> immense pain everywhere.

Leave Barrow heading E on A5087 2m to **Rampside**, a tiny seaside
village in a bleak, melancholy setting which has its own appeal. Prominent
in the single street is **Clarke's Hotel**, formerly a private house built in 1720
(traces of the original structure beneath the 1913 renovation are visible at
the back).

William and Dorothy Wordsworth stayed here in June 1794 with their
cousins, the Barkers. William later recalled the 'four summer weeks' of the
visit in his poem on 'Peel Castle'. It was probably also during this stay that
he crossed the nearby Leven Estuary and heard the news of Robespierre's
death, as recalled in *Prelude* X.

Notice the remarkable Rampside Hall, with its twelve chimneys (the
'Twelve Apostles'), now sadly out of place on the fringe of the modern
housing estate; and the curious pointed brick tower on the foreshore,
which is a leading light for ships steering towards the harbour at Barrow.

Follow the road S along the shore and take the causeway for Roa Island, a strange and fascinating little place with just room for a row of houses, a pub, a café and the lifeboat station. Though we are so close to Barrow, in some curious way the atmosphere is as tranquil and timeless as if we were in the Outer Hebrides. This is where you get the ferry for **Piel Island**, which you can see just offshore. the ferry is operated by Mr Alan Cleasby. For services on any given day, check with him by telephone (number from any tourist information office in the area) as sailings may vary depending on demand and weather.

On Piel Island is **Piel Castle** (*open, according to English Heritage, 'any reasonable time summer weekdays from 11 a.m., subject to tides'; for winter opening, weekends and other details it would be wise to ask on Roa Island, since the real point seems to be whether or not you can get there*), built by the monks of Furness Abbey in the early fourteenth century to defend the harbour from the Scots and other raiders. Ships came to trade for the wool from the Abbey's estates. Wordsworth was struck by the view of the Castle and remembered the visit in his 'Elegiac Stanzas suggested by a Picture of Peele Castle' (1806):

> I was thy Neighbour once, thou rugged Pile!
> Four summer weeks I dwelt in sight of thee:
> I saw thee every day; and all the while
> Thy Form was sleeping on a glassy sea ...

> How perfect was the calm! it seemed no sleep;
> No mood, which season takes away, or brings:
> I could have fancied that the mighty Deep
> Was even the gentlest of all gentle Things ...

The picture was 'A Storm: Peele Castle' by Sir George Beaumont; the poem, one of Wordsworth's most quietly powerful, expresses his response to the drowning of his brother John in 1805 and the shock which it gave to his sense of nature as a benevolent presence.

Return to Rampside and continue NE up the coast road 4½m to the signed turning for **Aldingham**, a tiny seaside hamlet. Wordsworth had friends here and during his summer stay at Rampside, whilst crossing 'the smooth and level sands/Of Leven's ample estuary ... beneath a genial sun' from Holker to Aldingham after visiting Cartmel Priory, he heard the news of Robespierre's death – a moment of exaltation described in *Prelude* X. He would have ended his journey coming up from the sands by the steps near **St Cuthbert's churchyard**.

While you are here, notice (by the sundial S of the church) the memorial tablet to Christopher Gaskell (1912–81), 'Scholar, Aesthete, Dilettante'. One would like to know more.

Continue N on the coast road for 2m until it enters a wood. Watch for an inconspicuous turning L (W). It passes the small but beautiful **Conishead Stone Circle**, on a common strewn with limestone boulders and overlooking Morecambe Bay, which has been suggested by some as the one (rather

PIEL CASTLE
Thomas Aspland, 1868

than Swinside) visited by Wordsworth from Hawkshead. It is reached by a grassy track which runs 150yds N from the road just after it emerges from Sea Wood.

Continue W, then go N at junction and follow signs to Urswick for **Great Urswick**, a remarkable and little-known village set on the shores of a magnificent tarn. ¼m S of the tarn is **Holme Bank**, a large old farm with many outbuildings and cottages, which is the starting-point of an epic fox-chase commemorated in the traditional 'Holm Bank Hunting Song':

> Three times round Low Furness they chased him full hard;
> At last he sneaked off and through Urswick churchyard;
> He listened to the singers (as I've heard them say),
> But the rest of the service he could not well stay.

> Of such a fox chase there never was known, –
> The horsemen and footmen were instantly thrown;
> To keep within sound didn't lie in their power,
> For the dogs chased the fox eighty miles in five hours.

The hunt ends at Grassguards on the Duddon.

'Urswick churchyard' is the old and beautiful precinct of **St Mary and St Michael, Great Urswick** near the tarn: a lovely church, and in spring the churchyard is full of flowers.

Return to the coast road and continue 2m N to **Conishead Priory**, now the Manjushri Kadampa Meditation Centre (*grounds generally open; house tours most weekends, but telephone to be sure*). Built on the site of a twelfth-century priory, this is a huge and ornate Gothic revival building of 1821–36. It is currently a Tibetan Buddhist centre and is being extensively restored. Both house and grounds are well worth seeing.

West's *Guide* (1778), describing it before the present enlargement, calls it 'the paradise of Furness':

> The house stands on the site of the priory of Conishead, at the foot of a fine eminence ... The slopes are planted with shrubs and trees in such a manner, as to improve the elevation; and the waving woods that fly from it on each wing, give it an airy and noble appearance. The south front is in the modern taste, extended by an arcade. The north is in the gothic stile, with a piazza and wings ... The variety of culminated grounds, and winding slopes, comprehended within this sweet spot, furnishes all the advantage of mountains and vales, wood and water ... It is a great omission in the curious traveller, to be in *Furness*, and not to see so wonderfully pretty a place.

From the Priory a path runs E through woods to the pebbly beach. This gives a good view of **Chapel Island** directly opposite, a long limestone ridge lifting its back out of the sea like a whale. The island features prominently in Book X of *The Prelude*, where Wordsworth gives his account, colourful as a Turner sketch, of crossing the estuary with a crowd at low tide, on his way to Aldingham:

> Upon a small
> And rocky island near, a fragment stood
> (Itself like a sea rock) the low remains
> (With shells encrusted, dark with briny weeds)
> Of a dilapidated structure, once
> A Romish chapel, where the vested priest
> Said matins at the hour that suited those
> Who crossed the sands at ebb of morning tide.
> Not far from that still ruin all the plain
> Lay spotted with a variegated crowd
> Of vehicles and travellers, horse and foot,
> Wading beneath the conduct of their guide
> In loose procession through the shallow stream
> Of inland waters.

The ruins of **St Catherine's Chapel** are still just visible towards the N end of the island.

Follow the A5087 N into Ulverston.

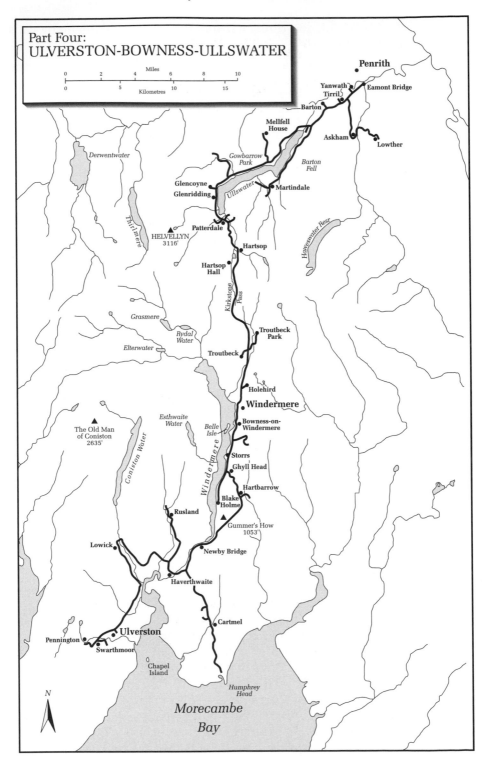

Part Four:
ULVERSTON-BOWNESS-ULLSWATER

Miles
0   2   4   6   8   10
0   5   10   15
Kilometres

Penrith
Yanwath Eamont Bridge
Tirril
Barton
Mellfell House
Askham
Lowther
Derwentwater
Gowbarrow Park
Barton Fell
Glencoyne
Glenridding
Ullswater
Martindale
Hawswater Resr
Thirlmere
Patterdale
HELVELLYN 3116'
Hartsop
Hartsop Hall
Kirkstone Pass
Grasmere
Rydal Water
Troutbeck Park
Elterwater
Troutbeck
Holehird
Windermere
Esthwaite Water
The Old Man of Coniston 2635'
Belle Isle
Bowness-on-Windermere
Coniston Water
Storrs
Ghyll Head
Windermere
Hartbarrow
Blake Holme
Rusland
Gummer's How 1053'
Lowick
Newby Bridge
Haverthwaite
Cartmel
Pennington Ulverston
Swarthmoor
Chapel Island
Humphrey Head
N
Morecambe Bay

PART FOUR

Ulverston – Bowness –
Ullswater

Ulverston, Swarthmoor, Pennington

We begin in what West (1778) called 'the key and mart of Furness': **Ulverston** (*several well-signed car parks*), the most important town in the Furness peninsula until the development of Barrow in the nineteenth century. Ulverston still has a good street market (Thursday and Saturday). In the eighteenth century it was a substantial port for fishing and trading vessels. Thomas West, a patriotic (though adoptive) Furnessman, thought well of its citizens:

> The people of Furness in general, and of Ulverston in particular, are civil and well-behaved to strangers, hospitable and humane. This universal civility and good manners is the characteristic of Furness … At church and market their appearance is decent, and sobriety is a general virtue. Quarrels and affrays are seldom heard of at fairs and public meetings. The modesty of the female sex and the sobriety of the men prevent irregularities before marriage, and secure conjugal love and affection through life. The women are handsome, the men in general robust. As the air of Furness is salubrious, so the inhabitants live to a good old age.

Thomas Pennant noted that the town had

> a good trade in iron ore, pig and bar iron, bark, lime-stone, oats and barley and much beans, which last are sent to *Leverpool*, for the food of the poor enslaved *negroes* in the *Guinea* trade.

The wear and tear of the steadily-increasing trade in iron (and later coal) left its marks, and when William and Dorothy Wordsworth visited in April 1827 Dorothy thought Ulverston a 'Dirty ugly town'. Parts of it still provoke this reaction, though Ulverston has plenty of character and improves on acquaintance.

Before the railways it was the final stage on the journey across the sands from Lancaster. West's *Guide* gives an evocative account of the crossing, and William Wilberforce, crossing the estuary here on one of his earliest visits to the Lakes in 1779, noted 'Crowds of young men and maidens hurrying to & from Ulverston (pronounced Ouston) market the scene was the most delightful I ever beheld'.

Ulverston's most famous son is the film comedian Stan Laurel (1890–1965) and fans will want to visit the **Laurel and Hardy Museum** (*open daily, February to December (except Christmas Day), 10 – 4.30; admission charge*). From Market Cross (top of Market Street) go E into King

SIR JOHN BARROW'S MONUMENT
1886

Street then first L into Upper Brook Street. Museum is on R. The museum has a huge (and amusingly chaotic) collection of memorabilia, including much of the furniture from Stan's childhood home. Laurel and Hardy films are shown continuously; film stills and other souvenirs on sale.

For Stan Laurel's birthplace, a tiny stone terrace house at **3 Argyle Street**, go down Market Street, across large roundabout, and S past the Stan Laurel pub (good painted sign). Opposite pub turn R along Chapel Street. Argyle Street is third L; house is on L with plaque. Mr Laurel senior was an actor and writer of melodramas.

Return to the Stan Laurel pub. Go downhill and at T-junction turn E, under railway bridge and along Dragley Beck. After ¼m the small white cottage on R with tall chimneys, now a shop (with plaque), is the birthplace of Sir John Barrow (1764–1848), diplomat, naturalist, oceanographer, and Secretary to the Admiralty 1804–45. He wrote many essays for the *Quarterly Review*, an interesting *Autobiography* and, most famously, *The Mutiny on the Bounty* (1831), the original account of the 1789 mutiny led by Fletcher Christian of Cockermouth. The story of his astonishing drive for world exploration, sending British expeditions on often disastrous missions to Africa, the polar regions and elsewhere, has been told by Fergus Fleming in *Barrow's Boys* (1998).

Look N from the cottage: the 'lighthouse' on the hill is his monument.

To reach the **Barrow Monument**, from the large roundabout take the A590 (signed Kendal); after ¾m turn L up Hoad Lane at sharp corner on crest of rise. (This is a nasty corner, and easy to miss: better to walk?) Walk up hill from gates in Hoad Lane. The splendid fake lighthouse was erected in 1850.

Return to large roundabout and for **Swarthmoor Hall** (*open for guided tours only, mid-March to mid- October, Thursdays, Fridays, and Sundays at 2.30pm, and at other times for groups by prior arrangement; voluntary admission charge*) go W on the A590 (signed Barrow). After 1m turn L (E) at the Miner's Arms; gates are on L after ¾m. The Hall is a fine late sixteenth-century manor with delightful gardens. In 1652 George Fox came here as an itinerant preacher, and convinced the family. Judge Thomas Fell, head of the household, gave his protection to Fox's movement, which spread from this house to become the Society of Friends (Quakers). After Fell's death Fox married his widow and came to live here, his visitors including William Penn, Quaker and founder of Pennsylvania. The house contains some of Fox's possessions and a small library with rare and early Bibles and Quaker works.

Fox's journal records his arrival at Swarthmoor:

> I came to Ulverston & soe to Swarth moore to Judge ffells. And there came uppe preist Lampitt which I perceived had beene & was stille a ranter ...

> I had a great deale of discourse with him before Margarett fell whoe soone then discerned ye preist cleerely & a convincement came upon her & her family of ye Lords truth ... And after this Judge ffell was come home ... & after dinner I aunswered him all his objections & satisfyed him by scripture soe as hee was thoroughly satisfyed & convict in his Judgement.

One cannot resist quoting Thomas Pennant's grotesquely unfair version of these events (from his *Tour in Scotland*, 1774):

> In after-time the melancholy spirit of *George Fox*, the founder of quakerism, took possession of *Swartz-moor* hall, first captivating, with grunts and groans, the kind heart of a widow, the then inhabitant, moving her congenial soul to resign herself to him. From thence this spiritual *Quixot* sallied out, and disturbed mankind with all the extravagancies that enthusiasm could invent.

To reach the **Swarthmoor Meeting House**, built by Fox and the earliest surviving meeting house, go L (E) from Swarthmoor Hall gates, cross junction into Meeting House Lane. Building is on L and has EX DONO G.F. 1688 carved over the door.

Return to the Hall gates and continue W to the Miner's Arms. Go L (S) on A590 for ¾m then first R (1m) to Pennington (*some parking near church*). From gate 80yds N of church cross field SE towards trees and over stone footbridge to **Ellabarrow**, an ancient burial mound where, according to tradition, 'Lord Ella sleeps with his golden sword'. Nothing more is known of Lord Ella or of the mound.

Lowick, Rusland, Haverthwaite

From Ulverston go R on A590 to Greenodd, then continue N on A5092; after 3m turn R (N) on A5084 (signed Torver) and continue 1m to the **Red Lion**, Lowick. This pleasant traditional village inn was a favourite around 1906 with the young Arthur Ransome and his friends, the poets Edward Thomas, Gordon Bottomley and Lascelles Abercrombie. The inn was frequented by charcoal-burners from the nearby woods and Edward Thomas was in the habit of leaving his clay pipes here for the charcoal-burners to 'sweeten' by burning them in their slow fires. Continue ½m SW from the inn to **Lowick Hall**, home of Arthur Ransome from 1948 to 1950. He was near the end of his career as a writer and wrote no children's fiction here, but edited a number of works on sailing and wrote much of his *Autobiography*.

From the Red Lion we shall follow the course of a favourite walk of Ransome, Thomas and their friends, adding a detour to other Ransome sites, including his grave. With detour, the distance is fourteen miles; without it, about seven. It is *not* circular, but it does end at another inn. There is an optional 'coda' to Wall Nook and Well Knowe. The walk as a whole takes us through delightful country, not the landscape of Ransome's well-known novels but of his quieter years and early associations with poets and essayists of the 'Georgian' period.

From Red Lion at Lowick, cross bridge (signed Spark Bridge); at Spark Bridge do not cross bridge but bear gently (not sharply) L uphill. At junction follow signs for Newby Bridge, then take turning to Bouth. From Bouth, to avoid detour go S for 1m then turn R (S) to Haverthwaite.

To take detour, from Bouth follow main road S for 2m. Where road forks (white house on corner) take L (W) fork (signed Rusland, Satterthwaite); after 150yds small cottage above road is **Ealinghearth Cottage**, which Arthur Ransome and his wife rented for the summer of 1951.

Return 150yds to corner and go uphill ¼m. White house on R is **Hill Top** (now kennels), which Ransome bought in 1960 and kept until his death in 1967. Here Ransome, now an old man, worked desultorily at his last books – *Mainly About Fishing* and the posthumously-published *Autobiography*.

Continue past Hill Top and take first L to rejoin valley road and continue N. After 2½m at group of cottages follow signs (Oxen Park and Ulverston) for **Rusland Church**. The grave of Arthur Ransome and his wife Evgenia is at the SE corner of the churchyard in a spot chosen by Ransome himself. Ransome met Evgenia in Russia: he was covering the Revolution as a journalist; she was Trotsky's secretary. Return past Ealinghearth Cottage and follow signs for Haverthwaite. At this point our detour ends and we return to Ransome's walk.

Heading S, cross A590 into Haverthwaite Village. At S side of village half way down steep hill, a large house with one wing named 'Melody Cottage' is the former **Hark to Melody Inn** – as Ransome wrote, 'a small inn with a delightful name, [and] with a painted signboard that I always believed to be a Morland, showing a pack of hounds in full cry.' Melody was a popular name for foxhounds. The inn was much loved by Ransome, who remembered it obliquely in his 1931 novel *Swallowdale*, where the hound that wins the hound trails is called Melody. (Ransome's 'Morland' is probably a mistake for Ibbetson: see p 25). Since the demise of the Hark to Melody those with a thirst must go ¾m NE to the Angler's Arms.

At this point we may consider our 'Ransome' walk complete but drivers, or those who want to match the walkers of those heroic days before World War I, should continue from Haverthwaite S over Low Wood Bridge and at once turn L (E). The road winds through steep woodland for 2m, then reaches a conifer plantation by pylons. From here: drivers should continue 1¼m then turn W (signed Speel Bank). First gate on L is entrance to Wall Nook. Walkers on the other hand may take small road R, then bridleway S through conifers to Wall Nook.

At **Wall Nook,** a much-renovated but still attractive farmhouse, Arthur Ransome spent the summers from 1905 to 1907. Here he wrote, walked and learned to wrestle with local youths training for the Grasmere Sports. For a time he also edited the London literary magazine *Temple Bar* here. Edward Thomas, Lascelles Abercrombie and Gordon Bottomley visited. Walkers can follow the poets' path to Well Knowe: take metal farm gate at R (S) of Wall Nook, go SE over field to stile (not gate). Cross next field to stile opposite, cross stream by footbridge and stile into next field. Then S, descending between rocks through gate into yard at Hardcrag. Take grassy lane W alongside Hardcrag House, then wooden gate into lane leading down to Well Knowe. Motorists should return from Wall Nook to road, then go S 1m past Garret House and first R, then first R again into lane. Well Knowe is first house on L (W) of lane.

Well Knowe was the home of the poet and dramatist Gordon Bottomley from 1894 to 1914. Now almost forgotten, Bottomley was prominent as a pioneer of modern verse drama. A few of his poems are still remembered, notably the haunting 'New Year's Eve 1913' (known as 'Cartmel Bells'):

> O, Cartmel bells ring soft tonight
> And Cartmel bells ring clear,
> But I lie far away tonight,
> Listening with my dear;
>
> Listening in a frosty land
> Where all the bells are still
> And the small-windowed bell-towers stand
> Dark under heath and hill ...

and 'To Iron-Founders and Others' with its much-quoted opening lines

> When you destroy a blade of grass
> You poison England at her roots.

His many literary friends included Edward Thomas, who stayed here in March 1906, to walk and 'read ... proofs of articles on stoats, reptiles etc.' and in June 1907, enjoying 'a perfectly happy & calm holiday that weaned me from my usual fidgets & discomforts in the most surprising way.' Bottomley dedicated his play *The Riding to Lithend* to Thomas with a splendid poem:

Here in the North we speak of you
And dream (and wish the dream were true)
That when the evening has grown late
You will appear outside our gate –
As though some Gipsy-Scholar yet
Sought this far place that men forget; ...
I bring my play, I turn to you
And wish it might to-night be true
That you would seek this small old house
Twixt laurel boughs and apple boughs.

His 1899 'Beam-Verses' – lines recording the house's history and his hopes for its future – are still carved on the joists of the sitting-room but at present are boxed in and cannot be seen.

Bottomley left the house for 'The Sheiling', Silverdale, in 1914. From Well Knowe take footpath opposite lower end of lane SE through woods; or follow road NE to T-junction and turn R (S) to Cartmel.

The contemporary Ulverston poet Neil Curry describes an attractive walk on the coast just S of here, beginning from the footbridge over the Leven and going E into **Roudsea Wood**, following the tracks of the old tramway used for moving gunpowder to the disused gunpowder shed near the shore, now a summerhouse, in his poem 'The Road to the Gunpowder House': see his book of the same name (2003).

Cartmel, Humphrey Head and Holker Hall

Cartmel (*several well-signed car parks*) is an entirely delightful village, and **Cartmel Priory** (with its unique double tower and undamaged architecture ranging in style from Norman to Perpendicular) is one of the wonders of England. In the churchyard (25yds due S of war memorial near gate from village) is the grave of William Taylor (1754–86), headmaster of Hawkshead Grammar School, friend and teacher of William Wordsworth, recalled in *The Prelude* Book X. Wordsworth visited the grave in the Summer of 1794 whilst staying at Rampside:

I gazed, and ... chanced to find
That morning, ranging through the churchyard graves
Of Cartmel's rural town, the place in which
An honoured teacher of my youth was laid ...
[The] sound of voice and countenance of the Man
Came back upon me, so that some few tears
Fell from me in my own despite. And now ...
I thought with pleasure of the verses graven
Upon his tombstone, saying to myself:
He loved the Poets, and, if now alive,
Would have loved me, as one not destitute
Of promise.

The grave is still as Wordsworth describes it; the epitaph is the final stanza of Gray's *Elegy*.

Inside the church, amongst many treasures, note a magnificent Victorian monument to Lord Frederick Cavendish, murdered with another politician in Phoenix Park, Dublin in 1882 (the so-called 'Phoenix Park Murders' which form a recurrent motif in Joyce's *Finnegans Wake* – 'O foenix culprit' and many other puns); at E, to R of altar, the tomb of Sir Edgar Harrington (see below). It used to be claimed that the animal under his feet (probably a lion) represented a wolf.

100yds S of the Priory, a splendid carved milestone gives distances to Lancaster and Ulverston over the sands. Take road S from milestone (soon signed Allithwaite) and after ¾m at crest of hill go R (signed Templand) then at sharp corner (oak tree with bench) turn down Locker Lane. Continue across main road (after ¼m note on L **Wraysholme Tower**, marvellous Tudor pele tower incorporated into farmhouse). At T junction after railway crossing go L (E) and continue to end of road (*small car park*). This is **Humphrey Head**, where according to tradition and a literary ballad of 1821 the last wolf in England was killed. Sir Edgar Harrington is said to have lived at Wraysholme Tower and to have been a great hunter of wolves:

> The sun hath set on Wraysholme's Tower,
> And o'er broad Morecambe Bay;
> The moon from out her eastern bower
> Pursues the track of day ...

> For know that on the morrow's dawn,
> With all who list to ride,
> Sir Edgar Harrington hath sworn
> To hunt the countryside.

> A wolf, the last, as rumour saith,
> In England's spacious realm,
> Is doomed that day to meet its death,
> And grace the conqueror's helm.

The ballad varies from the legend in making one Sir John De Lisle the killer of the wolf. It records the pursuit of the wolf to Windermere and back, and Sir John's return to find it threatening Harrington's daughter beneath the 'Fairy Church' on the Head. Sir John leaps his horse into the Church, killing both horse and wolf. He and the lady are married on the spot by a prior who happens to pass on his way to drink from the nearby **Holy Well**. Walk along base of cliff seaward 100yds for the Holy Well, very hard to see, a tiny spring emerging from the rock low down amongst boulders. The water tastes salty and is said to have medicinal properties. A few yards further seaward at the top of the cliff is the **Fairy Church**, an extraordinary bridge-like rock formation where a shaft from the top of the cliff emerges through its side. Both Well and Church are traditionally regarded as magical places.

To gain the top of the Head, return ¾m to the access point (*some parking by footpath sign 10yds N*) and walk up drive and path S to triangulation

CARTMEL PRIORY
W. Banks, 1872

point. The Head is the end of a limestone escarpment typical of South Lakeland, and gives a view over the whole of Morcambe Bay, S to Heysham, W to Piel Island, and NW to the Lakeland Fells.

Return to level crossing over railway and at first junction go L (W) on B5277 to Flookborough. At crossroads go R (N) still on main road (now B5278) 1m to **Holker Hall** (*house open daily except Saturday, 1 April to 29 October 10.30–4.30; gardens and park 10.30–6; car park, admission charge*), a seventeenth-century house hidden as you approach by its fine Victorian front wing, rebuilt after a fire in 1874.

The house appears as 'Severns Hall' in John Buchan's novel *The Dancing Floor* (1926), where Leithen, having sprained his ankle 'among the Cartmel fells' whilst heading for 'an obscure station' – Cark and Cartmel? – to catch the Lancaster train, hobbles up to the 'massive pillared porch' and is taken by the butler into 'a vast hall of the worst kind of Victorian Gothic', full of

> sham-medieval upholstered magnificence. It was Gothic with every merit of Gothic left out, and an air of dull ecclesiasticism hung about it. There was even an organ at one end, ugly and staring, as if it had come out of some *nouveau riche* provincial church. Every bit of woodwork was fretted and tortured into fancy shapes.

Here Leithen meets the owner, Vernon Milburne, and is drawn into strange adventures on a Greek island.

At the S edge of the Holker estate, in a house called **Quarrelflat**, Thomas De Quincey and his wife-to-be Margaret lived for a time in 1815-16, perhaps because their unmarried state would have caused a scandal at Grasmere, where they were well known. They used to bathe on the nearby shore, and one day went out leaving a flask of laudanum (De Quincey was a confirmed opium-addict) on the mantelpiece. A servant-girl, mistaking the red liquid for wine, picked it up and with the cheerful toast 'Here's to the bottom of the bottle!' drank most of it before realising her mistake. A doctor was summoned and the girl was saved by being 'continuously walked backwards and forwards along the sea shore between two men' to stop her from losing consciousness. By the time they left Quarrelflat, Margaret was pregnant with their first child. They married in 1817.

The road continues N to Haverthwaite; alternatively drive S to Cark and follow signs to Cartmel.

Gummer's How, Bowness and Windermere

Return to Cartmel or Allithwaite and follow signs for Newby Bridge, then take A592 (signed Windermere); after ¾m turn R (E) (signed Cartmel Fell, Bowland Bridge). Continue ¾m to Gummer's How car park. Path to **Gummer's How** starts 100yds up road. The How offers a justly famous view over Windermere and is the best place for viewing the country of Ransome's *Swallows and Amazons* books: as one authority says, the prospect is 'uncannily like the endpaper map of Swallows and Amazons' – most of all if you hold the book right way up (reversing real N and s) and forget about Rio.

Those who find bad weather obscuring the view may like to hear an explanation (1776) from the antiquarian William Stukeley, who thought the hills in this area acted like huge magnets:

> This country is exceedingly obnoxious to rain, and some of the hill-tops on one side or other are perpetually covered with clouds; I imagine the vast solidity of the stone that composed them attracts the clouds big with water at some considerable distance, and then the winds break and dash them into rain.

From Gummer's How car park continue 1¼m NE, turn L (N) opposite Lightwood and at junction L (N) then R (signed Winster) at fork. ¼m down is **Great Hartbarrow**, where Arthur Ransome and his wife had lodgings in 1925 whilst waiting to move into Low Ludderburn. From Great Hartbarrow continue NE and take first R. At grass triangle go R (signed Bowland Bridge). Just downhill at another grass triangle is private drive to **Barkbooth**, former home of Ransome's friend Colonel Kelsall. He and Ransome were keen fishermen and, having no telephones, devised a set of signals to arrange fishing-trips. Ransome would hoist black wooden diamonds, squares or triangles against the whitewashed wall of Low Ludderburn; Kelsall hoisted white shapes against the dark wall of his barn. The signals were used fictionally by the Swallows, Amazons and D's in *Winter Holiday*, where the barn appears as Dick's observatory, from which he signals to Mars and first makes contact with the Swallows. The grey and white buildings of Low Ludderburn are still just visible NW over treetops (which have grown since Ransome's day).

¼m S of Barkbooth is **Borderside**, home of William Pearson

BORDERSIDE
W. Wickes, 1863

(1780–1856), Quaker naturalist, folklorist and friend of Wordsworth. A statesman's son, born at Crosthwaite, Pearson spent twenty years as a banker in Manchester before returning to farm at Borderside in 1822. He built the present house in 1848 when he married. He was an authority on the local landscape, wildlife and traditions; his *Papers, Letters and Journals* were collected and published in 1863.

Continue S, then take first R (SW) and second L (S) to Cartmel Fell. Follow signs to **St Anthony's Church**, a fascinating and delightful pre-Reformation church. St Anthony was the patron saint of charcoal burners; the church is full of interesting features, notably its stained glass, described by Mrs Humphry Ward in her novel *Helbeck of Bannisdale*:

> Above the moth-eaten table that replaced the ancient altar there still rose a window that breathed the very *secreta* of the old faith – a window of radiant fragments, piercing the twilight of the little church with strange, uncomprehended things … For here … there stood a golden St Anthony, a virginal St Margaret … In the very centre of the stone tracery, a woman lifted herself in bed to receive the Holy Oil – so pale, so eager still after all these centuries! …

> But the children's dreams followed St Anthony rather – the kind, sly old man, with the belled staff, up which his pig was climbing.

Here the novel's heroine, Laura Fountain, comes to sit and ponder sadly after her separation from Alan Helbeck. The book and magazine illustrator Bertha Newcombe, active in the 1890s, evidently knew the church well: it features in several of her illustrations, which are displayed in the church.

From the church return to the road; follow it W then N; at junction go L, then immediately R and you will find yourself after ¾m at the junction above Great Hartbarrow. Go L (NW) ½m to **Low Ludderburn**, Arthur Ransome's home from 1925 to 1935. Of the many houses where he lived or stayed in the Lake District this one was longest and most fully his home. He was attracted to the house, with its 'low ceilings and walls so thick that the staircase was built within the thickness of the wall', partly by its views ('forty miles away down into Yorkshire' in one direction and in the other 'what I think the best panorama of Lake mountains, from Black Combe to Helvellyn and the high ground above the valleys of Lune and Eden') – and partly by its orchard-garden, which may be seen today in spring 'white with snowdrops' or full of daffodils, just as it was when he first saw it. There were also 'apples, damsons, gooseberries, raspberries, currants,' and water supplied by 'a Roman well just behind the house'. Ransome had the upper storey of the barn (large grey building at L) converted into a work-room, with a new window facing E, and added the wooden garage, which still has a distinctly Ransomesque look and resembles a boathouse. Here he wrote articles and leaders for *The Manchester Guardian*, as well as the paper's angling column, later collected in book form as *Rod and Line* (1929).

In this house he was visited by the Altounyan family, and to entertain them after their return to Syria wrote *Swallows and Amazons* (1930). *Swallowdale* (1931), *Winter Holiday* (1933), *Coot Club* (1936), and most of *Pigeon Post* (1936) were also written here.

Continue N ¼m and at junction go N (signed Bowness). After 1m pass Ghyll Head Outdoor Education Centre; immediately after it on L is a slate house called **The Cottage**. Here W.G. Collingwood, painter, novelist, and archaeologist lived in his early years as Ruskin's secretary, and wrote the first of a torrent of books reflecting his huge range of interests, among them *The Philosophy of Ornament* (1883), *The Limestone Alps of Savoy* (1884), *Astrology in the Apocalypse* (1886) and *John Ruskin: A Biographical Outline* (1889).

His son, the philosopher and archaeologist R.G. Collingwood, was born here in 1889. Soon afterwards the family moved to Lanehead, Coniston, to be nearer Ruskin.

At junction below The Cottage go N on A592. After 1m is the **Storrs Hall Hotel**, formerly Storrs Hall, an opulent early nineteenth-century mansion (note the ornate front with unusual 'Egyptian' pediment). Scott and Lock-hart (on their tour of the Lakes) and also Wordsworth and Canning stayed here for some days in August 1825 with the owner, Colonel Bolton:

> The weather was as Elysian as the scenery; there were brilliant cavalcades through the woods in the mornings, and delicious boatings on the Lake by moonlight

and, on the last day, 'one of the most brilliant regattas that ever enlivened Windermere' – organised by John Wilson.

Beatrix Potter, an expert scientific mycologist, often came here during

WINDERMERE AND STORRS HALL
Thomas Allom, 1832

her late-summer holidays in the 1890s to gather fungi. On one occasion, she notes in her journal (September 17, 1895) 'An old woodcutter warned me most kindly that "them aren't mushrooms".'

Take path NW from hotel front to lakeshore to reach the **Storrs Temple** (*NT*), a small stone viewing-house framing picturesque views of the lake. Built in 1804, it honours four British admirals (Duncan, St Vincent, Howe and Nelson), whose names are engraved on its sides.

Ransome fanatics may want to go 3½m S on the A592 from Storrs to look at **Blake Holme**, a small island close to the shore which was, according to Arthur Ransome, 'the island most used as Wild Cat Island' in *Swallows and Amazons*. Blake Holme is accessible to walkers from the waterside at the Hill of Oaks Caravan Park. A beautiful wooded island, it looks exactly right for Wild Cat Island but is just a few yards from shore, across water usually shallow enough to wade. Moreover, it has no harbour: Wild Cat Island's secret harbour was borrowed from Peel Island on Coniston Water.

From Storrs continue N towards Bowness and turn SE on B5284 (signed Kendal) crossing A5074. After 1m turn R (S) (signed Winster) and 1m further on take turn L just after Outmoss, for **Low Lindeth**. This farm was the model for Codlin Croft in Beatrix Potter's *The Fairy Caravan*, and is shown in the line-drawing of Charles and the turkey-cock at the head of Chapter XIII. The book gives an alluring description:

> The orchard ... is a long rambling strip of ground, with old bent pear trees and apple trees that bear little summer pears in August and sweet codlin apples in September. At the end nearest to the buildings there are clothes-props, hen-coops, tubs, troughs, old oddments; and pig-styes that adjoin the calf hulls and cow byres. The back windows of the farmhouse

look out nearly level with the orchard grass; little back windows of diamond panes not made to open. The far end of the orchard is a neglected pretty wilderness, with mossy old trees, elder bushes, and long grass,

but the farm has been greatly renovated and tidied-up since.

Return to A592 and follow it N into **Bowness-on-Windermere** (*many well-signed car parks*). Until the early nineteenth century Bowness was thought of as 'the port of Windermere', and was an important marketing centre for local products such as fish and charcoal. Heavier materials such as slate and timber would go on past Bowness to Newby Bridge and Ulverston for coastal shipping.

In the course of the nineteenth century Bowness became a great centre for moneyed tourists. Large hotels sprang up (one gets an idea of the tone from Harriet Martineau's cosy 1854 reference to The Crown, with its 'ten private sitting rooms and ... ninety beds. Nothing can well exceed the beauty of the view from its garden seats'). Now that the railway had arrived nearby a process of suburban development was under way, merging Bowness into the new village of 'Windermere'. Bowness is now commercialised and overcrowded, but it has been for well over a century, so there is no point in grumbling. One may as well enjoy the boats and the restaurants (some excellent) and be grateful to the National Trust for ensuring that the W bank of the lake has not been exploited in the same manner.

Bowness is the 'Rio' of Arthur Ransome's *Swallows and Amazons* – 'The little town is known in guide-books by another name, but the crew of the *Swallow* had long ago given it the name of Rio Grande'. The Victorian wooden boatsheds where 'Swallow' was repaired in *Swallowdale* used to

'That's a fine little ship ...' BOWNESS BAY ('RIO')
Clifford Webb, 1930

be by the waterside here (until c 1960 one had 'John Walker' painted over the door, perhaps suggesting the hero's name). They are now gone, though there are some half-hearted modern replicas 100yds N of the steamer pier.

From the main car park S of Steamer Pier walk S along Rectory Road 200yds between golf course and cemetery to drive opposite (signed Parson Wyke) for **Bowness Rectory** (now Parson Wyke House). Harriet Martineau loved this building,

> which is hardly less venerable than the church, ... and is approached through fields and a garden. The old-fashioned porch is there, of which this is said to be the last remaining instance in the whole district, – the roomy, substantial porch, with benches on each side, long enough to hold a little company of parishioners, and a round ivy-clad chimney immediately surmounting the porch.

The Rectory is all the more valuable as, in Martineau's words, 'Almost every other noticeable edifice in Bowness is new.'

In his *Guide to the Lakes*, Wordsworth recommended a boat-trip:

> None of the other Lakes unfold so many fresh beauties to him who sails upon them ... The Islands may be explored at any time of day; but one bright unruffled evening must, if possible, be set apart for the splendour, the stillness, the solemnity of a three hours' voyage upon the higher division of the Lake, not omitting, towards the end of the excursion, to quit the expanse of water, and peep into the calm and close River at its head.

Certainly you will not be in Bowness long before someone tries to get you aboard a boat.

The first steam-boats (with paddle-wheels) appeared on the lake in 1845, against much opposition. They were coalfired and smoky, and brought with them brass bands and day-excursion parties fetched by rail from industrial Lancashire. *Punch* published a splendid protest-sonnet in mock-Wordsworthian style:

> What incubus, my goodness! have we here
> Cumbering the bosom of our lovely lake?
> A steamboat, as I live! – without mistake!
> Puffing and splashing over Windermere!
> What inharmonious shouts assail mine ear?
> Shocking poor Echo, that perforce replies
> 'Ease her!' and 'Stop her!' – frightful and horrid cries,
> Mingling with frequent pop of ginger beer ...

Three elegant Victorian vessels with awnings and brass-banded funnels (which appear in the background in Ransome's novels and in a Clifford Webb illustration to early editions of *Swallows and Amazons*) still ply the lake. Perhaps one of these carried Thomas Hardy, who declined an invitation to George V's coronation (June 1911) on the grounds that he had already fixed up a Lakeland holiday, and reflected that, despite the rain, he 'probably got more satisfaction out of Coronation Day by spending it on

Windermere than he would have done by spending it in a seat at the Abbey.'

The lake gives the best view of the central group of islands which divide the lake into its northern and southern basins. Landing is allowed on all islands except Belle Isle, which is a private residence.

Lady Holme is mentioned in Wordsworth's *Prelude* (1850) Book II as the

> small Island, where survived
> In solitude the ruins of a shrine
> Once to Our Lady dedicate, and served
> Daily with chaunted rites

but except for the island's name and some rough steps cut into the rock, all traces of the medieval shrine have now gone. The two tiny **Lily of the Valley Holmes** are mentioned in *Prelude* II (amongst places to which the Hawkshead boys made holiday excursions) as

> an Island musical with birds
> That sang and ceased not; [and] a Sister Isle
> Beneath the oaks' umbrageous covert, sown
> With lilies of the valley like a field.

Belle Isle (the 'Long Island' of Ransome's novels) is the largest and most interesting island. Until the late eighteenth century it was the property of the Philipson family of Calgarth Hall, who had a house there. During the Civil War the head of the family, Robin Philipson ('Robin the Devil'), a Royalist, who had stowed the family treasures on the island for safekeeping, was besieged there by the Parliamentarians under Colonel Briggs. The siege was raised by Robin's brother and Briggs retreated, whereupon Robin set off to Kendal in pursuit of him. It was a Sunday and he expected to find Briggs in church so he rode into Kendal Church on horseback. Briggs was not there but the Parliamentarian congregation set on Robin and dragged him off his horse. He fought his way out of the church, resaddled his horse and escaped back to the island. A highly-coloured version of the story is used for the conclusion of Scott's narrative poem *Rokeby* (1813).

Celia Fiennes visited Sir Christopher Philipson here in 1698:

> the isle did not look to be so bigg at the shore but takeing boat I went on it and found it as large and very good barley and oates and grass; the water is very cleer and full of good fish.

Gilpin visited the island in 1772 and sang its praises:

> A more sequestered spot cannot easily be conceived. Nothing can be more excluded from the noise, and interruption of life; or abound with a greater variety of those circumstances, which make retirement pleasing.

The island contains two of West's 'stations' for obtaining ideal views of the lake and its surroundings: from the S side he recommended the view down the length of the lake; from the N side, the landscape form[s] as magnificent an amphitheatre and as grand an assemblage of mountains, dells, and chasms, as ever the fancy of Poussin suggested, or the genius of Rosa invented.

In 1774 the island acquired its most remarkable feature, the house – said to be both the first circular large house to be built in England and the earliest Lake District building to be consciously placed 'for picturesque reasons'. The house was built for a Mr English, who laid out formal gardens in a taste already outmoded: West's guide (1778) censured them as 'An unpleasing contrast to the natural simplicity and insular beauty of the place' and Gilpin commented that 'the proprietor [has] spent six thousand pounds upon it; with which sum he has contrived to do almost every thing, that one would wish had been left undone.' William Gell in 1797 thought the house 'wants only a little green paint and a label of Souchong or fine Hyson to make it exactly like a large shop tea canister'.

The island was acquired in 1781 by J.C. Curwen, whose wife Isabella was heiress to the Workington coalmines. He landscaped the grounds afresh but criticism continued, Dorothy Wordsworth noting (June 8 1802) that

> Mr Curwen's shrubberies looked pitiful enough under the native trees ... And that great house! Mercy upon us! if it *could* be concealed, it *would* be well for all who are not [*sic*] pained to see the pleasantest of earthly spots deformed by man. But it *cannot* be covered. Even the tallest of our old oak trees would not reach to the top of it.

In August 1831, however, she stayed there with the Curwens, though she found it 'dull' and reflected, 'What I like least in an island as a residence is the being separated from men, cattle, cottages, and the goings-on of rural life.'

Ironically enough, now that everyone admires the house and wants to see it, the trees have grown to the point where it cannot be seen at all except through a small gap at the middle of the E side. A glimpse of this elegant and remarkable building is well worth getting.

Windermere, like many of the lakes, has undergone various changes of name. Until the early nineteenth century two versions – 'Winandermere' and the familiar 'Windermere' – were current side by side; in time the simpler version won. Camden thought it was called '*Winander mere* ... probably from its windings on a bed of almost one stone continued for near ten miles with crooked banks' – though the name is probably from some tenth-century landowner, and its bed is as fragmented and muddy as that of any other lake.

At first the char, a trout-like fish confined to this and a few of the other lakes, interested visitors even more than its size (ten and a half miles long, it is the largest lake in England). Thus John Leland in 1540 notes that

> There is a very greate lake, or mere, wherof part is under the egge [edge] of Furnes Felles, cawlled Wynermerewath, wherin a straunge fisch cawlled a chare, not sene else there in the cuntery as they say.

Defoe too (in 1724) was interested in char, which 'is a curious fish, and, as a dainty, is potted, and sent far and near, as presents to the best friends; but the quantity they take also is not great.'

In 1698 Celia Fiennes tried to describe her impression of the landscape – without the aid of a 'picturesque' vocabulary which had not been invented:

> This great water seemes to flow and wave about with the wind or in one motion but it does not ebb and flow like the sea with the tyde ... but it seems to be a standing lake encompass'd with vast high hills that are perfect rocks and barren ground of a vast height from which many little springs out of the rock does bubble up and descend down and fall into this water.

Many poems have been written about the lake, perhaps the first being Richard Braithwaite's *The Fatall Nuptiall* (1636); though mainly concerned with the ferry accident of the previous year (see p 338), it has a preface which shows awareness of Windermere's beauty, referring to it as

> no less eminent and generously knowne for her Solebreeding, and peculiar kinde of fishes (commonly called Chares) as for those windy and labyrinthian mazes, with those curiously shaded, beauteously tufted, naturally fortifide, and impregnably seated Ilands in every part of the Mere interveined.

The earliest description to present the lake in truly picturesque terms seems to be an anonymous article in the *Gentleman's Magazine* for 1748:

> We came upon a high promontory [Orrest Head?] that gave us at once a full view of the bright lake; which, spreading itself under us, in the midst of the mountains, presented one of the most glorious appearances that ever struck the eye of a traveller with transport ... In some places the crags appear through the trees hanging over the water, in other places little valleys are seen opening between the hills, through which small torrents empty themselves into the lake; and, in all places, the border quite round shows itself delicate and beautiful.

As visitors became more numerous the poets followed. Typical of later eighteenth-century poetic descriptions is Budworth's *Windermere* (1798):

> No! not a fan of air the mirror moves,
> But then a rustling leaf falls from the groves:
> Or wanton wild-ducks on the surface skim,
> Shewing, by their long trains, how fast they swim;
> Or finny tribe their sportiveness display,
> And circles cause, till circles melt away ...

Windermere was a regular presence in Wordworth's earliest poetic experiments, supplying conventional landscape imagery for such poems as 'The Dog: An Idyllium' and 'Beauty and Moonlight' (?1786), and 'An Evening Walk' (1788–9).

As a boy Wordsworth probably skated on it: the twilight skating episode in *The Prelude* Book I owes something to memories of Esthwaite Water but probably refers mainly to the W bank of Windermere near the ferry:

> All shod with steel,
> We hissed along the polished ice in games
> Confederate ...
>
>   ... through the darkness and the cold we flew,
> And not a voice was idle; with the din,
> Meanwhile, the precipices rang aloud;
> The leafless trees and every icy crag
> Tinkled like iron.

On the shores of Windermere too (no doubt on the W side nearer to Hawkshead) the young Wordsworth often stood 'At evening when the stars had just begun/To move along the edges of the hills' and

> Blew mimic hootings to the silent owls,
> That they might answer him; and they would shout
> Across the watery vale, and shout again,
> Responsive to his call, with quivering peals.

During Wordsworth's schooldays he and his friends often rowed here:

> When summer came,
> It was the pastime of our afternoons
> To beat along the shores of Windermere
> With rival oars,

and returning from Bowness 'over the dusky lake' to Hawkshead at twilight they sometimes steered their boat to 'some small island' where they landed young Robert Greenwood, a skilled flute-player,

> And rowed off gently, while he blew his flute
> Alone upon the rock.

Stendhal viewed the lake on his English tour of 1826, noting simply 'Fine moonlight with its tender reverie on the shores of Wendermere' – a comment which, says a biographer unkindly, merely reveals 'his insensibility to nature and his persistent ignorance of English'. Perhaps we should forgive Stendhal: Windermere is delightful, but it is hard to say anything about it that is not obvious. Interestingly, both Wordsworth and Arthur Ransome, in their best writing about it, found the same solution – to picture the lake frozen.

Ransome was here as a schoolboy during the Great Frost of February 1895, when the Lake was frozen for several weeks. The boys of the Old College spent their days on the ice learning to skate. Carriages were driven across the lake, bonfires were lit on it and at night people skated with lanterns. Ransome would also have seen Herbert Crossley's ice yachts racing on the lake. Windermere froze again in 1929, and Ransome walked across from the steamer pier and noticed a boat (the *Maid Marion*) frozen into the ice. Memories of both 'freezes' combined to give him the basis for *Winter Holiday* (1933), where the immobilised boat becomes Captain Flint's houseboat, *alias* the *Fram*. Ransome sailed extensively on Windermere in the 1920s and '30s, mainly in his fourteen-foot dinghy *Swallow*.

Windermere, incidentally, has the honour of being the only Lakeland place named in James Joyce's *Finnegans Wake* – 'Die Windermere Dichter' (German: 'The Windermere Poets') on pp. 212–3, in the midst of a preposterous catalogue of books, being presumably a vague reference to the 'Lake Poets'.

For information about the Ferry and the W bank, see p 337ff.

We return to Bowness. 250yds N of the Steamer Pier is **St Martin's Church**, somewhat aggressively restored in 1870. The E window contains fine painted glass (pre-1523, restored 1871) from Cartmel Priory. Outside, near the SE corner of the church, is the tomb of Bishop Watson (see p 25), tastefully restrained and engraved with elegant Latin. Far more interesting is the headstone, under holly trees at the E end of the church, of Rasselas Belfield, 'a Native of ABYSSINIA' (d 1822):

> A Slave by birth I left my native land
> And found my Freedom on Britania's Strand:
> Blest Isle! Thou Glory of the Wise and Free!
> Thy Touch alone unbinds the Chains of Slavery!

Next to the church and a little uphill stands the **Royal Hotel**, formerly the White Lion. This is the hotel celebrated in *The Prelude* Book II, where Wordsworth describes visits in summer with his schoolfellows, recalling it as

> a splendid place, the door beset
> With chaises, grooms and liveries, and within
> Decanters, glasses, and the blood-red wine ...
> Yet, to this hour, the spot to me is dear
> With all its foolish pomp. The garden lay
> Upon a slope surmounted by the plain
> Of a small bowling-green; beneath us stood
> A grove, with gleams of water through the trees
> And over the tree-tops; nor did we want
> Refreshment, strawberries and mellow cream.
> And there, through half an afternoon, we played
> On the smooth platform.

Keats and Charles Brown dined here on 26 June 1818, on their walking tour to Scotland. Keats was overwhelmed by Windermere's scenery, but disconcerted by news of Wordsworth's Tory political activities: 'There is no such thing as time and space', he told his brother Tom,

> which by the way came forcibly upon me on seeing for the first hour the Lake and Mountains of Winander – I cannot describe them – they surpass my expectation – beautiful water – shores and islands green to the marge –

mountains all round up to the clouds ... we have walked to Bowne's [Bowness] to dinner – said Bowne's situated on the lake where we have just dined, and I am writing this present. I took an oar to one of the islands to take up some trout for dinner, which they keep in porous boxes. I enquired of the waiter for Wordsworth – he said he knew him, and that he had been here a few days ago, canvassing for the Lowthers. What think you of that – Wordsworth versus Brougham!!

'Pomp' (to use Wordsworth's term) was still evident (despite changes of name) in 1854, when Harriet Martineau tells us that

Ullock's Hotel, called Royal since the visit of Queen Adelaide in 1840, makes up between seventy and eighty beds. Close at hand is a little museum, where the birds of the district may be seen, exceedingly well stuffed and arranged by Mr. Armstrong, a waiter at the hotel.

Mr Armstrong's amateur taxidermy is no longer on display, but the Royal is still most impressive.

If you walk between the Church and the Royal Hotel heading N for 100yds you will reach **The Hole in the Wall**. A sign announces that Dickens was here in 1857; but as his biographers and his magazine *Household Words* are silent on the subject one may be sceptical. 100 yds N of the Royal Hotel, along the Ambleside Road and opposite the Old John Peel Inn, is **The World of Beatrix Potter Attraction** (*open 10.00 – 5.30 daily except Christmas; admission charge; pay and display car park nearby*). Children will enjoy the large-scale recreations of scenes from Beatrix Potter's books, and there are videos and displays about her life and work.

From the centre of Bowness follow the A592 ¼m N to the **Steamboat Museum** (*open 10 – 5 daily; car park, admission charge*). This is an excellent museum, even if you think you're not interested in steamboats. Among items with a literary resonance, the collection includes Beatrix Potter's strange, flat-bottomed rowing boat (salvaged from Moss Eccles Tarn in 1976); the original dinghy *Amazon* of Ransome's novels (actually called the *Mavis* in his day, and enormously evocative with its much-mended red sail); one of the ice-yachts that helped to inspire *Winter Holiday*; and the steam launch *Esperance*, built for the local magnate H.W. Schneider to commute to Barrow in the late nineteenth century and the main model for Captain Flint's houseboat in *Swallows and Amazons*:

She was a long narrow craft with a high raised cabin roof, and a row of glass windows along her side. Her bows were like the bows of an old-time clipper. Her stern was like that of a steamship. She had nothing that could properly be called a mast, though there was a little flagstaff, where a mast might have been, stepped just forward of the glass-windowed cabin.

⅓m further N and an easy walk is **Rayrigg Hall**, summer home of William Wilberforce between 1780 and 1787; and ⅓m N of Rayrigg is **Queen Adelaide's Hill** (*NT; small car park in lay-by*), formerly Rayrigg Bank. This is West's fifth 'station' or viewpoint: he advises the visitor to climb the hill (from the lakeshore) without looking back, then turn to receive the full impact of the view:

> You will be struck with astonishment at the prospect spread at your feet, which, if not the most superlative view that nature can exhibit, she is more fertile in beauties than the reach of my imagination will allow me to conceive. It would be mere vanity to attempt to describe a scene which beggars all description.

Harriet Martineau thought it

> a view unsurpassed for beauty in the whole Lake District. The entire lake lies below, the white houses of Clappersgate being distinctly visible at the north end and the Beacon at the south ... The Calgarth woods, for which we are indebted to Bishop Watson, rising and falling, spreading and contracting, with green undulating meadows interposed, are a treat to the eye; and so are the islands clustering in the centre of the lake. Wray Castle stands forth well above the promontory opposite; and at the head, the Langdale Pikes, and their surrounding mountains seem, in some states of the atmosphere, to approach and overshadow the waters; and shroud themselves in soft haze and delicate lines.

Modern eyes tend to prefer the higher view from Gummer's How, but this one has a panoramic sweetness which still gives it a special quality.

½m N of Queen Adelaide's Hill at roundabout take A592 (signed Kirkstone Pass, Ullswater). (At the roundabout our route crosses that of Part One: if you are taking the A591, turn to p 24).

Troutbeck

1m N of roundabout, clearly signed is **Holehird** (*house not open; gardens open; car park*), now a Cheshire Home, its fine gardens maintained by the Lakeland Horticultural Society. In this rather forbidding-looking Victorian mansion Beatrix Potter stayed with her parents for the summers of 1889 and 1895. The weather was poor but she had some success hunting for fossils and fungi in the woods. The present house was built in 1854 on the site of an older farmhouse, said to have had its name from 'Hird's Holding' as it was the house and land granted by the King to Hugh Hird, the 'Cork Lad of Kentmere' (see p 21). Continue N.

We are now travelling up through **Troutbeck**, a small settlement straggling along the beck of that name in the approaches to Kirkstone Pass. It now looks salubrious enough, but in 1864 Eliza Lynn Linton was lamenting that

> In a few years ... pretty, dirty, neglected Troutbeck will be cleaned, schooled, and ornamented, and made fit company for ambitious Windermere and respectable Ambleside. It is worth seeing, however, in its dirt and neglect; its tumbledown cottages – not one among them all straight according to the plumb-line – with ivied walls and casements patched with rags and paper; its one curious chateau-like house, with its formal courtyard, and formal terrace, and formal yew-trees clipped and closely

shaven; its destitution and penury; all so grandly enframed that its very poverty becomes a charm the more. It is one of the real bye-hamlets of the lake district, picturesque, wild, dirty, diseased, which the prosaic architect and schoolmaster will sweep away before many years are gone.

For such a small and scattered community, it has produced a surprising number of colourful characters. Harriet Martineau tells the story of two farmers, one a Troutbeck man, the other Josiah Brown of Orrest Head, who had 'prodigious' bulls:

> and what must they do but meet half-way, and have a bullfight; the terms being that the winner should have the fallen animal. Josiah actually came riding his bull. The battle was tremendous; and the Troutbeck animal went down before Josiah's, and was given by him to the poor of Troutbeck.

Troutbeck was also the home of one of the earliest recorded Cumbrian poets, Thomas Hoggart (c 1640–1709), known as 'Old Hoggart', said to be an uncle of the painter William Hogarth. According to Adam Walker he was a farmer, and

> the simple strains of this mountain Theocritus were fabricated while he held the plough, or was leading his fuel from the hills ... not an incident or absurdity in the neighbourhood escaped ... If anyone attempted to overreach his neighbour, or cast a leering eye at his wife, he was sure to hear himself sung over the whole parish, nay, to the very boundaries of the Westmorland dialect; so that his songs were said to have a greater effect on the manners of his neighbourhood, than even the sermons of the parson himself.

One might imagine a rough dialect poet, but what survives of his work, though tough and witty, is also polished and sometimes strewn with classical allusions. Recollections of his plays are fascinating and suggest that a theatre like that of Shakespeare and Marlowe was still thriving at Troutbeck in the 1730s. Walker recorded in 1780:

> I myself have had the honour to bear a part in one of his plays ... This play was called 'The destruction of Troy.' It was written in metre, much in the manner of Lope de Vega, or the ancient French drama; the unities were not too strictly observed, for the siege of ten years was all represented; every hero was present in the piece, so that the Dramatis Personae consisted of every lad of genius in the whole parish. The wooden horse – Hector dragged by the heels – the Fury of Diomed – the flight of Aeneas – and the burning of the city, were all represented. I remember not what Fairies had to do with all this; but as I happened to be about three feet high at the time ... I personated one of these tiny beings. The stage was a fabrication of boards placed about six feet high, on strong poles; the Green Room was partitioned off with the same materials; its ceiling was the azure canopy of heaven; and the boxes, pit and gallery were ... the green slope of a fine hill.

The production began with a grand procession led by 'a yeoman on bull-back' (could this be our friend Josiah Brown?) and 'there were more spectators for three days together than the three theatres in London will

TROUTBECK PARK
Beatrix Potter, 1929

hold'. There is also record of 'the Play called the Lascivious Queen, as it was acted on St. James' Day, 1693, upon a scaffold at the Moss Gap, in Troutbeck' whose title survives, sadly without any text.

Troutbeck Town Head is ⅓m N of the Limefitt Park gates. Go R (NE) just before the Queen's Head Hotel, and E down bridleway (signed Long Green Head). Follow bridleway to first corner below buildings. Looking N from this point Beatrix Potter made the line drawing at the end of Chapter IV of *The Fairy Caravan* (early editions only) showing Pony Billy in the Pound. The corner of the wall is shown, and beyond it Long Green Head farm with Troutbeck Tongue and High Street in the background. Continue ¾m to **Ing Bridge**, which appears in the landscape sketch at the head of Chapter XV of *The Fairy Caravan*. It is shown from the S, without the trees that have since grown up around it; Troutbeck Tongue is in the background.

¾m further N up the lane is **Troutbeck Park** (*NT*), a farm owned by Beatrix Potter (Mrs Heelis) in her later years and given to the National Trust. It was used for several *Fairy Caravan* illustrations. The house front, with its remarkable deeply-arched doorway, and the wall where the parrot-cage sits, is shown (viewed from the yard gate) in the drawing at the end of Chapter XIII (the beehives were fictitious) and the farmyard with the barn (looking from the house end along the slate-roofed bay) is the background for the drawing of the farmdogs Roy, Bobs and Matt lying lazily in the sun in Chapter XIII.

Above the farm buildings looms the beautiful **Troutbeck Tongue**, which is part of the farm's land. There is no footpath up it now, though there must have been once, for there is an old summit cairn, in bad repair. The Tongue makes a noble ridge-walk with fine views S down the Troutbeck valley to Windermere and N towards High Street and Kirkstone, but the approach demands a desperate struggle through waist-deep bracken. Seek the farmer's permission. Beatrix Potter must often have come up here: the drawing at the head of Chapter XI of *The Fairy Caravan* shows the view N from the summit; the tailpiece to Chapter XVII shows a pack of foxhounds descending E into Hagg Gill. And it was up here – in 'the lonely wilderness ... behind the table-land of Troutbeck Tongue' – that *The Fairy Caravan* was first conceived:

> In the midst of that waste of yellow bent grass and stones there is a patch of green grass and a stunted thorn. Round the tree, round and round it in measured canter went four of the wild fell ponies. Round then checked and turned, round and round reversed; dainty hoofs, arched necks, manes tossing and tails streaming.

> I watched a while, crouched behind a boulder ... Who had taught them? Who had learned them 'dance the heys' in that wilderness?

These thoughts led to the character of Pony Billy in the story. The thorn has gone, but the place is the flat area just N of the northernmost knoll on the summit.

Return to the Queens Head. 200yds N turn sharp L (signed Ambleside) for the **Mortal Man**. The inn and its curious signboard are famous. Originally a small cottage inn called the White House, it gained its present name around 1800 when a loyal customer, the painter Julius Caesar Ibbetson (who lived in Ambleside 1799–1802 and in Troutbeck 1802–5) painted a new sign for it. On one side it showed 'the face of a thin-lipped, lantern-jawed individual, the very picture of a modern teetotaler', and on the other 'a jolly-faced toper with rubicund nose'; both were 'well-known and worthy denizens of the vale'. From their mouths came 'labels' with appropriate couplets:

> Thou mortal man, who liv'st by bread,
> What is it makes thy nose so red?

> Thou silly fool, that look'st so pale,
> 'Tis drinking Sally Birkett's ale!

The sign was such a success that the inn soon became known as the Mortal Man. Alas, the then landlord took the sign away with him when he retired and it has been lost. The present sign is a modern replica.

The inn was popular with Victorian travellers and, inevitably, was greatly extended in so-called 'Domestic Gothic' style in 1889 to produce the present large hotel.

200yds SW of the hotel, running uphill from Lanefoot Farm, is **Nanny Lane**. In August 1895 Beatrix Potter was fossil-hunting with great success, having left her pony and

> walked up Nanny Lane leading to the foot path up Wansfell. I had to go high, nearly level with the quarries across the valley before I came to a part where the walls were crumbling stone.

Here she had her 'first great day of fossils' but does not tell us what she found. Another day she and her father left their pony at The Mortal Man ('which looks a nice little inn') and walked up the lane where they

> had great pleasure watching a pair of buzzards sailing round and round over the top of Wansfell. There was an old shepherd half way up the side of Troutbeck, much bent and gesticulating with a stick. He watched the collie scouring round over stone walls ... Four or five sheep louped over a wall at least three feet high on our right and escaped the dog's observation, whereupon the ancient shepherd, a mere speck in the slanting sunlight down the great hillside, this aged Wordsworthian worthy, awoke the echoes with a flood of the most singularly bad language.

The lane goes over to Ambleside *via* Wansfell and Stockgill Force.

Kirkstone Pass and Brothers Water

Return to A592 and continue N. This is **Kirkstone Pass**, the spectacular road linking Windermere to Ullswater. There are fine views E over Troutbeck Tongue, S to Ambleside and N to Brothers Water and Ullswater. Formerly a rugged mountain track, it is now a busy motor road and walkers in summer will find the traffic tiresome.

Celia Fiennes crossed the Pass in her 'Great Journey' of 1698:

> There is good marble amongst those rocks: as I walked down at this place I was walled on both sides by those inaccessible high rocky barren hills which hangs over ones head in some places and appear very terrible; and from them springs many little currents of water from the sides and clefts which trickle down to some lower part where it runs swiftly over the stones and shelves in the way, which makes a pleasant rush and murmuring noise and like a snow ball is encreased by each spring trickling down on either side of those hills.

William and Dorothy Wordsworth frequently walked this way to visit their friends the Clarksons at Eusemere. In November 1805, Dorothy was struck by the view of

> the fields of Hartsop, below Brotherswater ... first seen like a lake, tinged by the reflection of yellow clouds. I mistook them for the water; but soon we saw the lake itself gleaming with a steely brightness; then as we descended appeared the brown oaks, and the birches of lovely yellow and, when we came still nearer to the valley, the cottages and the lowly old Hall of Hartsop with its long roof and elegant chimnies.

The Wordsworths took De Quincey over the pass (riding, to his genteel surprise, in a 'common farmers' cart') in 1807; he describes the pass, and recalls a later journey over it, in his *Recollections*:

> In some parts it is almost frightfully steep; for the road, being only the original mountain track of shepherds, ... is carried over ground which no engineer, even in alpine countries, would have viewed as practicable ... Once, in utter darkness, after midnight, and the darkness irradiated only by continual streams of lightning, I was driven down the whole descent, at a full gallop, by a young woman – the carriage being a light one, the horses

frightened, and the descents, at some critical parts of the road, so literally like the sides of a house, that it was difficult to keep the fore wheels from pressing upon the hind legs of the horses

– for, he claims, Westmorland drivers always used to go down the hills full tilt.

In his poem 'The Pass of Kirkstone' (1817) Wordsworth summed up the 'Thoughts and feelings of many walks in all weathers, by day and night, over this Pass, alone and with beloved friends':

> Within the mind strong fancies work,
> A deep delight the bosom thrills,
> Oft as I pass along the fork
> Of these fraternal hills:
> Where, save the rugged road, we find
> No appanage of human kind,
> Nor hint of man: if stone or rock
> Seem not his handiwork to mock
> By something cognizably shaped:
> Mockery – or model roughly hewn,
> And left as if by earthquake strewn,
> Or from the flood escaped ...
> Wrinkled Egyptian monument;
> Green moss-grown tower; or hoary tent;
> Tents of a camp that never shall be razed –
> On which four thousand years have gazed!

At the top of the pass is the **Kirkstone Pass Inn** (*car park*), not (as Harriet Martineau claimed in 1854) 'the highest inhabited house in England', but (at 1500ft above sea level) the highest pub in Lakeland. Built in 1496, it is full of character and every kind of *bric-a-brac*.

To reach **The Kirkstone**, which gives the pass its name, take the path from the inn car park and walk ½m N. The stone is a pointed boulder some ten feet high on a knoll above the road. Some barely-legible initials (probably Victorian) are carved on its W face. Its likeness to a church or 'kirk' (ie a small chapel without a tower, like most old Lakeland churches) is best seen from the Red Pit car park ¾m N of the inn. A romantic description of the Stone (now rendered somewhat ironic by the constant traffic) is given by De Quincey:

> This church – which is but a phantom of man's handiwork – ... has a peculiarly fine effect in this wild situation, which leave[s] so far below the tumults of this world: the phantom church, by suggesting the phantom and evanescent image of a congregation, where never congregation met; of the pealing organ, where never sound was heard except of wild natural notes, or else of the wind rushing through these mighty gates of everlasting rock – ... serves to bring out the antagonist feeling of intense and awful solitude, which is the natural and presiding sentiment – the *religio loci* – that broods for ever over the romantic pass.

The pass descends to the valley bottom at **Brothers Water** (*NT*), said to be so called after two brothers drowned there centuries ago, falling

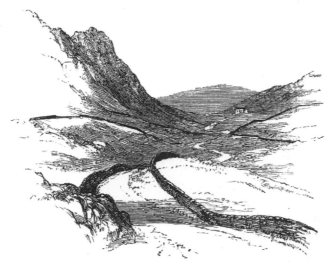

KIRKSTONE PASS
W.J. Linton, 1864

through the ice. Dorothy Wordsworth records the 'remarkable' coincidence that another pair had been drowned in about 1785 on a New Year's Day:

> Their mother had set them to thresh some corn, and they (probably thinking it hard to be so tasked when all others were keeping holiday) stole out to slide upon the ice, and were both drowned. A neighbour who had seen them fall through the ice, though not near enough to be certain, *guessed who* they were and went to the mother to inquire after her sons. She replied that 'they were threshing in the barn'. 'Nay', said the man, 'they are not there, nor is it likely to-day.' The woman then went to the barn and the boys were gone. He was then convinced of the truth, and told her that they were drowned. It is said that they were found locked in each other's arms.

Dorothy's account, with its grimly ironic dialogue, sounds suspiciously like a retelling of a folk-tale: perhaps what she was told had happened 'about twenty years since' was the local tradition of a much older legend. The name may anyway be an accident: the lake was previously called Broader Water or Broad Water.

Take the footpath from the Brotherswater Inn through the Sykeside campsite to reach the fine fifteenth-century **Hartsop Hall** (*NT*) – 'the lowly old Hall of Hartshop with its long roof and elegant chimnies' – then round the back of the Hall and along the lakeshore. Seen from this W side on a sunny day, Brothers Water is a Romantic landscape painting come to life: a picture of absolute tranquillity.

William and Dorothy Wordsworth took this path on 16 April 1802, returning from Eusemere to Grasmere. Dorothy

> left William sitting on the bridge, and went along the path at the right [i.e. w] side of the Lake through the wood. I was delighted with what I saw. The

water under the boughs of the bare old trees, the simplicity of the
mountains, and the exquisite beauty of the path. I repeated *The Glowworm*
as I walked along. I hung over the gate, and thought I could have stayed for
ever. When I returned, I found William writing a poem descriptive of the
sights and sounds we saw and heard ... William finished his poem before
we got to the foot of Kirkstone.

The bridge where Wordsworth sat was **Cow Bridge** (*car park*), and the
poem (though written in April) was 'Written in March while resting on the
Bridge at the foot of Brother's Water':

> The Cock is crowing,
> The stream is flowing,
> The small birds twitter,
> The lake doth glitter,
> The green field sleeps in the sun;
> The oldest and youngest
> Are at work with the strongest;
> The cattle are grazing,
> Their heads never raising;
> There are forty feeding like one!

Patterdale

The lane from the bridge rejoins the road at Hartsop. 2m further N is
Patterdale, a small village in a valley long admired for its picturesqueness.
Kathleen Raine's poem 'For Posterity' (1946) evokes an 1832 engraving of a
storm in Patterdale, where 'the crags stand out clear in the lightning' and
'trees, like animate things, tear at their roots and groan' – symbols of
emotional storms long past.

The valley's name is from 'Patrick's dale' and local legend claims that St
Patrick preached here and baptised converts at the spring near the lake (see
p 261).

Formerly there was some mining locally, and *The Excursion* Book V
tells the story – 'true to the letter', Wordsworth says – of a miner who lived
at Patterdale. He stayed on to prospect and dig after his companions had
given up hope of finding 'precious ore' – presumably copper. After ten
years' persistence he succeeded, but his new wealth turned his brain.
'Giddy and restless' by day, drinking 'immoderate cups' by night, he soon
died; but

> conspicuous to this day
> The path remains that linked his cottage-door
> To the mine's mouth; a long and slanting track,
> Upon the rugged mountain's stony side,
> Worn by his daily visits to and from
> The darksome centre of a constant hope.

The path cannot now be identified.

Also now unknown, though it was somewhere in Patterdale, is the
birthplace of Adam Walker (1731?–1821), philosopher and inventor. From

PATTERDALE, GOING TOWARDS AMBLESIDE
Thomas Allom, 1832

a poor family, he left school when he could hardly read but made his mark by building working models of local corn and paper mills. At fifteen he became a schoolteacher in Yorkshire; later he went to London, where he became the best-known popular lecturer of his day on philosophy, mathematics and astronomy. His many inventions included a rotating lighthouse lamp installed on the Scilly Isles in 1790.

At the S edge of the village, ½m N of the sign announcing Patterdale, on the E side of the road, is the Patterdale Youth Hostel, **Goldrill House**. This stands on the site of the original stone mansion (demolished 1970) where the novelist and feminist 'Edna Lyall' (Ada Ellen Bayly) stayed in August 1892:

> We are having a thoroughly lazy time, and have brought a whole boxful of novels to read, with just a sprinkling of sober literature. I am rather thinking of having an Irish heroine for my next story, and have brought Miss Lawless' *History of Ireland* …

The 'next story' was published as *Doreen*. Perhaps it was also here that she stayed in 1896, 'gleaning information from inhabitants of all classes' for her now forgotten *Hope the Hermit* (1898), a historical tale set in 1688, the best-selling novel about the Lake District until 1930 when Hugh Walpole brought out *Rogue Herries* (which, he confessed, was partly inspired by *Hope*).

200yds further N, between two lime trees on the E side of the road at a sharp corner, take small road over Goldrill Beck 200yds to **Broad How**, a Victorian house on the N side of the road. This site belonged (from 1805 to 1834) to Wordsworth, who bought it with help from his patron Lord Lowther. He intended to build a house here but never did. Dorothy records his discovery of the site in 1805, whilst staying at nearby Side Farm:

257

William went for a walk up Patterdale and pitched upon the spot where he should like to build a house better than in any other he had yet seen. Mrs Luff went with him by moonlight to view it. The vale looked as if it were filled with white light when the moon had climbed up to the middle of the sky; but long before we could see her face, while all the eastern hills were in black shade, those on the opposite side were almost as bright as snow.

Next door but one is a picturesque, long, white-rendered stone cottage called **Wordsworth Cottage**. Built in 1670, it has no connection with Wordsworth (the name comes from confused association with Broad How) but was the home of Ann Macbeth (1875–1948), embroidress and pioneer of craft education. Above the cottage at wooden gates the road meets the path running NW to Side Farm and Sandwick; and SE to Boredale Hause.

At the village centre is the **Patterdale Hotel**. Once a small inn called the King's Arms, since the eighteenth century it has swollen continuously with the tourist trade. This is probably 'the inn at Patterdale' where the young Wordsworth stayed in about 1783 (on his way from school at Hawkshead for holidays with his grandparents at Penrith) and ventured out by night to row a boat on Ullswater.

Other visitors included Joseph Budworth (1792) who notes that on his arrival

> The landlord had been in his hay-field. We asked him to sit down, and found him a very well-informed man; … He … had pencilled upon the wall the view from his house; he had some choice books in the room where we dined, and he conversed so *sensibly*, I felt even respect for him.

Ann Radcliffe stayed here in 1794. She walked out from the inn in the evening to enjoy the view, and

> The effect of a stormy evening upon the scenery was solemn. Clouds smoked along the fells … The lake was dark and tempestuous, dashing the rocks with a strong foam. It was a scene worthy of the sublimity of Ossian, and brought to recollection some touches of his gloomy pencil …

> We returned to our low-roofed habitation, where, as the wind swept in hollow gusts along the mountains and strove against our casements, the crackling blaze of a wood fire lighted up the cheerfulness.

This is probably also the 'Dobson's' where Charles Gough stayed in 1805 before his fatal accident on Helvellyn. Later that year Wordsworth, Scott and Humphry Davy stayed here before climbing Helvellyn together. The inn was crowded, and Wordsworth and Davy were to sleep in a room hired for the evening by Elizabeth Smith of Coniston and friends. The ladies, unaware that the room was needed, sat up late talking whilst Wordsworth and Davy tried to drive them out by walking under the windows like watchmen, calling out the hours in loud voices.

Side Farm, Blowick, Boredale Hause, Place Fell

250yds N of the Patterdale Hotel is the drive for **Side Farm**. William and

Dorothy Wordsworth stayed here in November 1805 with friends, Captain and Mrs Luff. Dorothy describes the view from her bedroom window:

> The two storm-stiffened black yew-trees on the crag above Luff's house were striking objects, close under or seen through the flying mists … Mrs Luff's large white dog lay in the moonshine upon the round knoll under the old yew-tree, a beautiful and romantic image – the dark tree with its shadow, and the elegant creature as fair as a spirit.

There are still yews on the crag over the house; and one yew on a knoll in the garden.

From the farmyard take the path (signed Howtown) ¾m NW through the campsite and along the lakeshore to **Blowick**, a pleasantly wooded bay. Dorothy Wordsworth, boating here in 1805, sums up the view: 'Place Fell steady and bold as a lion; the whole lake driving onward like a great river, waves dancing round the small islands.' The small picturesque farmhouse 200yds from the shore is **Blowick House**, home of the landscaper painter John Glover, 'The English Claude', between about 1805 and 1820. A successful but unremarkable painter in England, Glover – despite obesity and two club feet – made the courageous decision to embark for Tasmania in 1830 and was rewarded by a late flowering of his talent: he became the first significant Australasian landscape painter and is still regarded as one of the best.

Wordsworth and Coleridge were here in 1799. They stayed at the inn at Patterdale on November 16 and the next morning (according to Coleridge's notebook)

> left our bad Inn, & went down the lake by the opposite [E] shore – the hoar-frost on the ground, the lake calm & would have been mirrorlike but that it had been *breathed* on by the mist – & that shapely white Cloud, the Day-moon, hung over the snowy mountain opposite to us –.

A little further along the bank (perhaps near Scalehow Wood, 2m NE of Blowick) he recorded the view across to Lyulph's Tower:

> the fog begins to clear off from the Lake, … all the objects on the opposite Coast are hidden, and all those hidden are reflected in the Lake, Trees, & the Castle, [ie Lyulph's Tower] & the huge Cliff that dwarfs it! – Divine! – the reflection of the huge pyramidal Crag is still hidden, & the image in the water still brighter//but the Lyulph's Tower gleams like a Ghost, dim & shadowy – & the bright Shadow thereof how beautiful it is cut across by that Tongue of *breezy* water – now the Shadow is suddenly gone – and the Tower itself rises emerging out of the mist, two-thirds wholly hidden, the turrets quite clear – & a moment all is snatched away – Realities & Shadows –

The path continues to Sandwick.

Take the path SE from Side Farm to **Boredale Hause**. After 200yds turn uphill through gate, continuing SE up steep clear fellside path (at fork do *not* take upper path past iron bench). Path turns E and levels out at Hause; there is a cairn, and remains of a stone sheepfold at R (S). Bear L (N) round base of knoll, past iron shaft-cover. After 100yds the rectangular ruins of **Chapel in the Hause**, will be seen. From the chapel a clear path (1m, steep) runs N up **Place Fell**, which offers particularly fine views.

The chapel is the scene of an episode in *The Excursion*, suggested when the Wordsworths climbed Place Fell with the Luffs on November 8 1805. Mr Luff showed them 'a small ruin, which was formerly a Chapel, or place of worship where the inhabitants of Martindale and Patterdale were accustomed to meet on Sabbath days'. Dorothy had some doubt about whether it was really a chapel – it looked no different from 'a common sheepfold'. Visitors will agree; it is merely a nondescript heap of stones, interior dimensions 8ft by 20ft; but it is rectangular and 'stands east and west'. Dorothy records Luff's story of a 'poor old man' who, going up to collect peat 'last summer' (1804 or 1805) was overtaken by a storm but sheltered in the chapel ruins, whence he was rescued the next day. Wordsworth retold the story in *Excursion* II 730–895 and followed it with a passage based partly on Luff's account of the extraordinary dawn cloudscape he saw from Place Fell as he descended after the discovery of the old man, and partly on recollections of a similar panorama seen from above Hartsop:

> a step,
> A single step, that freed me from the skirts
> Of the blind vapour, opened to my view
> Glory beyond all glory ever seen
> By waking sense or by the dreaming soul!
> The appearance, instantaneously disclosed,
> Was of a mighty city – boldly say
> A wilderness of building, sinking far
> And self-withdrawn into a boundless depth,
> Far sinking into splendour – without end!
> Fabric it seemed of diamond, and of gold,
> With alabaster domes, and silver spires,
> And blazing terrace above terrace, high
> Uplifted ...

De Quincey later quoted the passage in *Confessions of an English Opium-Eater* (1821) to describe the opium-dreams he experienced at Dove Cottage. From Place Fell summit and from Boredale Hause paths continue to Sandwick and Martindale.

St Patrick's Church, Patterdale Hall and Glenridding

St Patrick's Church, Patterdale, is mid-Victorian, replacing a fourteenth-century chapel. Several eighteenth-century writers mention a curate of Patterdale, Mattinson, who (in Gilpin's words)

> was minister of this place sixty years; and died lately at the age of ninety ...
> With that singular simplicity, and inattention to forms which characterize
> a country like this; he himself read the burial-service over his mother; he
> married his father to a second wife; and afterwards buried him also. He

published his own banns of marriage in the church, with a woman, whom he had formerly christened; and himself married all his four children.

Mattinson, an exemplar of rugged rural piety rather like Robert Walker of Seathwaite, died in 1766.

The interior of the church has embroideries by Ann Macbeth; the large panel of *The Good Shepherd* shows as background the view towards Kirkstone from Wordsworth Cottage, the artist's home; beneath is the score of Parry's setting of Blake's 'Jerusalem' (wrong note in bar 11). At the E end of the churchyard a large irregular mound shows where the famous **Patterdale Yews** stood. A local meeting-point and tourist attraction, they were more than a thousand years old but were blown down in 1883.

200yds W of church go L (S) by bridge then first R for **Patterdale Hall** (now a residential centre), an elaborate early nineteenth-century Italianate mansion rebuilt near the site of the original hall, which was the 'Palace' of the once-famous Kings of Patterdale. Gilpin recorded in 1772 that

> Among the cottages of this valley, there is a house, belonging to a person of somewhat better condition; whose little estate ... has gained him the title of *King of Patterdale*, in which his family name is lost. His ancestors have long enjoyed the title before him. We had the honour of seeing this prince, as he took the diversion of fishing on the lake; and I could not help thinking, that if I were inclined to envy the situation of any potentate in Europe, it would be that of the king of Patterdale. The pride of Windsor and Versailles would shrink in a comparison with the magnificence of his dominions.

The then 'King' was called Mounsey, and according to Budworth (1792) was a miser and a glutton. His farm was the largest in the dale but its remoteness enabled him to avoid paying any taxes. He rented land to other farmers in exchange for the right to eat enormous meals at their houses, and drank ten to fourteen cups of tea a day, 'using an immoderate quantity of sugar, of which he is so fond, he generally carries some loose in his pocket.' He owned goats, which roamed free on his land, and a favourite joke was to sell one to a visitor on condition the purchaser caught it himself. Dorothy Wordsworth records in her journal (Dec 22 1801) that the Queen of Patterdale was 'brought to drinking by her husband's unkindness and avarice'. The last of the Mounsey dynasty died in 1824. The present house was built by the Marshall family; Scott and Lockhart stayed here in August 1825.

⅓m N of Patterdale, on the landward side of the road opposite the boat hire car park, is **St Patrick's Well** in a Victorian stone niche. From this spring (now generally dry) the Saint is said to have baptised converts.

¾m further N the road runs at the base of a sheer rockface, **Stybarrow Crag**. There is a small car park in a lay-by immediately at the N side of the crag. The crag is the scene of one of the most famous episodes in *The Prelude* (I 372–427), where Wordsworth recalls how as a boy, staying at the Patterdale Inn, he

> One evening ...
> Went alone into a shepherd's boat,
> A skiff that to a willow tree was tied
> Within a rocky cave, its usual home.

Untying the boat, he rowed out on to the lake – 'an act of stealth/And troubled pleasure' – fixing his gaze on a 'craggy ridge' until,

> ... from behind that craggy steep till then
> The bound of the horizon, a huge cliff,
> As if with voluntary power instinct
> Upreared its head. I struck and struck again,
> And growing still in stature the huge cliff
> Rose up between me and the stars, and still,
> With measured motion, like a living thing,
> Strode after me.

Turning back 'with trembling hands', he returned the stolen boat to its moorings and was troubled for many days afterwards by 'a dim and undertermined sense/Of unknown modes of being', of 'huge and mighty forms, that do not live/Like living men'. The date of the episode, one of Wordsworth's most powerful early initiations into the awesome grandeur and mystery of nature, is not known, but was probably about 1783.

The spot can be identified with confidence because in 1829, twenty-one years before *The Prelude* appeared, Sir Edward Baines (in his *Companion to the Lakes*) described how a local boatman showed him what is clearly the same sight that had so surprised Wordsworth:

> At the desire of the boatman, we crossed to the side of Gowbarrow Park, just where it terminates in the deep and secluded valley of Glencoin ... He contrived that we should creep along the shore, till we came close under a lofty crag, enveloped from the base to the summit in natural wood. Then, turning the head of the boat from the land, and desiring me to pull as strongly as I could, whilst he directed us all to keep our eyes on the crag, we shot out towards the middle of the lake. The effect was magical. The naked peak of a mountain, before concealed, seemed to rise up swiftly out of the woody eminence from which we were receding, till it stood in its just proportion before us, and appeared many hundred feet above our heads, leaving at its base the bold crag from under which we had darted.

This can only apply to Stybarrow Crag, above whose craggy, near-vertical base and wooded flanks Glenridding Dodd rises with a steep convex slope to some 1300ft. The Crag looks impressive from below, but from a distance is dwarfed by the Dodd, whose bare, rocky crown makes a sudden, delayed appearance because the slope is 'stepped back' at one point, creating a false summit. Wordsworth's 'rocky cave' and willow tree are gone, for an embankment has since been built to level the road. A little further N there are many rocky inlets, some overhung with willows, which give an idea of what the place must have been like.

Ullswater

Ullswater makes a brief appearance in *Poly-Olbion* (1619), where Drayton traces the various streams that feed the River Eden:

> next *Troutbeck* in she takes,
> And *Levenant*, then these, a somewhat lesser Rill,
> When *Glenkwin* greets her well, and happily to fill,
> Her more abundant Banks, from *Ulls*, a mightie Mere
> On *Cumberlands* confines, comes *Eymot* neat and cleere,
> And *Loder* doth allure, with whome she haps to meet.

Ullswater has always been counted one of the great sights of Lakeland and was early sought out by lovers of the picturesque. William Stukeley in 1776 blends science and aesthetics in an almost childlike effort to convey this impressive spectacle seen on his route to Keswick:

> In our way we had sight of that vast receptacle of water called Ulles lake ... These vast collections of fluid element are owing to the rocks, which suffer not the water thoroughly to drain out of the valleys. When one stands at the end of these lakes, the prospect is exceeding delightful; the mountains on each side rising to a great height, one behind another the whole length, and broke off into short ones, like the scenes at a playhouse: nor need a painter go to Italy for variety and grandeur of prospects.

Wordsworth thought it 'perhaps, upon the whole, the happiest combination of beauty and grandeur, which any of the Lakes affords.' Gilpin, in more pedantic style, said more or less the same thing in 1772: 'Among all the *visions* of this inchanting country, we had seen nothing so beautifully sublime, so correctly picturesque as this.' Others liked to deflate such rhetoric: Budworth (1792) thought it was shaped 'like the letter Z made by a bad penman; when we saw it from Helvellyn, the top arm was not visible, which occasioned its looking like a pair of breeches.' In the eighteenth century it was famous above all for its echoes, and life for local people in the tourist season must have been anything but tranquil. According to Gilpin,

> The duke of Portland ... has a vessel on the lake, with brass guns, for the purpose of exciting echoes ... The grandest effect of this kind is produced by a *successive* discharge of cannon; at the interval of a few seconds between each discharge ... Such a variety of awful sounds, mixing, and commixing, and at the same moment heard from all sides, have a wonderful effect on the mind; as if the very foundations of every rock on the lake were giving way; and the whole scene, from some strange convulsion, were falling into general ruin.

Alternatively, he suggests,

> Instead of cannon, let a few French-horns, and clarionets be introduced ... The *continuation of musical sounds* form a *continuation* of *musical ecchoes*; which reverberating around the lake, are exquisitely melodious ... and form a thousand symphonies, playing together from every part. The variety

of notes is inconceivable ... Every promontory seems peopled by aerial beings, answering each other in celestial music.

More peacefully, De Quincey records a night-time ride along the lakeshore in 1807 (he was heading for Penrith with Wordsworth):

All I remember is – that through those most romantic woods and rocks of Stybarrow – through those silent glens of Glencoin and Glenridding – through that most romantic of parks then belonging to the Duke of Norfolk, viz. Gobarrow Park – we saw alternately, for four miles, the most grotesque and awful spectacles – 'Abbey windows And Moorish temples of the Hindoos,' all fantastic, all as unreal and shadowy as the moonlight which created them; whilst, at every angle of the road, broad gleams came upwards of Ulleswater.

The Wordsworths passed the lake many times, usually on visits to the Clarksons at Eusemere or to Thomas Hutchinson at Park House. In November 1805 they took a boat trip on the lake and

In the grand bay under Place Fell saw three fishermen with a boat dragging a net, and rowed up to them. They had just brought the net ashore, and hundreds of fish were leaping in their prison. They were all of one kind, what are called Skellies. After we had left them the fishermen continued their work, a picturesque group under the lofty and bare crags.

The lake must also have impressed Mary Shelley, during her brief stay in Cumbria with Percy Shelley in 1811, since she placed Perdita, heroine of her 1826 novel *The Last Man*, in 'a cottage whose trim grass-plat sloped down to the waters of the lake of Ulswater; [whilst] a beech wood stretched up the hill behind, and a purling brook gently falling from the acclivity ran through poplar-shaded banks into the lake.'

By the Victorian period the lake was a major tourist attraction but local landowners kept its banks largely unspoilt despite the advent of the pleasure-steamers which still sail, so that in 1864 Eliza Lynn Linton could write that Ullswater

has a certain savageness and solitude about it which makes one forget its two grand hotels with their startling London prices ... Even its inconveniences are pleasant as a summer day's experience – its no market and its no shops, and the need of sending fifteen miles to Penrith for a cap-string or a fishing-fly ... All this is very delightful; though, to be sure, it is only playing at the life of long ago, with the steamboat hissing on the lake, and crinolines swelling on the mountains.

The lake's position between steep fells often makes it misty, giving rise to strange and beautiful visions. We have noted Coleridge's observations from the east bank near Blowick; the twentieth-century poet Norman Nicholson reports seeing (from Cockley Moor) 'very early one summer morning ... a new lake of mist, identical with Ullswater in size and shape, lying some fifty or a hundred feet above it, as if it had grown a second storey.'

Literary visitors have been countless; most have left no record. Charles

Darwin spent a holiday at Glenridding House; John Cowper Powys stayed with a friend in a cottage on the banks of the lake in 1894; he listened to his friend reading aloud 'those singular prefaces written by Wordsworth' for the *Lyrical Ballads*, but his chief memory was of the pink stocks growing in the cottage garden: 'The contrast between the wild, bare, Ullswater mountains and the sweet security of this heavily scented flower struck deep into my being.'

Stevie Smith has an eerie poem, 'The Frozen Lake', which seems to take Ullswater as the 'mere' to which 'Sir Bedivere/Consigned Excalibur'. Smith imagines the depths of the lake as haunted by 'the Lord of Ullan's daughter', who is 'a witch of endless might'. The lady's lover visits the lake in winter and 'can feel the water shiver/As the lady with a slither/Comes to tap the ice, to tear it'. Eventually he dives into the lake and is pierced by the magic sword.

Glencoyne, Aira Force, Lyulph's Tower

Take the A592 N from the Glenridding Steamer Pier. After 1m the road passes the drive entrance to **Glencoyne**. To park, go over a small stone bridge, Glencoyne Bridge: car park is on W side of road 100yds N of bridge. Walk back to Glencoyne: Wordsworth drew attention to it as

> a little recess called Glencoin, in which lurks a single house, yet visible from the road. Let the Artist and leisurely Traveller turn aside to it, for the buildings and objects around them are both romantic and exquisitely picturesque.

It is a fine example of a traditional lakeland farmhouse, complete with round chimneys, white render, crow-stepped porch and gables and a lovely garden inhabited on warm days by two cats, one black and one white. Ann Radcliffe in 1794 was entranced here by a moment of pastoral vision:

> Here, on the right, at the feet of awful rocks, was spread a gay autumnal scene, in which the peasants were singing merrily as they gathered the oats into sheafs; woods, turfy hillocks, and, above all, tremendous crags, abruptly closing round the yellow harvest. The figures, together with the whole landscape, resembled one of those beautifully fantastic scenes, which fable calls up before the wand of the magician.

Return to the car park and cross the road. ¼m NE along the lakeshore is the area where William and Dorothy Wordsworth saw the famous **daffodils**. They were walking southward along the lake on April 15 1802, and Dorothy recorded,

> When we were in the woods beyond Gowbarrow Park we saw a few daffodils close to the water-side. We fancied that the lake had floated the seeds ashore, and that the little colony had so sprung up. But as we went along there were more and yet more; and at last, under the boughs of the trees, we saw that there was a long belt of them along the shore, about the

breadth of a country turnpike road. I never saw daffodils so beautiful. They grew among the mossy stones about and about them; some rested their heads upon these stones as on a pillow for weariness; and the rest tossed and reeled and danced, and seemed as if they verily laughed with the wind, that blew upon them over the lake; they looked so gay, ever glancing, ever changing. This wind blew directly over the lake to them. There was here and there a little knot, and a few stragglers a few yards higher up; but they were so few as not to disturb the simplicity, unity, and life of that one busy highway.

The sight inspired Wordsworth's poem 'I wandered lonely as a cloud ...', written sometime between 1804 and 1807. Years later, Wordsworth liked to think that the daffodils 'probably may be seen to this day as beautiful in the month of March, nodding their golden heads beside the dancing and foaming waves'. They are still plentiful, mainly because of the efforts of the National Trust.

One mile NE of the Glencoyne car park is the A5091 junction, followed by the main car park for **Aira Force** (*NT*). There is a café. Smaller car parks are uphill on the A5091. Paths wind through the woods to this beautiful waterfall, which has a sheer 80ft drop. Best after heavy rain, it is attractive even in dry weather. In spate and on a sunny day its spray often carries spectacular rainbows.

Wordsworth and Coleridge visited the Force on their November 1799 walking tour, and Coleridge noted his (fanciful and somewhat discontented) impressions:

> We visited the water fall – too much water & no where ground low enough to view it from/the chasm is very fine – & violet-coloured Beeches & Hawthorns quite Trees, red & purple with fruits, as if the berries were flowers –/ the higher part of the water, the two streams running athwart each other is original but where the Wheel-part is broken, it spreads into a muslin apron, & the whole water looks like a long-waisted Lady-Giantess slipping down on her Back but on the bridge where you see only the Wheel, it is very fine/it circumvolves, with a complete half-wheel.

The gorge (though not the Force itself) is celebrated in Wordsworth's 1835 poem 'Airey-Force Valley', and in 'The Somnambulist' he recounts a tale connected with the waterfall: a knight-errant returns to find his lady-love, deranged by her longing for him, sleepwalking by the Force. He touches her and she wakes but loses her balance and drowns in the river. The lady's home is supposed to have been near the site now occupied by Lyulph's Tower, and the story was suggested to Wordsworth by one told by the landscape-painter John Glover:

> Mr Glover, the Artist, while lodging at Lyulph's Tower, had been disturbed by a loud shriek, and upon rising he had learnt that it had come from a young woman in the house who was in the habit of walking in her sleep: in that state she had gone downstairs, and, while attempting to open the outer door, either from some difficulty or the effect of the cold stone upon her feet, had uttered the cry.

In his *Recollections* De Quincey tells a story of the young scholar and translator Elizabeth Smith, then living in 'a cottage upon the banks of Ullswater', who lost her way one winter day in 1800 whilst sketching on the rocks near the Force. She was 'on the brink of a chasm' with no apparent route down when she saw her sister on the other bank. The sister guided her down by gestures, then vanished. Returning home, Miss Smith found that her sister had never left the house.

The stone bridges (replacing earlier wooden ones) commemorate Cecil Spring-Rice and his sons. Spring-Rice was a diplomat (his main achievement was to gain America's support for Britain in the First World War) and a witty writer of light verse (collected in *Poems* (1920)). He lived at Old Church House (now the Old Church Hotel) at Knotts on the shore of Ullswater.

From the top of the Force the path continues to Ulcat Row. Alternatively follow the path down almost to the car park and take the fork that goes off E under an enormous conifer. Take stile to the fellside and follow path E 1¼m to the **Memorial Seat**, a stone seat with the enigmatic inscription A THANK OFFERING OCT 1905, for a splendid view of Ullswater. (For a still better view, go to the cairn a few yards away).

On its way to the seat, the path gives the best view of **Lyulph's Tower**, a Gothic hunting lodge built by the Duke of Norfolk in 1780 and named 'from a tradition that a chieftain, named Lyulph, was the owner of these possessions about the time of the Conquest.' The tower is one of the earliest Gothic buildings in the district, but Eliza Lynn Linton writes contemptuously,

> if you are of the 'true sort', you will care nothing for [it] – a mere modern make-believe, with glazed windows among the ivy and cucumber frames at the tops of the towers.

To see its imposing fake-medieval front, you need to view it across the lake. From this side you can see what it really is – an honest Georgian house oddly embedded in huge castle ramparts.

The tower and its fabled owner feature in Scott's *The Bridal of Triermain* (1805), where Sir Roland de Vaux, having fallen in love with a fairy maiden, sends his page to seek Lyulph's advice:

> My fleetest courser thou must rein,
> And ride to Lyulph's tower,
> And from the Baron of Triermain
> Greet well that sage of power ...
> Gifted like his gifted race,
> He the characters can trace,
> Graven deep in elder time
> Upon Helvellyn's cliffs sublime;
> Sign and sigil well doth he know
> And can bode of weal and woe,
> Of kingdoms' fall, and fate of wars,
> From mystic dreams and course of stars.

Aira Force and the land behind the Tower make up **Gowbarrow Park** (*NT*), formerly a hunting ground and still visited by red deer. Celia Fiennes passed this way in 1698 and recalled

> I rode through a fine forest or parke where was deer skipping about and haires, which by means of a good Greyhound I had a little Course, but we being strangers could not so fast pursue it in the grounds full of hillocks and furse and soe she escaped us.

In Gowbarrow Park, wrote Wordsworth nearly a century and a half later,

> the lover of Nature might wish to linger for hours ... Here is a powerful Brook, which dashes among rocks through a deep glen, hung on every side with a rich and happy intermixture of native wood; here are beds of luxuriant fern, aged hawthorns, and hollies decked with honeysuckle; and fallow-deer glancing and bounding over the lawns and through the thickets. These ... constitute a fore-ground to ever-varying pictures of the majestic Lake.

On the day when the famous 'daffodils' were noted, Dorothy also noticed the poor condition of the deer in the park: 'NB Deer in Gowbarrow Park like skeletons.' By November 1805, their condition must have improved: passing the park again she observed 'a large troop of them ... either moving slowly, or standing still, among the fern', and was 'grieved' when two passers-by

> startled them with a whistle, disturbing a beautiful image of grave simplicity and thoughtful enjoyment ... I could have fancied that even they were partaking with me a sensation of the solemnity of the closing day.

Cockley Moor and Mellfell House

Take A5091 N from the junction by the main Aira Force car park and turn W (signed High Row and Dowthwaite Head) by the Royal Hotel at Dockray. After 1m the long stone house with many extensions on S side of the road is **Cockley Moor**. Built as a shooting-box for the Lowther family and later a farm, it was the home until 1962 of Helen Sutherland, collector and patron of the arts. The house held a collection of paintings by Picasso, Mondrian, Seurat and others; guests, for long or short stays, included artists such as Ben and Winifred Nicholson, Barbara Hepworth, Naum Gabo and David Jones, and the poets Norman Nicholson, Elizabeth Jennings and Kathleen Raine, who describes the Cockley Moor house-parties in her autobiographical *The Land Unknown* (1977). In 1942 T.S. Eliot visited, brought by the poet and editor Michael Roberts.

Later (1965–75) it was the home of Fred Hoyle (b 1915), Astronomer Royal, science-fiction writer and originator of the 'Steady State' theory of the universe. Whilst here he wrote general works such as *Man in the Universe* (1966) and *From Stonehenge to Modern Cosmology* (1974), and (with Geoffrey Hoyle) novels such as *October the First Is Too Late* (1966), *Seven Steps to the Sun* (1970) and *The Molecule Men* (1971).

Return to the Royal Hotel, Dockray and follow the main road S to the lakeside. Follow the A592 lakeside road E 3m to the next junction, which is at Knotts, and turn NW (signed Watermillock and Dacre). After 1½m at junction go L past Watermillock Church, then R (signed Bennethead and Dacre) then take L fork (*not* fork to Quiet Campsite) and then R after campsite to Mellfell House.

Mellfell House features as 'Nameless Grange' in the novel *A Cumberland Statesman* (1808) by Barbara Hofland, who was a friend of its early nineteenth-century owner, Tom Rumney, a well-known local character. The novel describes Mellfell House much as it is today, 'spread in a long line at the foot of a noble mountain' (Mellfell itself), with its 'large garden formed in terraces.' It also gives a vivid picture of Rumney as the forbidding but kindly eccentric 'Terence Nameless':

> His face was so weather-beaten, his skin so dried and tanned, that at the first glance he appeared at least sixty years of age; and his dress, which consisted of a worn-out shooting-jacket, ragged breeches, grey woollen stockings, and wooden clogs, by uniting the idea of poverty to years, made the impression stronger.

Much of the novel describes daily life at the house, and the character of its owner. Barbara Hofland, in her time a well-known writer, visited Rumney here in July 1805 with her husband, the angler-artist Hofland, and wrote a poem addressed to Mary Russell Mitford which incidentally mentions Rumney's construction of a road up Little Mell Fell.

Rumney's own letters and diary, giving an amusing account of his life and adventures, were published in 1936 as *Tom Rumney of Mellfell (1764–1835) by Himself*.

Dunmallard, Eusemere, Park House and Barton Fell

Return to the A592. At the foot of the lake is **Pooley Bridge**, an attractive eighteenth-century bridge over a broad, rippling reach of the River Eamont. There are car parks at both ends of the bridge. By the entrance of the W ('Dunmallard') car park is the gate giving access to **Dunmallard** or Dunmallet, a round wooded hill. In the early eighteenth century a progressive landowner planted the hill with symmetrical ranks of conifers, giving it a neat, striped appearance. By the end of the century picturesque taste had come to despise such regimentation and it was fashionable to grumble about Dunmallet for spoiling the view. Thus Ann Radcliffe in 1794:

> Dunmallet at the foot of the lake was a formal unpleasing object, not large enough to be grand, or wild enough to be picturesque.

It is now mainly planted with broadleaves (with the occasional tract of wild raspberries as a bonus). The summit cannot easily be reached, but a permissive path circles the base of the hill. From the car park take the path

N along the edge of the wood and fork L at the 'Viewpoint' sign. There is a good view up Ullswater. From the viewpoint a path leads S downhill to rejoin the circular path.

Cross Pooley Bridge to the E (Pooley Bridge) car park. From small gate at rear of car park take path signed Lakeshore footpath. On reaching a huge green boathouse follow the path that runs a little back from the lakeside above a row of trees. This gives the best view of **Eusemere House**, built by Thomas Clarkson, leader of the anti-slavetrade movement, and his wife Catherine, who were among the closest friends of the Wordsworths and lived here from 1796 to 1804, whilst Clarkson was resting to recover his health, injured by his tireless work in the cause of abolition. Rest did not mean idleness, for here he wrote his *Portrait of Quakerism* (1806) and *History of the Rise, Progress and Accomplishment of the Abolition of Slavery* (1808) and perhaps started work on his *Memoirs of the Private and Public Life of William Penn* (1813). The site was found for Clarkson, and the building supervised, by the Quaker poet and landscape gardener Thomas Wilkinson of Yanwath. The house is now much enlarged: only the central part is original.

William and Dorothy Wordsworth stayed here in April 1802 (one of many visits) and their walks in the district are detailed in Dorothy's journal.

Wordsworth and Coleridge came here on 18 November 1799 in the course of their walking tour, and Coleridge sat on the lakeshore indulging in Freudian jottings about the landscape in front of him:

> Monday Morning – sitting on a Tree Stump at the brink of the Lake by Mr Clarkson's – perfect serenity/that round fat backside of a Hill with its image in the water made together *one* absolutely undistinguishable Form – a kite or Paddle or keel turned to you/the road appeared a sort of suture, in many places exactly as the weiblich tetragrammaton is painted in anatomical Books! I never saw so sweet an Image!! –

('Weiblich tetragrammaton is German/Greek for 'female four-letter'.) The hill that inspired this remarkable vision is obvious from the lakeside below Eusemere: it is the wooded hill directly opposite, nameless on most maps but labelled 'Salmond's Plantation' on the 1:25,000 OS map. The road is now obscured by trees, but on a calm day one sees roughly what Coleridge had in mind.

From Pooley Bridge take the B5320 road NE, turning R (signed Martindale) at the church, and follow signs for Martindale ¾m to Park Foot Holiday Village. Walkers may approach **Park House** from here, although it is on private land and ruined, so cannot be entered. From 1804 it was the home of Wordsworth's brother-in-law Thomas Hutchinson, and the Wordsworths were frequent visitors. To see it, follow Fell Access signs from Park Foot clubhouse to back gate (behind Trekking Centre). From gate go SW to join boundary fence. Follow fence until it joins stone wall at corner of wood. Look NW over wall: large ruined building is Park House.

From this point, walk S ½m along beck to join bridleway along Barton Fell. Follow it R (W) to reach Howtown and Martindale (3m), or L (E) ⅓m to junction with another bridleway which leads SW to top of **Barton Fell**, continuing to High Street. Wordsworth recalled that the writing of 'Resolution and Independence' had arisen from the mood of despondency he felt as he crossed Barton Fell heading NE towards Askham on April 7 1802, his thirty-second birthday. 'The image of the hare' he said 'I then observed on the ridge of the Fell':

> on the moors
> The hare is running races in her mirth;
> And with her feet she from the plashy earth
> Raises a mist; that, glittering in the sun,
> Runs with her all the way, wherever she doth run.

Martindale

From the main gates of Park Foot follow the road SW 3m to the gate to **Bonscale**, a fellside farm where George Gissing stayed in the summer of 1884 as tutor to the sons of Frederick Harrison, the 'Positivist' author and sociologist. Gissing later set the opening chapter of his novel *Thyrza* at the farm. Continue 1m to **St Peter's Church**, a Victorian red sandstone church on S side of road (car park 200yds down hill). There is excellent modern stained glass by Jane Gray.

Downhill one meets a triangular road-junction. This is the entrance to **Martindale**, one of the most beautiful and secluded of all Lakeland valleys. The Wordsworths were here on December 29 1801, and Dorothy recalled:

> A sharp hail-shower gathered at the head of Martindale, and the view upwards was very grand – the wild cottages, seen through the hurrying hail-shower. The wind drove and eddied about and about, and the hills looked large and swelling through the storm ... O! the bonny nooks and windings and curlings of the beck, down at the bottom of the steep green mossy banks. We dined at the public-house on porridge, with a second course of Christmas pies.

The public house (the Star Inn) was the farm now called **Cotehow**, just visible up a steep bank E of the junction. The Wordsworths were here again – at 'the last house in the dale' – in 1805 and were shown 'a room built by Mr. Hazel for his accommodation at the yearly Chace of red deer in his forests at the head of these dales.' (There are still wild red deer in Martindale.) Here they were given a meal of 'excellent butter and new oaten bread' and 'Mr. Hazel's strong ale', which left them 'well prepared to face the mountain' – apparently Place Fell, which they climbed forthwith.

Bear L (S) at the junction for ⅓m to **St Martin's Church**, the original parish church. Sixteenth-century (on twelfth-century foundations) the church is a rectangular building of extreme simplicity and extraordinarily powerful atmosphere. It was abandoned in favour of a new parish church in 1882 for no very good reason, and local legend has it that on the day the new church was consecrated a storm tore the roof off the old one, which became derelict. Restored since, it is now used again for some services. The font is a Roman altar brought in the middle ages from a wayside shrine on High Street; the medieval bell carries lettering which defied interpretation until recently, when it was discovered that the letters are Lombardic characters, cast separately from the bell and naively welded on in alphabetical order by the presumably illiterate bellfounders.

In the churchyard, under the massive yew (said to be some 1,300 years old) E of the church, is the tomb of the Rev. George Woodley (1785–1845), 'an Author, A Poet and A Christian'. Woodley was a remarkable character: of poor parentage, he went to sea aboard a man-of-war before he was twelve and was soon composing verse to amuse his shipmates. In 1808 he settled in Cornwall, where he edited the *Royal Cornish Gazette* and wrote poetry, including such formidable titles as *Britain's Bulwarks, or the British Seaman* (1811) and *Redemption: a Poem in Twenty Books* (1816). In 1820 he ordained and went as a missionary to the Scilly Isles. He came to Martindale as Perpetual Curate in 1843. At the S side of the churchyard is the grave of another literary wanderer, Andrew Wilson (1830–81), 'Traveller, Orientalist and Man of Letters'. Born in Bombay, Wilson edited, at various times, the *China Mail*, the *Times of India*, the *Bombay Times* and the *Bombay Gazette* as well as contributing a prodigious number of articles to *Blackwood's Magazine*. He was best known for a book about his travels in China and Tibet, *The Abode of Snow* (1876), which is still well worth reading.

200yds SW of the church is **Christy Bridge**, 'the one-arched bridge above the Church' from which Dorothy Wordsworth in 1805 admired the 'beautiful view of the church with its 'bare ring of mossy wall' and single yew-tree.'

Return to the triangular junction and bear L (W) over small stone bridge. After ½m, take sharp turning downhill (signed Sandwick) and go 300yds to **The Old Vicarage**. The poet Kathleen Raine lived at Martindale Vicarage in 1940, a period chronicled in her autobiography *The Land Unknown* (1975). The house is unchanged, still

> the most beautiful little white house imaginable ... in its own field, with a great lime tree at the gate and a beck fringed with birch and alder bounding its little domain

– except that the lime tree has gone. In spring the snowdrops that welcomed her – 'multitudes ... emerging from the melting snow' – may still be seen. This small Georgian house, with its attractive garden under the steep fell, is surely a candidate for the most beautiful small house in England. Here Kathleen Raine wrote many of the poems collected in *Stone and Flower* (1943), such as 'Night in Martindale', praising

> the authentic utterance of cloud,
> the speech of flowing water, blowing wind,
> of silver moon and stunted juniper.

Literary visitors included the poet Michael Roberts, and William Empson, poet and author of *Seven Types of Ambiguity* and other works of literary theory, who turned up absentmindedly wearing two left shoes: he was going climbing with Roberts, but 'confessed to the blisters only afterwards'.

Follow the road NW until it ends at **Sandwick**. Take footpath signed to Howtown, which reaches the lake at Sandwick Bay. William and Dorothy Wordsworth landed here by boat with the Luffs in 1805, reaching Martindale village by

> a beautiful summer path, at first through a copse by the Lake-side, then through green fields. The Village and brook very pretty, shut out from mountains and lake.

Barton, Tirril, Sockbridge and Lowther

From Pooley Bridge, go 2m NW on B5320 and take first L (N) to **St Michael's Church, Barton**, a 12th-13th century church with unique double arches under the tower. The S chapel has monuments to Wordsworth's cousin John and his two wives – the second, young enough to be his granddaughter, outlived him by forty-four years. The N side of the chancel has a brass commemorating the poet's grandfather Richard Wordsworth of Sockbridge (1690–1760). Note the brass at L of E window with a poem by Lancelot Dawes in memory of his wife Frances (1650–1673):

> Under this stone Reader Interr'd doth lye
> beauty, and Vertues, true Epitomy,
> Att her appearance the noone sun
> blush'd & shrunke in cause quite outdone.
>
> In her concenter'd did all graces dwell
> god pluckt my Rose yt he might take a smell
> Ile say noe more, but weeping wish I may
> soone wth thy Deare chast ashes come to lay.

Return to the road and continue 1m NE to Tirril. As you enter the village, the white cottage on the corner of Quaker Lane is the old **Friends' Meeting House**, built in 1733 and now a private cottage. The small field in front of it is the old burial ground; many Quakers are buried here in unmarked graves. They include Thomas Wilkinson, and Charles Gough (whose death on Helvellyn in 1805 was the subject of poems by Wordsworth and Scott). The mathematician John Slee (1780-1819) for some reason has the sole memorial stone.

Go up Quaker Lane. At the top the lane runs round under the grey stone wall of **Wordsworth House**, an elegant gentleman-farmer's residence with DRE 1699 over the door. The house and attached land belonged to Wordsworth's grandfather Richard and then to his father John (providing a small income which helped him survive despite the refusal of his employer, the Earl of Lowther, ever to pay him for the work he did as agent). Later it

LOWTHER CASTLE, SOUTH FRONT
Thomas Allom, 1832

became the property of Richard Wordsworth, the poet's brother. William and Dorothy visited him here several times. In letters and journals they refer to it simply as 'Sockbridge', as it is in the hamlet of that name.

½m NE of Tirril, turn S to Askham (2½m). Follow village green NE and cross Askham Bridge. From the E side of the bridge a path runs S along the side of the River Lowther. This pleasant walk, with interestingly craggy rock formations on the opposite bank, was created by Thomas Wilkinson, who (according to Wordsworth) was 'Arbiter Elegantiarum, or master of the grounds at Lowther' and advised Lord Lonsdale on landscaping when he rebuilt Lowther castle in 1806–11. The walk rejoins the road 2m S of Askham.

200yds N of Askham Bridge the road enters **Lowther Park**. The land is private but roads and footpaths are open to the public. Much of the park is covered with forest, and Wordsworth read Burns's *Poems* – borrowed from Penrith circulating library – to Dorothy in these woods in the summer of 1787. Wordsworth also recalled his early wanderings here in his dedication of *The Excursion* to William, Earl of Lonsdale, in 1814:

> Oft, through thy fair demesnes, illustrious Peer!
> In youth I roamed, on youthful pleasures bent;
> And mused in rocky cell or sylvan tent,
> Beside swift-flowing Lowther's current clear.

Near the entrance to the Park is **St Michael's Church**, a Norman building restored in 1680 and again in late-Victorian times. Note the many elaborate Lowther family memorials, including the huge Victorian mausoleum outside. In the N transept is the large polished marble tomb of the Second

Earl of Lonsdale (1757–1844), Wordsworth's patron and dedicatee of *The Excursion* – 'the ardent and zealous patron of men of genius and the early friend of William Pitt'. In the S transept a frustrating tablet to Sir Richard Lowther (1530–1607) gives his complete family tree and the information that he 'kept plentifull hospitallitye for 57 yeares together' and died 'vttring at his last breth these verses followinge' – followed by a metal plate from which all trace of the verses has been cleaned off.

¼m S of the church, over a field, is **Lowther Castle**, former seat of the Lowther family, Earls of Lonsdale. A fascinating structure, it resembles an immense and intricate toy fort – an effect heightened by the fact that it has no roof and is merely a shell. The castle was first built in the 1690s, then burnt down in 1720, rebuilt 1806–1811 and abandoned in recent times as the family fortunes diminished.

Celia Fiennes visited the first Castle in 1698, when it was newly built, and was impressed especially by the large 'hall' upstairs, which was

> very lofty, the top and sides are exquisitely painted by the best hand in England [Antonio Verrio] which did the painting at Windsor; the top is the Gods and Goddesses that are sitting at some great feast and a great tribunal before them, each corner is the Seasons of the yeare with the variety of weather, raines and rainbows stormy winds sun shine snow and frost with multitudes of other fancyes and varietyes in painting, and looks very natural – it cost 500£ that roome alone.

In 1724 Defoe added that the Lowther stables were 'the wonder of England ... certainly the largest and finest that any gentleman or nobleman in Britain is master of.'

The First Earl (1736–1802), a ferociously eccentric man, indirectly affected the course of English poetry by his dogged refusal to pay Wordsworth (and his sister and brothers) the debt of some £8000 which he owed their father, his agent, when the latter died in 1783. The result was a poverty-stricken existence for the poet until the Earl's death, when his heir honoured the debt.

According to De Quincey, the First Earl 'was a true feudal chieftain': when he drove to Penrith with his battered coach and 'fine, but untrimmed' horses, 'such was the impression diffused about him by his gloomy temper and his habits of oppression, that the streets were silent as he traversed them, and an awe sate upon many faces'. As for his park,

> All was savage grandeur about these native forests: their sweeping lawns and glades had been unapproached, for centuries it might be, by the hand of art; and amongst them roamed – not the timid fallow deer – but thundering droves of wild horses.

He also records the story that the Earl had fallen in love with a young girl from a 'Cumberland farm-house' and persuaded her to live with him. When she died he 'could not bear the thought of a final parting' and had her embalmed under glass.

In the time of the Earl's more generous son, Wordsworth became a frequent visitor, spending 'a few days' here each year. 'Lines Written in the Album of the Countess of Lonsdale' (1834), a rather overwrought and sentimental tribute, suggests the sort of view – friendly but a little tense and overawed – which the poet had of his aristocratic patrons. The poet Samuel Rogers recalled meeting Wordsworth and Southey here in 1812:

> while the rest of the party were walking about, talking and amusing themselves, Southey preferred sitting solus in the library. 'How *cold* he is!' was the exclamation of Wordsworth – himself so joyous and communicative.

Scott and Lockhart stayed here on their August 1825 tour.

Wordsworth celebrated the Castle in an 1833 sonnet ('Lowther! In thy majestic pile are seen ...') which hails its 'Towers and Pinnacles' as a worthy defence against the 'democratic torrent' (an unexpected view from the once-radical poet whose youth had been impoverished by a former Lonsdale's avarice); and Southey addressed the Castle in 'Stanzas written in Lady Lonsdale's Album, at Lowther Castle, October 13, 1821'.

Thomas Wilkinson, in 'Lowther' (1824), makes the landscaping and rebuilding sound like a version of Coleridge's Xanadu:

> The Muse prophetic sees the hand of taste
> Conduct new beauties through the wild-wood waste; ...
> Sees the rude dome above your forest grow,
> The sparkling grotto hide its wealth below;
> Sees Phoenix-like, the mansion rise again,
> And look majestic o'er her native plain.
> 'Tis done – already, glittering from afar,
> Lowther's white towers salute the morning star.

Continue ½m up the road from the church to reach Lowther New Town, a village built c 1684 when Sir John Lowther pulled down the old village to improve the landscape around the rebuilt church; a further ½m brings us to **Lowther Village**, described by Arthur Young in 1770:

> Near the road is the new town of *Lowther*, where Sir *James* is building a town to consist of 300 houses, for the use of such of his domesticks, and other people, as are married: And it is highly worthy of remark, that he not only encourages all to marry, but keeps them in his service *after* they have families: Every couple finds a residence here, and an annual allowance of coals. This is a most incomparable method of advancing population, and consequently the good of the nation at large; nor can it be too much imitated.

'Coals', of course, were the Lowther family business. The 'domesticks' were lucky: these are attractive pink sandstone houses arranged in closes with lawns and garden beds. Young's earnest enthusiasm for 'advancing' the working population is typical of British economists on the verge of the industrial revolution. The original plan, for a large symmetrical housing estate, was never fulfilled.

Yanwath, Eamont Bridge

Return to B5320. ½m NE of Tirril, entering Yanwath, turn sharp L (N) immediately after bridge over railway and continue 200yds to **The Grotto**, a private house which was the residence of Thomas Wilkinson (1751–1836), Quaker poet, farmer, landscape gardener and friend of Wordsworth.

Wilkinson enlarged the house in 1773 and landscaped the grounds. Though many of his improvements have been lost, his concealed underground retreat, a kind of summerhouse-for-all-seasons, survives, its entrance behind a large beech tree in the field behind the house. This is private land with no public access. In his poem *Emont Vale* Wilkinson calls this 'grotto', in the language of the day, his 'hovel', but it was far from comfortless: plastered and furnished with cushions, it had a fireplace and a glazed window looking towards Penrith Beacon. On the wall were the lines

> Beneath this moss grown roof, this rustic cell
> Truth, Liberty, Content, sequester'd dwell;
> Say, you who dare our hermitage disdain,
> What drawing room can boast so fair a train?

In 'Emont Vale (1824) Wilkinson writes

> I am no solitary, but repair
> To woods and streams what time my duties spare:
> Musing my fancies, silent and unseen,
> I build my hovel 'mong thy alders green! –
> Emont! I wish – I will not say I pray –
> Thou wouldst not wash my little works away!

Wilkinson was aware of the tradition of poetic landscape-artists: his own gardens were inspired by a visit to Shenstone's gardens at Leasowes in Worcestershire, and contained a willow grown from a cutting from Pope's 'Grotto' at Twickenham.

Visitors to The Grotto included the Wordsworths, Coleridge, Charles Lloyd, George Canning and Elizabeth Fry. Here Wilkinson wrote his poems, including 'Lowther' and 'The River Emont', and his excellent *Tours to the British Mountains* (1824), one passage in which inspired Wordsworth's 'The Solitary Reaper'.

Dorothy's *Journal* mentions a visit to him on November 12 1805: she and William found him 'at work in one of his fields; he chearfully laid down the spade and walked by our side'. Wordsworth addressed this spade in 'Lines to the spade of a friend (An Agriculturist)', conceived whilst helping Wilkinson with some gardening at The Grotto:

> Spade! with which Wilkinson hath tilled his lands,
> And shaped these pleasant walks by Eamont's side,
> Thou art a tool of honour in my hands;
> I press thee, through the yielding soil, with pride.

Return to the B5320. ½m NE of Yanwath the road crosses the M6 motorway; immediately after the motorway bridge is the access road to **Mayborough** (*some parking space*), a circular mound-shaped earthwork about 120yds across. Made of heaped-up stones from the Eamont River bed, it has a nine-foot standing stone inside it and was probably built between 2000 and 1000 BC. Stone and bronze axe-heads have been found there but its purpose is unknown. Over the centuries it has lost several standing-stones: John Aubrey describes it as 'a great circular Bank of stones and earth [with] four stones of great magnitude' at the centre. 'These stones are very unshapen, hard boulder stones, not being capable of being wrought into any proportion'. William Stukeley adds that they were 'of a hard black kind of stone, like the altar at Stonehenge'. The three missing ones were 'blown to pieces with gunpowder', apparently for fun, in about 1775.

It was much visited by eighteenth-century tourists. Coleridge came here with Wordsworth in 1799 and jotted in his notebook:

> – Maybrough – a stone fence – between the stone-fence which is circular an irregular circle of Trees – in the centre of the green circle-plot thus inclosed an upright stone 10 foot high, with an ash close by its side umbrellaing it – a scene of religion & seclusion.

Go out of the gap in the Mayborough rampart and across the road. Some 400 yds E of Mayborough is **King Arthur's Round Table**, another mysterious monument. Leland in 1540 recorded it as

> a ruine, as sum suppose, of a castel within a flite shotte of Loder [Lowther] and as much of Emot Water, stonding almost as a *mediamnis* betwixt them; the ruin is of sum caulled the Round Table, and of summe Arture's Castel.

Celia Fiennes in 1698

> came by a round green spott of a large circumfference which they keep cut round with a banke round it like a bench; its story is that it was the table a great Giant 6 yards tall used to dine at and there entertained another of nine yards tall which he afterwards killed; there is the length in the Church yard [at Penrith] how farre he could leape a great many yards.

The raised platform in the middle was used for games until some time in the nineteenth century, spectators sitting on the banks around (Stukeley in 1776 said it was 'used to this day for a country rendezvous, either for sports or military exercises, shooting with bows etc'). It is thought to be from the same period as Mayborough and perhaps connected with it in some way.

Drayton's *Poly-Olbion* mentions both monuments, but misunderstands (and applies to Mayborough alone) an early suggestion that the two monuments together formed the ends of an oval race-track:

> So neere to *Loders* Spring, from thence not farre away,
> Be [stones] nine foot high, a myle in length that runne,

The victories for which these Trophies were begun,
From dark oblivion thou, O Time shouldst have protected;
For mighty were their minds, them that thus first erected:
And neere to this againe, there is a piece of ground,
A little rising Bank, which of the Table round,
Men in remembrance keepe, and *Arthurs* Table name.

They feature also in Scott's *The Bridal of Triermain*, where Sir Roland's page, hastening to Lyulph's Tower,

> passed red Penrith's Table Round,
> For feats of chivalry renown'd,
> Left Mayborough's mound and stones of power,
> By Druids raised in magic hour,
> And traced the Eamont's winding way,
> Till Ulfo's lake beneath him lay.

We are now entering **Eamont Bridge**, a small hamlet clustered round the bridge itself. One of these houses was the birthplace of Isaac Ritson (1761–89), poet, classical translator and author of the 'Borrowdale Letter', an early piece of comic dialect writing published in 1789. His works ranged from translations of Hesiod and the Homeric Hymns, to 'a poem, full of technical medical terms' and a ballad cataloguing twenty-five Cumbrian mountains (from which Coleridge borrowed lines for both *Christabel* and 'A Thought Suggested by a View'). All his poems except this last seem to have disappeared. He was 'too volatile to be a good author', says William Hutchinson (1794): 'It was difficult to prevail on him to revise and correct any thing.' He died 'after a short, but irregular life in London', where he had gone to seek his fortune.

At Eamont Bridge our road joins the A6, which runs N to Penrith and S to Shap. For Penrith, turn to p 99.

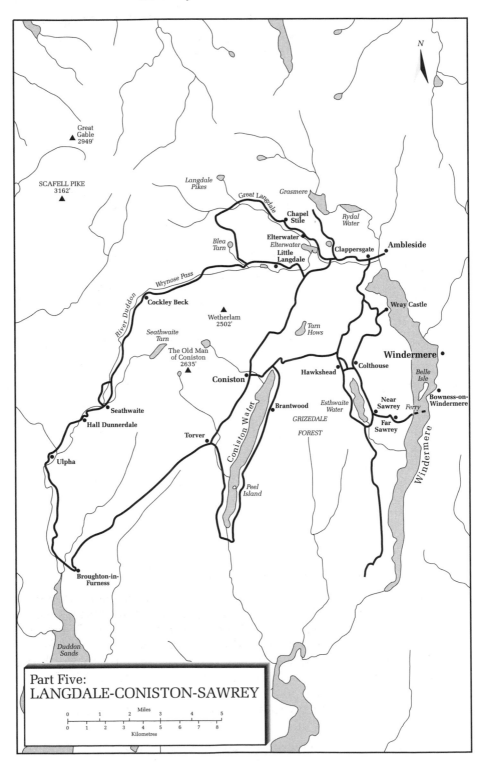

N

Great
Gable
2949'

SCAFELL PIKE
3162'

*Langdale
Pikes*

Great Langdale

Grasmere

**Chapel
Stile**

*Rydal
Water*

Elterwater

*Blea
Tarn*

Elterwater
**Little
Langdale**

Clappersgate

Ambleside

Wrynose Pass

River Duddon

Cockley Beck

Wetherlam
2502'

Wray Castle

*Seathwaite
Tarn*

*Tarn
Hows*

The Old Man
of Coniston
2635'

Windermere

Coniston

Hawkshead

Colthouse

*Belle
Isle*

Seathwaite

Brantwood

*Esthwaite
Water*

**Near
Sawrey**

Ferry

**Bowness-on-
Windermere**

Hall Dunnerdale

Coniston Water

GRIZEDALE

**Far
Sawrey**

Torver

FOREST

Windermere

Ulpha

*Peel
Island*

**Broughton-in-
Furness**

*Duddon
Sands*

Part Five:
LANGDALE-CONISTON-SAWREY

Miles
0   1   2   3   4   5
0 1 2 3 4 5 6 7 8
Kilometres

PART FIVE
Langdale – Coniston – Sawrey

Clappersgate and Skelwith Bridge

Leave Ambleside by A593 (signed Langdale, Coniston) and after ½m you reach the pretty hamlet of **Clappersgate**. In one of the houses 'on [the] north-west angle' – that is, at the corner by the turning to Hawkshead – lived the novelist Margaret Cullen, described by De Quincey in his *Recollections* (1840). She was author of two sentimental novels: *Home* (1802, 'in as many as seven volumes, I really believe' says De Quincey; actually a mere five) and *Mornton* (3 vols, 1829). Her house was probably the elegant early nineteenth-century **Howsley Cottage**, with its coach house, balcony and fine front door.

200yds S, turn downhill (signed Hawkshead) over Brathay Bridge. Immediately beside the bridge is **Low Brathay**, a large house with farm buildings. About 1780 the house is said to have been occupied by two gentlemanly brothers called Gilbert, who were highwaymen. From 1800 to 1815 it was the home of Charles Lloyd (1775–1839), minor poet, novelist, translator and (at times) friend of Wordsworth, Coleridge and De Quincey. Lloyd describes Skelwith Bridge in his 'Lines Written in Retirement':

> There is a scene
> To which I often turn; the rustic bridge
> 'Neath whose grey arch, in days of wintry gloom,
> Whitens far off the torrent's foam; ...
> The inn for tired foot-passenger, who haunts
> These seldom-trodden scenes; the village school,
> The village green, where little rustics sport,
> And dance, and sing; the mill, the waterfall,
> Make up the measure of its simple charms.

Talented but unstable, Lloyd managed to annoy almost everyone. His novel *Edmund Oliver* (1797) upset Coleridge by parodying his early career; and he fomented quarrels between Wordsworth and Hazlitt. De Quincey, who often visited him at Low Brathay, describes in his *Recollections* Lloyd's gradual descent into madness, culminating in his removal to an asylum. He escaped and visited De Quincey at Dove Cottage, full of strange delusions, but was recaptured.

De Quincey claims to have made nostalgic return-visits to Low Brathay after Lloyd's final departure

> and, seating myself on a stone, by the side of the mountain river Brathay,

SKELWITH BRIDGE
Thomas Allom, 1832

have staid for hours on end listening to the same sound to which so often Charles Lloyd and I used to hearken together with profound emotion and awe – the sound of pealing anthems, as if streaming from the open portals of some illimitable cathedral; for such a sound does actually arise, in many states of the weather, from the peculiar action of the river Brathay upon its rocky bed.

Behind Low Brathay a drive runs 250yds to **Brathay Hall** (now a management training centre), a Georgian house on a knoll with a good view down Windermere. This was the home (from 1804 to 1833) of John Harden, a significant amateur landscape painter, with whom John Constable sometimes stayed. An account of his life here, based partly on his wife Jessie's voluminous diaries, is given, with many of Harden's pictures, in Daphne Foskett's *John Harden of Brathay Hall* (1974).

200yds S of Low Brathay at road junction follow the lane W alongside the river: you will see signs to **Skelwith Fold** caravan park. The park is on the site of the large house, demolished in the 1960s, where the essayist and critic A.C. Benson frequently stayed with his cousin, a member of the wealthy Marshall family. Benson was in the habit of hiding small objects – silver trinkets, keys and other favoured items, which he called his 'fetishes' – in the course of his walks, under stones, in crevices in trees and so on. If you find such objects (they would date from the 1920s or earlier) they could be his.

Return to A593 and after 1¼m notice **Mill Brow Farm**, a white-rendered farmhouse up on the fellside. The novelist Elizabeth Gaskell and her family stayed here in late summer 1849. During the holiday they visited Edward Quillinan at Lesketh How, Ambleside, where they also met the elderly Wordsworth. On her return to Manchester Mrs Gaskell wrote exultantly to a friend who was holidaying in the Isle of Man,

> What sort of rooms have you? Grand proper rooms, I dare say, as dull as dust, with no amusing warming-pans, nor crockery, nor spurs, nor dresser, as Selina and we had at the Lakes; our dear charming farm-kitchen at Skelwith was worth a dozen respectable properly-furnished rooms. However, we're all at home now, and settled down into soberness.

Continue W into **Skelwith Bridge**, well known for its attractive water-fall, Skelwith Force, and by the Hotel take the turning R (W) on to B5343. After 1m turn R (N, signed Grasmere, High Close) and follow signs for High Close. After the second junction notice a pair of cottages just above the road. One is a recently-converted barn; the other, of white-rendered stone, rejoices in the name of **Scroggs**, and is the birthplace of Jonathan Otley (1756–1866), the pioneering geologist and author who spent most of his life at Keswick.

250yds SW of here is **Loughrigg Tarn**, hidden in a tranquil bowl of fells, circled by a footpath and overlooked by two white cottages. It was a favour-ite place of Wordsworth's, who gives it a splendid description in his little-known 'Epistle To Sir George Howland Beaumont' (1811), a poetic account of a Lakeland tour:

> Thus gladdened from our own dear Vale we pass
> And soon approach Diana's Looking-glass!
> To Loughrigg-tarn, round, clear and bright as heaven,
> Such name Italian fancy would have given ...
> The encircling region vividly exprest
> Within the mirror's depth, a world at rest –
> Sky streaked with purple, grove and craggy bield,
> And the smooth green of many a pendant field,
> And, quieted and soothed, a torrent small,
> A little daring would-be waterfall,
> One chimney smoking and its azure wreath,
> Associate all in the calm pool beneath,
> With here and there a faint imperfect gleam
> Of water-lilies veiled in misty steam.

A walk here in July 1844 inspired one of Wordsworth's last poems, 'So fair, so sweet, withal so sensitive,' when the poet noticed a 'mountain-daisy' and 'The beauty of its star-shaped shadow, thrown/On the smooth surface of [a] naked stone!'

Elterwater and the Langdales

Return to the valley road (B5343). Continue W and take signed turn L (SW) to **Elterwater** (*NT; car park at centre*). The village was the site of the old **Gunpowder Mills**, established in the early nineteenth century and closed in 1926. As Eliza Lynn Linton wrote,

> The place of the powder-mills alone is a poem in itself, and the bridge

across the Langdale Beck (the Brathay in its embryonic state) lets you into such a scene of river loveliness as you will never forget all your life long ...

To see the spot, look NW from the bridge. The site is now occupied by the Langdale Estate timeshare development, mercifully well-concealed from the beck. Several of the old grinding wheels and part of the mill-race from the powder works can still be seen.

Cross to the S side of the bridge; the second cottage, **St Martin**, was the original workshop of the hand-spinning and weaving industry revived by John Ruskin in 1883.

Continue ¾m S to **Colwith Bridge**, where the beck, says Eliza Linton, 'fret[s] out its life under the crags and about the tree roots, while the great rocks look down into the very heart of its turmoil'. As the carving on the parapet indicates, the beck marked the old boundary between Westmorland and Lancashire; this is the bridge over which Pigling Bland and Pig-wig are shown escaping into Westmorland in the last illustration to Beatrix Potter's *The Tale of Pigling Bland* (1913).

From the bridge go N 200yds and take turning W (signed Little Langdale, Wrynose), then after 250yds walkers may turn uphill through the large gate. This is the private drive (for much of the way also a public footpath) to **High Hacket** (at the top of the hill). This delightful, rambling old traditional farmhouse was the home of John Yewdale, quarryman, and his wife Betty, whose use of the Westmorland dialect was much admired by Wordsworth. A sample of her story-telling was recorded by Edith Southey and Sara Hutchinson and included in Southey's *The Doctor* (1837) as 'The Terrible Knitters i' Dent'.

The Wordsworth family stayed here in October 1810, hoping that a 'change of air' would help the children recover from whooping-cough. According to Dorothy, it was

> as poor a cottage as ever you saw ... but at the door chuse to the right or to the left and you have mountains, hamlets, woods, cottages, and rocks. The weather was heavenly, when we were there, and the first morning we sate in hot sunshine on a crag, twenty yards from the door, while William read part of the 5th book of the Paradise Lost to us. He read The Morning Hymn, while a stream of white vapour, which covered the Valley of Brathay, ascended slowly and by degrees melted away. It seemed as if we had never before felt the power of the Poet – 'Ye mists and exhalations, etc., etc.!'

The 'crag' where they sat is the outcrop just beyond the W end of the house. The cottage is mentioned in Wordsworth's 'Epistle to Sir George Beaumont' (1811).

Another view of Hacket, seen this time from the valley floor, is given by the Pastor in Book V of *The Excursion* (though the setting is moved to Grasmere Vale):

> 'tis a plot of cultivated ground,
> Cut off, an island in a dusky waste ...
> A house of stones, collected on the spot,

By rude hands built, with rocky knolls in front,
Backed also by a ledge of rock, whose crest
Of birch-trees waves over the chimney top.

Return to the road and continue W into **Little Langdale**, then turn NW following sign for Blea Tarn. There is a small car park after ¾m and a path leads W to the edge of **Blea Tarn**.

The first poem W.H. Auden ever wrote was about Blea Tarn: composed in 1922, it ended '… and in the quiet/Oblivion of the water let them stay.' The manuscript is lost, and Auden himself wrote later, 'Who or what *They* were, I cannot, for the life of me, recall.'

The Tarn and its surroundings are described by Wordsworth in *The Excursion* Book II, where the Author and the Wanderer walk over into the valley from the E:

BLEA TARN
John M'Whirter, 1882

    all at once, behold!
Beneath our feet, a little lowly vale …
Urn-like it was in shape, deep as an urn;
With rocks encompassed, save that to the south
Was one small opening, where a heath-clad ridge
Supplied a boundary less abrupt and close;
A quiet treeless nook, with two green fields,
A liquid pool that glittered in the sun,
And one bare dwelling; one abode, no more!

The narrator and his friend watch a funeral procession leaving the S end of the valley, heading for Little Langdale; then they descend the crags behind Bleatarn House, finding 'a platform – that lay, sheepfoldwise,/Enclosed between an upright mass of rock/And one old mossgrown wall;' in this enclosure, a kind of cragside garden, the Wanderer picks up a bedraggled copy of Voltaire's *Candide*, which occasions much philosophical reflection.

Bleatarn House, a fine old stone farmhouse (enlarged since Wordsworth's day) stands alone ¼m N of the car park. For the spot where the

Wanderer found the book, take grassy path up slope beside gill just SE of house, going up until you reach gap in stone wall, then go L along wall to stream. The book belongs to the Solitary, a disillusioned Stoic who, in the fiction of the poem, inhabits Bleatarn House. The characters 'clomb the cottage-stairs' (on the outside of the building: now gone) to 'a small apartment dark and low' where, in a north-facing room, they share a meal and the Solitary tells them the story of an old man who nearly died of exposure on the fells – a true story which Wordsworth had heard at Patterdale in 1804. The characters also discuss the Langdale Pikes:

> 'Those lusty twins,' exclaimed our host, 'if here
> It were your lot to dwell, would soon become
> Your prized companions... . there the sun himself,
> At the calm close of summer's longest day,
> Rests his substantial orb'.

William Knight's 1886 note to the poem confirms that on Midsummer Day the sun, viewed from Blea Tarn, does indeed set between the Pikes.

In Book III the Solitary, the Wanderer and the Author leave the house and walk across the valley past the Tarn to the crag at the W of the Tarn, which is the 'barrier of steep rock' which stops their walk. Here,

> Upon a semicirque of turf-clad ground,
> The hidden nook discovered to our view
> A mass of rock, resembling, as it lay
> Right at the foot of that moist precipice,
> A stranded ship, with keel upturned, that rests
> Fearless of winds and waves.

The philosophical conversations of the poem's third and fourth books take place here. The area has now been fenced and planted with conifers; it is boggy and inaccessible, and the rocks are concealed by trees.

You may follow the road (very steep, and impassible in bad winter conditions) NW over the fell to Great Langdale; otherwise, as we shall do here, return to Colwith Bridge, cross it to the S side and join A593, following it L (NE) to Skelwith bridge and turning for Great Langdale. Pass the two turnings for Elterwater and watch for the main entrance to the Langdale Estate timeshare development.

Directly opposite the Hotel across the road is a wooden gate; if you look over this, uphill and some 50yds into the wood you will see a stone barn; it is on private land and there is no public access. This was formerly the **Merzbarn**, housing a sculptural environment created in 1947 by the German Dadaist poet, painter and sculptor Kurt Schwitters (1887–1948). Schwitters, a fugitive from the Nazis exiled in Ambleside, was offered the barn by its owner, Harry Pierce. Helped by a grant from the Museum of Modern Art in New York, he set to work in freezing weather to transform it with plaster, stone and other materials but was already seriously ill and completed only one wall before he died in January 1948. In 1965 it was removed to the Hatton Gallery at Newcastle University, where it can now be seen. The move was made for conservation purposes, but may have been ill-judged: for Schwitters, the relationship between the barn and its environment was vital. Of the barn's owner, he wrote:

> He is a genius ... he lets the weeds grow, yet by means of slight touches he transforms them into a composition as I create art out of rubbish. He wants to give me every assistance. The new Merz construction will stand close to nature, in the midst of a national park, and afford a wonderful view in all directions.

The site of the barn was formerly known as **Cylinders Farm**: an odd name – but then we are just opposite the former gunpowder works. Could this have been the site of the cylinders used to make the 'cylinder gunpowder' invented (see p 25) by Bishop Watson?

Continue W into **Great Langdale**, a huge and beautiful glaciated valley with a broad, flat, pastoral floor. Slate quarrying is still carried on here and you are likely to hear the dull thud of blasting. Even in the eighteenth century quarrying dominated. According to Clarke (1787),

> the slate quarries and the slaters ... debauch the natives so far, that even the poor *Curate* is obliged to sell ale to support himself and family; and at his house I have played *Barnaby* with him on the sabbath-day morning, when he left us with the good old song, 'I'll but preach, and be with you again.'

On 'playing *Barnaby*', see p 20.

Wordsworth thought Great Langdale

> a Vale which should on no account be missed by him who has a true enjoyment of grand separate Forms composing a sublime Unity, austere but reconciled and rendered attractive to the affections by the deep serenity that is spread over every thing

– and this is the valley through which the narrator and his friend the Wanderer begin their walk in Book II of *The Excursion*.

Entering the valley from Little Langdale in 1831, John Stuart Mill thought it a scene 'wholly unlike any we had yet beheld. We might have fancied ourselves at the wall of the world.'

Michael Roberts, poet and mountaineer, depicts a winter aspect of the valley in 'Langdale: Nightfall January 4th', a poem of the 1940s:

> Dark are the shrouded hills, and vague, and the rain,
> as the wind changes,
> halts, and clouds over the fells
> drift, and the pleiads drown.

> The hooded fells are uncertain, the track to the tarn
> is lost, the fields are in flood,
> and at six the lane is in darkness,
> the beck is a ghost.

Roughly ¾m W of the Merzbarn is **Chapel Stile**, with **Holy Trinity Church** prominent just N of the village. In the churchyard, 20yds SW of the tower, is the grave of Owen Lloyd, son of the poet Charles Lloyd and Vicar here from 1829 to 1842. His epitaph (rendered a little obscure here by poor punctuation in the first lines) is by Wordsworth and was published as 'Epitaph in the Chapel-Yard of Langdale, Westmoreland'. Just beyond the E end of the church is a finely lettered headstone to G.M. Trevelyan, 'Historian of England' – a phrase chosen perhaps with his classic *English Social History* (1944) in mind.

The church, rebuilt in 1875, was formerly extremely dilapidated. According to Harriet Martineau,

> A few years since, the rotten old pulpit fell, with the clergyman, Mr Frazer in it, just after he had begun his sermon from the text 'Behold, I come quickly.' The pulpit fell on an elderly dame, who escaped wonderfully … She tartly refused [the minister's] sympathy, saying, 'If I'd been kilt, I'd been reet serrat, (rightly served), for you threatened ye's be comin doon sune.'

The annual 'Wake' or Fair at Chapel Stile is described in Book II of *The Excursion* in a passage that also offers a glimpse of the valley in the early sunlight of a May morning.

Return to the main road. Heading NW out of the village we pass under the jagged brow of **Thrang Crag**, whose quarries (now abandoned) were, according to Eliza Lynn Linton,

> noted for their picture slates, which are very curious; for sometimes a whole landscape is figured on a slab, with trees and lakes and mountains and rivers, just like their own larger natural selves. If you go into the excavation you may knock your head against the propped-up roof, and see where the last block has been cut; and stumble on the loose shingle, and cut your hands, and bruise your feet, without being much the wiser for the ordeal; … and take in the whole beauty and desolateness, in the solitude and the wreck of slates heaped up about.

Beside the craft shop at the foot a small road winds up into the quarry. From this the workings can be explored, with extreme caution.

John Stuart Mill cast a critical (and geologically-trained) eye over the quarryman's cottages hereabouts: they lacked the flowers and creepers 'so general in the south of England', he noted, and he disliked the white render on the outsides:

> I should like their houses much better if they would but leave them as they leave their barns. These are built of the same material, but there is no attempt to hide it; and the masses of solid slate, some blue, some red with iron, intermixed with masses of greenstone, or trachytic amygdaloid of the country, have a singular, and not unpleasing effect.

After ½m notice **Robin Ghyll**, an attractive cottage above the road. Between 1904 and 1911 G.M. Trevelyan spent the summers in this house working on his definitive three-volume study of Garibaldi's life and campaigns.

Continue 1¾m to the Dungeon Ghyll Hotel, right under the splendid and extraordinary Langdale Pikes. There is a large car park (*NT*) opposite the Hotel. Take path at E end of Hotel; it bears a little L uphill to gap at corner of two fences. From here, for Dungeon Ghyll Force go L uphill to gate. Path follows ghyll and after 250yds reaches a cleft in the rock: hollies grow thickly around it, and a rectangular block of stone has fallen to make a natural bridge.

This is **Dungeon Ghyll Force**, where a waterfall drops in front of a recess in the rock which, shaded by rocks and trees, appears unfathomably deep. It is a most beautiful spot, though the waterfall is peculiarly difficult to see and you have to clamber about with great caution. If you feel intrepid, walk back 30yds downstream, remove your boots and socks and scramble upstream into the 'dungeon' itself, where the great vertical column of water thunders down into the cool, dark stone cell: a memorable experience.

This is the scene of Wordsworth's anecdotal poem 'The Idle Shepherd-Boys' and, as the poet says,

> Into a chasm a mighty block
> Hath fallen, and made a bridge of rock:
> The gulf is deep below;
> And, in a basin black and small,
> Receives a lofty waterfall.

Instead of watching their sheep the shepherd-boys are running a race; one of them is halfway over the block, daring his friend to follow, when he sees a lamb which has fallen into 'the pool … Within that black and frightful rent'. Luckily 'a Poet' is passing; he pulls the lamb out and 'gently' tells them to 'mind their trade' better in future.

Coleridge recorded his impressions in the summer of 1800:

> the Stream widens from a foot to a yard and a half, as it widens, varying from a vivid white to a blue thro' all the intermediate shades – … plumy ferns on the side, & over the second pool, on the left side, the light umbrella of a young Ash –

and claims in *Christabel* that when a bell tolls at Langdale Hall,

> In Langdale Pike and Witch's Lair,
> And Dungeon-ghyll so foully rent,
> With ropes of rock and bells of air
> Three sinful sextons' ghosts are pent,
> Who all give back, one after t'other,
> The death-note of their living brother.

Return to the gate by the Hotel, and go straight uphill (alongside Stickle Ghyll) for **Stickle Tarn**, reached by a short but strenuous scramble. Wordsworth was once (the date is unknown) startled by the bleat of a lamb re-echoed from **Pavey Ark**, the great wall of crag that runs NW of the tarn, as he stood by the water. He based a passage in *The Excursion* Book IV on the memory of the sound,

> sent forth
> As if the visible mountain made the cry
> ... the unanswer'd bleat
> Of a poor lamb – left somewhere to itself,
> The plaintive spirit of the solitude!

¾m NE across rugged terrain is **Blea Rigg**, a steep rise leading to the precipitous rockface of **Eagle Crag** where George and Sarah Green, in 1808, perished in a blizzard trying to cross to Blindtarn Gill (see p 75).

Just SW of the tarn is the massive head of **Harrison Stickle** and, ½m due W, its companion **Pike of Stickle**. These are the famous **Langdale Pikes**. Dramatically craggy and giving wonderful views, yet not really difficult to get to, they early attracted tourists.

Joseph Budworth climbed 'Langdale Pike' (ie Pike of Stickle) in August 1792, guided by a young farmer, Paul Postlethwaite, who

> never remembered 'foine folk aiming at et afore;' ... We had many rough rocks to scramble up, and in a deep recess, impenetrable to the sun, I observed a large quantity of snow that I should suppose never completely dissolves. We had again to haul ourselves by rocks to bring us to the crown of Langdale Pike, which is about twenty yards in circumference; in the centre is a natural stone seat, with moss and small rocks around it.
> *PP*: 'Ith neome oh fackins, wot a broughtin you here?'
> *Rambler*: 'Curiosity, Paul.'
> *PP*: 'I think you mun be kurious enuff; I neor cum here but after runnaway sheop, an I'me then so vext at um, I cud throa um deawn th' Poike...'

They came down on the W side of the Pike; Budworth found the steep slope so terrifying that he 'tied up my right eye, which could not have borne the vast precipice almost perpendicularly under me.' He followed Postlethwaite, who merely remarked, with quintessential Cumbrian brevity, that 'a man might surely goa wheor sheep cud'.

Thomas Wilkinson climbed the Pikes sometime before 1805 with the Smith sisters of Coniston. Elizbeth Smith, intrepid as always, left the party to scramble among the summits, and her absence

> was terribly extended ... I knew not whether she might be clambering up the cliffs above us, or falling down the precipices below; ... but we were at length relieved by her calling to us from the cliffs over our heads. In her descent she had missed her way, and got on a shelf of rocks higher than that on which we sat.

Wordsworth's sonnet 'November 1' describes the year's first sight of snow on the Pikes, as seen from the Brathay valley in 1815.

Ruskin in a letter of August 1867 judges the Pikes

> the loveliest rock-scenery, chased with silver waterfalls, that I ever set foot or heart upon ... the sweet heather and ferns and star mosses nestled in close to the dashing of the narrow streams ... Fancy what a place for a hot afternoon after five, with no wind, and absolute solitude; no creature, except a lamb or two, to mix any ruder sound or voice with the splash of the innumerable streamlets!

Wrynose and Cockley Beck

Return to the road and make your way to Little Langdale either by the pass at the W end of Great Langdale or *via* Skelwith Bridge. From Little Langdale take road W (signed Wrynose). The road climbs to the head of Little Langdale to reach the **The Three Shire Stones**, beside the road 200yds E of the top of the pass. They mark the point at which three pre-1974 counties touched – Lancashire to the S, Cumberland to the NW and Westmorland to the NE. There are five stones altogether: a tall one with the inscription LANCASHIRE on the S face towards the Furness peninsula and 'W.F 1816' on the N (for William Field of Cartmel, the Roadmaster who had the original stone made), three smaller stones with the letters C, W and L indicating the directions of the three counties, and another giving some information. In 1854 Harriet Martineau suggested that

> Young tourists, who happen to have long limbs, may enjoy the privilege of being in three counties at once, by setting their feet on two of the three stones, and resting their hands on the third.

– but their present position would make that very difficult. The original small initialled stones are said to have been buried nearby during the Second World War and never found. The present ones are replicas. The 'Lancashire' pillar was broken into four pieces by a vehicle in 1997 but expertly restored soon afterwards.

The road continues W, gradually veering S, into the **Duddon Valley**. Richly pastoral and scattered with small areas of woodland, this is delightful walking country, less visited than much of Lakeland. The river is strikingly beautiful in many places; buildings and landscape are full of interest. The valley is the 'Dundale' often mentioned but never actually portrayed in Arthur Ransome's novels.

Wordsworth, who explored the valley in childhood, described the Duddon as his 'favourite river' and recalled how he came to fish in it during his schooldays at Hawkshead, having, he says,

> fallen into the common delusion that the farther from home the better sport would be had. Accordingly, one day I attached myself to a person living in the neighbourhood of Hawkshead, who was going to try his fortune as an angler near the source of the Duddon. We fished a great part of the day with very sorry success, the rain pouring torrents, and long before we got home I was worn out with fatigue; and, if the good man had not carried me on his back, I must have laid down under the best shelter I could find.

The valley's main literary association is with Wordsworth's *The River Duddon: A Series of Sonnets* (1820), whose course we shall follow. The Duddon rises just W of the top of the pass, in a saucer-like depression full of bog and meandering streams. Wordsworth's *Duddon Sonnet* II stresses the wildness of the place where the stream has its birth:

Child of the clouds! remote from every taint
Of sordid industry thy lot is cast;
Thine are the honours of the lofty waste ...
  – to chant thy birth, thou hast
No meaner Poet than the whistling Blast,
And desolation is thy Patron-saint!

and NW of the small car park at the pass-top is a pulpit-like rock outcrop on top of a grassy knoll. Wordsworth imagines himself sitting here to write *Duddon Sonnet* III: 'How shall I paint thee? – Be this naked stone/My seat, while I give way to such intent ... ' A clear path leads from the car park to the foot of the knoll. Running W, the stream (as Wordsworth says, addressing it in *Duddon Sonnet* IV)

a loosely scattered chain doth make;
Or rather thou appear'st a glittering snake,
Silent, and to the gazer's eye untrue,
Thridding with sinuous lapse the rushes, through
Dwarf willows gliding, and by ferny brake.

– though the dwarf willows are no longer to be seen. 1½m W of the Three Shires Stone is **Cockley Beck**, described in the *Duddon Sonnet* V:

now, to form a shade
For Thee, green alders have together wound
Their foliage; ashes flung their arms around;
And birch-trees risen in silver collonade.
And thou hast also tempted here to rise,
'Mid sheltering pines, this Cottage rude and grey;
Whose ruddy children, by the mother's eyes
Carelessly watched, sport through the summer day.

The trees by the cottage are now sycamore and ash; but this is clearly the place Wordsworth has in mind. (The bridge also features in Richard Adams's novel *The Plague Dogs*).

Birks Bridge and Seathwaite

Here the road forks. NW over the bridge lie Hardknott Pass (with its Roman fort, mentioned in *Duddon Sonnet* X) and Eskdale, for which turn to p 214. We continue S 1½m to the beautiful **Birks Bridge**, over a weirdly-eroded rocky gorge, the 'Faery Chasm' of *Duddon Sonnet* XI, where Wordsworth notes that fairy footprints can be seen in the stone. Though the marks cannot now be found, the spot is a strange and lovely one. The river hereabouts takes on a remarkable blue-green colour which justifies Wordsworth's calling it, in *Duddon Sonnet* VIII, 'blue Streamlet' and 'pellucid current'.

From the bridge either follow road parallel to E bank of river to Seathwaite; or (strictly for the adventurous) take path on W bank. Be warned that it does not stay close to the river all the way. Twice it seems to

BIRKS BRIDGE
W. Conway, 1854

go right to the brink, becoming rocky, dangerous and finally impassable:
these points should be treated as viewpoints for looking down the river at
its strange, eroded rocks and the details described in Sonnet XII, 'Hints for
the Fancy':

> Wild shapes for many a strange comparison!
> Niagaras, Alpine passes, and anon
> Abodes of Naiads, calm abysses pure,
> Bright liquid mansions ...

Then, as Wordsworth puts it, 'Turn from the sight, enamoured Muse – we
must;/And, if thou canst, leave them without regret!': go back a little, to get
round above and behind the crags which overhang the riverbank. You will
soon join the clearly waymarked Permissive Path to Seathwaite through
conifer woods to stepping-stones with a steel hawser for handrail (Fickle
Steps). Cross the steps to the road or continue on the woodland path until
you reach a slender stone footbridge. This is Seathwaite Footbridge
(details on p 295). Cross it and follow the river down to its junction with
the Tarn Beck, then follow the Beck to a small footbridge and path to the
road.

Turn L (E) for **Seathwaite**, a hamlet consisting of a church, a few houses
and the Newfield Inn. **Holy Trinity Church** is mentioned in *Duddon
Sonnet* XVIII, which recalls

those days
When this low Pile a Gospel Teacher knew
Whose good works formed an endless retinue

– the Rev Robert Walker (1709–1802), curate of Seathwaite for over sixty-six years. Known as 'Wonderful Walker', he was a famous local figure. Wordsworth admired him greatly and published a long 'Memoir' of him with the Duddon sonnets. He was remarkable for his goodness, generosity and austere religious life, spent contentedly in a very poor parish. He was also one of those Lakeland 'characters' whom early tourists loved to visit: one traveller in 1754 describes finding him at home,

> sitting at the head of a long square table, such as is commonly used in this country by the lower class of people, dressed in a coarse blue frock, trimmed with black horn buttons; a checked shirt, a leathern strap about his neck for a stock, a coarse apron, and a pair of great wooden-soled shoes, plated with iron to preserve them (what we call clogs in these parts), with a child upon his knee, eating his breakfast.

As his costume suggests, Walker added to his meagre stipend by farming. He also taught the village school, in the chapel: there was no heating, even in winter, so 'he used to send the children in parties either to his own fire at home, or make them run up the mountain's side.'

A detailed description of Walker is given in *The Excursion* Book VII, and a fictional account of Walker's preaching in his crowded church features in Chapter X of Richard Parkinson's novel *The Old Church Clock* (1843).

The church, formerly a primitive chapel, was rebuilt in 1874. Beside the porch is Walker's 'clipping stone', the rock on which he sat to shear sheep at Gateskell Farm (on Wrynose Pass, ¾m above Cockley Beck), now adorned with a sundial. Walker's grave is on the E side of the path, midway between the porch and the S gate. The gravestone, with its simple but finely-lettered inscription, is not of local stone but 'was sent as a mark of respect', Wordsworth says, 'by one of [his] descendants from the vale of Festiniog, a region almost as beautiful as that in which it now lies!' The donor was a grandson who had become a slate-quarrying magnate. Inside, at the W end of the aisle, is a plain, upright wooden chair said to have been made by Walker himself. The N wall carries a brass plaque commemorating Walker and his wife.

Fine shearing is a Seathwaite tradition: in July 1890 the journalist and social reformer H.W. Nevinson, on his way to see Ruskin at Brantwood, walked through Seathwaite and

> watched an old farmer and his two sons shearing sheep – a miraculous process. Catch your sheep in your arms, sit astride the broad seat, with the sheep held down on its back in front of you, its head under your left arm for choice. Make an incision underneath, between the front legs, and cut away all the under wool to the tail, clearing the tail with great care. Tie the four legs all together with a rope; turn the sheep over, and clip its back in the same way. The whole fleece comes away at last in one piece, the sheep escaping from it like a nice white ghost from its coil.

Opposite the church is **Walker House**, formerly the parsonage, greatly enlarged since Walker's day, when it was 'a mere cottage, with a peat-house at one end and an out-house of some kind at the other.'

Half a mile N of the church, up a short unmarked drive, is Walker's birthplace, **Undercrag**, a small white-rendered farmhouse with an attractive garden nestling under a jagged rock outcrop.

Return to Walker House. From its N corner opposite the church a footpath leads by a ford across the **Tarn Beck**, which flows down from Seathwaite Tarn and is the subject of Wordsworth's *Duddon Sonnet* XIX, 'Tributary Stream'. In the 1820s a yarn-spinning mill stood on the beck just below the chapel; Wordsworth thought it

> A mean and disagreeable object, though not unimportant to the spectator, as calling to mind the momentous changes wrought by such inventions in the frame of society – changes which have proved especially unfavourable to these mountain solitudes.

All trace of the mill has now vanished.

The path leads after a rambling route of about ½m to **Seathwaite Footbridge**. (For a direct route, follow the road SW from church to large stone house with pine trees, set back from road. Take gate opposite house, cross beck by footbridge and go downstream to junction with Duddon, then follow Duddon upstream to footbridge.) Note the engraved stone tablets set into the parapets of this lovely bridge. That on the S side is inscribed 'AB'; on the N is a magical-looking symbol combining Alpha, Omega and a star.

100yds downstream from the footbridge are **Seathwaite Stepping-Stones**, the subject of *Duddon Sonnets* IX and X. Placed in a beautiful curving line, they

> might seem a zone
> Chosen for ornament – stone matched for stone
> In studied symmetry, with interspace
> For the clear waters to pursue their race
> Without restraint.

The other sonnet, depicting a pair of lovers crossing the steps, imagines the 'frolic Loves' – presumably Cupids – watching from 'yon high rock' – which must be Wallowbarrow Crag, the rock face which overlooks the gorge on its west side. Walk 100yds or so upstream and you will see the jagged face of the Crag above trees opposite. This is probably the place mentioned in *Duddon Sonnets* XIV and XV:

> From this deep chasm, where quivering sunbeams play
> Upon its loftiest crags, mine eyes behold ...
> A gloomy NICHE, capacious, blank and cold;
> A concave free from shrubs and mosses grey;

The 'niche' cannot now be identified: possibly it was caused by a mass of rock falling into the stream – there are plenty to be seen in the riverbed hereabouts.

Opposite the Crag, the slope running up E is Hollin House Tongue. There is no path up it, but its rocky summit, known as **The Pen**, has been suggested as the viewpoint for *Duddon Sonnet* XIII, 'Open Prospect', which describes the view over Seathwaite:

> Hail to the fields – with Dwellings sprinkled o'er,
> And one small hamlet, under a green hill
> Clustering, with barn and byre, and spouting mill!

The 'spouting mill' was the yarn-mill mentioned above; the 'barn and byre' belonged to Newfield, which in Wordsworth's day was both farm and inn.

Return to the road and continue 250yds S to **The Newfield Inn**. Wordsworth concludes *Duddon Sonnet* XIII by imagining himself taking refuge there in winter,

> Reckless of angry Duddon sweeping by,
> While the warm hearth exalts the mantling ale,
> [To] laugh with the generous household heartily
> At all the merry pranks of Donnerdale!

Strictly, though confusingly, the name 'Dunnerdale' is given only to the part of the valley below Ulpha Bridge, which we have not yet reached. Wordsworth uses the name loosely; the spelling 'Donnerdale' reflected local pronunciation.

Newfield in the later nineteenth century became solely a farm, but retained a reputation for hospitality, the last farmer-innkeeper on his deathbed having insisted that 'no stranger in the valley who requested a night's lodging was ever to be refused'. Now it has become an inn again. It has a comfortable traditional interior with a fine banded slate floor.

Hall Dunnerdale and Ulpha

Go 1m SW to **Hall Dunnerdale Bridge**, in a delightful pastoral setting, which seems to be the viewpoint for *Duddon Sonnet* XX, 'The Plain of Donnerdale', and where, in Sonnet XXI, Wordsworth recalls walking with 'friends and kindred tenderly beloved' whilst staying at Broughton-in-Furness during holidays from Cambridge in his student days.

Coleridge was here in 1802: losing his way in the fells near Ulpha he came down to the road about here and saw

> an [old] man with his Daughter, a sweet Girl, burning Bracken – went up to him & talked with him & the lovely Girl in the [midst] of the huge Volumes of Smoke, & found I had gone two miles wrong.

They directed him to the road (on the E side of the bridge) to Broughton Mills. To follow the Duddon take the other road, W over the bridge towards Ulpha. The shallower parts of the river between Hall Dunnerdale and Ulpha are the probable setting for *Duddon Sonnet* XXIII, 'Sheep-Washing'.

Continue 2m to S **Ulpha**. At N edge of village (250yds N of turning signed Eskdale and Whitehaven) take metal gate into field. Walk down to riverbank then downstream 200yds. Look for a large semicircular pool scooped out of sheer rock in the opposite bank. This is **Long Dubs** – setting for *Duddon Sonnet* XXII, 'Tradition', which tells of a girl who drowned in the river attempting to reach a primrose growing 'Upon the steep rock's breast' over the pool.

Return to road and turn NW uphill (signed Eskdale and Whitehaven). The house on the corner 50yds up was

VIEW FROM DUDDON BRIDGE
W.J. Linton, 1864

formerly the **Traveller's Rest Inn**. Wordsworth and Coleridge stayed here in 1802, the latter noting 'The public house at Ulpha a very nice one,/& the Landlord, a very intelligent man'.

The 'very intelligent' landlord was probably the same who early in the nineteenth century is said to have taught some arrogant students a lesson: they

> wrote a note in Latin to the Landlord, asking for the bill, and gave it to the girl who waited. Mr Gunson, the landlord, ... immediately sent in the bill in Greek. It was too much for the students, who were obliged to ask for it in English.

At this inn too Philip Irvine, villain of Hugh Walpole's novel *The Bright Pavilions*, stays and plots before his final confrontation with Nicholas Herries. He is making with his henchmen for Muncaster, and his final journey through a blizzard (in one of the more violent and vivid chapters of the novel) takes him 1½m further up this road to **Crosbythwaite**, which is, as Walpole describes it, 'a little bunch of trees and a farmhouse beside them'. The intruders quarrel and end by murdering the farmer and his wife before fleeing across Ulpha Fell to Devoke Water. The road continues to Eskdale. We, however, return to the Duddon Valley road and Ulpha.

Because of its prominent church, the village was formerly known as Ulpha Kirk. Coleridge was here, travelling S through the valley from Eskdale in August 1802, and somewhere in the fells just S of the road, perhaps at the top of Yew Pike, he noted:

> Here it was seated on this Mount, on Saturday, August 7, that I resolved to write under the name of The Soother of Absence, the topographical poem

which I had long mummel'd about in my mind, & the day before thought of under the name of the Bards of Helvellin or the Stone Hovels/-

The 'Soother of Absence' was never written. Coleridge got lost in the region of Tarn Hill and Stickle Pike, eventually finding his way down to the road somewhere near Hall Dunnerdale.

St John's Church, Ulpha, is described by Wordsworth in *Duddon Sonnet* XXXI:

> The Kirk of Ulpha to the pilgrim's eye
> Is welcome as a star, that doth present
> Its shining forehead through the peaceful rent
> Of a black cloud diffused o'er half the sky.

The church was always white-rendered, and seen from the fields on the other side of the river when there were fewer trees than now it looked high and radiant – hence the 'star' image of the poem. Late medieval but much-restored, the church is of simple, barnlike construction with exposed roof-timbers, thick walls and small, square windows. The walls have eighteenth-century painted texts and fragments of earlier pictorial work. The bells are still rung by ropes in the porch.

Harriet Martineau in 1854 calls Ulpha 'one of the primitive places where the old manners of the district may be traced yet', and tells the story of a blind clergyman who officiated there 'not long since':

> One Sunday morning, the bell rang before the people were all ready; and especially the stoutest farmer in the neighbourhood, who, detained by some cow, pig, or sheep, entered the church last of all, 'thunnerin down the aisle.' 'Wha's comin now?' asked the blind priest; and, being informed by the clerk that it was John T-, he inquired further, 'a-foot or a-horse-back?'

Wordsworth revisited Dunnerdale in 1844, in old age, with Mary, Edward Quillinan and others. They stayed at the 'little farm-house inn' – the Travellers' Rest – for the night. Wordsworth got up early to walk in the churchyard, reflecting sadly on old times and lost friends: 'the recollection of former days and people crowded in upon him'.

At Ulpha Bridge, take the road SW (keeping on the N bank of the river). After ½m it runs alongside a wooded gorge with a small stream. This is **Holehouse Gill**, probably referred to in *Duddon Sonnets* XXIV and XXV as the 'Nook – with woodbine hung and straggling weed ... Half grot, half arbour' where the poet rests. Soon after leaving the woods, the road passes between the buildings of **Old Hall Farm**. By the W end of the farmhouse are the ruins of the 'Old Hall', a medieval fortified farmhouse which is the subject of *Duddon Sonnet* XXVII:

> quietly self-buried in earth's mould,
> Is that embattled House, whose massy Keep
> Flung from yon cliff a shadow large and cold.

The building was never the impressive 'Keep' Wordsworth suggests; today little is left but the walls, some six feet high, of a single room with window and fireplace, now used as an animal-pen. The poem claims that the inhabitants were driven out by a haunting, a legend Wordsworth borrowed from Rydal Hall. Return to Ulpha Bridge.

To reach **The Sepulchre**, a Quaker burial-ground which is the subject of *Duddon Sonnet* XXIX, take gate by cattle grid at SE end of bridge. Walk N, parallel to the river, to edge of wood, then follow waymarked path through wood. When path reaches gate of house (New Close) go E across field to gap in wall, then SE uphill to clump of conifers. The conifers grow inside the burial-ground.

Wordsworth's sonnet celebrates 'the loyal and the brave, who lie/In the blank earth, neglected and forlorn', for the graves are unmarked and the enclosure is completely wild and untended. The Sepulchre has not been used since 1755 and there is, really, nothing whatever to see: just the stone walls, three living pine trees and the stumps of three more dead ones, some bracken and long grass. It is a strange, peaceful, neglected spot. Return to the road, which follows the river S through some 5m of pleasant country to join the coast road, A595.

Torver and Coniston

Follow this E 1m to Broughton-in-Furness (see p 219) then turn N onto A593 which runs NE through some 10m of pleasant farming country to the hamlet of **Torver**. Coleridge in 1802

> observe[d] from Torva thro' Coniston the force of imitation in the Gardens & sweet Porches, & every where clipped yews, in obelisks, & fine arches …

CONISTON HALL
W. Conway, 1854

Splendid topiary was plentiful in the cottage gardens of Torver until the 1950s but now, sadly, has largely disappeared, though there is one splendid example ¾m N of the village on A593. A few good examples survive also at High Nibthwaite, which we visit later.

Torver was the home of an eminent scholar of Icelandic, the Rev Thomas Ellwood. Rector of the former Torver Chapel, he wrote a small history of the village, *Leaves from the Annals of a Mountain Parish* (1888), which is less interesting than it sounds.

Continue N to Coniston. As you enter the village watch for sign on R to the quite extraordinary sixteenth-century **Coniston Hall** *(NT)*. *Anne Radcliffe passed along the opposite shore in 1794 and noted (perhaps confusing it with Conishead Priory) that 'on the edge of the water, the antient hall, or priory, shows its turret and ivyed ruins among old woods. The whole picture is reflected in the liquid mirror below'.*

Coleridge admired it, 'with its four Round Chimneys, two cloathed so warmly cap a pie with ivy & down on the wall far below'. Wordsworth too was delighted by the ivy:

> The rustic inmates of the beautiful fabric of Coniston Hall must take some pains to exclude the ivy from their chambers, or it would otherwise present itself as a bold intruder &, not content with possession of the window, would advance till it had entwined the bedposts & decorated them like the Thyrsus of Bacchus.

Having been discussed and illustrated by Ruskin in 'The Poetry of Architecture' (1837), the hall can claim to be one of the classic examples of Lakeland architecture. It is certainly remarkable, with its gigantic chimneys, its cart-ramp up to the first-floor granary, and its windows ranging from the enormous to the minuscule. But stripped of its ivy, conscientiously restored and heavily rendered, backed by the car and boat park of the local boat club, is it now beautiful? It seems blasphemy to say so, but one cannot quite banish recollections of Battersea Power Station.

Continue into **Coniston** *(large car park 250yds E of church)*, a pleasant and mainly Victorian village, built of slate and excitingly dominated by the craggy foothills of Coniston Old Man. Formerly a tiny cluster of houses associated with the local slate quarries, it grew into a tourist centre during the nineteenth century. A good starting point is the **Black Bull**, easily found at the village centre. This is a comfortable sixteenth-century inn where Coleridge stayed on his 1802 walking tour and 'Dined on Oatcake & Cheese, with a pint of Ale, & 2 glasses of Rum & water sweetened with preserved Gooseberries'. It is also the 'little rustic inn ... at Church Coniston' where the young De Quincey stayed in 1805 and 1806. Here in 1806 he wrote an essay on 'The Constituents of Happiness', setting the goals of his future life; and from here, in both years, he walked over towards Grasmere hoping to visit Wordsworth but lost his nerve and turned back.

75yds N of the inn is the **Ruskin Museum** *(open 10-5.30 daily; admission charge)*. The Museum has extensive displays on the history of Coniston, the geology, archeology and mining of the area; local crafts (slate working, violin-making, pottery). It also presents Ruskin's life and activities. There are displays of his personal belongings, among them his paintbox, his set of musical stones and the billhooks he used to coppice the woods at Brantwood. A selection of his sketchbooks and paintings is displayed, together with parts of his fine collection of minerals and many other objects. His encouragement of local skills and crafts is represented by displays of 'Ruskin lace' and other products. There are excellent interactive computer presentations on Ruskin, local history and other topics. A substantial display is devoted to Donald Campbell, who died on Coniston Water on 4 January 1967 in his jet-powered craft Bluebird K7 whilst attempting to break his own world water speed record.

Those interested in the Museum's history and significance should consult Canon H.D. Rawnsley's *Ruskin and the English Lakes* (1901), whose fourth chapter is an elaborate meditation on the contents and meaning of the museum as it was before modernisation.

Opposite the Black Bull, the present Yewdale Hotel probably stands on the site of the older **Bank House** which was the home of Alexander Craig Gibson (though between 1844 and 1851 he is said to have lived near Yewdale Bridge, ¼m E of here on the way to Brantwood). He wrote dialect poetry and fiction, collected in *The Folk-Speech of Cumberland* (1869), and a kind of crazy guidebook, full of local information, called *The Old Man, or Ravings and Ramblings Around Coniston* (1849). The present building is probably the one where Arthur Ransome rented rooms in 1903 on his first adult visit to the Lake District.

A few yards E of the Hotel is **St Andrew's Church**, built in 1891 to replace an earlier small chapel. W.G. Collingwood made an entertaining recreation of the life of a seventeenth-century curate of this church in his novel *Dutch Agnes, Her Valentine* (1910), based partly on parish records. At the E side of the churchyard is John Ruskin's grave, marked by a splendid Celtic cross designed by Collingwood and carved by a local craftsman from Tilberthwaite stone, resting on a rock from Elterwater.

The designs are symbolic, indicating Ruskin's interests and writings: the shaft carvings include a boy with a lyre (for poetry and music); St George and the Dragon (for Ruskin's craft organisation, the Guild of St George); an artist sketching a landscape; the Lion of St Mark (for *Stones of Venice*); a seven-branched candlestick (*Seven Lamps of Architecture*); the parable of the labourers in the vineyard (*Unto This Last*); lilies and sesame-cakes (*Sesame and Lilies*); a woman holding a club, a key and a nail (*Fors Clavigera*); and a crown of wild olive for the book of that title. Designs of animals, birds and wild flowers recall Ruskin's interest in nature and science.

On the R of Ruskin's grave are those of his cousin Joanna and her husband, Arthur Severn, artist and disciple of Ruskin; further R are Ruskin's secretary, the artist and antiquarian W.G. Collingwood, and his wife; and their son, the Oxford philosopher and archaeologist R.G. Collingwood, and his wife.

Gondola and Coniston Water

Continue E for ⅓m to signed turning to the pier for **Gondola** (*NT*), an ornate Victorian steam-yacht (its design, according to Arthur Ransome, 'formally approved by Mr Ruskin' himself) restored by the National Trust and plying for passengers on the lake from spring to autumn (*details of sailings from Tourist Information Offices*).

As a small child on holiday Arthur Ransome was allowed by the captain to steer the vessel; later it contributed to his conception of Captain Flint's houseboat in *Swallows and Amazons* and *Winter Holiday*. Ransome sent a postcard of *Gondola* with details added in ink to his first illustrator, Clifford Webb; Ransome's own drawings, which replaced Webb's after 1934, show the houseboat as more like the *Esperance* at Bowness.

The *Gondola* Pier is a good point from which to survey **Coniston Water**. Formerly known as Thurstonmere, it apparently acquired its present name from the village of Coniston about 1800, for Ann Radcliffe in 1794 calls it 'Thurston-lake', yet in 1823 Jonathan Otley writes that it was 'called in some old books Thurston Water'. It has recovered from early industrial development, for the woods on the E shore of the lake still have many traces of the iron bloomeries and charcoal burners' pitsteads common in these areas until the end of the nineteenth century. According to Collingwood,

> At one time the woods were nearly destroyed, and we can imagine a period when the barren hills were only varied by smoking 'pitsteads,' where charcoal was made, and flaming 'hearths' where grimy workers toiled at the bellows, or shovelled the red ore and black coals.

Wordsworth in *The Prelude* records memories of the shores of the lake with their

> gentle airs,
> Birds, running streams, and hills so beautiful
> On golden evenings, while the charcoal pile
> Breathed up its smoke

– though acknowledging that the charcoal-burner himself might well

> languish with disease
> Induced by sleeping nightly on the ground
> Within his sod-built cabin, Indian-wise.

To the western shore of the lake Wordsworth came with schoolfriends for a picnic in the summer of 1783. He floated in a boat under

> the shade of a magnificent row of sycamores, which then extended their branches from the shore of the promontory upon which stands the ancient, and at that time, the more picturesque Hall of Coniston

and vowed lifelong allegiance to the Lake Country:

> Dear native Region, wheresoe'er shall close
> My mortal course, there will I think on you;
> Dying, will cast on you a backward look;
> Even as this setting sun ...
> Doth with the fond remains of his last power
> Still linger, and a farewell lustre sheds
> On the dear mountain-tops where first he rose.

Coniston Water is said to have had at one time a floating island, and Eliza Lynn Linton in 1864 claimed it was possible to see where it 'got stranded among the reeds at Nibthwaite during a high wind and heavy flood, and has never been able to get off again'.

The lake is the setting of W.G. Collingwood's historical novel *Thorstein of the Mere* (1895), dealing with the adventures of the Norse settler who gave the lake its old name of Thurstonmere. As a child Arthur Ransome formed a close acquaintance with its waters when his father dropped him in from a boat to find out if, like other mammals, the human child could swim by instinct. He sank. Later Ransome learned to row here in a 'heavy farm-boat with oars that worked on pins instead of in rowlocks (so that a fisherman could drop them instantly if a pike or a char took his trailed spinner)' and started to fish there, catching perch. In adult life he sailed on the lake frequently, and we shall be visiting many of the places used as fictional settings in his novels.

A circuit of Coniston Water: East Bank

From the *Gondola* Pier return to the road. 200yds E is the **Waterhead Hotel**, a massive product of the Victorian tourist vogue. It was probably here that C.L. Dodgson ('Lewis Carroll') stayed during his Lakeland holiday of 1857; Charles Darwin spent a holiday here in August 1879, resting from his research for two small but classic works, *The Power of Movement in Plants* (1880) and *The Formation of Vegetable Mould through the Action of Earthworms* (1881); and Ruskin escaped here when domestic tensions (the result of his mental instability) drove him from Brantwood temporarily in 1887.

100yds E of the hotel is the drive to **Thwaite Court**, home (1827-1893) of John Beever, author (under the pseudonym 'Arundo') of *Practical Fly-Fishing: founded on nature, and tested by the experience of more than forty years* (1869) and his botanist sisters Mary and Susannah. They were friends of Ruskin: Susannah edited *Frondes Agrestes* (1875), a popular selection of extracts from *Modern Painters*; Ruskin in turn published a selection of Susannah's letters in his *Hortus Inclusus* (1887).

At the junction turn on to lakeside road (signed Brantwood). After ¼m on a steep corner is **Tent Lodge**, a squarish Georgian house of no very distinguished design but with a rich history. Its name commemorates the death of the young scholar and translator Elizabeth Smith (b 1776), who died of tuberculosis on August 7 1806 in a tent near the spot where the house now stands. Miss Smith had taught herself nine languages, published a new translation of the Book of Job, made linguistic studies of Welsh, Chinese and some African languages and wrote poetry. Her literary remains were published as *Fragments in Prose and Verse* (1810), edited by Dr H.M. Bowdler the censoring editor of Shakespeare whose name gave us the word 'Bowdlerise'.

The Smith family lived at **Townson Ground** (long known as **Tent Cottage**; now a guest house) across the road. Its gardens, including the present site of Tent Lodge, were landscaped for the Smiths by Thomas Wilkinson of Yanwath. Tent Lodge stands on the former Townson Ground lawn, and Elizabeth slept in the tent here because tubercular patients were supposed to benefit from fresh air. Her own account of the onset of her illness is poignant:

> One very hot evening in July, I took a book, and walked about two miles from home, where I seated myself on a stone beside the lake. Being much engaged by a poem I was reading, I did not perceive that the sun was gone down, and was succeeded by a very heavy dew; till in a moment I felt struck on the chest as if with a sharp knife. I returned home, but said nothing of the pain. The next day being also very hot, and every one busy in the hay-fields, I thought I would take a rake, and work very hard, to produce perspiration, in the hope that it might remove the pain, but it did not.

She declined rapidly and died just over a year later. Before her death she pointed out the site of the present Tent Lodge as 'a good situation for a new cottage'.

Her accomplishments included intrepid fell-walking, an aspect which features in both De Quincey's *Recollections* and Wilkinson's *Tours to the British Mountains*. Harriet Martineau adds that

> The boat-house is at the bottom of the slope, down which she used to take her mother's guests; and she and her sister were so well practised at the oar that they could show the beauties of the scene from any point of the lake.

In the mid-nineteenth century Tent Lodge changed hands and was often let as a holiday home. The Tennysons stayed here on their honeymoon tour in 1850 and entertained a vast range of visitors, including Matthew Arnold, Carlyle, Coventry Patmore and Edward Lear. They walked and boated and Tennyson (though not Emily) climbed mountains with Patmore. Tennyson also worked on *The Princess*, which he composed on long walks. He was so wrapped up in the poem that he several times walked past the entrance without noticing it. Emily had the gatepost painted white so that he could not miss it.

The Tennysons returned in August and September 1857; this time Charles Dodgson, Oxford mathematician and photographer (who had not yet written his *Alice* books as 'Lewis Carroll') visited and noted in his diary:

> After I had waited some little time the door opened, and a strange shaggy-looking man entered: his hair, moustache and beard looked wild and neglected: these very much hid the character of the face.

This was Tennyson.

William Smith, poet, essayist and philosopher and his wife Lucy Cumming, newly married, spent the summer of 1861 here. Here Smith wrote poetry and worked at *Gravenhurst, or Thoughts on Good and Evil.*

250yds S of Tent Lodge, by How Head Cottage, the two openings of the turning to Hawkshead make a small wooded triangle. The gate above this opens into a field with a small rocky beck and a grassy knoll. This is probably the point H.D. Rawnsley says was locally called **'Tennyson's Seat'** at the end of the nineteenth century, 'and one can well believe that for so fair a view the late Lord Laureate would often have strolled thither.' Harriet Martineau also recommends this view:

> Some people think this the finest view in the whole district ... Nowhere else, perhaps, is the grouping of the mountain peaks, and the indication of their recesses so striking; and as to the foreground, with its glittering waterfall, its green undulations, its diversified woods, its bright dwellings, and its clear lake, – it conveys the strongest impression of joyful charm, – of fertility, prosperity and comfort, nestling in the bosom of the rarest beauty.

Directly up the fellside from here, and now covered with conifers, is **Monk Coniston Moor**, where Gilbert Armstrong and Nicholas Herries, in Hugh Walpole's *The Bright Pavilions*, fight and defeat Captain Winterset and his four thugs (sent by Herries's enemy Irvine) in 'an old tower', which is probably fictitious. If it does exist, you would now need a helicopter to find it.

CONISTON, FROM THE WOOD ABOVE BANK GROUND
Thomas Aspland, 1868

From How Head cottage continue 200yds S to **Lanehead**, now an outdoor pursuits centre, a large well-proportioned mid-Victorian house on a site formerly occupied by the Halfpenny Alehouse, where Turner is said to have stayed in 1797, sketching in preparation for his first Royal Academy exhibit, 'Morning Among the Coniston Fells'.

The present house was the home of W.G. Collingwood, painter, author, archaeologist and secretary to John Ruskin. Arthur Ransome became a family friend and was a frequent visitor between 1903 and 1913; he gives a vivid and affectionate account of the Collingwoods' family life in his *Autobiography*. A particularly close friend was the young Robin, later famous as the philosopher R.G. Collingwood. With the Collingwoods Ransome took up sailing, which soon became an obsession; they would sail in the Collingwoods' boat *Swallow* to picnic on Peel Island, and after 1908 Ransome would borrow a boat called *Jamrach* from Tent Lodge to race against *Swallow*.

Later Lanehead provided the principal model for 'Beckfoot', home of Peggy and Nancy Blackett (the Amazons), their longsuffering mother and her brother Jim Turner ('Captain Flint') in Ransome's *Swallows and Amazons* and its sequels.

R.G. Collingwood in his autobiography recalls his childhood here: his father was poor, and Robin was educated at home, beginning 'Latin at four and Greek at six', learning to paint from his father's artist friends and at eight trying to read Kant's *Theory of Ethics*: he could not understand a word of it, but felt 'intense excitement' and knew that he must become a philosopher.

200yds S of Lanehead is the gate to the sloping drive down to **Bank Ground Farm**, a long, old, rambling farmhouse and the original of 'Holly Howe', where the Walker family spend the summer in *Swallows and Amazons*. It was formerly the holiday home of Arthur Ransome's friend Ernest Altounyan, a doctor with literary interests who married W.G. Collingwood's daughter Dora. In 1928 Altounyan and Ransome together bought two dinghies, *Swallow* and *Mavis*, and the exploits of the five Altounyan children, as they learned to sail on Coniston Water, inspired aspects of *Swallows and Amazons*, Ransome's first novel for children. The place looks just as it should, with a field below the house stretching down to the lake and a gate from the yard into the field. Ransome brought his first illustrator Clifford Webb here to draw the picture of Roger Walker 'tacking' in zig-zags up the field in the opening scene.

200yds S of the Bank Ground drive, a bridleway leads up into the woods, continuing parallel to the road for 1¼m to **Lawson Park**, an old, lonely, strange-looking group of farm buildings on the edge of forbidding pine woods above Brantwood. Richard Adams chose this as the fictional site for his sinister Animal Research station in *The Plague Dogs*. The bridleway continues to Low Parkamoor and High Nibthwaite, where it rejoins the road – a delightful walk through varied but gentle terrain. We continue, however, to follow the lakeside road.

Continue ½m to **Brantwood** (*open 11–5.30 every day mid-March to*

'HOLLY HOWE': BANK GROUND FARM
Clifford Webb, 1931

mid-November; winter season 11–4 Wednesday to Sunday; admission charge, car park), an eighteenth-century house with a complex patchwork of additions and extensions in a commanding site above Coniston Water. Best known as John Ruskin's home from 1872–1900, it has an extensive literary history.

Brantwood was bought in a dilapidated state in 1851 by W.J. Linton, Chartist, republican and wood-engraver, who in 1858 married the novelist Eliza Lynn. She describes the state of the garden, the house, and Linton's seven children from a previous marriage:

> Playing in the neglected, untrimmed garden, where never tree or bush were lopped or pruned, ... was a troop of little children ... all dressed exactly alike – in long blouses of that coarse blue flannel with which housemaids scrub floors ... But they were as lovely as angels ...
>
> The house itself was found and furnished on the same lines. There were no carpets, but there were rare pictures and first proofs unframed; casts of noble cinque-cento work, darkened with dust; superb shells; and all the precious lumber of an artist's home, crowded on shelves of roughhewn, unvarnished deal set against the unpapered whitewashed wall. There were not enough chairs for the family and empty packing-cases eked out the deficiency.

In 1863 the Lintons collaborated on *The Lake Country*, a guidebook written by Eliza with Linton's engravings, and at Brantwood Eliza wrote *Witch Stories* (1861) and her novels *Lizzie Lorton of Greyrigg* (1866) – set in a composite Cumbrian landscape – and *Sowing the Wind* (1867). But she soon tired of Linton's fecklessness and domestic chaos. The marriage broke up; she went to London and Linton to America. The house was let briefly to Gerald Massey (1828–1907), now forgotten but once a popular poet and the author of many strange books on religion and mythology.

Ruskin bought the house in 1871. He loved Coniston Water so much that in the delirium of a fever a few months before in Derbyshire he had longed to lie down in the lake, and when Brantwood came on the market he bought it without seeing it. He was pleased and amused when he arrived to find Linton's printing-press 'still in one of the outhouses, and "God and the People" scratched deep in the whitewash outside'.

Ruskin built the boathouse and the turret room with its view over the lake. He delighted in the changing beauty of the landscape with dangerous intensity: it came to dominate his wildly fluctuating moods so that at times a change of light could hurl him into ecstasy or, more often, terrible depression. One brief extract, chosen from many such passages in his diaries, will give the flavour:

> *February 22nd, 1883. Thursday*. Yesterday a fearfully dark mist all
> afternoon with steady south plague-wind of the bitterest, nastiest,
> poisonous blight and fretful flutter. I could scarcely stay in the wood for
> the horror of it. To-day, really rather bright blue and bright semi-cumuli,
> with the frantic Old Man blowing sheaves of lancets and chisels across the
> lake; not in strength enough, or whirl enough, to raise it in spray, but
> tracing every squall's outline in black on the silver grey waves, and
> whistling meanly, as if on a flute made of a file.

Visitors included Charles Darwin and J.A. Froude, the artists Burne-Jones, Holman Hunt, Kate Greenaway and Walter Crane, and the book designer and fine printer Sidney Cockerell. Major works written here include Ruskin's autobiography *Praeterita* and *Fors Clavigera*. He died of influenza in the house in 1900.

Brantwood today contains a major collection of Ruskin's drawings and paintings, with his mineral, shell and other scientific collections, and paintings by his friends and associates. Much of the original furniture is on display, as are his boat and the double Brougham carriage he designed for his 1875 tour.

The appearance of the house in Ruskin's day has been recreated and makes an effective introduction to Ruskin's various and inspiring activities. There are also a bookshop and an excellent restaurant. For a modern novel dealing with Ruskin's increasingly strange and hallucinatory life here, see Peter Hoyle's *Brantwood* (1986).

The view from Brantwood is famous, and may be sampled from the car park or from the terrace in front of the restaurant. Coleridge admired the view from somewhere about this point in 1802, commenting

> The head of the Lake is an admirable junction of awful & of pleasing
> Simplicity./it is beyond all the other lakes perfectly intelligible – Conceive
> a crescent of Hills, or rather a crescent hill, enfolding the first mile of
> water/this hill of various height and various outline, but no where
> high/above this hill at the head of the Lake ... high mountain[s] of a

remarkable sternness & simplicity, one-coloured, as seen at a distance, & dark-coloured/its boldest parts are first, the Bell & the Scrow, two black peaks, perfectly breast-shaped & lying abreast of each other, the whole Bosom of a Brobdignag Negress, & on one side of them the Lever's water-fall.

One sees exactly what he means, but cannot help wondering what Ruskin would have made of this cheerfully erotic interpretation. Ruskin, in fact, had his own names for several of these features, calling the **Bell** (the left 'breast') 'St George's Hill' and its partner, **Scrow Crag**, 'Lion Crag', with the crag to R of that on the other side of Church Beck (actually **Long Crag**) renamed 'Tiger Crag'.

1m S of Brantwood, above the road, is **The Heald**, a long stone bungalow, home of Arthur Ransome from 1940 to 1945. Ransome loved the view of the Old Man from the windows – 'better even than the view from Brantwood' – and the house itself, 'of grey Coniston Stone ... roofed with green slate from the Old Man'. Here in 1941 Ransome wrote *Missee Lee*, in 1942 *The Picts and the Martyrs* and in 1944 part of *Great Northern?* He also began a historical novel, *The River Comes First*, which he never finished. The wood above the house (imaginatively transferred to the other side of the lake) suggested 'Heald Wood', where Titty and Roger meet the charcoal burners in Chapter 30 of *Swallowdale*.

Continue S for 2m. Where the road moves away from the lakeshore in a wood a picturesque, rocky, tree-covered promontory juts out into the lake. This is **High Peel Near** and is reached by a stile and path from the road. There is no good parking-place nearby. It is a pleasant place to explore and scramble about on, and is West's second 'station' for viewing Coniston Water, giving what he judged 'the finest view of the lake'. Possibly the first 'station' was where the large house of **Water Park** now stands, near Nibthwaite.)

A couple of hundred yards offshore from High Peel Near is **Peel Island**, so-called from the fact that there was once a small tower or 'pele' on it. The island was a favourite picnicking-place

'THE HIDDEN HARBOUR': PEEL ISLAND
Clifford Webb, 1931

of Arthur Ransome and the Collingwood family, and in 1910 Ransome corrected the proofs of his book *Edgar Allan Poe* on the island; Collingwood's youngest daughter, Ursula, delivered them, swimming out from shore with the proofs tied to her head. The following year, Ransome nearly wrecked his borrowed boat, *Jamrach*, on the island's rocks, an adventure he later used fictionally for John's accident with *Swallow* in *Swallowdale*. Peel Island was the chief model for the 'Wildcat Island' of *Swallows and Amazons*, contributing in particular the 'secret harbour' which lies concealed by jagged rocks at its S end. Ransome took a sprig of heather from the island when he went as a foreign correspondent to Russia in 1913 and kept it with him through the Russian Revolution.

Continue 1½m S to **High Nibthwaite**. At the centre of the village by the post box, its gardens hidden by a wall and laurel hedge, is **Laurel House**, formerly a farm. Arthur Ransome spent his summer holidays here from early childhood until 1897, when he was thirteen. He remembered the farm as 'paradise', with its familiar smells, old butter-churn, 'the grandfather clock in the kitchen still whirring wheezily as it struck the hours', its 'sociable' three-seater earth-closet in the garden, the damson-orchard, bee-hives and blue-and-red haycart and, best of all, the boat, drawn up by the old stone dock at the lakeside in 'shallow, clear water which always seemed alive with minnows'. Here Ransome would perform a secret rite:

> Without letting the others know what I was doing, I had to dip my hand in the water, as a greeting to the beloved lake or as a proof to myself that I had indeed come home. In later years, even as an old man, I have laughed at myself, resolved not to do it, and every time I have done it again.

The farm features in Ransome's novels as 'Swainson's Farm'. It does not resemble the illustrations but the back of the house, with its stonepaved passage and kitchen, corresponds to the description in *Swallowdale*, where Peggy, Titty and Roger come here for milk and listen to old Mr Swainson's songs.

Go through the gate behind the house. 'Sharp to the right through the gate', recalled Ransome, 'a grass track led up the sides of Brockbarrow' where was a group of rocks 'something like a boat' which Ransome called 'the Gondola' and from which the steamer pier on Coniston Water and the real *Gondola* could be seen. The outcrop, which has a grassy boatshaped hollow in the top, is 150yds up the track at a corner. Look NW and you can see the pier.

Go down again to the gate and follow the unpaved road to Bethecar and Parkamoor; about ¼m up this road on R is the roughly cube-shaped **'Knickerbockerbreaker'** – 'a smooth precipitous rock easy to climb from one side for the pleasure of sliding down its face' on which Ransome wore out many pairs of shorts and which he introduced (shifting its location to the novel's hidden valley) into *Swallowdale*: readers will remember the illustration of Roger being darned over Mary Swainson's knee. The rock is alarmingly large; a child sliding down it would seem more likely to get a broken ankle than torn trousers.

½m S of High Nibthwaite, turn R (w; signed Water Yeat). A footpath leads upstream along the River Crake for ¼m towards, but not reaching, **Allan Tarn**, a rushy circular pool surrounded by bog and willows which was the model for the 'Octopus Lagoon' of *Swallows and Amazons*. The tarn is surrounded by private land and there is no right of way. Continue to Water Yeat and at the junction turn R (N) on A5084.

Beacon Tarn

After ¾m notice sign for Lake Bank and just after it the Blawith Common car park. Immediately up the fell about 1m due W of here is **Beacon Tarn**, completely hidden until you are almost upon it yet unexpectedly large – almost a lake – and beautiful. This is the 'Trout Tarn' of Arthur Ransome's *Swallowdale*, where Jacky teaches Roger to 'guddle' trout. Easily identified as the highest craggy outcrop ⅓m NNE of the tarn is **Beacon Hill**, which probably suggested the 'Watch Tower' of *Swallowdale* and appears on an early sketchmap drawn for the novel by Arthur Ransome.

The question which naturally arises now is, where is **Swallowdale** itself? Arthur Ransome, like his characters, always refused to reveal the location of the real Swallowdale. Many people have found it, but so far the secret has been kept, and it would be a pity to deprive others of the opportunity of finding it for themselves. The latest authority, Roger Wardale, gives the clue that it is in the triangular area between the A593, A5084 and A5092 roads. One may add that it is by no means easy to find, and that you are perhaps most likely to discover it as Roger and Titty did, by following a beck.

From the Blawith car park follow the road 2¼m N to join A593 at Torver.

The Old Man and Walna Scar

Coniston is the obvious starting point for climbing **Coniston Old Man**, one of Lakeland's most impressive peaks and peculiarly difficult of access because of its wealth of steep and rugged foothills. Several ascents begin from the Walna Scar Road (discussed below). For detailed guidance on the approaches, see Wainwright or another fellwalker's guide.

The mountain's name is Celtic: originally it was *allt maen*, 'high cairn', and until the early nineteenth century it was more commonly known simply as 'Coniston Fell'. For centuries it has been a major centre of slate-quarrying. Wordsworth gives a fine description of one of the quarries in his early poem 'An Evening Walk':

> I love to mark the quarry's moving trains,
> Dwarf panniered steeds, and men, and numerous wains:
> How busy all the enormous hive within,
> While Echo dallies with its various din!

Some (hear you not their chisels' clinking sound?)
Toil, small as pigmies in the gulf profound;
Some, dim between the lofty cliffs descried,
O'erwalk the slender plank from side to side;
These, by the pale blue rocks that ceaseless ring,
In airy baskets hanging, work and sing.

The slate was carried by pack-ponies to Waterhead on Coniston Water, whence it was shipped in barges to the foot of the lake. Quarrying still goes on, and from time to time you may hear strange rumblings and the boom of blasting.

In a sense, the Old Man's summit is referred to in Wordsworth's sonnet 'Nuns fret not at their convent's narrow room', where, expressing his own happiness as a poet within the limitations of the sonnet, he notes that

> bees that soar for bloom
> High as the highest peak of Furness-fells,
> Will murmur by the hour in foxglove bells.

In Wordsworth's day 'Furness Fells' meant most of the high ground of SW Lakeland, including the Coniston fells; hence their 'highest peak' would be the Old Man. The foxgloves, of course, will be found in the valleys, not at the summit: the poem's point is that the same bees are happy to visit both.

Thomas Wilkinson (who calls it quaintly 'The Man Mountain') climbed the Old Man early in the nineteenth century and reports

> I added seven stones to the fabric [of the summit cairn] but declined looking down, for I wished not my present tranquillity to be disturbed by giddiness.

Tennyson and Coventry Patmore climbed it in 1850. On the way they refreshed themselves from a bottle, got 'rather glorious', and raced down the mountain, according to Patmore, 'six times faster than we had ascended'.

CONISTON OLD MAN FROM BRANTWOOD
W. J. Linton, 1864

The Old Man is the 'Kanchenjunga' of Arthur Ransome's novels, and held great personal significance for Ransome, who was carried up to the summit as a baby by his father. 'I think no younger human being can ever have been there,' he reflects in his *Autobiography*. In 1903, on holiday from his publishing job in London, he was lying on a flat rock between two torrents of the Coppermines Beck trying to write a poem, when a voice hailed him: 'Young man, are you alive?' It was W.G. Collingwood, who quickly became his friend and mentor. Ransome carried a 'lucky stone' from the summit of the Old Man in his boat *Racundra* when he cruised in the Baltic collecting material for his book *Racundra's First Cruise* in 1923. Later he kept the stone on his writing desk.

In his novel *Swallowdale* the children climb 'Kanchenjunga' by following Church Beck and making a half-way camp at the head of Coppermines Valley. They then climb Brim Fell (SSE from Levers Water) past Low Water to the summit. They could hardly have chosen a more awkward approach, and not surprisingly it is on Brim Fell –

> a steep face of rock, not really difficult, because there were cracks running across it which made good footholds and handholds, but not a good place to tumble down, because there was nothing to stop you and there were a lot of loose stones at the bottom of it

– that Roger loses his footing on the rock, badly spraining his ankle.

In the summit cairn (the same one augmented a century before by Thomas Wilkinson) the children find 'a small round brass box' with a note commemorating the Amazons' relatives' climb of thirty years before (August 2 1901), and add their own message before replacing it; "'And now perhaps it won't be found for ages and ages till people wear quite different sorts of clothes," said Titty.'

From Coniston village an ancient unpaved road leads SW past the base of the Old Man. This is the **Walna Scar Road**, once used by packhorses and quarrymen, which continues W over into the Duddon Valley. To reach it, take the signed path by the Sun Inn at the W edge of Coniston, then take turning above Dixon Ground Farm (signed Old Man, Walna Scar). Ignore a well-used route with many tyre tracks leading off uphill and continue ahead but at a very large pile of stones after 2m go straight ahead for Walna Scar and the Duddon Valley, or R (NE) uphill on grassy track for **Goat's Water** and the Old Man. (You can also reach Seathwaite Tarn and the Duddon by going 1¼m NNW from Goat's Water).

In decent weather all these are very fine though strenuous walks. Of the route to Goat's Water, Geoffrey Winthrop Young writes,

> The long-winding and springing grass track up round the Old Man of Coniston, to the tarn under Dow Crag [i.e. Goat's Water] in the autumn when the bracken was red-russet and the silver birches a bright gold and the snow-covered domes of the fells enormous as Himalaya upon the cold-blue evening skies, I have often thought to be the most beautiful walk in Europe.

Andrew Young's 1939 poem 'The Thunderstorm' records impressions of the same walk in the opposite direction, beginning at Goat's Water and heading to the old road:

> When Coniston Old Man was younger
> And his deep-quarried sides were stronger
> Goats may have leapt about Goat's Water;
> But why the tarn that looks like its young daughter
> Though lying high under the fell
> Should be called Blind Tarn, who can tell?
>
> For From Dow Crag, passing it by,
> I saw it as a dark presageful eye.

The name is easily explained, for Blind Tarn (one of several in the Lake District), like a 'blind' alley, has no outlet. Goat's Water itself is hugely impressive, a Stygian pool enclosed between charcoal-grey screes, the only speck of colour the bright blue of an ominously-placed first-aid box at the foot of the fearsome **Dow Crag** (from which the unpleasant Geoffrey Westcott falls to his death in Adams's *The Plague Dogs*). Until the turn of the century there were goats here, descended from escapers from a local farm.

The other route, following the road over to the Duddon Valley and descending into Seathwaite, features in Richard Parkinson's 1843 novel *The Old Church Clock*: the hero and his family, bound for Seathwaite, meet Robert Walker, the curate, cutting peat up here with his family.

Yewdale and Tarn Hows

Take the main road (A593) N from Coniston. At the road junction as you leave the village you will see the sign for the youth hostel. This is **Holly How**, a large Victorian stone house whose name Arthur Ransome transferred to Bank Ground Farm for the purposes of *Swallows and Amazons*. The road continues into the beautiful valley of **Yewdale**, described (from the N) in Wordsworth's 'Epistle to Sir George ... Beaumont':

> Descend and reach, in Yewdale's depths, a plain
> With haycocks studded, striped with yellowing grain –
> An area level as a Lake and spread
> Under a rock too steep for man to tread,
> Where sheltered from the north and bleak north-west
> Aloft the Raven hangs a visible nest,
> Fearless of all assaults that would her brood molest.

As we shall see, Wordsworth knew all about those ravens. ¾am after leaving Coniston, however, look out for the sign to **Low Yewdale**, a delightful white-rendered stone farmhouse. At the E end of the house is a small cottage where Arthur Ransome spent the summer of 1908 'under Raven Crag [he means **Yewdale Crag**, across the road to the W], at the head of the Coniston Valley'. In bad weather he worked in the house; in good weather he used a tent 'on a small mound close to Yewdale Beck a few hundred yards up the valley'. The mound is the rocky knoll 200yds E of the cottage. Later he used the farmhouse as the model for Dixon's Farm in his novel *Winter Holiday*.

Yewdale Beck and indeed the whole valley were favourite spots of Ruskin's; they are often mentioned in his works, and he used the Beck to illustrate his strange and fascinating geological lecture *Yewdale and its Streamlets* (1877).

⅓m further N on the road take the turning L (N; signed Tilberthwaite Ghyll) and continue to car park. 250yds S of car park is **Penny Rigg Quarry**, the model for Slater Bob's Mine in Ransome's *Pigeon Post*. You will see two tunnels, one of them with the rusted iron rails of a tramway vanishing into the darkness. A source of fine-quality green slate, the mine was shown to Ransome in 1935 by John William Shaw, its operator and the original of Slater Bob. Its layout matches the description of Slater Bob's mine, and it was formerly connected to the Tilberthwaite Copper Mine (higher up Weatherlam) by a thousand-yard-long tunnel, Tilberthwaite Deep Level, depicted as the tunnel used by the children in *Pigeon Post* to escape after the entrance collapses behind them.

We are now at the base of **Weatherlam**, which slopes straight up W above us and is the 'Grey Screes' of Arthur Ransome's *Swallowdale* and *Pigeon Post*, where its SE slopes, the Yewdale Fells, modelled as 'High Topps' (though Ransome placed them S of the Old Man's summit). Ransome explored the slate quarries and tunnels ('the hundred holes of Weatherlam') here in March 1935 with his friend Oscar Gnosspelius, a former prospector (and model for Timothy, *alias* Squashy Hat), whilst researching for *Pigeon Post*.

On no account should these tunnels or any other openings in this area be entered. Many apparently safe levels contain dangerous floors or roofs and concealed vertical drops. Here is a cautionary tale (1886) from John Barrow:

> On our descent [from the Old Man] we visited the coppermines ... I led the way, and walked steadily on through the tunnel, till it got darker and darker, and my only thought at the moment was, how far daylight might still penetrate, looking up to the roof of the tunnel. My companion suddenly asked me if I had a match. I stopped on the instant, and lit one. He made an exclamation, and I the remark, 'It was lucky you asked me for a light, or I should have knocked my head against those beams.' 'Those beams!' he said; 'look at your feet!' and on looking down I found myself on the very verge of a shaft (which neither he nor I could possibly have seen), down which another step would inevitably have taken me ...
>
> On subsequent inquiry, I found that had I fallen into this shaft, I should have struck a narrow platform some twenty feet below, and if I had bounded off it, which was nearly certain to have happened, I should have gone down fifty fathoms!

Return to A593. Some 200yds E of the junction is a stone bridge over

Yewdale Beck. Look due N from the bridge: you will see a small wood with a row of steep crags above it. The L (W) end of the series is **Raven Crag**, the probable site of the young Wordsworth's perilous assaults on ravens' nests described in a splendid passage of the first book of *The Prelude*:

> Nor less when spring had warmed the cultured Vale,
> Moved we as plunderers where the mother-bird
> Had in high places built her lodge; though mean
> Our object and inglorious, yet the end
> Was not ignoble. Oh! when I have hung
> Above the raven's nest, by knots of grass
> And half-inch fissures in the slippery rock
> But ill sustained, and almost (so it seemed)
> Suspended by the blast that blew amain,
> Shouldering the naked crag, oh, at that time,
> While on the perilous ridge I hung alone,
> With what strange utterance did the loud dry wind
> Blow through my ear! The sky seemed not a sky
> Of earth – and with what motion moved the clouds!

A bounty was paid for ravens' nests, as the birds were thought to harm lambs.

Continue N for 1½m and note the sign for **High Arnside Farm**, the model for 'High Tarn Farm', setting of Marjorie Lloyd's *Fell Farm* children's books. *Fell Farm Holiday* (1951) describes the 'low, whitewashed farm', which 'nestled into a grassy, rocky knoll, that rose as high as the chimneys at the back.' (You cannot park or drive up the approach road to the farm; but there is a small lay-by offering a few parking-places ¼m back towards Coniston). 100yds up the approach to the farm a bridleway goes off S. Look L (E) from this path after ¼m to see a small tarn, beautiful, hidden and apparently nameless. This is the tarn frequently mentioned (as **High Tarn**) in the Fell Farm books – readers may recall it as the one where Jan found the heron with its leg frozen into the ice.

Another ¼m brings us to that magical place **Tarn Hows** which, despite having appeared on more calendars than Marilyn Monroe, keeps a mysteri-

'HIGH TARN': VIEW NORTH-WEST FROM HIGH ARNSIDE
Marjorie Lloyd, 1951

ous and pristine beauty. This delightfully irregular miniature lake with its densely wooded shores and promontories is certainly one of the loveliest places in the Lake District, and it is hard to believe that it is artificial, created in the nineteenth century by damming a beck – a uniquely success-ful piece of landscaping. (It can also be reached from car parks on the small road that runs N off the Coniston-Hawkshead road just opposite Monk Coniston.)

Its literary associations are modest but attractive. Arthur Ransome skated here in 1933 with Titty, Taqui and Susan Altounyan; their exploits whilst learning to skate inspired parts of Chapter 5 of *Winter Holiday*. And Jan and Hyacinth are marooned on Tarn Hows Island in Chapter 17 of Marjorie Lloyd's *Fell Farm Campers* (1960), which gives a vivid descrip-tion of the island's thickly wooded interior. The road continues NE to Skelwith Bridge.

Hawkshead

Leave Coniston heading E on B5285, as if making for Brantwood, but at the junction ⅓m after the Waterhead Hotel keep on the main road (signed Hawkshead). On the corner after ¼m you reach **Boon Crag Cottage**, a long, low traditional house described in Richard Parkinson's *The Old Church Clock* (1843), set partly in Yewdale in the 1780s and 90s. Poor enough as literature, the book gives an interesting sketch of daily life here. The hero lives in this house: it was

> low, and built of cobbles, ... one end ... had fallen in, and was used as a hen-roost and cart-house, but the main part of the house was well slated with good brown flat stones, out of Coniston Old Man, and had two chimneys at the top as tall and round as a church ... There was a great broad plane tree at the end of it ... and a large thorn before the door ... with the top of it cut into the shape of a cock.

The reference to local topiary is interesting. The trees are gone and the house has been renovated, but it is still recognisable.

200yds further uphill is the gateway to **Monk Coniston**, a large mansion which is now a hotel. In Victorian times it was one of the several Lakeland properties of the influential Marshall family. Tennyson brought C.L. Dodgson ('Lewis Carroll') here in July 1857 to lunch with them. Dodgson 'lunched and dined' here again two days later; possibly he found the company less than sparkling, for he recorded that 'it rained hard all the afternoon, which gave me an opportunity for some Integral Calculus.'

Continue (some 3m) along B5285 over Hawkshead Hill to **Hawkshead** (*several large car parks, clearly signed*). From the early sixteenth century until the nineteenth the town (little more than a village to modern eyes) was an important marketing centre for local industries of spinning and weaving, the woollen thread and cloth being taken S by pack-horse. Like most of the Furness area it also supplied forest products such as baskets, hurdles and charcoal.

A local delicacy, and a favourite with the young Wordsworth, was Hawkshead Cake, a round pasty nearly two inches thick and eleven across made from puff pastry and filled with currants, brown sugar, butter and cream. It is no longer made but deserves a revival.

At the centre of the town in Main Street is the **Beatrix Potter Gallery** (*NT, open 1 April – 1 October, Monday-Friday 10.30–4.30 (last admission 4); admission charge*). The Gallery occupies the former offices of William Heelis, Beatrix Potter's solicitor husband; some rooms recreate the offices as they might have been during his occupancy, with original furniture, books and papers, and even a set of his golf-clubs in a corner. Other rooms display a selection of Beatrix Potter's watercolour paintings and book-illustrations. (At any time 80 out of some 500 are on display; the selection is changed annually, so return visits are worthwhile). The rich colouring and sharp outlines of the illustrations are a revelation even when you know the printed versions. Look for the fine details of the background landscapes, and for pictures with small areas covered by sections of paper meticulously pasted on to alter a detail.

There are also photographs of Potter and the Lake District farms which she left to the National Trust; landscape photographs by her father, Rupert Potter; and a collection of trophies won at shows by her Herdwick sheep.

Opposite the Gallery is the **Co-op**, used by Potter for the line drawing of Tuppeny's house in *The Fairy Caravan*. L (S) of the Gallery and opposite Post Office is **Thimble Hall**, model for the Misses Pussycats' shop in *The Fairy Caravan*, where a drawing shows Louisa and Mary Ellen creeping towards the door. Across the street is the **Queen's Head Inn**, formerly 'Postlethwaite's', where in August 1896 Beatrix Potter watched the arrival of Bostock and Wombwell's Menagerie, a sight which also contributed to *The Fairy Caravan*:

> the two first Vans, driven by elephants and camels, ... stopped to take
> water out of buckets at Postlethwaite's Inn. One of the elephants
> appreciated a heap of road sweepings which it sprinkled all over its back,
> and blew the dust on to its belly and legs. They doubled up their legs into
> strange contortions, kicking at the flies, the school-children dancing round
> the road and screaming.

Continue S along Main Street and R after the Sun Inn for **Hawkshead Grammar School** (*open Easter to October, weekdays 10–12.30, 1.30–5.00 (4.30 in October); Sundays 1–5; admission charge*), a substantial two-storey sixteenth-century building. William Wordsworth and his brothers attended the school (founded 1585 by Archbishop Sandys of York), Wordsworth being there from 1779 to 1787. The school gave an excellent education to about a hundred boys.

The lower room contains oak desks and benches heavily carved with boys' names and initials; Wordsworth cut his name into the desk just to R of the entrance. (Malcolm Lowry visited in 1957 and told a friend, 'we sat at the desk of the old man himself in Hawkshead, which is exactly like Tlaxcala in Mexico, examining the words mysteriously written thereon: W

Wordsworth'.) On the opposite wall is the 'tablet' listing the names of the schoolmasters, as described in Wordsworth's poem 'Matthew' (of the two wooden boards only the R one, which ends in 1758, was here in Wordsworth's time). The initials 'WW' can be found carved on the desk facing it, so perhaps he sometimes sat here.

Wordsworth was inspired, and probably introduced to recent poetry, by the schoolmaster William Taylor and his successor after 1786, James Bowman. He later drew on memories of Taylor for the character of Matthew, the 'village schoolmaster/With hair of glittering grey' described in 'Expostulation and Reply', 'Matthew', 'The Two April Mornings' and the other elegiac 'Matthew' poems. 'Address to the Scholars of the Village School of – 1798' seems to have Taylor in mind, sympathising with the long hours he spent in the classroom:

> Here did he sit confined for hours;
> But he could see the woods and plains,
> Could hear the wind and mark the showers
> Come streaming down the streaming panes.

The upper schoolroom, where the older boys were taught, displays the account-book of Ann Tyson (with whom Wordsworth lodged during his schooldays) and other items. The S window-sill has the name 'I. Wordsworth' carved by the poet's brother John. The school library, still complete, includes Archbishop Sandys's personal copy of the *Bishops' Bible*, which he helped to translate.

Wordsworth wrote his first poems whilst a pupil at the school. For its bicentenary in 1785 he produced 'Lines Written as a School Exercise' in what he later ruefully called 'a tame imitation of Pope's style'; of more significance was *The Vale of Esthwaite* (1787), 'a long poem running upon my own adventures and the scenery of the country in which I was brought up' and thus a forerunner of *The Prelude*. Its best passages were worked into his first published poem, *An Evening Walk*. Finally, he celebrated his departure from the school in 1786 with a poem that survives as the fragment 'Extract from the Conclusion of a Poem, Composed in Anticipation of Leaving School'. The school still has two books given jointly by Wordsworth and two other boys on leaving: they are a *History of Greece* and Hoole's translation of Tasso's *Jerusalem Delivered*.

Amongst Wordsworth's schoolfellows were the brothers Charles and John Farish, both of whom were minor poets: Charles's *The Minstrels of Winandermere* (1811) gives an account of the school; John published nothing, but his poem 'The Heath' gave Wordsworth an image for 'Guilt and Sorrow'.

Uphill just behind the school is **St Michael's Church**. It was attended by Wordsworth and his schoolfellows on most Sundays, and is the

> Snow-white church upon her hill
> Sit[ting] like a throned lady, sending out
> A gracious look all over her domain

above the 'azure smoke' of the town in Book IV of *The Prelude*. Its white rough-cast (a protection against damp in the days before modern cement) was removed in 1875–6, exposing the darker local stone. Its beautiful interior is light and finely proportioned, and the nave, with not-quite-circular piers supporting not-quite-semicircular arches, is unique in England. It is also rich in memorial tablets and has elaborate wall-paintings, many executed about 1680 by Joseph Addison of Hornby. In *The Excursion*'s Book V Wordsworth describes a church where

> Admonitory texts inscribed the walls,
> Each, in its ornamental scroll, enclosed;
> Each also crowned with wingèd heads – a pair
> Of rudely painted cherubim.

In other details that church seems to be Grasmere; but the murals there had gone before his time so he may well be remembering Hawkshead's: there are several fine cherubim to be seen here. Towards the E end of the S side of the nave is a white marble tablet to Elizabeth Smith of Coniston and her parents. De Quincey thought the inscription

> the scantiest record that, for a person so eminently accomplished, I have ever met with … Anything so unsatisfactory or so commonplace I have never known. As much, or more, is often said of the most insipid people; whereas Miss Smith was really a most extraordinary person.

Also on the S side is a tablet to James Bowman, friend and schoolmaster to Wordsworth at the Grammer School.

The churchyard has a fine view of the mountains to the N. In 'There was a Boy' Wordsworth recalls a friend (largely a self-portrait) who he says died before he was twelve and was buried

> Upon a slope above the Village School,
> And there, along that bank, when I have pass'd
> At evening, I believe that oftentimes
> A full half hour together have I stood
> Mute – looking at the grave in which he lies.

The passage describes this churchyard, and at least one of Wordsworth's schoolfellows, John Tyson, was buried here (in 1782), though the spot is now unknown. Against the E end of the church is the long stone seat known as 'Church End' where Wordsworth, like other villagers, frequently sat. Against the same wall is a gravestone praising Thomas Cowperthwaite, ironmonger (d 1782), for his 'facetious disposition, together with his other good qualities'. Cowperthwaite figures in Wordsworth's poem 'The Fountain' as 'Leonard', who

> sang those witty rhymes
> About the crazy old church-clock,
> And the bewildered chimes.

He was well known as a local wit and several scraps of his humorous doggerel survive.

Leave churchyard by lychgate and turn R to Market Square. On R is the **Market House**, built in 1790 and enlarged in 1887. It contained Assembly Rooms where meetings and balls were held. In *The Prelude* Wordsworth recalls his disgust at finding, on a return visit to Hawkshead, that

> A grey stone
> Of native rock, left midway in the square
> Of our small market village…

where an old lady had kept a stall for sixty years

> was split, and gone to build
> A smart Assembly-room that perked and flared
> With wash and rough-cast elbowing the ground
> Which had been ours.

The building has now lost its white roughcast.

Across the square is the **King's Arms Hotel**. The arch at R of the Hotel is shown in Beatrix Potter's *The Tale of Johnny Town-Mouse* (1918) with the carrier's cart standing under it. The hamper containing Timmy Willie is being handed to a maid, who stands at the door of the house which is now a café. (Beatrix Potter has moved this door back towards the arch.) The interior of the house (whose owner had a hamper of vegetables sent from Sawrey every week) was also used for illustrations of Johnny Town-Mouse's residence.

Go through the King's Arms arch and L through another arch (this one appears in a line-drawing for *The Pie and the Patty-Pan* showing Ribby and Duchess passing in the street) to reach **Ann Tyson's Cottage**, a picturesque traditional Lakeland stone house where Wordsworth lodged (1779–83), one of several Grammar School boys who lived here. Ann kept a small grocery and haberdashery shop in the house; her husband Hugh was a joiner. (Claims that Wordsworth worshipped in the chapel up the steps to the left are probably mistaken.) The Tysons and their boarders moved to Colthouse, ½m away, in 1783.

ANN TYSON'S COTTAGE
John M'Whirter, 1882

Esthwaite Water (West Bank), Graythwaite and Finsthwaite

½m SE of Hawkshead is **Esthwaite Water**, a beautiful though not a spectacular lake: as De Quincey says,

> though a lovely scene in its summer garniture of woods, [it] has no features of permanent grandeur to rely upon. A wet or gloomy day, even in summer, reduces it to little more than a wildish pond, surrounded by miniature hills.

It was therefore slow to attract visitors: De Quincey could write in 1839 that 'few tourists ever trouble the repose' of the lake or of nearby Hawkshead. But Beatrix Potter thought it 'The most beautiful of the Lakes' and used it for the setting of *The Tale of Mr Jeremy Fisher* (1906).

During his schooldays Wordsworth spent countless hours exploring the borders of the lake. His early poem *An Evening Walk* (1793) gives a glimpse of a hot summer afternoon there, and one of his best-known poems, 'Expostulation and Reply', is set (despite having been written in Somerset) 'One morning ... by Esthwaite's lake,/When life was sweet, I knew not why'. Although its advocacy of 'a wise passiveness' against bookish philosophy probably arose out of arguments with Hazlitt, the 'Matthew' with whom the poet disagrees is based on William Taylor, master at Hawkshead Grammar School.

Wordsworth probably skated here when the lake froze in hard winters, though the skating episode in *The Prelude* Book I draws on memories of both Esthwaite and Windermere: the 'cottage windows' that 'through the twilight blazed' could have been those of nearby Colthouse. There were swans on Esthwaite (described in *An Evening Walk*) and the young poet relished 'the daily opportunities [he] had of observing their habits'. Two pairs 'divided the lake ... between them,' he recalled in old age, 'never trespassing a single yard upon each other's separate domain.'

Not all Esthwaite's associations were so pleasant: he recalls in *The Prelude* how in 1779, during his first week at school, he noticed on the shore 'A heap of garments, left, as I supposed,/By one who there was bathing.' The clothes were still there next day and the nine-year-old Wordsworth watched as men

> Sounded with grappling irons and long poles.
> At length, the dead man, 'mid that beauteous scene
> Of trees and hills and water, bolt upright
> Rose with his ghastly face, a spectre shape
> Of terror.

Take the road (signed Newby Bridge) S from Hawkshead. After 1m at a small wood we pass **Esthwaite Lodge** (now Hawkshead Youth Hostel), home of the novelist Francis Brett Young from 1928 to 1932.

Young found this fine Regency house, beautiful and mysteriously empty, the front door ajar, as he drove S after a visit to Hugh Walpole in September 1928. He rented it at once and here, in the 'beautiful ... library with its soft apple-green walls' he wrote *Jim Redlake* (1930), *Mr and Mrs Pennington* (1931) and his best-known novel, *The House Under the Water* (1932) – all of them set in Wales or his native West Midlands.

He worked with the window open, and kept a tin of nuts on his desk for squirrels, who would come in and help themselves. Visitors included (in July 1930) Thomas Hardy's widow, Florence, and in the same month Hugh Walpole, who finished the Parisian section of *Judith Paris* in the bed-sitting room (now the hostel's Dormitory 2) overlooking Esthwaite Water. (The view inspired him to add the room over the library at Brackenburn.) Edward Marsh, aesthete and editor of the famous *Georgian Poetry* anthologies, also stayed: his prolonged mutterings in the bath aroused fears for his sanity, but it turned out he was merely learning *Paradise Lost* by heart. In 1932 Young moved to Worcestershire, where, he explained, 'rainfall is twenty-three inches against eighty'.

The house still has its fine oval staircase and extravagantly ornate plaster and woodwork. The dining-room, probably once the library, contains a collection of books by Young and one of his huge built-in floor-to-ceiling bookcases.

¼m further S the road passes the gentle green slopes of **Strickland Ees**, probably the 'green peninsula' 'shaped like [an] ear' from which the young Wordsworth looked across the lake and saw the drowned man's pile of clothes.

Another ½m brings us to **Esthwaite Hall**, a pleasant white-rendered farmhouse (the older-looking unrendered building beside it is a modern barn conversion), birthplace of Archbishop Edwin Sandys (1516–1588), founder of Hawkshead Grammar School, translator of the 'Bishops' Bible' and a dedicated ecclesiastical politician.

Two of Sandys' sons are also of importance: Edwin (1561–1629) was Treasurer of the Virginia Company and in 1619 helped organise the Assembly of Burgesses at Jamestown Church, the first representative assembly to be summoned in America. George (1578–1644) emigrated to Virginia and there completed a fine translation of Ovid's *Metamorphoses*, possibly the first significant English-language literary work to be written in America.

Graythwaite and Finsthwaite

Continue S 4m, partly through pleasant woods (the edge of Grizedale Forest). By the telephone box turn sharp L (NE) and go 1m until road comes for a moment to edge of lake. On a sharp corner after 200yds is a large stone barn. Take signed footpath over stile alongside lake (boots needed) to a wooded promontory, **Rawlinson Nab**, the 'interior nab' of which was West's fourth viewing-station for Windermere. It does not seem a very good viewpoint now; perhaps it was less treeclad in West's day. The tip of the promontory gives a better view. Return to the road junction.

200yds S are the imposing gates of **Graythwaite Hall**. The 'extensive woods' around the hall were a favourite haunt of the young Wordsworth, and the poem 'Nutting' arose out of memories of gathering hazel-nuts here.

The woods around the hall also provided settings for Beatrix Potter's *The Fairy Caravan*. Pony Billy is shown trotting through the woods, startled by roe-deer and the 'strange dwarfy figures' of the Oakmen (miniature versions of the charcoal-burners who worked here).

One of the Sandys dynasty living at the Hall is the hero of the traditional 'Holm Bank Hunting Song':

> One morning last winter to Holm Bank there came
> A brave noble sportsman, Squire Sandys was his name.

The Squire and his companions chase Reynard all over Low Furness before killing him at Grassguards in the Duddon Valley:

> You gentlemen and sportsmen, wherever you be,
> All you that love hunting, draw near unto me,
> Since Reynard is dead, we have heard his downfall,
> Here's a health to Squire Sandys of High Graythwaite Hall.
> Tally ho, tally ho! Hark forward away, tally ho!

This is 'High' Graythwaite Hall because some 300yds S is the humbler **Graythwaite Old Hall** (or 'Low Graythwaite Hall'), which family status outgrew some time in the eighteenth century. This is a seventeenth-century house notable for its superb topiary, a row of yews like giant chessmen running along the top of the front hedge.

¾m S on the lakeward (E) side of the road (we are now running alongside Windermere) is the beginning of the lakeside footpath which you must take N for half a mile to see **Silverholme**, a tiny island which is the 'Cormorant Island' of Arthur Ransome's *Swallows and Amazons*. In 1937 Ransome wrote that

> until a year or two ago the cormorants were there, and did a great deal of good by eating eels and thinning down the huge shoals of small perch. But now, alas, people have shot the cormorants.

There are now a fair number of cormorants around Windermere again. The island is less barren than Ransome described it, but in the middle is still to be seen the large fallen treetrunk under which Titty and Roger found Captain Flint's box. According to Collingwood, it used to be said that there was 'a kist [chest] of silver ligging under t' watter' near the island – a notion which may have suggested it as the hiding place for the Captain's literary treasure.

Return to road and continue 3m S to **Finsthwaite House** (set back from the road, ¾m S of Stott Park Bobbin Mill), an imposing Georgian mansion with pillared porch and well-clipped yew hedges, former home of Barbara Sneyd, whose account of her childhood (recorded in her diaries and watercolours) has been published as *Riding High, 1896–1903: Scenes from a Lakeland Childhood*. Barbara's charmed life of hunting, boating, picnics and balls ended in mysterious tragedy: a breakdown (perhaps precipitated by her fiancé's death in the Boer War) was followed by half a century spent obscurely in nursing-homes; she died, forgotten, in the 1950s.

The road continues S to Newby Bridge. We return to Hawkshead.

Outgate and Colthouse

1½m N of Hawkshead is the **Outgate Inn**. NW of it are a number of rocky knolls and small crags, which seem the most likely location for the 'crag … from the meeting-point/Of two highways ascending' where Wordsworth waited for the horses which were being sent to take him and his brothers home from school at Christmas 1783:

> 'twas a day
> Stormy, and rough, and wild, and on the grass
> I sate half-sheltered by a naked wall;
> Upon my right hand was a single sheep,
> A whistling hawthorn on my left, and there,
> With those companions at my side, I watched,
> Straining my eyes intensely, as the mist
> Gave intermitting prospect of the wood
> And plain beneath.

When he returned home it was to find his father ill, and within ten days he was dead. Wordsworth later found a mysterious symbolic quality in his memories of that eager waiting in the mist, looking down on the two roads and unaware of the approaching tragedy. The experience and its meaning are explored in *The Prelude* Book XI.

Later it was while walking along this road at sunset – 'in the way between Hawkshead and Ambleside' – in the summer of (probably) 1784, when he was fourteen, that Wordsworth was struck by the beauty of an oak tree. As he said in old age,

> The moment was important in my poetical history; for I date from it my consciousness of the infinite variety of natural appearances which had been unnoticed by poets of any age or country, so far as I was acquainted with them: and I made a resolution to supply in some degree the deficiency.

He made an attempt at sketching the fateful tree in his first published poem, *An Evening Walk*. The road continues N to Low Brathay and Clappersgate.

To reach **Colthouse**, if possible walk the ½m from Hawkshead as there is very little parking space. Leave Hawkshead by roads signed Windermere by ferry then take first turning L (signed Wray). By the sign announcing Colthouse turn L into small unmetalled lane. The white-rendered house on the corner with wooden fence, iron-hooped gate and slated porch is **Greenend Cottage** (*NT*), the most popular (though not the only) candidate for the house where Wordsworth lodged with Ann Tyson after her move from Hawkshead.

In *The Prelude* Book IV Wordsworth affectionately recalls Ann, 'my aged Dame', the garden with its 'spreading pine/And broad stone table underneath the boughs' and the brook, 'boxed/Within our garden' into a stone channel where it 'dimple[d] down' silently. The brook, still in its stone channel, can be seen flowing under the lane in front of the house after crossing a corner of the Greenend garden. Houses which now stand E of Greenend did not exist in Wordsworth's time, and from the cottage he could have had an uninterrupted view of Spring Wood, the

<blockquote>
copse,
An upright bank of wood and woody rock,
That opposite our rural dwelling stood,
</blockquote>

from which on sunny afternoons he would see 'a sparkling patch of diamond light' shining – probably the sun reflected from rock drenched by a beck in the wood, but seeming 'To have some meaning which I could not find'.

He and the other boarders had plenty of freedom: the excursions described in 'Nutting' were made from here, as were the other escapades (fishing, skating, wildfowling, roaming the fells) recalled in the first two books of *The Prelude*. The wildfowling probably took place on the hills to E and W of Hawkshead, on Claife Heights and Hawkshead Moor. Woodcock could be sold for the table and were a useful source of pocket-money.

One of Wordsworth's earliest poems, 'A Ballad' ('And will you leave me thus alone ... ') was written about the death of Mary Rigge, a young woman who had lived in Greenend and died in 1760, abandoned by her lover after giving birth to an illegitimate son. Wordsworth heard her story from Ann Tyson and wrote the poem when he was seventeen.

Wordsworth returned here in June 1788, after his first year at Cambridge, to stay for nine weeks. He looked at the valley and its people with 'something of another eye', now that he had experienced a more urban and sophisticated way of life, and later described the visit in *The Prelude*'s Book IV, 'Summer Vacation'. It was probably also this visit that he recalls in his sonnet '"Beloved Vale! ..."'

During the same summer holiday he began to write *An Evening Walk* (published in 1793), completing it here the following summer.

But all this may not have happened at Greenend, for local tradition insists that Beatrix Potter, herself drawing on information from neighbours, indicated a different site for Wordsworth's lodging, a building which no longer stands. To reach the site, follow the road uphill 200yds to the corner where the road forks. Opposite the post box and sign to the Friends' Meeting House is a neat garden which may well be the site of the house where Wordsworth lived. The 'brook' here too runs through the garden, and Spring Wood here is certainly 'fronting' the cottage (as the 1850 *Prelude* puts it) far more directly than at Greenend.

Follow the sign R here to the **Friends' Meeting House**, through a white door in a high wall on the R (W) side of the road. Ann Tyson used to bring her boarders here on Sundays when it was too hot or wet to go to church at

Hawkshead. Beatrix Potter also occasionally attended the Meeting House during holidays in the area, and noted (in September 1896)

> I liked it very much. It is a pretty little place, peaceful and sunny, very old-fashioned inside, with a gigantic old key to the door.
> I thought it so pleasant in the stillness to listen to a robin singing in the copperbeach outside the porch. I doubt if his sentiments were religious ... There was one child present, a little boy, who sat behind me on the women's side. He was very quiet, except for audibly sucking sweeties and sighing deeply at intervals. I fear, but do not wonder, that backsliders are frequent in the young generation.

New locks have been installed, but note the huge, elaborate keyhole in the left-hand door.

We shall now make a detour to Wray. If you prefer to continue directly along the lake to Near Sawrey, pass the Meeting House and go downhill through Town End Farm to rejoin the main road.

Wray

For Wray, take the road N from Colthouse. We are now on the route taken in November 1799 by Coleridge, who noted:

> leave Esthwaite on the road survey the whole of the Lake on my right, straight before me a peep of Wynandermere, and over a Gate on my left 5 huge ragged mountains, rising one above another in wild relations of posture – our road turns – we pass by Blellum Tarn, the 5 Mountains now facing us –

(at which point he must have been passing Tock How farm) and after Blelham Tarn, drawing into sight of the opulent, obtrusively white-painted houses of the new gentry, spluttered in an ecstasy of disgust

> Head of the Lake of Wyandermere – Mr Law's White palace – a bitch! – Matthew Harrison's House where [the Bishop of] Llandaff lived/these and more among the mountains! – Mrs Taylor's House! – ... damned scoundrel on the right with his house & a barn built to represent a chapel – 'tis his brother's cow-pen.

Most of these would have been houses around Clappersgate and Ambleside Waterhead, now mainly hidden by trees. But we are in the land of peculiar and extravagant mansions, for ¾m after Tock How we reach the drive to **Wray Castle** (*NT; grounds open to walkers; house not open*), in the form of a grey gothic castle whose exaggeratedly massive proportions give a weird feeling of elephantine playfulness. (Hawthorne aptly called it 'a great, foolish toy of gray stone'.) The building, which must be seen to be believed, is now rented to private tenants. It was built in 1840 by James Dawson, a Liverpool surgeon whose wife's fortune came from gin.

Beatrix Potter and her parents spent a summer holiday here in 1882, at which time she met the Rev (later Canon) H.D. Rawnsley, then vicar of the nearby church. They became firm friends; Beatrix Potter took up

Rawnsley's conservation interests and in 1895 they helped to found the National Trust.

Beatrix Potter visited the Castle again in September 1896 with a friend and

> had a very pleasant time ... I went to the top of the tower with Mary Foxcroft, peeping over amongst the soot and the jackdaws, and she describing how the Ainsworths had had the beams afire through too great a stove in the front hall ... Down in the scullery of the great kitchen Jane had a clothes-basket full of elder-berries for wine, some greeny-white, a variety I never saw. She had already made damson wine and ginger, and outside was a litter of walnuts blown down by the gale.

Beside the Castle gates, built at the same time as the Castle and reduced by the other building's scale to a kind of ecclesiastical summer-house, is **St Margaret's Church, Low Wray**. Rawnsley (cousin of the owner of Wray Castle) was Vicar here from 1878 to 1883. Note the brass at NE corner of chancel commemorating Richard Fletcher Broadrick, 'Drowned when crossing Windermere on the ice January 31 1879': the goodish sonnet on the brass is thought to be by Rawnsley. The road continues N to Pull Wyke and Clappersgate. We return to Colthouse.

Esthwaite Water (East Bank) and Sawrey

200yds S of Colthouse the road passes **Priest Pot**, a round pool, fringed with scrub and rushes, at the N end of Esthwaite Water. The name suggests that it was once an ecclesiastical fishpond. It is on private land without access; in appearance it resembles Allan Tarn.

Priest Pot formerly played host to a floating island smaller but much more substantial than the famous one on Derwentwater. It is well-authenticated: in the *Guide* Wordsworth says it 'may sometimes be seen, a mossy Islet, with trees upon it, shifting about before the wind' and Coleridge in 1802 noted 'Priest-pot and its floating Isle with Trees'. That reliable observer Jonathan Otley gave details in 1830: the island, he says, is twenty-four yards long and five or six wide,

> supporting several trees of alder and willow of considerable size ... when the water is high it is frequently moved from side to side [of the pool] by a change of wind; and has undoubtedly been thus torn from the bank at some remote period.

William Knight, in 1886, describes its demise:

> This island had a few bushes on it: but it became stranded some time ago. One of the old natives of Hawkshead described the process of trying to float it off again, by tying ropes to the bushes on its surface, – an experiment which was unsuccessful.

The road continues S along the E shore of the lake. A favourite evening walk 'in the latter part of my school-time', said Wordsworth, was along this side of the lake, where there was a yew-tree that had been 'taught ... to bend his arms in circling shade', forming a seat with its lower branches. Wordsworth later celebrated the seat, and the melancholy Rev William Braithwaite who made it, in his poem 'Lines left upon a Seat in a Yew-Tree'. The **Yew-Tree Seat** has gone; its approximate position was just above the road, on the E side, a few yards S of the signed drive to Broomriggs. The shore is no longer 'desolate', as Wordsworth calls it, but it still 'command[s] a beautiful prospect'.

Continue S ¾m to **Near Sawrey**, an attractive village pleasantly suspended in time because of its strong associations with Beatrix Potter, who visited frequently from 1896, and from 1913 made it her home. Near Sawrey and the surrounding countryside figure prominently in her books and the whole neighbourhood has become a carefully-tended environ-ment, alive and muddy but shielded even more carefully than the rest of the district from incongruous development. Potter gives a view of the village from the E, Coniston Old Man beyond, at the head of Chapter XIV of *The Fairy Caravan*.

The chief attraction of Near Sawrey is Beatrix Potter's house, **Hill Top** (*NT; open 1 April – 1 November, 11–5 (last admissions 4.30) except Thurs-day and Friday; admission charge. Delays possible at peak times. Car park for visitors to Hill Top and the Tower Bank Arms only at N edge of village*). Beatrix Potter bought this seventeenth century farmhouse and land in 1905 with royalties from her books supplemented by a legacy. It was never a permanent home, but she made long and frequent stays, stocking the farm and running it through a manager, writing most of her books from *The Tale of Mr Jeremy Fisher* (1906) onwards here, and returning here to write after she moved to Castle Cottage following her marriage in 1913. In her will she stipulated that 'the rooms and furnishings ... be kept in their pres-ent condition' and left many detailed instructions. Many parts of the house were used for illustrations in her books.

The fine traditional cottage garden is easily recognisable as Tabitha Twitchit's garden, illustrated in *The Tale of Tom Kitten* (1907). At R of the path are the stone wall and white wicket gate where Tom and his sisters sit and where Tom loses his clothes to Mr Drake Puddle-Duck. The picture of Tabitha smacking the kittens at the end of the book shows this gate again, with Castle Cottage beyond. The rose-covered slate-slab porch is illus-trated as the one where the kittens 'tumbled about the doorstep and played in the dust'. The exterior of the house also features in several line-drawings for the *The Tale of Pigling Bland* (1913).

Opposite the front door is the wrought-iron *art nouveau* gate by which Jemima hides her eggs in rhubarb in *The Tale of Jemima Puddleduck* (1908). Crane over the gate: there is still a wooden beehive in the recess to R of gate. (Children should look for Jemima's egg in the rhubarb patch.) Potter's illustration shows the gate from outside; the children shown are those of John Cannon, manager at Hill Top.

The wing at L of the front door was added by Potter in 1906 as a home for

HILL TOP: ALEXANDER AND THE POLICEMAN
Beatrix Potter, 1913

Cannon. It is still a working farm with no public access. Note Potter's monogram HBP with horseshoe and date on a stone tablet set into the wall. Hill Top was pebbledashed against damp when the extension was built; formerly it was white roughcast as shown in Potter's books. The extension appears in the penultimate illustration to *The Tale of Jemima Puddleduck*, viewed from the bottom of the farmyard; down there, in the fields away from the house through the farm, Jemima found the sandy-whiskered gentleman and his shed. In the same book Mr Cannon's wife is shown feeding poultry at the back door.

The entrance hall has several views used in *The Tale of Samuel Whiskers* (written in 1906 when the house was overrun with rats). Note in particular the front door and porch (shown in the illustration of Cousin Ribby's arrival), the kitchen range through which Tom climbs up into the chimney and, facing the front door, the ornate kitchen dresser past which Anna Maria runs with her plate to steal the dough. (The same dresser appears in *The Tale of Pigling Bland* (1913): Pig-Wig sits on a chair beside it in Mr Piperson's house.) Children will enjoy the cuckoo-clock, which does not feature in the books but performs effectively on the hour.

The parlour contains books from Potter's own library. Those who think of her as a naive writer may be surprised to notice works by Sterne, Hume, Addison, Coleridge, several editions of Shakespeare and a Latin version of Homer.

The staircase features in several illustrations for *Samuel Whiskers*: note the half-landing with red curtains and long-case clock where Tabitha stands (the stair-carpet has been removed) and the first floor landing across which Samuel Whiskers pushes the rolling-pin 'like a brewer's man trundling a barrel'.

For the view Tom saw from the chimney stack, go into the New Room and look L from the window. The unmetalled road winding uphill between stone walls is Stoney Lane; the hill beyond is Oatmeal Crag. Both were favourite places of Potter's. None of the Hill Top chimneys is visible, however.

Walking back past the Hill Top entrance, stand in front of the white wicket gate, looking NW along the road towards the cottage at the corner, Buckle Yeat. This is the view in front of which the three puddleducks stand to stare up at the kittens (Potter reversed the drawing in tracing it).

Beside Hill Top is the **Tower Bank Arms** (NT), instantly recognisable from an illustration in *The Tale of Jemima Puddle-Duck* as the inn where Kep met the fox-hound puppies. Beatrix Potter has compressed the building a little, moving in the bay at L to stand beside the front door.

On the corner just NW of the inn, is **Buckle Yeat**. Its front garden is seen in an illustration to *The Pie and the Patty-Pan* (1905), where Duchess stands on the path to read Ribby's invitation. The wooden fence has gone but the garden is otherwise much the same.

The field opposite Buckle Yeat is **Post Office Meadow**; in *The Pie and the Patty-Pan* Ribby is shown crossing this field bringing butter and milk from a farm for her tea with Duchess. The farm building shown is Hill Top, which Beatrix Potter has 'moved' to the spot where Buckle Yeat actually stands.

The unmetalled lane running alongside the meadow opposite Buckle Yeat is **Stoney Lane**, whose undulating upper reaches appear in several Potter illustrations. 60yds along the lane, passing (not following) a sign To the Tarns, is a row of cottages. The second, with the ornate doorway, is **Low Green Gate**, formerly The Old Post Office, which has the elaborate classical doorway used for Duchess's house in *The Pie and the Patty-Pan*. Further along the path, the white house set back behind a lawn and orchard is Castle Cottage, where Beatrix Potter, as Mrs Heelis, spent most of her married life.

The metalled road opposite Buckle Yeat is Smithy Lane. The house on the corner with the spectacular gilded weather-vane was formerly the village shop, portrayed as Ginger and Pickles' shop in *The Tale of Ginger and Pickles* (1909), which was dedicated to John Taylor, whose wife kept the shop. Its front garden is also the one where Duchess stands holding her basket in *The Pie and the Patty-Pan*. The garden is now less spectacular, but the slate path is clearly recognisable.

High Green Gate, on the opposite side of the lane, was the farmhouse of Mr Postlethwaite, Potter's tenant, who appears as 'Farmer Potatoes' in *The Tale of Samuel Whiskers*. He was reluctant to appear in a book, so the illustration shows him from behind, as surreptitiously photographed by Potter herself. The picture of the rats leaving with their wheelbarrow shows the view from the lane in front of High Green Gate, looking towards the village centre. The doll-like figure of Beatrix Potter stands roughly where the post box now is. Look the other way, uphill along Smithy Lane, for the scene through which the Puddle-Ducks take their departure wearing Tom's clothes in *The Tale of Tom Kitten*.

The last house on R before the gate is **Castle Cottage**, the farm which Beatrix Potter bought in 1909 and where she lived from her marriage in 1913 until her death in 1943. It was enlarged before William and Beatrix Heelis made it their home, but retains its original white rendering, more attractive than Hill Top's drab pebbledash. During her time here Mrs Heelis was mainly occupied with farming, and with conservation of the Lake District; she produced only a few published works: *Appley Dapply's Nursery Rhymes* (1917); *The Tale of Johnny Town-Mouse* (1918); *Cecily Parsley's Nursery Rhymes* (1922); *The Fairy Caravan* (1929); and *The Tale of Little Pig Robinson* (1930).

Uphill through the gate the lane continues as Stoney Lane (very muddy in wet weather): its winding upper sections appear in many of Potter's books and drawings. A line drawing for *The Fairy Caravan* ('My! What a mop of hair!') shows the caravan parked in a disused quarry ¼m up the lane. The rocky slopes behind the quarry are known as Bull Banks (see below). The lane continues N and after ½m it is joined from R by an unmetalled bridleway, Cuckoo Brow Lane (see p 334). For a pleasant circular walk of some three miles, continue N to Moss Eccles Tarn then turn back and at fork take Cuckoo Brow Lane down to Far Sawrey, returning to Near Sawrey by the road.

From the entrance to the Hill Top car park, the view back towards the village centre is shown in the penultimate illustration to *The Tale of Johnny Town-Mouse* where Timmy Willie waves goodbye to Johnny. The corner of the village shop, with its weather vane, is clearly visible, but the wall on which Timmy Willie sits does not exist.

Turning L out of the car park, take first L downhill for ¼m to the wooden signpost (at the road's second junction) shown in the frontispiece to *The Tale of Pigling Bland* as the starting-point for Alexander's and Pigling Bland's journey to market. A full-page illustration in *The Fairy Caravan* ('They fetched a load of provisions') shows Pony Billy dragging a loaded sledge in the snow along this lane, which leads down to Ees Bridge at the foot of Esthwaite Water.

Return to main road and go NW out of Near Sawrey; lane opposite Beech Mount Hotel leads N under **Oatmeal Crag** and its lower slopes, **Bull Banks**, which provided the setting for *The Tale of Mr Tod* (1912), where we are told that 'In winter and early spring [Mr Tod] might generally be found in an earth amongst the rocks at the top of Bull Banks, under Oatmeal Crag.' Illustrations to the book show a number of places among these thickly wooded, rocky outcrops.

This was a favourite spot of Beatrix Potter's; as she wrote in 1896,

> I think one of my pleasantest memories of Esthwaite is sitting on Oatmeal Crag on a Sunday afternoon, where there is a sort of table of rock with a dip, with the lane and fields and oak copse like in a trough below my feet, and all the tiny fungus people singing and bobbing and dancing in the

grass and under the leaves all down below, like the whistling that some people cannot hear of stray mice and bats, and I sitting up above and knowing something about them.

The exact place may be impossible to identify, especially since the summit of Oatmeal Crag is now thickly planted with conifers; if she means one of the lower slopes, it would be one of the rocky outcrops just above Bank Head, the farmhouse whose drive begins ¼m up the lane on R (N) side.

Return to B5286 and turn L (downhill) after the Beech Mount Hotel. The small unmetalled lane opposite the Garth Guest House is the private drive leading to **Lakefield Cottages**.

In 1902 Beatrix Potter made drawings of the third of these (at S end), for Ribby's cottage in *The Pie and the Patty-Pan*. The porch is clearly recognisable as the one where Duchess stands holding the bunch of flowers. The house still contains the cupboard which Duchess opens whilst searching Ribby's house for the mouse pie. Duchess herself was based on two Pomeranian dogs kept by the cottage's occupant.

Near Beech Mount is **Ees Wyke**, a large Victorian country house overlooking Esthwaite Water, now a hotel. Beatrix Potter stayed here with her parents, who rented the house (then called Lakefield) in the summer of 1896. The weather was wet, and besides exploring the damp woods for fungi (in which they are still rich) she and her brother

> Poked about amongst the lumber in the attics, and watched the rain rushing down a sort of runnel into the cistern. There are some ancient pistols and an ancient case and velvet hunting-cap. Bertram turned out a portfolio of chalk drawings, figures and heads, in the style of Fuseli, such as young ladies drew at school sixty years since.

She was here again in 1900 and 1902, when she did much sketching in Near Sawrey; many of the drawings later suggested settings for her books.

A drawing of Mrs Rogerson, wife of the Ees Wyke caretaker, was used for the housemaid who carries out the hamper in *The Tale of Johnny Town-Mouse*.

Return to Hill Top and follow the road E towards Far Sawrey. After ¼m a tiny bridge crosses **Wilfin Beck**. The colour plate of the Herdwick ewes in *The Fairy Caravan* shows the ewes on the bank of the beck just S of the bridge.

This road is the probable scene of Wordsworth's encounter (in autumn 1788) with the

BULL BANKS: TOMMY BROCK WATCHES
MR TOD
Beatrix Potter, 1912

discharged soldier described in *The Prelude* Book IV. Returning late at night from a dance in the Windermere area (perhaps at Rayrigg Hall) Wordsworth seems to have crossed the lake by ferry and taken the road to the Sawreys and Hawkshead when, near the crest of a ridge,

> It chanced a sudden turning of the road
> Presented to my view an uncouth shape …
> A milestone propped him, and his figure seemed
> Half-sitting, and half standing. I could mark
> That he was clad in military garb,
> Though faded, yet entire.

After watching him fearfully for a while Wordsworth spoke to him. The soldier explained that he had lately been 'dismissed' on returning from service in the tropics, and was making his way home on foot, asking for no help but trusting 'in the God of Heaven,/And in the eye of him that passes me!' Wordsworth took him to a nearby cottage where he could find food and shelter. The place is impossible to identify exactly (though a mention of 'the brook/That murmured in the vale' seems to refer to Wilfin Beck): the road has many 'sudden turning[s]' which would fit the account.

Continue ¼m to Far Sawrey. The unmetalled lane on L (N) side of road at village entrance (signed Colthouse and Wray) is **Cuckoo-Brow Lane**, one of Beatrix Potter's favourite walks. The last line-drawing in *The Fairy Caravan* shows the caravan parked in the lane, and in the book's last colour plate Xarifa tells her tale under one of the lane's hawthorn trees. Follow it to cattle-grid where it passes a small copse. This was the 'Pringle Wood' of *The Fairy Caravan*, where Paddy Pig ate the toadstool tartlets. Wilfin Beck flows along the far (W) edge of the wood; this spot is the 'Eller-Tree Camp' shown in a colour-plate to the book. Return to the road.

After ¼m we reach the tiny village of **Far Sawrey** (far, that is, from Hawkshead, as compared with Near Sawrey). Note the Sawrey Hotel's bar,

NEAR WILFIN BECK
Beatrix Potter, 1929

The Claife Crier, commemorating a character we shall encounter a little further on. Opposite the Hotel a small gate and flight of steps leads to **Spout House**. A fireplace here was used in illustrations of the sinister Mr Piperson's house in *The Tale of Pigling Bland*.

Continue along the undulating road ¾m until it nears the shore of Windermere. Watch for car park which soon appears on L (N). From car park take footpath signed Claife Heights, Hawkshead. It leads up to **The Station** (*NT*), a viewing-house built in the 1790s on the site of West's first 'station' for viewing Windermere. Originally it was just a rock from which one might 'command all the beauties of the lake', with Ramp Holme in front and 'To the north … a glorious sheet of water expand[ing] itself to the right and left, in curves bearing from the eye'. Tree growth has now abolished the view. Wordsworth recalled:

> So much used I to be delighted with the view from it, while a little boy, that I led thither from Hawkshead a youngster about my own age, an Irish boy, who was a servant to an itinerant conurjer. My notion was to witness the pleasure I expected the boy would receive from the prospect of the islands below and the intermingling water. I was not disappointed.

The pleasure-house (originally called 'Belle View') was built, according to Wordsworth, by William Braithwaite, the recluse commemorated in the poem on the 'Yew-Tree Seat'. Later it belonged to the Curwens of Belle Isle. Now a ruin consisting of a dilapidated octagonal tower and Gothic arch, it was formerly quite elaborate. The path wound so as to hide the view until the visitor had reached the upper room of the tower; the lower room was a lodge for the caretaker and guide. In the upper chamber (equipped with chairs, a fireplace and an Eolian harp) three large windows commanded the view, each bordered with coloured glass (yellow, blue and purple) so the visitor could tint the scene with the chill of winter or the mellow hues of late summer and autumn. Within living memory it was still possible to pick up fragments of the glass.

The Station was well known in the early nineteenth century; in Southey's *Letters from England* Don Espriella visits it, judging it

> a castellated building in a style so foolish, that, if any thing could mar the beauty of so beautiful a scene, it would be this ridiculous edifice.

A visitors' book was kept there, and Wordsworth, visiting in about 1829, found an absurdly pompous entry:

> Lord and Lady Darlington, Lady Vane, Miss Taylor and Captain Stamp pronounce this Lake superior to Lac de Geneve, Lago de Como, Lago Maggiore, L'Eau de Zurich, Loch Lomond, Loch Katerine, or the Lakes of Killarney.

This provoked Wordsworth into a delightful and wholly untypical piece of comic verse.

> My Lord and Lady Darlington,
> I would not speak in snarling tone;

Nor to you, good Lady Vane,
Would I give one moment's pain;
Nor Miss Taylor, Captain Stamp,
Would I your flights of memory cramp ...
I, not insensible, Heaven knows,
To all the charms this Station shows,
Must tell you, Captain, Lord and Ladies,
For honest worth one poet's trade is,
That your praise appears to me
Folly's own hyperbole.

We are now going to visit the **Crier of Claife**. This is a pleasant walk of some five miles over fairly rough, often boggy ground. Go through the arch of the Station, following path NW uphill. At kissing gate go L (NW) (signed Hawkshead and Sawrey); at next junction go N (signed Hawkshead); and at next, go ahead (signed Belle Grange). Where a path runs off L uphill to signed 'viewpoint' go up if you like (for a view that compensates for the loss of the Station's prospect), but then return to main path and continue NW following waymarks. At next junctions go R (N; signed Hawkshead) and then L (NW; signed Hawkshead). When path meets a forest road, with stone chippings, go N along it. After 400yds take R (E) turning off it to foot of TV mast.

Having rested to steady your nerves by the TV mast, take the small (probably muddy) path than runs E into wood just by transmitter gate. It soon joins another path, which you should follow, heading N. Where this path divides and rejoins, forming a loop of 50yds or so, go *cautiously* NE a few yards. You will find you are on the top of a precipitous overhang. Retreat a little and make your way down one side or the other; you will see a small rough quarry where a rock outcrop has been partly cut away. This is said to be the abode of the Claife Crier.

There are several versions of the story, but Harriet Martineau's is as good as any.

> It was about the time of the Reformation, one stormy night, when a party of travellers were making merry at the Ferryhouse – then a humble tavern, – that a call for the boat was heard from the Nab. A quiet, sober boatman obeyed the call, though the night was wild and fearful. When he ought to be returning, the tavern guests stepped out upon the shore, to see whom he would bring. He returned alone, ghastly and dumb with horror. Next morning, he was in a high fever; and in a few days he died, without having been prevailed upon to say what he had seen at the Nab. For weeks after, there were shouts, yells, and howlings at the Nab, on every stormy night: and no boatman would attend to any call after dark.

The thing was eventually exorcised by a local monk, who confined it to this quarry 'until a man could walk across Windermere dryshod'. Since then the lake has frozen several times, so it is not clear how effective this treatment has been. There are many stories of weird howlings on Claife Heights, and there are reports into recent times of people being followed in dark or mist on the heights by a hooded, heavily-breathing figure, perhaps in a monk's habit. The legend of the Crier was used as the theme of a weird one-act play by Gordon Bottomley, *The Crier by Night* (1902). Look at the 1:25000 map at ref. 386982 (where we are) and you will see the words 'Crier of Claife'. This must be the only bogle to have its location baldly stated on an OS map.

Return to the path and continue N; in ¼m it turns E and winds down to the lakeshore. You can return S along the shore to the Ferry and Station.

From the Station car park follow the road NE 200yds to **Ferry House**, now headquarters of the Freshwater Biological Association. On this site stood a small and picturesque cottage-inn, the **Ferry Inn**. John Wilson established an annual wrestling-meet here which developed into a sports day, moving to Grasmere in the 1860s as the Grasmere Sports.

The Inn was a favourite base for sailing, and Ellen Weeton's *Journal of a Governess* for April 1810 gives a glimpse of innocent enjoyments here:

> A few weeks ago [we] walked to the ferry, where there is an Inn on the edge of the lake, delightfully situated ... the weather was *peculiarly* favourable, and I would not have missed such a romantic walk, to have rode in the most elegant carriage in the universe. I was so sailing mad, that once or twice when Mr. P. and Mrs. P. were more inclined to indulge by the fire, Joe [the footman], and I, took the boat ourselves, he at one oar, and myself at the other, for several miles down the lake; and one morning, ... I went in a small row boat round one of the islands alone. At this early part of the year, there is no company, or you may suppose I should not have done *anything* that would attract the gaze of spectators.

She also describes the Windermere Regattas, which were then held just offshore from the Inn and were an uneasy mixture of sailing races and more plebeian sports:

> After a rowing match or two, which began the entertainment, there followed a footrace by four men. Two of them ran without shirts; one had breeches on, the other only drawers ... Expecting they would burst or come off, the ladies durst not view the race, and turned away from the sight. And well it was they did, for during the race, and with the exertion of running, the drawers did actually burst, and the man cried out as he run – 'O Lord! O Lord! I cannot keep my tackle in, G-d d-n it! I cannot keep my tackle in.'

> The ladies, disgusted, every one left the ground; there were many of fashion and rank; amongst others, Lady Diana Fleming, and her daughter Lady Fleming, and the Bishop of Landaff's daughters; several carriages, barouches, curricles; but all trooped off.

The charming inn met the predictable fate and was demolished in 1879 to make way for a large unlovely Hotel (the present building). Beatrix Potter stayed here with her parents in September 1895 and noted that it was

> reasonable in charge, cooking and attendance excellent, but I thought the company more than usually disagreeable, and did not at all like it.
> It is much frequented by the Yacht Club, who ... lounge about to such

an extent that one feels almost constrained to kick their shins before one can get out at the door.

Beside the Ferry House is the **Ferry** itself (*operating, roughly, spring to autumn: 0650–2150; winter: 0650–2050; about every ten minutes*) which has a long and fascinating history. A ferry has been here as long as people have lived around the lake; formerly there were several boats for different purposes, including a small passenger boat and a large flat boat rowed with immensely long oars and able to carry a horse and cart.

Its first poetic appearance seems to be in Richard Braithwaite's *The Fatall Nuptiall: Or, Mournfull Marriage* (1636), which mourns the drowning of forty-seven people ('and some of those of especiall quality') when the ferry, with a party returning from a wedding at Hawkshead, sank 'either through the pressure and weight which surcharged her, or some violent and impetuous windes and waves that surpriz'd her'. Braithwaite addresses the lake eloquently:

O WINDERMERE, who art renown'd afarre
For thy sole-breeding there unvalued *Charre*,
And with thy spatious channell doest divide
Two antient Counties seated on each side;
May thy fresh waters salt and brackish turne,
And in their chang'd condition henceforth mourne;
May these distilling conduits of thine,
Loosing their native sweetness flow with brine:
Tuning each accent of this accident
To Swanlike Odes of dying dreriment.

Many of those drowned were involved in the Kendal woollen industry:

These were such
Who, to relieve their Meniey, labour'd much
In their industrious Wool-worke; justly fam'd,
And for their Manuall labour *Sheare-men* nam'd.
An usefull mystery! which though it make
Course cloaths, and such as ne'er did *Alnage* take,
Yet 'tis commodious to the Common-weale,
And fit for Sale, although unfit for Seale.

('Alnage' was a tax on fine cloth, its payment marked by an official seal.)

Wordsworth crossed by ferry to Hawkshead with his brother John and Coleridge during their tour of the Lakes in November 1799: he was 'much disgusted with the New Erections and objects about Windermere' – the new whitewashed villas which were springing up round the head of the lake. In *An Evening Walk* he mentions as a common night-time sound the 'shout that wakes the ferry-man from sleep/Soon followed by his hollow-parting oar' for if he was on the far side you had to yell for him. Charles Farish, in *The Minstrels of Winandermere* (1811), describes the ferryman in Winter 'Winning his way across the lake/With battering Maul and iron crow', smashing his way through the ice.

FERRY HOUSE REGATTA
Thomas Allom, 1832

Budworth's *Windermere* (1798) gives us a glimpse of the vehicle ferry (the 'horse-boat') and lets us hear its tuneful rowers:

> Hark! ere the horse-boat opens to the eye,
> How gaily true the sturdy rowers ply;
> Whilst on her little stage she glides along,
> Tugg's to the charm of many a vacant song:
> The magic tones of undulating sound,
> Through the calm air, from hill to hill rebound.

A steampowered ferry was introduced in 1869; one of its successors was adapted in the mid-twentieth century to diesel, and this is the one that still operates. It takes 18 cars and gives a delightful crossing to Bowness, pulling itself along on cables. Children (and indeed all persons of taste) love it.

Taking the ferry is not for the impatient. If the queue extends much round the corner from the Ferry House, forget it. Drive S through the wonderful woods to Newby Bridge; or else return to Far Sawrey, telephone to cancel your engagements and decide where to go next.

REFERENCES

Where sources are clearly indicated in the main text, no reference is given here. Full details of published sources are given at the first occurrence; thereafter, author and short title. Where no source is given, information is either from readily-accessible reference works (the *British Library Catalogue*, the *Ordnance Survey Gazetteer*, the *Dictionary of National Biography* etc) or is based on personal knowledge supplied by local residents.

Wordsworth's notes on his poems, dictated to Isabella Fleming, are referred to as 'IF note to ...' followed by the title of the poem. The notes are reprinted in *The Poetical Works of William Wordsworth*, ed E De Selincourt, 5 vols, Oxford (OUP), 1940–9, or (selectively) in *William Wordsworth: The Poems*, ed John O. Hayden, 2 vols, New Haven and London (Yale University Press), 1977.

Abbreviations are used to refer to books which appear frequently, as follows:

Budworth	Joseph Budworth, *A Fortnight's Ramble to the Lakes* ... 3rd edn, London (Cadell and Davies), 1810.
Camden	William Camden, *Britannia*, tr R. Gough, 4 vols, London (Stockdale), 1806.
CL	*Collected Letters of Samuel Taylor Coleridge*, ed E.L. Griggs, 6 vols, Oxford (Clarendon Press), 1956–71.
CN	*The Notebooks of Samuel Taylor Coleridge*, ed K. Coburn, 3 vols, NY (Pantheon), 1957–73 (references give the numbers of the notebook entries)
Clarke	James Clarke, *A Survey of the Lakes of Westmoreland, Cumberland and Lancashire*, London (the Author), 2nd ed, 1789
Collingwood	W.G. Collingwood, *The Lake Counties*, London (Warne), 2nd ed, 1930
De Quincey	Thomas De Quincey, *Recollections of the Lakes and the Lake Poets*, ed David Wright, Harmondsworth (Penguin Books), 1970
D.W. Journals	*The Journals of Dorothy Wordsworth*, ed E. de Selincourt, 2 vols, London (Macmillan), 1941
Fiennes	Celia Fiennes, *The Illustrated Journeys*, ed Christopher Morris, London (Macdonald), 1982
Hardyment	*Arthur Ransome and Captain Flint's Chest*, London (Cape), 1984
Knight	*The Poetical Works of William Wordsworth*, ed William Knight, 11 vols, Edinburgh (Paterson), 1882–9
Linder	*A History of the Writings of Beatrix Potter*, London (Warne), 1971
Leland	Leland, John, *The Itinerary*, Part IX, ed L.T. Smith, London (Bell), 1910
Linton	Eliza Lynn Linton, *The Lake Country*, London (Smith, Elder), 1864
Martineau	Harriet Martineau, *A Complete Guide to the English Lakes*, Windermere (Garnett), 1854
Mason	William Mason, *The Works of Thomas Gray, Esq ... with Memoirs of his Life and Writings*, London (Dove), 1827
Moorman	Mary Moorman, *William Wordsworth: A Biography*, 2 vols, Oxford (Clarendon Press), 1965
Otley	Jonathan Otley, *A Concise Description of the English Lakes and Adjacent Mountains*, 4th edition, Keswick (the author) 1830

Poly-Olbion	Michael Drayton, *Works*, IV, *Poly-Olbion* (1619), ed J.W. Hebel, Oxford (Blackwell), 2nd ed, 1961
Radcliffe	Ann Radcliffe, *A Journey made in the Summer of 1794 ... to which are added, Observations During a Tour to the Lakes*, Dublin (Porter et al), 1795
Rawnsley	H.D. Rawnsley, *Literary Associations of the English Lakes*, 2 vols, Glasgow (MacLehose), 1901
Wardale	Roger Wardale, *Arthur Ransome's Lakeland*, 2nd ed, Lancaster (Dalesman), 1988
West	Thomas West, *A Guide to the Lakes in Cumberland, Westmorland and Lancashire* (1784), Oxford (Woodstock Books), 1989
Wilkinson	Thomas Wilkinson, *Tours to the British Mountains*, London (Cadell and Davies), 1824
W Letters	*The Letters of William and Dorothy Wordsworth*, ed E. De Selincourt, 2nd ed, revised (variously) by Mary Moorman, C.L. Shaver and A.G. Hill, 7 vols, 1967–85 (for clarity, each volume is referred to by its number in the seven-volume sequence).
W.W. Prose	*The Prose Works of William Wordsworth*, ed W.J.B. Owen and J.W. Smyser, 3 vols, Oxford (Clarendon Press), 1974
Young	Young, Arthur, *A Six Months' Tour Through the North of England*, 3 vols, London (W. Strachan et al) 1770

Epigraphs

John Keats, *The Letters*, ed H.E. Rollins, Cambridge, Mass, (Harvard UP), 1958, 1299.

Rupert Hart-Davis, *Hugh Walpole: A Biography*, London (Macmillan), 1952, 238.

User's Guide

John Wilson, *The Recreations of Christopher North*, Edinburgh (Blackwood), 1842, III 356.

Part One

Hest Bank W.W. Prose II 160; Radcliffe 498; Edwin Waugh, *Works* VII, Manchester (1882), 188; **Silverdale: Gibraltar Farm**, Winifred Gerin, *Elizabeth Gaskell: A Biography*, Oxford (Clarendon Press), 1976, 110, 135–6; 205; **The Sheiling**, *Letters from Edward Thomas to Gordon Borromley*, ed R.G. Thomas, London (OUP), 1968, 5, 274; **Arnside: Crossfield's Boatyard**, Wardale 17; **Levens Hall** D. Hill, *In Turner's Footsteps* 78–9; Noakes, Vivien, *Edward Lear*, London (Weiudenfeld)1985, 94; Sutherland, J.A., *Mrs Humphry Ward*, Oxford (Clarendon Press), 1988, 154–5; Letter 7 March 1897 to Dorothy Ward in Library of Pusey House, Oxford; *A Writer's Recollections*, 315; *Helbeck of Bannisdale*, ed B. Worthington, Harmondsworth (Penguin), 1983, 166; **Lyth Valley**, *Helbeck* 339; Anne Pearson, ed, *Papers, Letters and Journals of William Pearson*, London (privately printed), 1863, 90; **Crosthwaite** Collingwood 11; **Sizergh** Mason, 301–2; **Kendal** Poly-Olbion XXX 8–32; Fiennes 165–166; Young III 591–2, Mason, 300, 302; Arthur Ransome, *The Autobiography*, ed Rupert Hart-Davies, London (Cape), 1976, 112; Budworth 38–9; Radcliffe 389; **King's Arms** CL II 1033; D.W. Journals I 102n; Camden III, 339; **Oxenholme** K.M.E. Murray, *Caught in the Web of Words*, Oxford (OUP), 1977,129; Eliza Lynn Linton, *Lizzie Lorton of Grayrigg*, 3 vols, London, 1866, I 56–9; **Endmoor** Keats *Letters*, 1424; **Longsleddale** Mrs Humphry Ward, *Robert Elsmere*, London (Smith and Elder), 9th ed, 3, 34, 131; **Blea Water Crag** Clarke 41–2; **High Street** Otley 73; W.G. Collingwood, *Lake District History*, Kendal (T. Wilson), 1928, 150; **Kidsty Pike** Wordsworth's note to 'The Brothers'; Wilkinson, 162; **Mardale** *Elsmere* 99100;

Linton 132–3; **Wallow Crag** CN510; **Helton Dale** Linton 129; **Swindale** Collingwood 175; **Burneside** *Transactions of the Cumberland and Westmorland Archaeological and Antiquarian Society*, NS xiii 147; R. Braithwaite, *Barnabae Itinerarium*, Penguin 1932; Collingwood *Lake District History* 145; **A 591** Young III 580; **Staveley** D.W. Journals I 182; **Kentmere** Martineau 175–6; **Kentmere Hall** Clarke *Survey* 136; **Ings** Wordsworth, 'Michael' 264–276; D.W. Journals I 182–3; **Windermere** Martineau 8; Linton 4–5; **The Terrace** Ransome, *Autobiography* 44; **Orrest Head** Martineau 6; **Elleray** Moorman II 425; **Sun Inn** R.B. Martin, *Tennyson: The Unquiet Heart*, Oxford (Clarendon Press), 1980, 203; **Calgarth Hall** Clarke, *Survey* 133–4; **Calgarth Park** *Life of Bishop Watson ... by Himself* London (Cadell), 1818, I, 241–2, 389; De Quincey, 83–90; Ellen Weeton, *Miss Weeton's Journal of a Governess*, 2 vols, Newton Abbott (David and Charles), 1969, 289; **Briery Close** Winifred Gerin, *Charlotte Brontë*, Oxford (OUP), 1967, 445; **Low-wood Hotel** D.W. Journals I 37; West 73n; Moorman II 157; Mill, *Works* XXVII, *Journals and Debating Speeches II*, ed J.M. Robson, London (Routledge), 1988, 515; Hawthorne, *English Notebook*, ed R. Stewart, N.Y. and London (MLA), 1941, 161–2; E.M. Forster, *Selected Letters*, ed M. Lago and P.N. Furbank, London (Collins), 1985, I 89; **Dove Nest** Kathleen Coburn, ed, *The Letters of Sara Hutchinson*, London (RKP), 1954, 370; Moorman I 244; IF note to 'There is a little unpretending Rill'; **Galava Roman Fort** Camden III 399; Wardale 21; **Ambleside** R. Gittings and J. Manton, *Dorothy Wordsworth*, Oxford (Clarendon Press), 1985, 187; Linton 18, 158; **Salutation** Mason, 299; Keats *Letters* I 300; Budworth 196; W.W. Prose II 340n; Mill *Works* XXVII 516; Martin *Tennyson* 203; **Post Office** Jessie Harden's Journal, quoted in *William Green: Crags, Fells and Forces*, exhibition catalogue, Dove Cottage, 1985; **2 Gale Crescent** W. Schmalenbach, *Kurt Schwitters*, London (Thames and Hudson), 1970, 66–70; **Laurel Villa** L. Linder, ed, *The Journal of Beatrix Potter*, London (Warne), 1974, 138, 388; **The Knoll** Harriet Martineau, *Autobiography*, London (Smith, Elder), 1877, II passim.; **Lesketh How** Gerin, *Gaskell*, 103; **Walks about Ambleside** Linton 11; **Eller How** Sutherland, *Mrs Humphry Ward*, 15; **High Sweden Bridge** Mrs Humphry Ward, *A Writer's Recollections*, 88–9; **Scandale Tarn** Clare Boyle, *A Servant of Empire: A Memoir of Harry Boyle*, London (Methuen), 1938, 22; **Stockghyll Force** Keats *Letters* I 300–301; **Under Loughrigg** D.W. Journals 37; **Fox How** Park Honan, *Matthew Arnold: A Life*, London (Weidenfeld and Nicholson), 1981, 23, 127; Matthew Arnold, *Poems* ed M. Allott, Longman 1965, 41; Sutherland 13; Ward, *A Writer's Recollections* 23–4; **Fox Ghyll** Lindop, *The Opium-Eater*, 278–9; **Stepping Stones** Moorman II 427; Rawnsley II 121; **River Rothay** Hawthorne, *English Notebook* 167–8; **Rydal Hall** Rawnsley II 120; Collingwood *Lake District History* 155; CN514; **Rydal Cascades** Tyson, B., 'The Rydal Grotto', *Trans Ancient Monuments Society* 1980 49–56; Mason, 299n; Budworth 56; Mill, Works, XXVII 520; Linton 37–8; Green, R. L., ed, *The Diaries of Lewis Carroll*, Westport (Greenwood Press), 1971 2 vols, I 90; IF note to 'Lyre, though such power ...'; D.W. Journals I 75; **Rydal Park** Moorman I 463 Knight WPW II 167; **Rydal Mount** Lindop *The Opium-Eater* 214–5; Keats *Letters* I 302–3; Gittings DW 214; Moorman II 293n, 426, 429, 604; Martin *Tennyson* 203; Henderson, P, *Swinburne: The Portrait of a Poet*, London (RKP), 1974, 17; Emerson, *Journals and Miscellaneous Notebooks* ed Ferguson A.R., Cambridge, Mass (Harvard UP), 1964, IV 222–3, X 558; Blanchard, Paula, *Margaret Fuller*, NY (Delaeourte Press), 1978, 249; Ward, *Writer's Recollections* 88; **Rydal Church** Burd, V.A. and Dearden, J.S., eds, *A Tour to the Lakes in Cumberland: John Ruskin's Diary for 1830*, 46; **Rydal Water** West 79; CN 768; D.W. Journals I 104, 413; Moorman II 74; **Nab Cottage** W Letters II (i) 372; **White Moss Quarry** IF note to 'Beggars'; Brothers' Wood IF note to 'The Brothers'; **Dove Cottage** Knight II 102; W Letters I 124; W Letters III 378; D.W. Journals I 91; Moorman II 69; D.W. Journals I 46; Hayden, *Wordsworth: The Poems* I 1008; D.W. Journals I 144; IF note to 'The Redbreast and the Butterfly'; De Quincey

128; De Quincey, *Confessions of an English Opium-Eater and Other Writings*, ed G. Lindop, Oxford (OUP), 1985, 241; **Rock of Names** Knight III 115; CN 1163; D.W. Journals I 142; **Sunny Bank** Breit, H. and Lowry, M. B., ed, *Selected Letters of Malcolm Lowry*, London (Jonathan Cape), 1967, 413; **Sykeside Farm** D.W. Journals I 434–5; **Ashburner's Cottage** D.W. Journals I 433–4; **Rose Cottage** Moorman II 426; **How Top** D.W. Journals I 59; **Dry Close** *Times* June 17 1978 3; **John's Grove** Moorman I 471; D.W. Journals I 109, 139–140; **Wishing Gate** headnote to 'The Wishing-Gate'; D.W. Journals I 185; **Glow-Worm Rock** IF note to 'The Primrose of the Rock'; D.W. Journals I 138; **White Moss Common** West 79; D.W. Journals I 152, 109; **Brockstone** Knight II 171, 176; IF note to 'To the Clouds'; **Coleridge's Bower** D.W. Journals I 137; **The Nab Well** D. McCracken, *Wordsworth and the Lake District*, Oxford (OUP), 1985, 246; **Point Rash-Judgment** IF note to 'A Narrow Girdle of rough stones and crags …'; **Bainriggs** D.W. Journals 66; **Grasmere Lake** D.W. Journals I 137; D.W. Journals I 105; D.W. Journals I 96; Fanny Alford, *Life of Dean Alford*, London, 1873, 62–3, D.W. Journals I 48; CL 1612; D.W. Journals I 53; D.W. Journals I 48; **Grasmere Vale** Wilberforce, W, *Journey to the Lake District from Cambridge 1779*, ed C.E. Wrangham, Stocksfield (Oriel Press), 1983, 48; Moorman II 77; **Sports Field** Potter *Journal* 387; **Grasmere Village** C.C. Abbott and A. Bertram, ed, *Poet and Painter*, London, 1955, 71; Forster *Letters* 189–90; **Rectory** Gittings DW 188; W Letters II (i) 524; **St Oswald's Churchyard** Knight V 272n; St Oswald's Church Mill, Works XXVII 526; *Ecclesiastical Sonnets* III xxxii; IF note to 'Epistle to Sir G. Beaumont'; De Quincey 372–3; Millgate, M, ed, *The Life and Work of Thomas Hardy*, London (Macmillan), 1984, 383; **Gingerbread Shop** D.W. Journals I 188; **Church Stile** Budworth 65–6, 127–8; Moorman I 51, 244; **Wordsworth Hotel** Sean Day-Lewis, *C. Day-Lewis: An English Literary Life*, London (Weidenfeld and Nicholson), 1980, 190; **Red Lion** Martineau 50; **Pavement End Farm** D.W. Journals I 82; **Kelbarrow** Linder 156; **Silverhow** D.W. Journals I 42, 46, 48; Moorman I 463n; **The Wyke** Knight V 226, VIII 151; D.W. Journals I 38; **Loughrigg Terrace** D.W. Journals I 39, 43, 52; **Hammerscar** De Quincey 122–3; **Allan Bank** W Letters I 534, 539; De Quincey 292–3; Moorman II 109; Moorman II 134–5; Rawnsley II 164; **Dockwray Cottage** D.W. Journals I 42; **Butharlyp How** D.W. Journals I 118; **Easedale Lodge** Day-Lewis, *C. Day-Lewis*, 65; **Easedale footbridge** D.W. Journals I 90; **Easedale** De Quincey 250; D.W. Journals I 91; CN 948; D.W. Journals I 136; D.W. Journals I 183; **Blindtarn Gill** Dorothy Wordsworth, *George and Sarah Green: A Narrative*, ed E. De Selicourt, Oxford (Clarendon Press), 1936; De Quincey 248ff; **Sourmilk Gill** CN516; Linton 42; De Quincey 251; K.M.E. Murray, *Caught in the Web of Words* 131; **Helm Crag** D.W. Journals I 91; Knight II 160; D.W. Journals I 88; **Packhorse bridge** CN 516; **The Hollins** D.W. Journals I 116; **Forest Side** D.W. Journals I 84; **Swan Inn** Rawnsley II 197; Emerson *Notebooks* X 560; **Greenhead Gill** D.W. Journals I 66; IF note to 'Michael'; CN 1782; Moorman II 1, 487; **Grisedale Tarn** D.W. Journals I 62; **Fairfield** Weeton *Journal* 272–4; **Helvellyn** William Gilpin, *Observations on Cumberland and Westmoreland, relative … to Picturesque Beauty* (1786), Richmond (Richmond Publishing Co.), 2 vols in 1, 1973, 1170–1; CN515; D.W. Journals I 58; Wilkinson, 169, 173; D.W. Journals I 78; J.C. Powys, *Autobiography*, London (MacDonald), 1967, 203–4; Collingwood 161; De Quincey 272–4n; Pyatt and Noyce, *British Crags and Climbers*, London, 1952, 54–5; M.E. Braddon, quoted in John Barrow, *Mountain Ascents*, London (Sampson Low), 1886, 94; original source unknown; **Brownrigg Well** Otley 62; **High Broadrayne** Letters I 140; **Helm Crag Summit rocks** Otley 105–6; Radcliffe 470; **Dunmail Raise** Gilpin I 166–7; CN 535; Mason, 297–8; De Quincey 160; Edward Baines, *Companion to the Lakes*, London (Hurst, Chance) 1829, 81–2; **Thirlmere** West 82; Clarke 116; Linton 44; Mason, 297; Gilpin I 172; CN 1607; Barrow, *Mountain Ascents*, 137; Collingwood, 155; W.W. Prose, II 163; CN 1696; Honan 23; **Armboth House** Martineau 70; **Wythburn Church** Rawnsley II 208;

Collingwood 159; Keats *Letters* I 303–4; **Cherry Tree** Budworth 197, 201–2; Knight III 114; **Rock of Names** D.W. Journals I 142–3; **Clarke's Leap** Clarke 118; **Fisher Place** Caine, *Recollections of Rossetti*, London (Century), 1990, 103; Rawnsley II 232; **High Bridge End** Rawnsley II 227; De Quincey 228–229; **Piper House** Rawnsley II 240; **Castle Rock** Otley 107; **St John's in the Vale** Gilpin II 32; Mason, 289; **St John's in the Vale Church** Collingwood 156.

Part Two

Penrith Fiennes 169; Mason, 287; Radcliffe 432–3; **Arnison's** Gittings DW 18; Wilberforce 51; **George Hotel** Young III 591; D.W. Journals II 339; **St Andrew's Church** Ellman, *James Joyce*, NY (OUP), 1959, 594–5; *Finnegans Wake* 3; Defoe, *A Tour through the Whole Island of Great Britain*, London (Dent), 1974, 276; J.G. Lockhart, *Memoirs of Sir Walter Scott*, 10 vols, Edinburgh (A. and C. Black), 1869, X 107; **Robin Hood Inn** Reed *Wordsworth: Chronology of the Early Years* 159; **Wordsworth House** Moorman I 501; De Quincey 215; **Wordsworth Street** Kathleen Raine, *The Land Unknown*, London (Hamilton), 1975, 109, 111–113; **Beacon Pike** Moorman I 15; *Prelude* VI 230–236; **Red Hill** William Walker, *History of Penrith* 99, 201; Robert Woof, in Erskine-Hill, E. and McCabe, R.A., *Presenting Poetry*, Cambridge (CUP), 1995, 157n.; **Carletonhill** T.A. Trollope, *What I Remember*, 2 vols, London, 1887, II 36; **Penrith Castle** Gilpin II 85; Radcliffe 436; **Penrith Station** Wilfred Owen, *Letters*, ed H. Owen and J. Bell, London (OUP), 1967, 150; **Giant's Cave**, Defoe, *Tour* 277; CN560; Barbara Hoole, *Poems*, Sheffield, 1805; Edenhall T.A. Trollope, *What I Remember*, 11, 38; **River Eden** Poly-Olbion XXX 69–74; Stagg, *Miscellaneous Poems*, 195; **Long Meg and her Daughters** Poly-Olbion XXX 317–323; John Aubrey, *Monumenta Britannica*, 2 vols in 1, ed J. Fowles, Milborne Port (Dorset Publishing), 1980, I 115; Fiennes 172; Martineau 96; **Brougham Castle** Leland 47; Radcliffe 425–9; Clarke 4; D.W. Journals I 420; John Stagg, *The Cumbrian Minstrel* 35–43; **Countess' Pillar** Defoe *Tour* 275; **Hartshorn Tree** CN496; J.P. White, *Lays and Legends of the English Lake Country*, London (J.R. Smith) 1873, 5–7; Moorman I 555n; **View above Stainton Bridge** D.W. Journals I 99; **Dacre Castle** *The Anglo-Saxon Chronicles*, tr Anne Savage, London (Heinemann) 1982, 119; Bede *History*, Chapter XXXII; **Hutton John** D.W. Journals I 169; IF note to 'The Horn of Egremont Castle'; **Greystoke** Shelley, *Letters*, ed F.L. Jones, 2 vols, Oxford (Clarendon Press), 1964, I 199; **Threlkeld** Radcliffe 442; CN559; **Wescoe** Humphrey Carpenter, W.H. *Auden: A Biography*, London (Allen and Unwin), 1981, 39–40, 107–8, 140, 217; **Ormathwaite Hall** Thomas Pennant, *A Tour in Scotland*, 3rd ed, Warrington (Eyres), 1774, 42; Royal Society, *Philosophical Transactions* LXIV, 445; W.W. Prose II 124; **Applethwaite** Moorman I 588; W.W. Prose II 274; Mirehouse Clarke 99; Martin *Tennyson* 199, 338; Rawnsley I 183–4; **Bassenthwaite Lake** Linton 96; Mason, 295–6; West 124; **High Ireby** Rupert Hart-Davis, *Hugh Walpole: A Biography*, London (Macmillan), 1952, 320; **Ireby** Keats *Letters* I 307; **Caldbeck** Walter and Clare Jerrold, *Cumberland in Prose and Verse*, London (Matthews and Marrot), 1930, 118–9; F.J. Carruthers, *Around the Lakeland Hills*, London (Robert Hale), 1976, 52–5; **Caldbeck Howk** CN 828; D.W. Journals I 195; **Rose Castle** Fuller, Thomas, *The History of the Worthies of England*, 3 vols, London (Tegg), 1840, 338; D.W. Journals I 195–6; CN1427; **Hesket Newmarket** D.W. Journals I 195; CN 1426; Dickens, *Christmas Stories*, ed M. Lane, London (OUP), 1956, 661–4; **Mungrisdale** D.W. Journals I 195 CN 794; **Carrock Fell** CL 1 638; *Christmas Stories* 365–8; **Bowscale Tarn** Linton 87; Collingwood 291; **Souther Fell** Martineau 99; David Brewster, *Letters on Natural Magic*, London (1882), 201–3; **Scales Tarn** Linton 88; Mill *Works* XXVII 550; **Blencathra** Wilkinson 193; Collingwood 152; Keswick Leland 54; Fuller 1338; D.W. Journals I 89; Young III 155–6; CL 1610 Budworth 210, 213; Keats *Letters* I 306;

Hester Lynch Piozzi, MS *Journey Book*, John Rylands University Library of Manchester; William Gell, *A Tour in the Lakes made in 1797*, ed William Rollinson, Newcastle (Graham), 1968, 14; Collingwood 148; Beer, 'Coleridge, Hazlitt and Christabel', *Review of English Studies*, NS XXXVII (1986), 40–54; Dobbs, B. and J, *Rossetti: An Alien Victorian*, London (Macdonald), 1977, 219; **King's Head Court** Rawnsley I 126–7; **Oasis Restaurant** *A Prayer for My Son* 291; **St John's Church** Hart-Davies, 344; **Derwentwater Place** Rawnsley I 41–5; **Shelley Cottage** Shelley *Letters* I 142, 200–201; **Castlerigg Stone Circle** Mason, 295, 297; Keats *Letters* I 306; *Hyperion* II 34–7; **Old Windebrowe** W Letters I 114–6; Moorman 514; *Christopher Kirkland*, repr NY (Garland), 3 vols in 1, 1976, I 188–9; **Greta Hall** Richard Holmes, *Coleridge: Early Visions*, London (Hodder and Stoughton), 1989, 278; CL 1605, 612; CN 1252; *Letters of Charles and Mary Lamb* ed E.H. Marrs II 69; CN 798; Rawnsley I 47; De Quincey 215, 238; Mill, *Collected Works* XXVII 551; B.K. Mudge, *Sara Coleridge: A Victorian Daughter*, New Haven (Yale UP), 1989, 257–9; **River Greta** CL 1 632; Knight VII 335; **St Kentigern's Church** The Historians of Scotland, Edinburgh (Edmondston and Douglas), 1874, V; Linton, *Christopher Kirkland* 127–8; Ruskin, *A Tour to the Lakes*, ed Burd and Dearden, 42; **Crosthwaite Vicarage** Mason, 294; West 108; Linton, *Christopher Kirkland* 133–4, 49, 85; Van Thal, *Eliza Lynn Linton: The Girl of the Period*, London (Allen and Unwin), 1979, 76, 161; EF Rawnsley *Canon Rawnsley* 55–75 passim; **Keswick Convention** Owen *Letters* 151, 187; **Latrigg** West 103; CN 781, 830; **Whitewater Dash** CN 825; **Skiddaw** Gilpin II 3; Linton 93n; Blake, *Jerusalem* 80; Dalton, *Descriptive Poem* 288–96; Poly-Olbion XXX 183–190; Noakes, *Lear*, 95; Weeton, *Journal* 288; Collingwood 150–1; William Stukeley, *Itinerarium Curiosum*, 2nd ed, London (Baker and Leigh), 1776, 48; Wilberforce, *Journey*, 60, 62, CL 1618; Lamb *Letters* II 69; Keats *Letters* I 306–7; Norman Nicholson, *The Lakers: The First Tourists*, London (Hale), 1972, 108; **Crow Park** Mason, 294; Clarke 91; West 87; Poly-Olbion XXX 166–174; Pennant 39; Gilpin I 183; Ruskin *Iteriad* II 294; **Derwent Island** Collingwood 147; Walpole, *The Bright Pavilions* 120; W.W. Prose II 208–9; CN 541–2; Samuel Ladyman, *Thoughts and Recollections of Keswick*, 1885; Walpole, *Judith Paris*, London (Macmillan), 1932, 73–95; West 124; Clarke 66; **Lord's Island** Martineau 75; Linton 53; Collingwood 148; **St Herbert's Island** Bede, *A History of the English Church and People*, tr Leo Shelley-Price,. Harmondsworth (Penguin), 1968, 264–5; West 112n; **Floating Island** Otley 169, 172; W.W. Prose II 184; Knight VIII 114; Otley 172; Mill *Works* XXVII 534; **Friar's Crag** Ruskin, *Modern Painters* IV, xvii 13; H.D. Rawnsley, *Ruskin and the English Lakes*, Glasgow (MacLehose), 1901, 207, 216; Southey, *Sir Thomas More or Colloquies*, London (Murray), 1829, 2 vols, I 238; **Calfclose Bay** Mason, *Life*, 290; **Cat Gill** Southey, *Colloquies* I 119; **Lady's Rake** Budworth, 231; **Barrow House** documents at Derwentwater Youth Hostel; Linton 74–5; **Lodore** Martineau 81; Southey, *Letters from England* ed J. Simmons London (Cresset Press) 1951, 238; Potter, *Journal* 148; Young III 147–8; Mason, *Life*, 291; West 91; Keats *Letters* I 306; Chiang Yee, *The Silent Traveller: A Chinese Artist in Lakeland*, London (Country Life), 1938, 44; **Newton Place** D.W. Journals I 425; Gittings DW 215; Rawnsley I 145; **Grange** Mason, 292–3; Wilberforce 94n; **Copperfield** Hart-Davis, *Hugh Walpole* 349; **Brackenburn** Hart-Davis, *Hugh Walpole* 327, 329, 341, 347, 380; **Skelgill Farm** Stephen Spender, *World Within World*, London (Hamilton), 1951, 87; **Newlands Valley** West 127; **Lingholme** Linder 135; **Fawe Park** Linder 92; West 103; **Thornthwaite view of Skiddaw** D.W. Journals II 40; **Ouse Bridge** Roberts, Williams, *Thomas Gray's Journal*, Liverpool (Liverpool U.P.), 2001, 71-2, 151; **Armathwaite Hall** Pennant 43; **Surprise View** Otley 120; CN 161; **Watendlath** Wilkinson 209; Gilpin I 207; Norman Nicholson, *The Lakers*, 43; CN762n; Linton 78; **Steps End Farm** Michael Holrovd, *Lytton Strachey*, London (Heinemann), 1968, II 442–3; **Borrowdale** Mason, 290 (citing Dante, *Inferno* III 51); Radcliffe 465; Ruskin, *Iteriad*, Works ed. Cook and

Wedderburn II 298; Clarke 75; Martineau 80; Wilkinson 211; EF Rawnsley, *Canon Rawnsley* 51; **Bowder Stone** Gilpin II 94; Clarke 82; Southey, *Letters from England* ed J. Simmons London (Cresset Press) 1951, 243; Rosthwaite Gilpin II 97–8; **Royal Oak** Moorman II 222; **Castle Crag** West 93; **St Andrew's Church** D.W. Journals I 61; **Seatoller House** Levy, Paul, *G.E. Moore and the Cambridge Apostles*, London (Weidenfeld and Nicholson), 1979, 150–1; G.R. Elton, *C.E. Montague: A Memoir*, London, 1929, 237; **Graphite Mines** Camden III 422; Otley 177; Gilpin 1205; W.W. Prose II 346–7; **Borrowdale Yews** W.W. Prose II 275; IF note to 'Yew Trees'; Knight V, 429–32; **Seathwaite** Mason 292; **Styhead Pass** *Diaries of Lewis Carroll*, I 89; **Grey Knotts, Brandreth** Geoffrey Winthrop Young, *Mountains With a Difference*, London (Eyre and Spottiswoode), 1951, 147; **Honister Pass** Linton 196–7; **Lower Gatesgarth** J. Saltmarsh and P. Wilkinson: *A.C. Pigou*, Cambridge (King's College), 1960, 22; **Buttermere** Melvyn Bragg, *The Maid of Buttermere*, London (Hodder and Stoughton), 1987, 89; Budworth 249; **Fish Inn** Budworth 252, 385, 398, 407; RLLP 72–3; *Prelude* (1850) VII 296–308; **Hause Point** Noakes, *Lear*, 94; **Lorton Vale** Gilpin II 8–9; **Lorton Yew** D. Denman and M. Baron, *Wordsworth and the famous Lorton yew tree*, Lorton and Derwent Fells Historical Society, 2004; **Cockermouth** Leland, 52; **Wordsworth House** Moorman I 9; *Prelude* (1805) 1271–296; W Letters I (1787–1805), 616; D.W. Journals II 401; **Low Sand Lane** Rawnsley I 197; **All Saints' Church** Wordsworth, *Ecclesiastical Sonnets* III xxii; Moorman I 299; **Cockermouth Castle** Stukeley 49; **Bridekirk** Collingwood 105; WPW II 341.

Part Three

Allonby G. Head, *A Home Tour through the Manufacturing Districts of England in the Summer of 1835*, quoted in Weeton, *Journal* 271n; *Lazy Tour* 411; N.P. Davis, *The Life of Wilkie Collins*, Urbana (Illinois UP), 1956, 205–6; **Maryport** Abbott, C.C., ed., *Letters of G.M. Hopkins to Robert* Bridge, London (OUP), 1935, 140, 143; *Lazy Tour*, 413; **Brigham** George Fox, *The Journal*, ed Penney, N, New York (Octagon Books),1911, repr 1973, 112; Rawnsley I 203; **Moorland Close** Collingwood 105; **Eaglesfield** Rawnsley I 210–11; **Pardshaw** George Fox, *Journal* I 292; **Workington** Leland Part IX 54; Defoe, *Tour* 275; D.W. Journals II 402; **Aldingham** Rawnsley I 8; **Moresby** Moorman II 444n, 495; IF note to 'On a High Part of the Coast …'; R.H. Super, *Walter Savage Landor*, NY (NYUP), 1954, 227; **Whitehaven** Linton 239; Collingwood 92–3; Defoe *Tour* 273; Pennant 49–50; Stukeley 52; Wilberforce 67; IF note to 'On a High Part of the Coast of Cumberland'; Ehrenpreis, Irvin, *Swift*, London (Methuen), 1962, I 32; Shelley *Letters* I 248; D.W. Journals II 402; Wilson, D, *Thomas Carlyle*, London (RKP), 1923–4, II 221; Aird, *Poetical Works* ed Wallace, Edinburgh (Blackwood), 1878, xliii; **Whitehaven Castle** Moorman, II 233; **Hensingham** Thomas Blackburn, *A Clip of Steel*, London (MacGibbon and Kee), 1969, 106; **Ennerdale** E.F. Rawnsley, *Canon Rawnsley* 53; CN 1209; CN 1208; **Pillar** CN 540 f35; Moorman I 451–2; Alan Hankinson, *The First Tigers*, London (Dent), 1972, 60; **Egremont** CN 1211; **St Bees** Collingwood 90; Defoe, *Tour* 273; Linton 239n; Fuller *Worthies* 343; De Quincey 272–276; James Payn, *Poems*, Cambridge 1853; **Wotobank** Linton 223–4; Calder Abbey CN 1211; Martineau 122–3; **Red Admiral Inn** CN 1212; **Gosforth** Martineau, 122; Chiang Yee, *The Silent Traveller* 29; **Seascale** Green, R.L., ed, *Diaries of Lewis Carroll*, II 383; *Helbeck*; Abse, Joan, *The Passionate Moralist*, London (Quartet), 1980, 327; **Whitriggs** Pennant 26–27; **Sowermyrr** Hart-Davis, 27; Hugh Walpole, *A Note … on the Origins of the Herries Chronicle*, Doubleday (NY), 1940, 7; **Wasdale** Wilkinson, 223; W.W. Prose II 165, 172; CL II 839; Otley 29; Noakes, *Lear*, 94; Richard Parkinson, *The Old-Church Clock*, London (Rivington), 1843, 69–70; Mary Gordon, *Christopher North* (1879) 92–3; W.W. Prose II 172; W.G. Collingwood, *Lake District History* 115; Martineau 120;

Wasdale Head Inn M.J.B. Baddely, *The Thorough Guide to the Lake District*, London (Dulau), 1880, entry for Wasdale Head; Geoffrey Winthrop Young, *Mountains With a Difference* 19; Wilberforce, 15; **Rowhead** Sir Arthur QuillerCouch, *Memories and Opinions*, Cambridge (CUP), 1944, 85; R.L. Green, *A.E.W. Mason*, London (Max Parrish), 1952, 31; **Burnthwaite** K.M.E. Murray, *Caught in the Web of Words*, 129–30; **Scafell** Wilberforce 73; CL II 840; Newsome, D, *On the Edge of Paradise*, London (Murray), 1980, 227; CN 1215–1218; Otley 13; **Scafell Pike** D.W. Journals I 427–30; **Great Gable** Linton 205; W.W. Prose II 280; Otley 68; **Sty Head** D.W. Journals I 426–7; **Bridge Inn** Hankinson *The First Tigers* 40; **Holmrook** Carroll, *Diaries*, II 383; **Irton** CN 1213; **Ravenglass** *Poly-Olbion* XXX 103–120; Camden, III 421; Defoe, *Tour* 273; **Muncaster Castle** Linton 258 n; Collingwood, LDH 75; **Eskdale** CN 1221–2; **Black Combe** Collingwood *Lake District History* III; Farish quoted in W.W. Prose II 161; **Millom** Hugh Brogan, *The Life of Arthur Ransome*, London (Cape), 1984, 225; Ransome, *Autobiography* 128; **Furness Peninsula** Collingwood 45; J. Stockdale, *Annales Carmoelenses*, Ulverston, 1872, 18–19; Camden III 380; Martineau 22–3; **Furness Abbey** Linton 277; Radcliffe 490–1; W.W. Prose 294–5; Hawthorne, *English Notebook*, 157; **Barrow-in-Furness** Collingwood 58–9; Lawrence, *Letters*, 309–310; **Rampside** Moorman I 257–8; **Conishead** Priory West 44–5; Collingwood *Lake District History* 166.

Part Four

Ulverston Thomas West, *Antiquities of Furness*, Ulverston (Ashburner), 1805, 15–17; Pennant 25; Gittings *Dorothy Wordsworth* 247; Wilberforce 46; **Swarthmoor Hall** Fox *Journal* I 49–51; Pennant 28; **Pennington** Collingwood 48; **Lowick** Brogan, 225; **Lowick Hall** Brogan, 413–6; **Hark to Melody Inn** Ransome *Autobiography* 111; *Swallowdale*, 244; **Wall Nook** Ransome, *Autobiography*, 107–110; **Well Knowe** Thomas/Bottomley Letters 102, 142; Bottomley, *Poems and Plays*, London (Bodley Head), 1953, 69; **Humphrey Head** *Lonsdale Magazine* 1821; **Gummer's How** Hardyment 45; Stukeley II 39; Martineau 22; **Great Hartbarrow** Ransome *Autobiography* 324; **Barkbooth** Brogan, 286–90; **Borderside** Collingwood 23; Rawnsley II 73; Anne Pearson, ed, *Papers, Letters and Journals of William Pearson*; **Low Ludderburn** Ransome, *Autobiography* 323–4; **The Cottage** Ransome, *Autobiography* 92; **Storrs Hall** Lockhart, VIII 50–1; Potter *Journal* 393; Hardyment, 46; **Blake Holme** Hardyment 45; **Low Lindeth** Linder 297; **Bowness** Wardale 17; Hardyment *Arthur Ransome and Captain Flint's Trunk* 84; **Bowness Rectory** Martineau 11; **Belle Isle** Clarke, 133; Fiennes 166; Gilpin I 135, 138–9; West 59, 62; Gell, 1; D.W. Journals I 154–5; W Letters V (1829–34), 428; **Windermere [lake]** W.W. Prose II 158; Martineau 20; Wardale 63; Camden III 380; Leland Part IX 47; Defoe 269–70; Finnes, 166; CWAAS NS XIII 148; *Gentleman's Magazine*, 1748, 563; *Prelude* I 451–489, II 170–180, V 389–411; Moorman I 37; IF note to 'There was a boy...'; Richardson, Joanna, *Stendhal*, London (Gollancz), 1974, 200; Hardyment 55; Brogan, *Arthur Ransome* 12–19, 320, 303; **Royal Hotel** Keats *Letters* I 298–8; Martineau 10; **Rayrigg Hall** Wilberforce 20; **Queen Adelaide's Hill** West 67; Martineau 15; **Holehird** Potter *Journal* 382–3; **Sour Howes** Potter *Journal* 386; **Troutbeck** Linton 31n, 35; Martineau 34–5; Clarke 136; Hoggart, T., *Remnants of Rhyme*, Kendal (George Lee), 1853, ii–iii, 8; **Troutbeck Tongue** Linder 293; **Mortal Man** Linton 33; *Notes and Queries*, 2nd series, VIII (1859), 96; Henderson, B.L.K., *Morland and Ibbetson*, London (Phillip Allen), 1923, 127–8; Hoggart, *Remnants of Rhyme* 7; Iveagh Bequest: *J.C. Ibbetson* (Exhibition Catalogue), London County Council, 1957, 5; **Nanny Lane** Potter *Journal* 383, 385; **Kirkstone Pass** Fiennes 168; D.W. Journals I 414; De Quincey 212–3; CN 1189; **Kirkstone Pass Inn** Martineau 36; **Kirkstone** De Quincey 213–4; **Brothers Water** D.W. Journals I 133, 418–9; Clarke 153;

Collingwood 293; Otley 16; **Hartsop Hall** D.W. Journals I 414; **Goldrill House** Escreet, J.M., *The Life of Edna Lyall*, London (Longman), 1904, 119; **Broad How** D.W. Journals I 415; **Patterdale Hotel** Budworth 100; Radcliffe 423; Rawnsley II 60; **Side Farm** D.W. Journals I 415; **Blowick** D.W. Journals I 415; CN 551, 553; **Blowick House** John Glover (Exhibition Catalogue), Art Gallery of South Australia, Adelaide, 1985, passim; **Chapel in the Hause** D.W. Journals I 417–8; **St Martin's Church, Patterdale** Gilpin II 65; **Patterdale Hall** Gilpin II 64; Gell 42n; D.W. Journals I 95; Lockhart VIII 51; Collingwood 163; **Stybarrow Crag** Edward Baines, *Companion to the Lakes*, 204–5; Ullswater *Poly-Olbion* XXX 80–85; Stukeley II 48; W.W. Prose II 165; Gilpin II 52, 61–2; Budworth 327; De Quincey 214; D.W. Journals I 416; Linton 49; Nicholson, *Lakers* 62; Powys, *Autobiography* 203; **Glencoyne** W.W. Prose II 282; Radcliffe 416; **daffodils** D.W. Journals I 131–2; IF note to 'I wandered lonely as a cloud ...'; **Aira Force** CN 549; IF note to 'The Somnambullist'; De Quincey 344–6; **Lyulph's Tower** Gell *Tour* 40n; Linton 100; **Gowbarrow Park** Fiennes 169; W.W. Prose II 281; D.W. Journals I 42, 132; **Mellfell House** Barbara Hofland, *The Cumberland Statesman* 129; A.W. Rumney, ed, *Tom Rumney of Mellfell*, Kendal (Wilson), 1936, 144; **Dunmallard** Radcliffe 389; **Eusemere** Rawnsley II 1; CN 555; **Barton Fell** Moorman I 540; IF Note to 'Resolution and Independence'; **Bonscale** *Gissing Newsletter* October 1980, July 1984; **Martindale** D.W. Journals I 97, 417; **Old Vicarage** Raine, *Land Unknown* 114, 124; **Tirril** Rawnsley II 34, 39; **Wordsworth House** Moorman I 8; **River Lowther walk** Rawnsley II 32; **Lowther Castle** Fennes 171; Defoe 270; De Quincey 149–151; Moorman II 233; *Recollections of the Table Talk of Samuel Rogers*, ed A. Dyce, New Southgate, 207; Lockhart VIII 51; **Lowther Village** Young III 160–1; **The Grotto** Moorman I 73n; D.W. Journals I 420; IF Note to 'Lines to the spade ...'; Arnison, Janet: *A Glimpse into the History of The Grotto, Yanwath*, Yanwath (compiled for The Grotto), 1989; **Mayborough** Aubrey 113–4; Stukeley II 44; CN 496; **King Arthur's Round Table** Leland Part IX 48; Fiennes 171; *Poly-Olbion* XXX 324–331; William Hutchinson, *History of the County of Cumberland*, Carlisle, 1794, I 334–8.

Part Five

Clappersgate De Quincey 302; **Low Brathay** Moorman I 474; De Quincey 332; IF note to *The Excursion*; Budworth, 160–1; **Brathay Hall** Moorman II 232; **Pull Wyke** Clarke 136; **Loughrigg Tarn** IF note to 'Epistle to ... Beaumont'; **High Close** Martineau 49; **Mill Brow Farm** Gerin, *Gaskell* 103; Rawnsley II 175; Elizabeth Gaskell, *Letters* ed J. Chapple and A. Pollard, Manchester (MUP) 1966, 83, **Gunpowder Mills** ELL 255; **Colwith Bridge** ELL 256; **High Hackett** W Letters II (i) (1806–11), 447; IF note to *The Excursion*; **Blea Tarn** Knight V 108; Carpenter, *Auden* 29; **Bleatarn House** Knight V 93; **Merzbarn** John Elderfield, *Kurt Schwitters*, London (Thames and Hudson), 1985, 221; **Great Langdale** Clarke, *Survey* 146; W.W. Prose II 269; Mill, *Works* XXVII 522–3; **Chapel Stile** Martineau 147; **Thrang Crag** ELL 162; Mill, Works XXVII 523; **Robin Ghyll** Trevelyan, *Autobiography*, London (Longman), 1949, 29 ff, 41; **Dungeon Ghyll Force** CN 753; **Langdale Pikes** Budworth 271; Wilkinson 98–100; Ruskin quoted in Collingwood 36; **Three Shire Stone** Martineau 115–6; **Duddon Valley** Moorman II 248; Knight VI 300; **Seathwaite** Knight VI 326, 335; H.W. Nevinson, *Changes and Chances*, London (Nisbet), 1923, 106; **Walker House** Knight VI 324n; **Newfield Inn** Knight VI 377; **Hall Dunnerdale Bridge** CN 1225 f27; **Broughton Mills** CN 1225; **Travellers' Rest Inn** CN 1225 f27; Martineau 109; **Ulpha** CN 1225 f26,27; Martineau 108–9; Moorman II 583; **Old Hall Farm** Knight VI 344–5; **Torver** CN 1228 f32; Rawnsley II 191; **Coniston Hall** Radcliffe 480; CN 1228 f32; W.W. Prose 308; **Black Bull** CN 1227; De Quincey 122–3; **Bank House** Ransome *Autobiography*, 80; Collingwood 64; **Gondola** Ransome, *Autobiography* 27,

31; **Coniston Water** Radcliffe 481, Otley 17; Collingwood, 61–2; IF note to 'Extract ... Leaving School'; Prelude (1850) VIII 437–49, 459–75; ELL 264; **Waterhead Hotel** Abse, *The Passionate Moralist* 317; **Tent Lodge** Rawnsley I 145, 179, II 32, 186; Elizabeth Smith, *Fragments*, Bath (R Cruttwell), 1810, 236; De Quincey 334–48; Martineau 28; Martin, *Tennyson* 339–40; Carroll *Diaries*, I 125–7; **Tennyson's Seat** Rawnsley II 187; Martineau 28; **Lanehead** R.G. Collingwood, *Autobiography*, OUP 1939, 1–4; **Brantwood** Rawnsley II 187; Van Thal, *Eliza Lynn Linton*, 60–1; Abse, *The Passionate Moralist*, 252, 303, 316, 328; Rawnsley, *Ruskin and the English Lakes*, 67–8, 111; CN 1228 f31; Ruskin *Diaries* ed J. Evans and J. Whitehouse, III (1874–1889), Oxford (OUP) 1959, 1047; **The Heald** Hardyment 92; Brogan, 373–404 *passim*; Wardale 68; **High Peel Near** West, 47–48; **Peel Island** Wardale 19; Collingwood 61; Brogan, *Ransome* 47, 68, 71, 131; **High Nibthwaite** Ransome, *Autobiography* 26–27; **Beacon Tarn** Hardyment 74; **Beacon Hill** Hardyment 74–5; **Swallowdale** Wardale 68; **Coniston Old Man** Moorman I 25; Wilkinson, *Tours* 104; Martin *Tennyson* 339; Ransome *Autobiography* 24; **Walna Scar Road** Parkinson, *Old-Church Clock* 35–6; **Low Yewdale** Ransome, *Autobiography*, 128; Hardyment 63; **Yewdale** Ruskin *Works* ed Cook and Wedderburn, XXVI 243–266; **Weatherlam** Hardyment 72; Brogan 344; Barrow *Mountain Ascents* 28–9; **Raven Crag** Knight III 141; **Boon Crag Cottage** Parkinson, *Old-Church Clock* 4; **Monk Coniston** Lewis Carroll *Diaries* I 127; **Hawkshead Grammar School** Moorman I 31, 51–2, 61; Lowry *Letters* 414; **Queen's Head** Potter *Journal* 420; **St Michael's Church, Hawkshead** De Quincey 348; **Café** Linder 243; **Esthwaite Water** De Quincey 157; Moorman I 38; IF note to *An Evening Walk*; McCracken, D, *Wordsworth and the Lake District*, 226; *Prelude* (1805) V, 450–481; **Esthwaite Lodge** J.B. Young, *Francis Brett Young: A Biography*, London (Heinemann), 1962, 162–83; **Graythwaite Hall** IF note to 'Nutting'; **Silverholme** Hardyment 28, 48; Collingwood 25; **Outgate Inn** Knight III 416–20; IF note to EW; **Colthouse** Moorman I 84–5; **Friends' Meeting House** Moorman I 29; Potter *Journal* 421; **Wray** CN511; **Wray Castle** Hawthorne, *English Notebooks* 162; Potter *Journal* 421; **Priest Pot** W.W. Prose II 184; CN 1228 f32; Otley 19; Knight VIII 114; **Yew Tree Seat** IF note to 'Yew Tree Seat'; McCracken 227; **Oatmeal Crags** Potter *Journal* 422; **Lakefield Cottages** Linder 169; **Ees Wyke** Potter *Journal* 416; **Cuckoo Brow Lane** Linder 299; **The Station** West 55; IF note to 'Yew-Tree Seat'; Otley 13; Southey, *Letters from England*, 229; **Claife Crier** Martineau 31; John Wyatt, *Reflections on the Lakes*, London (Allen), 1980, 168–82; **Ferry Inn** Collingwood 26; Weeton, *Journal* 249, 294; Potter, *Journal* 393–4; **Ferry** CWAAS NS XIII 151; WW *Letters* I (1787–1805), 271; Moorman I 35; Budworth, *Windermere, A Poem*, London (Cadell and Davies), 1798, 13.

The passage from Mrs Humphry Ward's letter of 7 March 1897 on pages 5-6 is quoted by permission of the Custodian of the Library of Pusey House, Oxford. The extract from the manuscript *Journey Book* of Hester Lynch Piozzi on pages 165–6 is quoted by permission of the Librarian of the John Rylands University Library of Manchester.

The illustration on page 144 is reproduced by permission of Penguin Books Ltd from *A Pictorial Guide to the Lakeland Fells Book Five: The Northern Fells* by A. Wainwright (Michael Joseph, 1992), copyright © Michael Joseph Ltd, 1992. The illustration on page 174 is reproduced by permission from *The Collected Poems of Stevie Smith* (Penguin Twentieth Century Classics) © the Estate of Stevie Smith. The illustrations on pages 209 and 316 are reproduced from *Fell Farm Holiday* (Puffin Books, 1951) by permission of Penguin Books Ltd. The illustration on page 218 is reproduced by permission from *Provincial Pleasures* by Norman Nicholson (Robert Hale Ltd 1959).

INDEX OF PEOPLE

INDEX OF PLACES